Miss Leslie's Directions for Cookery

An Unabridged Reprint of the 1851 Classic

Miss Leslie's Directions for Cookery

An Unabridged Reprint of the 1851 Classic

Eliza Leslie

With A New Introduction by
Janice (Jan) Bluestein Longone

DOVER PUBLICATIONS, INC.
Mineola, New York

Copyright

Copyright © 1999 by Dover Publications, Inc.
All rights reserved under Pan American and International
Copyright Conventions.

Published in Canada by General Publishing Company, Ltd., 30
Lesmill Road, Don Mills, Toronto, Ontario.
Published in the United Kingdom by Constable and Company,
Ltd., 3 The Lanchesters, 162–164 Fulham Palace Road, London
W6 9ER.

Bibliographical Note

This Dover edition, first published in 1999, is an unabridged
republication of the 1863 printing of the 1851 edition of *Miss
Leslie's Complete Cookery: Directions for Cookery*, first published by
E. L. Carey and A. Hart, Philadelphia, 1837. The 1851 edition and
this 1863 printing were published by Henry Carey Baird,
Philadelphia. Portions of the new "Introduction to the Dover
Edition" by Jan Longone originally appeared in *The American
Magazine and Historical Chronicle, Vol. 4, No. 2 Autumn–Winter
1988–89*, published by the Clements Library, The University of
Michigan, Ann Arbor, Michigan and in *AB Bookman's Weekly*
(August 12, 1996). The text of the original book begins on page 7.

Library of Congress Cataloging-in-Publication Data

Leslie, Eliza, 1787–1858.
    [Miss Leslie's complete cookery]
    Miss Leslie's directions for cookery : an unabridged reprint of
the 1851 classic / Eliza Leslie ; with a new introduction by Janice
(Jan) Bluestein Longone. — Dover ed.
        p.   cm.
    ISBN 0-486-40614-8 (pbk.)
    1. Cookery, American.   I. Title.
TX715.L646   1999
641.5—dc21
                                          98-55116
                                            CIP

Manufactured in the United States of America
Dover Publications, Inc., 31 East 2nd Street, Mineola, N.Y. 11501

Introduction to the Dover Edition

Throughout its history, America has been blessed with a remarkable group of talented and influential cookery writers, none more so than Eliza Leslie, perhaps the 19th century's most popular and prolific.

Eliza Leslie's *Directions for Cookery* was probably the most successful American cookbook of the last century; a 60th edition appeared in 1870, thirty-three years after its first appearance in 1837 and twelve years after the author's death.

In her classic bibliography *American Cookery Books, 1742–1860* (Worcester, 1972), Eleanor Lowenstein lists more entries for Miss Leslie than for any other author. There are seventy-two citations for her works in various editions and printings; her nearest rivals in popularity, Sarah Josepha Hale and Lydia Maria Child, have twenty-seven and twenty-six entries respectively. In addition, Miss Leslie's works were reissued with regularity well after the Civil War. As late as 1890, more than thirty years after her death, her first book was included in an omnibus collection published in Chicago, the *Complete Library of Cookery*. Nor has interest in Miss Leslie's works waned; at least three reprints of her cookbooks have appeared within the past twenty years.

Who was Miss Eliza Leslie and why did her books claim such a loyal following?

Every writer on America's gastronomic history has lauded Miss Leslie. Some culinary historians have gone so far as to judge that American cookery, with Eliza Leslie as its guide, had reached its highest level in the second quarter of the 19th century: "From then on, it was downhill all the way."[1] One need not agree unreservedly with this assessment to appreciate the excellence of Miss Leslie's writings and her contribution to the shaping of American cuisine.

---

1 John and Karen Hess in the *Taste of America* (New York, 1977).

Typical of many of America's prominent culinary writers, Miss Leslie was more than *simply* a cookbook author. She was involved with numerous other literary and social pursuits. She was, in fact, a bit ashamed of the fame and fortune she received from her cookbooks, and assumed that her reputation would survive based upon her novels, children's books, and stories. By and large, however, these works have been forgotten; her reputation rests on her culinary works.

Much of our information about Eliza Leslie's early life is derived from a charming autobiographical letter that is included in J. S. Hart's *Female Prose Writers of America* (Philadelphia, 1852). Here she proudly records that her Scottish great-grandfather had arrived in America in 1745, but that her parents and all her grandparents were natives of Cecil County, Maryland. Soon after her parents' marriage, they moved to Philadelphia where her father was a respected watchmaker and friend to Franklin and Jefferson.

Eliza Leslie was born in Philadelphia on November 18, 1787. When she was five years old her family moved to England where they lived for six and a half years. Her literary education was shaped during those early years in England. In her autobiographical letter she writes:

My chief delight was in reading and drawing. I could read at four years old, and before I was twelve I was familiar, among a multitude of other books, with Goldsmith's admirable Letters on England, and his histories of Rome and Greece (Robinson Crusoe and the Arabian Nights, of course), and I had gone through the six octavo volumes of the first edition of Cook's Voyages.

The 'Elegant Extracts' made me acquainted with the best passages in the works of all the best British writers who flourished before the present century. From this book I first learned the beauties of Shakespeare.

Like most authors, I made my first attempts in *verse*. . . . At thirteen or fourteen, I began to despise my own poetry, and destroyed all I had. I then, for many years, abandoned the dream of my childhood, the hope of one day seeing my name in print.

This idyllic existence ended with the family's return to Philadelphia and her father's illness and subsequent death in 1803. Her father died heavily in debt and Miss Leslie comments: "My mother and her five children (of whom I was the eldest) were left in circumstances which rendered it necessary that she and myself should make immediate exertions for the support of those who were yet too young to assist themselves."

In her account Miss Leslie proceeds rather directly from her father's death in 1803 to the publication of her first book, *Seventy-five Receipts for Pastry, Cakes and Sweetmeats* (Boston, 1828). She neglects to mention that one "immediate exertion" she and her mother undertook for the support of the family was the running of a boardinghouse. This was one of the few occupations considered respectable enough at that time for a genteel woman to undertake when she found herself in need. Respectable enough to *do* perhaps, but obviously not respectable enough for Miss Leslie to mention in print.

She does reveal that her first book was compiled from a "tolerable collection of receipts, taken by myself while a pupil of Mrs. Goodfellow's cooking school in Philadelphia." However, when *Seventy-five Receipts* appeared, there was no mention of Mrs. Goodfellow, no attribution of any kind. Miss Leslie simply stated that the recipes were "all original, and have been used by the author and many of her friends with uniform success."

From its first printing in 1828, *Seventy-five Receipts* went on to become one of America's most popular cookbooks. At least twenty editions appeared by 1847, with additional printings of the "20th edition" being recorded as late as 1875. It was also published as an addendum to various other 19th-century cookbooks.

In her autobiographical letter, Miss Leslie almost apologetically explains that she wrote *Seventy-five Receipts* only because of the many requests from her friends for the recipes. The fact that this book and her later cookery works were so successful commercially that they supported her for the rest of her life was, she made quite obvious, never very pleasing to her.

In her preface to *Seventy-five Receipts*, Miss Leslie stresses the fact that the recipes are "in every sense of the word, American; but the writer flatters herself that (if exactly followed) the articles produced from them will not be found inferior to any of a similar description made in the European manner."

Her second cookbook was decidedly *not* American. In 1832, she published *Domestic French Cookery, chiefly translated from Sulpice Barué* (Philadelphia). There were at least six printings of this book in twenty-three years. Strangely, in her autobiographical letter, Miss Leslie makes no mention of this work, a very early American volume on French cookery.

Directions for Cookery, Miss Leslie's most influential cookery book, was published by Carey and Hart in Philadelphia in 1837. As previously indicated, it appears to have been the most popular cookbook printed in America during the 19th century; a 60th edition (including variant titles such as *Miss Leslie's Complete Cookery*) appeared in 1870 and was itself reprinted as late as 1892. This book was so successful and so well received that later, when she published a new cookbook, the advertisements took great pains to explain that the new work was "supplemental" to *Directions*: "all persons who have had Miss Leslie's former book, entitled 'Directions for Cookery,' should get this at once, *as all the receipts in this book are new*, and have been fully tried and tested by the author since the publication of her former book, and *none of them whatever are contained in any other work but this*." (Advertisement in and for *New Receipts for Cooking* [Philadelphia, 1854]).

It is easy to agree with the many culinary authorities who consider Miss Leslie's *Directions* to be one of America's great cookbooks. The writing and instructions are clear and elegant; the author's comments on the nuances of good cooking, on the importance of quality ingredients, on honesty in the kitchen—all combine to make this work an American classic.

To examine the recipes is to open a window into the 19th-century American larder: Apees, Beef-Steak Pudding, Moravian Sugar Cake, Sassafras Beer, Rye and Indian Bread, Cat-Fish Soup, Chestnut Pudding, Fricasseed Chickens, Clam Soup, Chilli Vinegar, Green Corn Muffins, Cranberry Sauce, Election Cake, Federal Cakes, Flannel Cakes, Fox Grape Shrub, Hominy, Huckleberry Cake, Indian Pudding, Johnny Cake, Lobster Catchup, Molasses Candy, New York Cookies, Ochra Soup, Oyster Pie, Pepper Pot, Pine-apple Ice Cream, Pork and Beans, Potato Snow, Pumpkin Chips, New England Pumpkin Pie, West India Cocoa-Nut Pudding, Fine Tomata Catchup, White Gingerbread. The titles alone stimulate the appetite!

But look beyond the titles; observe how carefully written are the recipes. Most ingredients are given in specific measurements—pounds, tablespoons, teaspoons, pints—a practice hardly routine in her day. But note also the many helpful hints and comments: "It is best the second day." "This is a very good plain cake; do not attempt it unless you have excellent yeast." For her Cinderellas or German Puffs, "Send them round whole, for they will fall almost as soon as cut." For her Apple Dumplings, "Do not take them up till a moment before they are wanted . . . The apples should never be sweet ones." For her Potato Snow, "This preparation looks well; but many think it renders the potatoes insipid."

Her concern for quality extends beyond the kitchen. The Cat-Fish Soup recipe, for example, begins, "Cat-fish that have been caught near the middle of the river are much nicer than those that are taken near the shore where they have access to impure food. The small white ones are the best." The soup is flavored with ham, parsley, sweet marjoram stripped from the stalks, pepper, and celery. The broth uses rich milk, butter, and egg yolks and the whole is garnished with toasted bread cut into small squares. A splendid American dish.

After the success of *Directions*, Miss Leslie turned her attention to *The House Book*, first published in Philadelphia in 1840, and appearing (sometimes called *Miss Leslie's Lady's House-Book*) in a 19th edition in 1863. This book was meant to teach the American woman how to manage a household and was a companion to her cookbooks. In her preface, Miss Leslie explains: "The design of the following work is to impart to novices in house-keeping some information on a subject which is, or ought to be, important to every American female so that they may be enabled to instruct unpracticed domestics, or, in case of emergency, to assist personally in forwarding the indispensable work of the family."

The book is subtitled "A Manual of Domestic Economy, containing approved directions for Washing, Dress-Making, Millinery, Dyeing, Cleaning, Quilting, Table-Linen, Window-Washing, Wood-Fires, Straw Bonnets, Silk Stockings, Rag Carpets, Plated-Ware, Porcelain, House-Cleaning, Laundry-Works, Coal-Grate Fires, Evening Parties, &c." It appears that Miss Leslie's years at her mother's boardinghouse were well remembered. This work was the only book one needed to run a proper household of the day. It is invaluable to modern social historians.

Although *Directions* was still then in print, a new cookbook by Miss Leslie, *Lady's Receipt-Book* (Philadelphia) appeared in 1846 followed by her *Lady's New Receipt-Book* (Philadelphia) in 1850. With varying titles (*New Receipts*, *More Receipts*, *Miss Leslie's Cook Book*, *New Cookery*) and often slightly varying content, these books appeared in at least ten editions prior to the Civil War, with additional printings in the 1870s and 1880s. It is virtually impossible to ascertain the definitive publishing history of these various printings, as there is no one location where all the editions can be found for direct examination and comparison.

As mentioned earlier, the advertising for her book titled *New Receipts* was replete with comments on the "newness" of the recipes and the need for the customer to buy *this* volume as a companion for *Directions*. In her preface for the 1854 printing of *New Receipts*, Miss Leslie forcefully repeats this plea. She explains that since her last book, she has "obtained new and fresh accessions of valuable knowledge, and new receipts for cooking . . . connected with the domestic improvement of my countrywomen, all of which I have been careful to note down . . . to carefully try and have them fully tested, and have now given them all in this work—minutely explaining them in a language intelligible to all persons." She further tells us that a large number of recipes in this new volume were obtained from the South and that many were "dictated by colored cooks, of high reputation in the art." These books do contain new recipes as well as fascinating sections on household hints, remedies, information on embroidery and needlework, and many pages on menu planning and entertaining.

In her autobiographical letter (written in 1851), Miss Leslie writes that "the work from which I have, as yet, derived the greatest pecuniary advantage, are my three books on domestic economy. The 'Domestic Cookery Book' (*Directions*), published in 1837, is now in its forty-first edition, no edition having been less than a thousand copies; and sales increase every year. 'The House Book' came out in 1840 and the 'Lady's Receipt Book' in 1846. All have been successful and profitable."

Miss Leslie ends the letter by indicating that she hopes "soon to finish a work (undertaken by particular desire) for the benefit of young ladies, and to which I purpose giving the plain, simple title of 'The Behavior Book.'" This book, first published, I believe, in 1853 went through at least half a dozen printings, sometimes entitled *The Ladies' Guide to True Politeness and Perfect Manners*. The work offers invaluable insight into contemporary manners and etiquette.

Miss Leslie never mentions in her 1851 letter a cookbook she had already authored, *The Indian Meal Book*. This volume has a most interesting printing history. It has often been assumed that the first edition was published by Carey & Hart in Philadelphia in 1847. There are, however, two earlier printings, both published in London. Why, one might ask, would a cookbook devoted entirely to Indian meal (cornmeal), until then a much-despised and little-known article of food in Europe, be first issued in London? The date reveals all. It was published to introduce and teach the Irish how to use corn-meal as a staple to survive the great potato famine. In fact, it was one of a series of little-known books and pamphlets explaining the use of cornmeal that were published during the famine years.

The preface states: "The author is sanguine in her hope, that this little book may be found a valuable accompaniment to the introduction of Indian Meal to Great Britain and Ireland. She believes also that it may be useful to strangers newly arrived in the British American provinces, and conse-quently unacquainted with the various modes of preparing for the table unground or green Indian corn.

"Miss Leslie, having lived in England, flatters herself that she has been enabled to make her directions clear to the com-prehension of English cooks. She has indicated the utensils used in America for preparing Indian meal, supposing that if any of them are found indispensably necessary, they will either be made in England or imported from the United States."

When *The Indian Meal Book* was published in the United States, there was no mention of the previous English editions or of the original purpose of the work. How Miss Leslie came to write this book I do not know. The answer to that mystery may lie in her papers which are at The Library Company of Philadelphia. Whatever the facts behind the publication of *The Indian Meal Book*, we must be grateful for its existence as there are few such wondrous and imaginative compilations of recipes using cornmeal. There are puddings and porridges, cakes and cupcakes, pone, flappers, fritters, mush, gruel, dumplings, biscuits, breads, grits, hominy, griddle cakes, hasty pudding, johnny cakes, muffins, puffs, samp, slip-jacks, and both summer and winter saccatash.

Miss Leslie died on January 1, 1858. Her works, especially those on cookery and domestic economy, have lived on. We have just begun to appreciate anew and assess her contributions to America's culinary history; more work remains to be done.

Once again, I must thank Dover Publications for its continuing commitment to publishing milestones of American culinary history, of which this is the sixth volume.[2] Dover has wisely chosen to reprint this later edition (59th edition, 1851), as it not only contains the complete text of the first edition (1837), but offers the reader the benefit of later addenda and additional recipes by the inimitable Miss Eliza Leslie.

JANICE (JAN) BLUESTEIN LONGONE
The Wine and Food Library
Ann Arbor, Michigan
July 1998

---

2 The others are: *The First American Cookbook: A Facsimile of "American Cookery," 1796*, Amelia Simmons [1984; ISBN 0-486-24710-4]; *The Virginia Housewife* (1869), Mary Randolph [1993; ISBN 0-486-27772-0]; *Boston Cooking School Cook Book: A Reprint of the 1884 Classic*, Mary J. Lincoln [1996; ISBN 0-486-29196-0]; *Early American Cookery: "The Good Housekeeper."* 1841, Sarah Josepha Hale [1997; ISBN 0-486-29296-7]; and *Original 1896 Boston Cooking-School Cook Book*, Fannie Merritt Farmer [1997; ISBN 0-486-29697].

PREFACE.

In preparing a new and carefully revised edition of this, my first work on general cookery, I have introduced improvements, corrected errors, and added new receipts, that I trust will, on trial, be found satisfactory. The success of the book (proved by its immense and increasing circulation,) affords conclusive evidence that it has obtained the approbation of a large number of my countrywomen; many of whom have informed me that it has made practical housewives of young ladies who have entered into married life with no other acquirements than a few showy accomplishments. Gentlemen, also, have told me of great improvements in the family-table, after presenting their wives with this manual of domestic cookery; and that, after a morning devoted to the fatigues of business, they no longer find themselves subjected to the annoyance of an ill-dressed dinner.

No man (or woman either) ought to be incapable of distinguishing bad eatables from good ones. Yet, I have heard some few ladies boast of that incapacity, as something meritorious, and declare that they considered the quality, the preparation, and even the taste of food, as things entirely beneath the attention of a rational being; their own minds being always occupied with objects of far greater importance.

Let no man marry such a woman.* If indifferent to her own food, he will find her still more indifferent to his. A wife who cares not, or knows not what a table ought to be, always has bad cooks; for she cannot distinguish a bad one

---

* My instructress, the late Mrs. Goodfellow, remarked, in allusion to the dullness or silliness of some of her pupils, "It requires a head even to make cakes."

The text of the original book begins here. No material has been omitted.

7

from a good one, dislikes change, and wonders how her husband can attach any importance to so trifling a circumstance as his dinner. Yet, though, for the sake of "preserving the peace," he may bring himself to pass over, as "trifling circumstances," the defects of his daily repasts, he will find himself not a little mortified, when, on inviting a friend to dinner, he finds his table disgraced by washy soup, poultry half raw, gravy unskimmed, and vegetables undrained; to say nothing of sour bread, ponderous puddings, curdled custards tasting of nothing, and tough pastry.

Let all housekeepers remember that there is no possibility of producing nice dishes without a liberal allowance of good ingredients. "Out of nothing, nothing can come," is a homely proverb, but a true one. And so is the ancient caution against being "penny-wise and pound-foolish." By judicious management, and by taking due care that nothing is wasted or thrown away which might be used to advantage, one family will live "excellently well," at no greater cost in the end than another family is expending on a table that never has a good thing upon it.

A sufficiency of wholesome and well-prepared food is absolutely necessary to the preservation of health and strength, both of body and mind. Ill-fed children rarely grow up with vigorous constitutions; and dyspepsia, in adults, is as frequently produced by eating food that is unpalatable or disagreeable to their taste, as by indulging too much in things they peculiarly relish. For those who possess the means of living well, it is a false (and sometimes fatal) economy to live badly; particularly when there is a lavish expenditure in fine clothes, fine furniture, and other ostentations, only excusable when *not* purchased at the expense of health and comfort.

ELIZA LESLIE.

Philadelphia, Jan. 16, 1851.

INTRODUCTORY HINTS.

WEIGHTS AND MEASURES.

WE recommend to all families that they should keep in the house a pair of scales, (one of the scales deep enough to hold flour, sugar, &c., conveniently,) and a set of tin measures; as accuracy in proportioning the ingredients is indispensable to success in cookery. It is best to have the scales permanently fixed to a small beam projecting (for instance) from one of the shelves of the store-room. This will preclude the frequent inconvenience of their getting twisted, unlinked, and otherwise out of order; a common consequence of putting them in and out of their box, and carrying them from place to place. The weights (of which there should be a set from two pounds to a quarter of an ounce) ought carefully to be kep in the box, that none of them may be lost or mislaid.

A set of tin measures (with small spouts or lips) from a gallon down to half a jill, will be found very convenient in every kitchen; though common pitchers, bowls, glasses, &c. may be substituted. It is also well to have a set of wooden measures from a bushel to a quarter of a peck.

Let it be remembered, that of liquid measure—

Two jills are half a pint.

Two pints — one quart.

Four quarts — one gallon.

9

Of dry measure—

> Half a gallon is a quarter of a peck.
> One gallon   — half a peck.
> Two gallons   — one peck.
> Four gallons   — half a bushel.
> Eight gallons   — one bushel.

About twenty-five drops of any thin liquid will fill a common sized tea-spoon.

Four table-spoonfuls or half a jill, will fill a common wine glass.

Four wine glasses will fill a half-pint or common tumbler or a large coffee-cup.

A quart black bottle holds in reality about a pint and a half.

Of flour, butter, sugar, and most articles used in cakes and pastry, a quart is generally about equal in quantity to a pound avoirdupois, (sixteen ounces.) Avoirdupois is the weight designated throughout this book.

Ten eggs generally weigh one pound before they are broken.

A table-spoonful of salt is generally about one ounce.

GENERAL CONTENTS.

MISS LESLIE'S COOKERY

SOUPS.

GENERAL REMARKS.

ALWAYS use soft water for making soup, and be careful to proportion the quantity of water to that of the meat. Somewhat less than a quart of water to a pound of meat, is a good rule for common soups. Rich soups, intended for company, may have a still smaller allowance of water.

Soup should always be made entirely of fresh meat that has not been previously cooked. An exception to this rule may sometimes be made in favour of the remains of a piece of roast beef that has been *very much* under-done in roasting This may be *added* to a good piece of raw meat. Cold ham, also, may be occasionally put into white soups.

Soup made of cold meat has always a vapid, disagreeable taste, very perceptible through all the seasoning, and which nothing indeed can disguise. Also, it will be of a bad, dingy colour. The juices of the meat having been exhausted by the first cooking, the undue proportion of watery liquid renders it, for soup, indigestible and unwholesome, as well as unpalatable. As there is little or no nutriment to be derived from soup made with cold meat, it is better to refrain from using it for this purpose, and to devote the leavings of the table to some other object No person accustomed to really good soup, made from fresh meat, can ever be deceived in the taste, even when flavoured with wine and spices. It is not true that French cooks have the art of producing *excellent* soups from cold scraps. There is much *bad* soup to be found in France, at inferior houses; but *good* French cooks are not, as is generally supposed, really in the practice of concocting any dishes out of the refuse of the table. And we repeat, that cold meat, even when perfectly good, and used in a large quantity, has not sufficient substance to flavour soup, or to render it wholesome.

Soup, however, that has been originally made of raw meat entirely, is frequently better the second day than the first; provided that it is re-boiled only for a very short time, and that no additional water is added to it.

Unless it has been allowed to boil too hard, so as to exhaust the water, the soup-pot will not require replenishing. When it is found absolutely necessary to do so, the additional water must be boiling hot when poured in; if lukewarm or cold, it will entirely spoil the soup.

Every particle of fat should be carefully skimmed from the surface. Greasy soup is disgusting and unwholesome. The lean of meat is much better for soup than the fat.

Long and slow boiling is necessary to extract the strength from the meat. If boiled fast over a large fire, the meat becomes hard and tough, and will not give out its juices.

Potatoes, if boiled in the soup, are thought by some to ren der it unwholesome, from the opinion that the water in which potatoes have been cooked is almost a poison. As potatoes are a part of every dinner, it is very easy to take a few out of the pot in which they have been boiled by themselves, and to cut them up and add them to the soup just before it goes to table. Remove all shreds of meat and bone.

The cook should season the soup but very slightly with salt and pepper. If she puts in too much it may spoil it for the taste of most of those that are to eat it; but if too little, it is easy to add more to your own plate.

The practice of thickening soup by stirring flour into it is not a good one, as it spoils both the appearance and the taste. If made with a sufficient quantity of good fresh meat, and not too much water, and if boiled long and slowly, it will have substance enough without flour.

FAMILY SOUP.

TAKE a shin or leg of beef that has been newly killed; the hind leg is best, as there is the most meat on it. Have it cut into three pieces, and wash it well. To each pound allow somewhat less than a quart of water; for instance, to ten pounds of leg of beef, nine quarts of water is a good proportion. Put it into a large pot, and add half a table-spoonful of salt. Hang it over a good fire, as early as six o'clock in the morning, if you dine at two. When it has come to a hard boil, and the scum has risen, (which it will do as soon as it has boiled,) skim it well. Do not remove the lid more frequently than is absolutely necessary, as uncovering the pot causes the flavour to evaporate. Then set it on hot coals in the corner, and keep it simmering steadily, adding fresh coals so as to continue a regular heat.

About nine o'clock, put in four carrots, one parsnip, and a large onion cut into slices, and four small turnips, and eight tomatas, also cut up; add a head of celery cut small. Put in a very small head of cabbage, cut into little pieces. If you have any objection to cabbage, substitute a larger proportion

of the other vegetables. Put in also a bunch of sweet marjo
ram, tied up in a thin muslin rag to prevent its floating on
the top. To grate the carrots is an improvement.

Let the soup simmer unceasingly till two o'clock, skimming
it well : then take it up, and put it into a tureen. If your
dinner hour is later, you may of course begin the soup later ;
but it will require at least eight hours' cooking ; remembering
to put in the vegetables three hours after the meat.

If you wish to send the meat to table, take the best part of
it out of the soup, about two hours before dinner. Have ready
another pot with a dozen tomatas and a few cloves. Moisten
them with a little of the soup, just sufficient to keep them from
burning. When the tomatas have stewed down soft, put the
meat upon them, and let it brown till dinner time over a few
coals, keeping the pot closely covered : then send it to table
on a dish by itself. Let the remainder of the meat be left in
the large pot till you send up the soup, as by that time it will
be boiled to rags and have transferred all its flavour to the
liquid, which should be served up free from shreds.

This soup will be greatly improved by the addition of a few
dozen ochras cut into very thin slices, and put in with the
other vegetables. You may put Lima beans into it, green
peas, or indeed any vegetables you like : or you may thicken
it with ochras and tomatas only.

Next day, take what is left of the soup, put it into a pot,
and simmer it over hot coals for half an hour : a longer time
will weaken the taste. If it has been well made and kept in
a cool place, it will be found better the second day than the
first.

If your family is very small, and the leg of beef large and
the season winter, it may furnish soup for four successive
days. Cut the beef in half; make soup of the first half, in

the manner above directed, and have the remainder warmed next day : then on the third day make fresh soup of the second half.

We have been minute in these directions; for if strictly followed, the soup, though plain, will be found excellent.

If you do not intend to serve up the meat separately, break to pieces all the bones with a mallet or kitchen cleaver. This, by causing them to give out their marrow, &c., will greatly enrich the liquid. Do this, of course, when you first begin the soup. It is a slovenly and vulgar practice to send soup to table with shreds. of meat and bits of bone in it.

FINE BEEF SOUP.

BEGIN this soup the day before it is wanted. Take a good piece of fresh beef that has been newly killed : any substantial part will do that has not too much fat about it: a shin is very good for this purpose. Wash it well. Cut off all the meat, and break up the bones. Put the meat and the bones into a large pot, very early in the day, so as to allow eight or nine hours for its boiling. Proportion the water to the quantity of meat—about a pint and a half to each pound. Sprinkle the meat with a small quantity of pepper and salt. Pour on the water, hang it over a moderate fire, and boil it slowly : carefully skimming off all the fat that rises to the top, and keeping it closely covered, except when you raise the lid to skim it. Do not, on any account, put in additional water to this soup while it is boiling; and take care that the boiling goes steadily on, as, if it stops, the soup will be much injured. But if the fire is too great, and the soup boils too fast, the meat will become hard and tough, and will not give out its juices

After the meat is reduced to rags, and the soup sufficiently boiled, remove the pot from the fire, and let it stand in the corner for a quarter of an hour to settle. Then take it up, strain it into a large earthen pan, cover it, and set it away in a cool dry place till next day. Straining it makes it clear and bright, and frees it from the shreds of meat and bone. If you find that it jellies in the pan, (which it will if properly made,) do not disturb it till you are ready to put it into the pot for the second boiling, as breaking the jelly may prevent it from keeping well.

On the following morning, boil separately, carrots, turnips, onions, celery, and whatever other vegetables you intend to thicken the soup with. Tomatas will greatly improve it. Prepare them by taking off the skin, cutting them into smal. pieces, and stewing them in their own juice till they are entirely dissolved. Put on the carrots before any of the other vegetables, as they require the longest time to boil. Or you may slice and put into the soup a portion of the vegetables you are boiling for dinner; but they must be nearly done before you put them in, as the second boiling of the soup should not exceed half an hour, or indeed, just sufficient time to heat it thoroughly.

Scrape off carefully from the cake of jellied soup whatever fat or sediment may still be remaining on it; divide the jelly into pieces, and about half an hour before it is to go to table, put it into a pot, add the various vegetables, (having first sliced them,) in sufficient quantities to make the soup very thick; hang it over the fire and let it boil slowly, or simmer steadily till dinner time. Boiling it much on the second day will destroy the flavour, and render it flat and insipid. For this reason, in making fine, clear beef soup, the vegetables are to be cooked separately. They need not be put in the first day, as the soup is to be strained; and on the second day, if put in raw, the length of time required to cook them would spoil the soup by doing it too much. We repeat, that when soup has been sufficiently boiled on the first day, and all the juices and flavour of the meat thoroughly extracted, half an hour is the utmost it requires on the second.

Carefully avoid seasoning it too highly. Soup, otherwise excellent, is frequently spoiled by too much pepper and salt. These condiments can be added at table, according to the taste of those that are eating it; but if too large a proportion of them is put in by the cook, there is then no remedy, and the soup may by some be found uneatable.

Many persons prefer boiling all the vegetables in the soup on the first day, thinking that they improve its flavour. This may be done in common soup that is not to be strained, but is inadmissible if you wish it to be very bright and clear. Also, unless you have a garden and a profusion of vegetables of your own, it is somewhat extravagant, as when strained out they are of no further use, and are therefore wasted.

MUTTON SOUP.

Cut off the shoulder part of a fore quarter of mutton and having cut all the meat from the bone, put it into a soup pot with two quarts of water. As soon as it boils, skim it well, and then slacken the fire and simmer the meat for an hour and a half. Then take the remainder of the mutton, and put it whole into the soup-pot with sufficient boiling water to cover it well, and salt it to your taste Skim it the moment the fresh piece of meat begins to boil, and about every quarter of an hour afterwards. It should boil slowly five hours. Prepare half a dozen turnips, four carrots,* and three onions, (all cut up, but not small,) and put them in about an hour and a half before dinner. You may also put in some small dumplings. Add some chopped parsley.

Cut the meat off the scrag into small pieces, and send it to table in the tureen with the soup. The other half of the mutton should be served on a separate dish, with whole turnips boiled and laid round it. Many persons are fond of mutton that has been boiled in soup.

You may thicken this soup with rice or barley that has first been soaked in cold water; or with green peas; or with young corn, cut down from the cob; or with tomatas scalded, peeled, and cut into pieces; or with grated carrots.

Cabbage Soup may be made in the same manner, of neck of mutton. Omit all the other vegetables, and put in a large head of white cabbage, stripped of the outside leaves, and cut small.

Noodle Soup can be made in this manner also. Noodles are a mixture of flour and beaten egg, made into a stiff paste, kneaded, rolled out very thin, and cut into long narrow slips, not thicker than straws, and then dried three or four hours in the sun, on tin or pewter plates. They must be put in the soup shortly before dinner, as, if boiled too long they will go to pieces.

With the mutton that is taken from the soup you may send to table some suet dumplings, boiled in another pot, and served on a separate dish. Make them in the proportion of half a pound of beef suet to a pound and a quarter of flour. Chop the suet as fine as possible, rub it into the flour, and mix it

---

* It will be best to grate the carrots, or at least two of them.

into a dough with a little cold water. Roll it out thick, and cut it into dumplings about as large as the top of a tumbler, and boil them an hour.

VEAL SOUP.

THE knuckle or leg of veal is the best for soup. Wash it and break up the bones. Put it into a pot with a pound of ham or bacon cut into pieces, and water enough to cover the meat. A set of calf's feet, cut in half, will greatly improve it. After it has stewed slowly, till all the meat drops to pieces, strain it, return it to the pot, and put in a head of celery cut small, three onions, a bunch of sweet marjoram, a carrot and a turnip cut into pieces, and two dozen black pepper-corns, but not any salt. Add some small dumplings made of flour and butter. Simmer it another hour, or till all the vegetables are sufficiently done, and thus send it to table.

You may thicken it with noodles, that is paste made of flour and beaten egg, and cut into long thin slips. Or with vermicelli, rice, or barley; or with green peas, or asparagus tops.

RICH VEAL SOUP.

TAKE three pounds of the scrag of a neck of veal, cut it into pieces, and put it with the bones (which must be broken up) into a pot with two quarts of water. Stew it till the meat is done to rags, and skim it well. Then strain it and return it to the pot.

Blanch and pound in a mortar to a smooth paste, a quarter

of a pound of sweet almonds, and mix them with the yolks of six hard boiled eggs grated, and a pint of cream, which must first have been boiled or it will curdle in the soup. Season it with nutmeg and mace. Stir the mixture into the soup, and let it boil afterward about three minutes, stirring all the time. Lay in the bottom of the tureen some slices of bread without the crust. Pour the soup upon it, and send it to table.

CLEAR GRAVY SOUP.

HAVING well buttered the inside of a nicely tinned stew-pot, cut half a pound of ham into slices, and lay them at the bottom, with three pounds of the lean of fresh beef, and as much veal, cut from the bones, which you must afterward break to pieces, and lay on the meat. Cover the pan closely, and set it over a quick fire. When the meat begins to stick to the pan, turn it; and when there is a nice brown glaze at the bottom, cover the meat with cold water. Watch it well, and when it is just coming to a boil, put in a pint of water. This will cause the scum to rise. Skim it well, and then pour in another pint of water; skim it again; pour in water as before, a pint at a time, and repeat this till no more scum rises. In skimming, carefully avoid stirring the soup, as that will injure its clearness.

In the mean time prepare your vegetables. Peel off the outer skin of three large white onions and slice them. Pare three large turnips, and slice them also. Wash clean and cu into small pieces three carrots, and three large heads of celery If you cannot obtain fresh celery, substitute a large table-spoonful of celery seed, tied up in a bit of clear muslin. Put the vegetables into the soup, and then place the pot on one side of the fire, where the heat is not so great as in the middle. Let it boil gently for four hours. Then strain the soup through a fine towel or linen bag into a large stone pan, but do not squeeze the bag, or the soup will be cloudy, and look dull instead of clear. In pouring it into the straining cloth, be careful not to disturb the ingredients at the bottom of the soup-pot.

This soup should be of a fine clear amber colour. If not perfectly bright after straining, you may clarify it in this manner. Put it into the stew-pan. Break the whites of two eggs into a basin, carefully avoiding the smallest particle of the yolk. Beat the white of egg to a stiff froth, and then mix it gradually with the soup. Set it over the fire, and stir it till it boils briskly. Then take it off, and set it beside the fire to settle for ten minutes. Strain it then through a clean napkin, and it will be fit for use. But it is better to have the soup clear by making it carefully, than to depend on clarifying it afterward, as the white of egg weakens the taste.

In making this (which is quite a show-soup) it is customary to reverse the general rule, and pour in cold water.

SOUPE À LA JULIENNE.

MAKE a gravy soup as in the preceding receipt, and strain it before you put in the vegetables. Cut some turnips and carrots into ribands, and some onions and celery into lozenges or long diamond-shaped pieces. Boil them separately. When the vegetables are thoroughly boiled, put them with the soup into the tureen, and then lay gently on the top some small squares of toasted bread without crust; taking care that they do not crumble down and disturb the brightness of the soup, which should be of a clear amber colour.

MACCARONI SOUP.

THIS also is made of clear gravy soup. Cut up and boil the maccaroni by itself in a very little water, allowing a quarter of a pound to a quart of soup. The pieces should be about an inch long. Put a small piece of butter with it. It must boil till tender, but not till it breaks. Throw it into the soup shortly before it goes to table, and give it one boil up. Send to table with it a plate or glass of rasped Parmesan or other rich cheese, with a dessert spoon in it, that those who like it may put it into their soup on the plate.

While the maccaroni is boiling, take care that it does not get into lumps.

RICH MACCARONI SOUP.

TAKE a quart of clear gravy soup, and boil in it a pound of the best maccaroni cut into pieces. When it is tender, take out half of the maccaroni, and add to the remainder two quarts more of the soup. Boil it till the maccaroni is entirely dissolved and incorporated with the liquid. Strain it: then return it to the soup-pan, and add to it the remainder of the maccaroni, (that was taken out before the pieces broke,) and put in a quarter of a pound of grated Parmesan cheese. Let it simmer awhile, but take it up before it comes to a boil.

It may be made with milk instead of gravy soup.

VERMICELLI SOUP.

Cut a knuckle of veal, or a neck of mutton into small pieces, and put them, with the bones broken up, into a large stew-pan. Add the meat sliced from a hock or shank of ham, a quarter of a pound of butter, two large onions sliced, a bunch of sweet herbs, and a head of celery cut small. Cover the pan closely, and set it without any water over a slow fire for an hour or more, to extract the essence from the meat. Then skim it well, and pour in four quarts of boiling water, and let it boil gently till all the meat is reduced to rags. Strain it, set it again on the fire, and add a quarter of a pound of vermicelli, which has first been scalded in boiling water. Season it to your taste with a little cayenne pepper, and let it boil five minutes. Lay a large slice of bread in the bottom of your tureen, and pour the soup upon it.

For the veal or mutton you may substitute a pair of large fowls cut into pieces; always adding the ham or a few slices of bacon, without which it will be insipid. Old fowls that are fit for no other purpose will do very well for soup.

MILK SOUP.

Boil two quarts of milk with a quarter of a pound of sweet almonds, and two ounces of bitter ones, blanched and broken to pieces, and a large stick of cinnamon broken up. Stir in sugar enough to make it very sweet. When it has boiled, strain it. Cut some thin slices of bread, and (having pared off the crust) toast them. Lay them in the bottom of a tureen, pour a little of the hot milk over them, and cover them close, that they may soak. Beat the yolks of five eggs very light.

Set the milk on hot coals, and add the eggs to it by degrees; stirring it all the time till it thickens. Then take it off instantly, lest it curdle, and pour it into the tureen, boiling not, over the bread.

This will be still better if you cover the bottom with slices of baked apple.

RICH BROWN SOUP.

TAKE six pounds of the lean of fresh beef, cut from the bone. Stick it over with four dozen cloves. Season it with a tea-spoonful of salt, a tea-spoonful of pepper, a tea-spoonful of mace, and a beaten nutmeg. Slice half a dozen onions; fry them in butter; chop them, and spread them over the meat after you have put it into the soup-pot. Pour in five quarts of water, and stew it slowly for five or six hours; skimming it well. When the meat has dissolved into shreds, strain it, and return the liquid to the pot. Then add a tumbler and a half, or six wine glasses of claret or port wine. Simmer it again slowly till dinner time. When the soup is reduced to three quarts, it is done enough. Put it into a tureen, and send it to table.

RICH WHITE SOUP.

TAKE a pair of large fat fowls. Cut them up. Butter the inside of the soup-pot, and put in the pieces of fowl with two pounds of the lean of veal, cut into pieces, or with four calf's feet cut in half. Season them with a tea-spoonful of salt, a half tea-spoonful of cayenne pepper, and a dozen blades of mace. Cover them with water, and stew it slowly for an hour, skimming it well. Then take out the breasts and wings of the fowls, and having cut off the flesh, chop it fine. Keep the pot covered, and the veal and the remainder of the fowls still stewing.

Mix the chopped chicken with the grated crumb of about one quarter of a loaf of stale bread, (a six cent loaf,) having soaked the crumbs in a little warm milk. Have ready the yolks of four hard boiled eggs, a dozen sweet almonds, and half a dozen bitter ones blanched and broken small. Mix the egg and almonds with the chopped chicken and grated bread, and pound all in a mortar till it is well incorporated. Strain the soup from the meat and fowl, and stir this mixture into the liquid, after it has stewed till reduced to two quarts. Having boiled separately a quart of cream or rich milk, add it hot to the soup, a little at a time. Cover it, and let it simmer a few minutes longer. Then send it to table.

These two soups (the brown and the white) are suited to dinner parties.

MEG MERRILIES' SOUP.

TAKE four pounds of venison, or if you cannot procure venison you may substitute the lean of fresh beef or mutton. Season it with pepper and salt, put it into a large pot, (break the bones and lay them on the meat,) pour in four quarts of water, and boil it three hours, skimming it well. Then strain it, and put it into another pot.

Cut up a hare or a rabbit, a pair of partridges, and a pair of grouse; or one of each, with a pheasant, a woodcock, or any other game that you can most easily obtain. Season them and put them into the soup. Add a dozen small onions, a couple of heads of celery cut small, and half a dozen sliced potatoes. Let the soup simmer till the game is sufficiently done, and all the vegetables tender.

This is the soup with which the gipsy, Meg Merrilies, regaled Dominie Sampson.

When game is used for soup, it must be newly killed, and quite fresh.

VENISON SOUP.

TAKE four pounds of freshly killed venison cut off from the bones, and one pound of ham in small slices. Add an onion minced, and black pepper to your taste. Put only as much water as will cover it, and stew it gently for an hour, keeping the pot closely covered. Then skim it well, and pour in a quart of boiling water. Add a head of celery cut into small pieces, and half a dozen blades of mace. Boil it gently two hours and a half. Then put in a quarter of a pound of butter, divided into small pieces and rolled in flour, and half a pint of port or Madeira wine. Let it boil a quarter of an hour longer, and then send it to table with the meat in it.

HARE OR RABBIT SOUP.

TAKE a large newly killed hare, or two rabbits; cut them up and wash the pieces. Save all the blood, (which adds much to the flavour of the hare,) and strain it through a sieve. Put the pieces into a soup-pot with four whole onions stuck with a few cloves, four or five blades of mace, a head of celery cut small, and a bunch of parsley with a large bunch of

sweet marjoram and one of sweet basil, all tied together.
Salt and cayenne to your taste. Pour in three quarts of
water, and stew it gently an hour and a half. Then put in
the strained blood and simmer it for another hour, at least.
Do not let it actually boil, as that will cause the blood to
curdle. Then strain it, and pound half the meat in a mortar, and
stir it into the soup to thicken it, and cut the remainder of the
meat into small mouthfuls. Stir in, at the last, a jill or two
glasses of red wine, and a large table-spoonful of currant jelly.
Boil it slowly a few minutes longer, and then put it into your
tureen. It will be much improved by the addition of two
or three dozen small force-meat balls, about the size of a
nutmeg. This soup will require cooking at least four hours.

Partridge, pheasant, or grouse soup may be made in a
similar manner.

If you have any clear gravy soup, you may cut up the hare,
season it as above, and put it into a jug or jar well covered
and set in boiling water till the meat is tender. Then put it
into the gravy soup, add the wine, and let it come to a boil.
Send it to table with the pieces of the hare in the soup.

When hare soup is made in this last manner, omit using
the blood.

MULLAGATAWNY SOUP,

AS MADE IN INDIA.

TAKE a quarter of an ounce of China turmeric, the third of
an ounce of cassia, three drachms of black pepper, two
drachms of cayenne pepper, and an ounce of coriander seeds.
These must all be pounded fine in a mortar, and well mixed
and sifted. They will make sufficient curry powder for the
following quantity of soup:

Take two large fowls, or three pounds of the lean of veal. Cut the flesh entirely from the bones in small pieces, and put it into a stew-pan with two quarts of water. Let it boil slowly for half an hour, skimming it well. Prepare four large onions, minced, and fried in two ounces of butter. Add to them the curry powder, and moisten the whole with broth from the stew-pan, mixed with a little rice flour. When thoroughly mixed, stir the seasoning into the soup, and simmer it till it is as smooth and thick as cream, and till the chicken or veal is perfectly tender. Then stir into it the juice of a lemon ; and five minutes after take up the soup, with the meat in it, and serve it in the tureen.

Send to table separately, boiled rice on a hot water dish to keep it warm. The rice is to be put into the plates of soup by those who eat it.

To boil rice for this soup in the East India fashion :—Pick and wash half a pound in warm water. Put it into a sauce-pan. Pour two quarts of boiling water over it, and cover the pan closely. Set it in a warm place by the fire, to cook gradually in the hot water. In an hour pour off all the water, and setting the pan on hot coals, stir up and toss the rice with a fork, so as to separate the grains, and to dry without hardening it. Do not use a spoon, as that will not loosen the grains sufficiently. You may toss it with two forks.

MOCK TURTLE OR CALF'S HEAD SOUP.

THIS soup will require eight hours to prepare. Take a large calf's head, and having cleaned, washed, and soaked it, put it into a pot with a knuckle of veal, and the hock of a ham, or a few slices of bacon; but previously cut off and reserve enough of the veal to make two dozen small force-meat balls. Put the head and the other meat into as much water as will cover it very well, so that it may not be necessary to replenish it: this soup being always made very rich. Let it boil slowly four hours, skimming it carefully. As soon as no more scum rises, put in six potatoes, and three turnips, all sliced thin; with equal proportions of parsley, sweet marjoram, and sweet basil, chopped fine; and cayenne pepper to your taste. The ham will salt it sufficiently.

An hour before you send the meat to table, make about two dozen small force-meat balls of minced veal and beef-suet in equal quantities, seasoned with pepper and salt; sweet herbs, grated lemon-peel, and powdered nutmeg and mace. Add some beaten yolk of egg to make all these ingredients stick together. Flour the balls very well, and fry them in butter. Before you put them into the soup, take out the head, and the other meat. Cut the meat from the head in small pieces, and return it to the soup. When the soup is nearly done, stir in half a pint of Madeira. Have ready at least a dozen egg-balls made of the yolks of hard boiled eggs, grated or pounded in a mortar, and mixed with a little flour and sufficient raw yolk of egg to bind them. Make them up into the form and size of boy's marbles. Throw them into the soup at the last, and also squeeze in the juice of a lemon. Let it get another slow boil, and then put it into the tureen.

We omit a receipt for *real* turtle soup, as when that very expensive, complicated, and difficult dish is prepared in a private family, it is advisable to hire a first-rate cook for the express purpose.

An easy way is to get it ready made, in any quantity you please, from a turtle-soup house.

OX TAIL SOUP.

THREE ox tails will make a large tureen full of soup. Desire the butcher to divide them at the joints. Rub them with salt, and put them to soak in warm water, while you prepare the vegetables. Put into a large pot or stew-pan four onions peeled and quartered, a bunch of parsley, two sliced carrots, two sliced turnips, and two dozen pepper corns. Then put in the tails, and pour on three quarts of water.

Cover the pot, and set it on hot coals by the side of the fire. Keep it gently simmering for about three hours, supplying it well with fresh hot coals. Skim it carefully. When the meat is quite tender, and falls from the bones, strain the soup into another pot, and add to it a spoonful of mushroom catchup, and two spoonfuls of butter rubbed in flour.

You may thicken it also with the pulp of a dozen onions first fried soft, and then rubbed through a cullender. After it is thickened. let it just boil up, and then send it to table, with small squares of toasted bread in the tureen.

OCHRA SOUP.

TAKE a large slice of ham (cold boiled ham is best) and two pounds of the lean of fresh beef; cut all the meat into small pieces. Add a quarter of a pound of butter slightly melted: twelve large tomatas pared and cut small; five dozen ochras cut into slices not thicker than a cent; and a little cayenne pepper to your taste. Put all these ingredients into a pot; cover them with boiling water, and let hem stew slowly for an hour. Then add three quarts of *hot* water, and increase the heat so as to make the soup boil. Skim it well, and stir it frequently with a wooden or silver spoon.

Boil it till the tomatas are all to pieces, and the ochras entirely dissolved. Strain it, and then serve it up with toasted bread cut into dice, put in after it comes out of the pot.

This soup will be improved by a pint of shelled Lima beans, boiled by themselves, and put into the tureen just before you send it to table.

BEAN SOUP.

Put two quarts of dried white beans into soak the night before you make the soup, which should be put on as early in the day as possible.

Take five pounds of the lean of fresh beef—the coarse pieces will do. Cut them up, and put them into your soup pot with the bones belonging to them, (which should be broken to pieces,) and a pound of bacon cut very small. If you have the remains of a piece of beef that has been roasted the day before, and so much under-done that the juices remain in it, you may put it into the pot, and its bones along with it. Season the meat with pepper only, and pour on it six quarts of water. As soon as it boils take off the scum, and put in the beans (having first drained them) and a head of celery cut small, or a table-spoonful of pounded celery-seed. Boil it slowly till the meat is done to shreds, and the beans all dissolved. Then strain it through a cullender into the tureen, and put into it small squares of toasted bread with the crust cut off.

Some prefer it with the beans boiled soft, but not quite dissolved. In this case, do not strain it; but take out the meat and bones with a fork before you send it to table.

~~~~~~~~~~~~~~

PEAS SOUP.

Soak two quarts of dried or split peas over-night. In the morning take three pounds of the lean of fresh beef, and a pound of bacon or pickled pork. Cut them into pieces, and put them into a large soup-pot with the peas, (which must first be well drained,) and a table-spoonful of dried mint rubbed to powder. Add five quarts of water, and boil the soup gently for three hours, skimming it well, and then put in four heads of celery cut small, or two table-spoonfuls of pounded celery seed.

It must be boiled till the peas are entirely dissolved, so as to be no longer distinguishable, and the celery quite soft. Then strain it into a tureen, and serve it up with toasted bread cut in dice. Omit the crust of the bread.

Stir it up immediately before it goes to table, as it is apt to settle, and be thick at the bottom and thin at the top.

~~~~~~~~~~~~~~

GREEN PEAS SOUP.

Take four pounds of knuckle of veal, and a pound of bacon Cut them to pieces, and put them into a soup kettle with a sprig of mint and five quarts of water. Boil it moderately fast, and skim it well. When the meat is boiled to rags, strain it out, and put to the liquor a quart of young green peas. Boil them till they are entirely dissolved, and till they have thickened the soup, and given it a green colour.*

Have ready two quarts of green peas that have been boiled in another pot with a sprig of mint, and two or three lumps of loaf sugar, (which will greatly improve the taste.) After they have boiled in this pot twenty minutes, take out the mint, put the whole peas into the pot of soup, and boil all together about ten minutes. Then put it into a tureen, and send it to table.

Never use hard old green peas for this soup, or for any other purpose. When they begin to turn yellow, it is time to leave them off for the season.

Lima bean soup may he made in the same manner.

ASPARAGUS SOUP.

ASPARAGUS soup may he made in a similar manner to that of green peas. You must have four or five bunches of asparagus. Cit off the green tops, and put half of them into the soup, after the meat has been boiled to pieces and strained out. The asparagus must be boiled till quite dissolved, and till it has given a green colour to the soup. Then take the remainder of the asparagus tops (which must all this time have been lying in cold water) and put them into the soup, and let them boil about twenty minutes. Serve it up with small squares of toast in the tureen.

You may heighten the green of this soup by adding the juice of a handful of spinach, pounded in a mortar and

* You may greatly improve the colour by pounding a handful of spinach in a mortar, straining the juice, and adding it to the soup about a quarter of an hour before it has done boiling.

strained. Or you may colour it with the juice of boiled
spinach squeezed through a cloth. The spinach juice should
be put in fifteen or ten minutes before you take up the soup,
as a short boiling in it will take off the peculiar taste.

FRIAR'S CHICKEN.

Cut up four pounds of knuckle of veal; season it with
white pepper and salt: put it into a soup-pan and let it boil
slowly till the meat drops from the bone. Then strain it off
Have ready a pair of young fowls skinned, and cut up as you
carve them at table. Season them with white pepper, salt,
and mace. Put them into the soup, add a handful of chopped
parsley, and let them boil. When the pieces of chicken are
all quite tender, have ready four or five eggs well beaten.
Stir the egg into the soup, and take it immediately off the
fire lest it curdle. Serve up the chicken in the soup.

Rabbits may be substituted for fowls.

CAT-FISH SOUP.

Cat-fish that have been caught near the middle of the
river are much nicer than those that are taken near the shore
where they have access to impure food. The small white
ones are the best. Having cut off their heads, skin the fish,
and clean them, and cut them in three. To twelve small cat-
fish allow a pound and a half of ham. Cut the ham into
small pieces, or mouthfuls, and scald it two or three
times in boiling water, lest it be too salt. Chop together a
bunch of parsley and some sweet marjoram stripped from the

stalks. Put these ingredients into a soup kettle and season them with pepper: the ham will make it salt enough. Add a head of celery cut small, or a large table-spoonful of celery seed tied up in a bit of clear muslin to prevent its dispersing. Put in two quarts of water, cover the kettle, and let it boil slowly till every thing is sufficiently done, and the fish and ham quite tender. Skim it frequently. Boil in another vessel a quart of rich milk, in which you have melted a quarter of a pound of butter divided into small bits and rolled in flour. Pour it hot to the soup, and stir in at the last the beaten yolks of four eggs. Give it another boil, just to take off the rawness of the eggs, and then put it into a tureen, taking out the bag of celery seed before you send the soup to table, and adding some toasted bread cut into small squares. In making toast for soup, cut the bread thick, and pare off all the crust.

Before you send it to table, remove the back-bones of the cat-fish.

Eel soup may be made in the same manner: chicken soup also.

LOBSTER SOUP.

HAVE ready a good broth made of a knuckle of veal boiled slowly in as much water as will cover it, till the meat is reduced to rags. It must then be well strained.

Having boiled three fine middle-sized lobsters, extract all the meat from the body and claws. Bruise part of the coral in a mortar, and also an equal quantity of the meat. Mix them well together. Add mace, nutmeg, cayenne, and a little grated lemon-peel; and make them up into force-meat balls, binding the mixture with the yolk of an egg slightly beaten.

Take three quarts of the veal broth, and put into it the meat of the lobsters cut into mouthfuls. Boil it together about twenty minutes. Then thicken it with the remaining coral, (which you must first rub through a sieve,) and add the force-meat balls, and a little butter rolled in flour. Simmer it gently for ten minutes, but do not let it come to a boil, as that will injure the colour. Pour it into a tureen, and send it to table immediately.

OYSTER SOUP.

Season two quarts of oysters with a little cayenne. Then take them out of the liquor. Grate and roll fine a dozen crackers. Put them into the liquor with a large lump of fresh butter. When the grated biscuit has quite dissolved, add a quart of milk with a grated nutmeg, and a dozen blades of mace; and, if in season, a head of celery split fine and cut into small pieces. Season it to your taste with pepper.

Mix the whole together, and set it in a closely covered vessel over a slow fire. When it comes to a boil, put in the oysters; and when it comes to a boil again, they will be suficiently done.

Before you send it to table put into the tureen some toasted bread cut into small squares, omitting the crust.

ANOTHER OYSTER SOUP.

Take two quarts of large oysters. Strain their liquor into a soup pan; season it with a tea-spoonful of whole pepper, a tea-spoonful of grated nutmeg, the same quantity of whole cloves, and seven or eight blades of mace. If the oysters are fresh, add a large tea-spoonful of salt; if tney are salt oysters, none is requisite. Set the pan on hot coals, and boil it slowly (skimming it when necessary) till you find that it is sufficiently flavoured with the taste of the spice. In the mean time (having cut out the hard part) chop the oysters fine, with some hard-boiled yolk of egg. Take the liquor from the fire, and strain out the spice from it. Then return it to the soup pan, and put the chopped oysters into it, with whatever liquid may have continued about them. Add a quarter of a pound of butter, divided into little bits and rolled in flour. Cover the pan, and let it boil hard about five minutes. If oysters are cooked too much they become tough and tasteless.

CLAM SOUP.

HAVING put your clams into a pot of boiling water to make them open easily, take them from the shells, carefully saving the liquor. To the liquor of fifty opened clams, allow three quarts of water. Mix the water with the liquor of the clams and put it into a large pot with a knuckle of veal, the bone of which should be chopped in four places. When it has simmered slowly three hours, put in a large bunch of sweet herbs, a beaten nutmeg, a tea-spoonful of mace, and a table-spoonful of whole pepper, but no salt, as the salt of the clam liquor will be sufficient. Stew it slowly an hour longer, and then strain it. When you have returned the liquor to the pot, add a quarter of a pound of butter divided into four and each bit rolled in flour. Then put in the clams, (having cut them in pieces,) and let it boil fifteen minutes. Send it to table with toasted bread in it cut into dice.

This soup will be greatly improved by the addition of small force-meat balls. Make them of cold minced veal or chicken, mixed with equal quantities of chopped suet and sweet marjoram, and a smaller proportion of hard-boiled egg, grated lemon-peel, and powdered nutmeg. Pound all the ingredients together in a mortar, adding a little pepper and salt. Break in a raw egg or two (in proportion to the quantity) to bind the whole together and prevent it from crumbling to pieces. When thoroughly mixed, make the force-meat into small balls, and let them boil ten minutes in the soup, shortly before you send it to table. If you are obliged to make them of raw veal or raw chicken they must boil longer.

It will be a great improvement first to pound the clams in a mortar

Oyster soup may be made in this manner.

PLAIN CLAM SOUP.

TAKE a hundred clams, well washed, and put them into a large pot of boiling water. This will cause the shells to open. As they open take them out, and extract the clams, taking care to save the liquor. Mix with the liquor a quart of water, (or what will be much better, a quart of milk,) and thicken it with butter rolled in flour. Add a small bunch of sweet-marjoram, and a large table-spoonful of whole pepper. Put the liquid into a pot over a moderate fire. Make some little round dumplings (about the size of a hickory nut) of flour and butter, and put them into the soup. When it comes to a boil, put in the clams, and keep them boiling an hour. Take them out before you send the soup to table.

When the soup is done, take out the sweet marjoram. Have ready some toasted bread cut into small squares or dice Put it into the soup before you send it to table.

You may make oyster soup in a similar manner.

WATER SOUCHY.

CUT up four flounders, or half a dozen perch, two onions, and a bunch of parsley. Put them into three quarts of water, and boil them till the fish go entirely to pieces, and dissolve in the water. Then strain the liquor through a sieve and put it into a kettle or stew-pan. Have ready a few more fish with the heads, tails, and fins removed, and the brown skin taken off. Cut little notches in them, and lay them for a short time in very cold water. Then put them into the stew-pan with the liquor or soup-stock of the first fish. Season with pepper, salt, and mace, and add half a pint of white wine or two table-spoonfuls of vinegar. Boil it gently for a quarter of an hour, and skim it well.

Provide some parsley roots, cut into slices and boiled till very tender; and also a quantity of parsley leaves boiled nice and green. After the fish-pan has boiled moderately fifteen minutes, take it off the fire, and put in the parsley roots; also a little mushroom catchup.

Take out the fish and lay them in a broad deep dish, or in a tureen, and then pour on the soup very gently for fear of breaking them. Strew the green parsley leaves over the top. Have ready plates of bread and butter, which it is customary to eat with water souchy.

You may omit the wine or vinegar, and flavour the soup just before you take it from the fire with essence of anchovy, or with any other of the essences and compound fish-sauces that are in general use.

Water souchy (commonly pronounced *sookey*) is a Dutch soup. It may be made of any sort of small fish; but flounders and perch are generally used for it. It is very good made of carp.

FISH.

REMARKS.

In choosing fresh fish, select only those that are thick and firm, with bright scales and stiff fins; the gills a very lively red, and the eyes full and prominent. In the summer, as soon as they are brought home, clean them, and put them in ice till you are ready to cook them; and even then do not attempt to keep a fresh fish till next day. Mackerel cannot be cooked too soon, as they spoil more readily than any other fish.

Oysters in the shell may be kept from a week to a fortnight, by the following process. Cover them with water, and wash them clean with a birch broom. Then lay them with the deep or concave part of the shell undermost, and sprinkle each of them well with salt and Indian meal. Fill up the tub with cold water. Repeat this every day; first pouring off the liquid of the day before.

The tub must stand all the time in a cool cellar, and be covered well with an old blanket, carpeting, or something of the sort.

If carefully attended to, oysters kept in this manner will not only live but fatten.

It is customary to eat fish only at the commencement of the dinner. Fish and soup are generally served up alone, before any of the other dishes appear, and with no vegetable but potatoes; it being considered a solecism in good taste to accompany them with any of the other productions of the garden except a little norse-radish, parsley, &c. as garnishing.

In England and at the most fashionable tables in America, bread only is eaten with fish. To this rule salt cod is an exception.

TO BOIL FRESH SALMON.

SCALE and clean the fish, handling it as little as possible, and cutting it open no more than is absolutely necesesry. Place it on the strainer of a large fish-kettle and fill it up with cold water. Throw in a handful of salt. Let it boil slowly. The length of time depends on the size and weight of the fish. You may allow a quarter of an hour to each pound; but experience alone can determine the exact time. It must however be thoroughly done, as nothing is more disgusting than fish that is under-cooked. You may try it with a fork. Skim it well or the colour will be bad.

The minute it is completely boiled, lift up the strainer and rest it across the top of the kettle, that the fish may drain, and then, if you cannot send it to table immediately, cover it with a soft napkin or flannel several folds double, to keep it firm by absorbing the moisture.

Send it to table on a hot dish. Garnish with scraped horse-radish and curled parsley. Have ready a small tureen of lobster sauce to accompany the salmon.

Take what is left of it after dinner, and put it into a deep dish with a close cover. Having saved some of the water in which the fish was boiled, take a quart of it, and season it with half an ounce of whole pepper, and half an ounce of whole cloves, half a pint of the best vinegar, and a tea-spoonful of salt. Boil it; and when cold, pour it over the fish, and cover it closely again. In a cold place, and set on ice, it will keep a day or two, and may be eaten at breakfast or supper.

If much of the salmon has been left, you must proportion a larger quantity of the pickle.

Boil salmon trout in a similar manner.

TO BAKE FRESH SALMON WHOLE.

HAVING cleaned a small or moderate sized salmon, season it with salt, pepper, and powdered mace rubbed on it both outside and in. Skewer it with the tail turned round and put to the mouth. Lay it on a stand or trivet in a deep dish or pan, and stick it over with bits of butter rolled in flour. Pu it into the oven, and baste it occasionally, while baking, with its own drippings.

Garnish it with horseradish and sprigs of curled parsley, laid alternately round the edge of the dish ; and send to table with it a small tureen of lobster sauce.

Salmon trout may be drest in the same manner.

SALMON BAKED IN SLICES.

TAKE out the bone and cut the flesh into slices. Season them with cayenne and salt. Melt two ounces of butter that has been rolled in flour, in a half pint of water, and mix with it two large glasses of port wine, two table-spoonfuls of catchup, and two of soy. This allowance is for a small quantity of salmon. For a large dish you must proportion the ingredients accordingly. You may add the juice of a large lemon. Mix all well. Then strain it and pour it over the slices of salmon. Tie a sheet of buttered paper over the dish, and put it into the oven.

You may bake trout or carp in the same manner.

SALMON STEAKS.

SPLIT the salmon and take out the bone as nicely as possible, without mangling the flesh. Then cut it into fillets or steaks about an inch thick. Dry them lightly in a cloth, and dredge them with flour. Take care not to squeeze or press them. Have ready some clear bright coals, such as are fit for beef-steaks. Let the gridiron be clean and bright, and rub the bars with chalk to prevent the fish from sticking. Broil the slices thoroughly, turning them with steak tongs. Send them to table hot, wrapped in the folds of a napkin that has been heated. Serve up with them anchovy, or prawn, or lobster sauce.

Many epicures consider this the best way of cooking salmon

Another way, perhaps still nicer, is to take some pieces of white paper and butter them well. Wrap in each a slice of salmon, securing the paper around them with a string or pins. Lay them on a gridiron, and broil them over a clear but moderate fire, till thoroughly done. Take off the paper, and send the cutlets to table hot, garnished with fried parsley.

Serve up with them prawn or lobster sauce in a boat.

PICKLED SALMON.

TAKE a fine fresh salmon, and having cleaned it, cut it into large pieces, and boil it in salted water as if for eating. Then drain it, wrap it in a dry cloth, and set it in a cold place till next day. Then make the pickle, which must be in proportion to the quantity of fish. To one quart of the water in which the salmon was boiled, allow two quarts of the best vinegar, one ounce of whole black pepper, one nutmeg grated, and a dozen blades of mace. Boil all these together in a kettle closely covered to prevent the flavour from evaporating. When the vinegar thus prepared is quite cold, pour it over the salmon, and put on the top a table-spoonful of sweet oil, which will make it keep the longer.

Cover it closely, put it in a dry cool place, and it will be good for many months.

This is the nicest way of preserving salmon, and is approved by all who have tried it. Garnish with fennel.

SMOKED SALMON.

CUT the fish up the back; clean, and scale it, and take out the roe, but do not wash it. Take the bone neatly out. Rub it well inside and out with a mixture of salt and fine Havanna sugar, in equal quantities, and a small portion of saltpetre. Cover the fish with a board on which weights are placed to press it down, and let it lie thus for two days and two nights. Drain it from the salt, wipe it dry, stretch it open, and fasten it so with pieces of stick. Then hang it up and smoke it over a wood fire. It will be smoked sufficiently in five or six days.

When you wish to eat it, cut off slices, soak them awhile in lukewarm water, and broil them for breakfast.

TO BOIL HALIBUT.

HALIBUT is seldom cooked whole; a piece weighing from four to six pounds being generally thought sufficient. Score deeply the skin of the back, and when you put it into the kettle lay it on the strainer with the back undermost. Cover it with cold water, and throw in a handful of salt. Do not let it come to a boil too fast. Sk'm it carefully, and when it has boiled hard a few minutes, hang the kettle higher, or diminish the fire under it, so as to let it simmer for about thirty or thirty-five minutes. Then drain it, and send it to table, garnished with alternate heaps of grated horse-radish and curled parsley, and accompanied by a boat of egg-sauce.

What is left of the halibut, you may prepare for the supper-table by mincing it when cold, and seasoning it with a dressing of salt, cayenne, sweet oil, hard-boiled yolk of egg, and a large proportion of vinegar.

HALIBUT CUTLETS.

CUT your halibut into steaks or cutlets about an inch thick. Wipe them with a dry cloth, and season them with salt and cayenne pepper. Have ready a pan of yolk of egg well beaten, and a large flat dish of grated bread crumbs.

Put some fresh lard or clarified beef dripping into a frying pan, and hold it over a clear fire till it boils. Dip your cutlets into the beaten egg, and then into the bread crumbs. Fry them of a light brown. Serve them up hot, with the gravy in the bottom of the dish.

Salmon or any large fish may be fried in the same manner.

Halibut cutlets are very fine cut quite thin and fried in the best sweet oil, omitting the egg and bread crumbs.

TO BROIL MACKEREL.

MACKEREL cannot be eaten in perfection except at the sea side, where it can be had immediately out of the water. It loses its flavour in a very few hours, and spoils sooner than any other fish. Broiling is the best way of cooking it.

Clean two fine fresh mackerel, and wipe them dry with a cloth. Split them open and rub them with salt. Spread some very bright coals on the hearth, and set the gridiron over them well greased. Lay on the mackerel, and broil them very nicely, taking care not to let them burn. When one side is quite done, turn them on the other. Lay them on a hot dish, and butter and pepper them before they go to table. Garnish them with lumps or pats of minced parsley mixed with butter, pepper and salt.

BOILED MACKEREL.

Clean the mackerel well, and let them lie a short time in vinegar and water. Then put them into the fish-kettle with cold water and a handful of salt. Boil them slowly. If small, they will be sufficiently cooked in twenty minutes. When the eye starts and the tail splits they are done. Take them up immediately on finding them boiled enough. If they stand any time in the water they will break.

Serve them up with parsley sauce, and garnish the dish with lumps of minced parsley.

They are eaten with mustard.

For boiling, choose those that have soft roes.

Another way is to put them in cold salt and water, and let them warm gradually for an hour. Then give them one hard boil, and they will be done.

TO BOIL SALT CODFISH.

THE day previous to that on which it is to be eaten, take the fish about four o'clock in the afternoon, and put it into a kettle of cold water. Then place it within the kitchen fire-place, so as to keep it blood-warm. Next morning at ten, take out the fish, scrub it clean with a hard brush, and put it into a kettle of fresh cold water, into which a jill of molasses has been stirred. The molasses will be found an improvement. Place the kettle again near the fire, until about twenty minutes before dinner. Then hang it over the fire, and boil it hard a quarter of an hour, or a little more.

When done, drain it, and cut it into large pieces. Wrap them closely in a fine napkin and send them to table on a large dish, garnished round the edge with hard-boiled eggs, either cut in half, or in circular slices, yolks and whites together. Have ready in a small tureen, egg-sauce made with drawn butter, thickened with hard-boiled eggs chopped fine. Place on one side of the fish a dish of mashed potatoes, on the other a dish of boiled parsnips.

The most usual way of preparing salt cod for eating when it comes to table, is (after picking out all the bones) to mince it fine on your plate, and mix it with mashed potato, parsnip, and egg-sauce; seasoning it to your taste with cayenne and mustard. What is left may be prepared for breakfast next morning. It should be put into a skillet or spider, which must be well buttered inside, and set over hot coals to warm and brown. Or it may be made up into small cakes and fried.

You may add to the mixture onions boiled and chopped.

TO BOIL FRESH COD.

HAVING washed and cleaned the fish, leave out the roe and liver; rub some salt on the inside, and if the weather is very cold you may keep it till next day. Put sufficient water in the fish-kettle to cover the fish very well, and add to the water a large handful of salt. As soon as the salt is entirely melted put in the fish. A very small codfish will be done in about twenty minutes, (after the water has boiled ;) a large one will take half an hour, or more. Garnish with the roe and liver fried, or with scraped horseradish. Send it to table with oyster-sauce in a boat. Or you may make a sauce by flavouring your melted butter with a glass of port wine, and a table-spoonful or more, of soy.

ANOTHER WAY OF BOILING FRESH COD.

PUT the fish into cold water with a handful of salt, and let it slowly and gradually warm for three hours if the cod is large, and two hours if it is small. Then increase the fire, and boil it hard for a few minutes only.

BAKED SHAD.

KEEP on the head and fins. Make a force-meat or stuffing of grated bread crumbs, cold boiled ham or bacon minced fine, sweet marjoram, red pepper, and a little powdered mace or cloves. Moisten it with beaten yolk of egg. Stuff the inside of the fish with it, reserving a little to rub over the outside, having first rubbed the fish all over with yolk of egg.

Lay the fish in a deep pan, putting its tail to its mouth. Pour into the bottom of the pan a little water, and add a jill of port wine, and a piece of butter rolled in flour. Bake it well, and when it is done, send it to table with the gravy poured round it. Garnish with slices of lemon.

Any fish may be baked in the same manner.

A large fish of ten or twelve pounds weight, will require about two hours baking.

TO BROIL A SHAD.

SPLIT and wash the shad, and afterwards dry it in a cloth. Season it with salt and pepper. Have ready a bed of clear bright coals. Grease your gridiron well, and as soon as it is hot lay the shad upon it, and broil it for about a quarter of an hour or more, according to the thickness. Butter it well, and send it to table. You may serve with it melted butter in a sauce-boat.

Or you may cut it into three pieces and broil it without splitting. It will then, of course, require a longer time. If done in this manner, send it to table with melted butter poured over it.

BOILED ROCK-FISH.

HAVING cleaned the rock-fish, put it into a fish-kettle with water enough to cover it well, having first dissolved a handful of salt in the water. Set it over a moderate fire, and do not let it boil too fast. Skim it well.

When done, drain it, and put it on a large dish. Have ready a few eggs boiled hard. Cut them in half, and lay them closely on the back of the fish in a straight line from the head to the tail.   Send with it in a boat, celery sauce flavoured with a little cayenne.

SEA BASS OR BLACK FISH.

MAY be boiled and served up in the above manner.

PICKLED ROCK-FISH.

HAVE ready a large rock-fish.   Put on your fish-kettle with a sufficiency of water to cover the fish amply ; spring or pump water is best.   As soon as the water boils, throw in a tea-cup full of salt, and put in the fish.   Boil it gently for about half an hour, skimming it well.   Then take it out, and drain it, laying it slantingly.   Reserve a part of the water in which the fish has been boiled, and season it to your taste with whole cloves, pepper, and mace.   Boil it up to extract the strength from the spice, and after it has boiled add to it an equal quantity of the best vinegar.   You must have enough of this liquid to cover the fish again.   When the fish is quite cold, cut off the head and tail, and cut the body into large pieces, extracting the back-bone.   Put it into a stone jar, and when the spiced liquor is cold, pour it on the fish, cover the jar closely, and set it in a cool place.   It will be fit for use in a day or two, and if well secured from the air, and but into a cold place will keep a fortnight.

FRIED PERCH.

HAVING cleaned the fish and dried them with a cloth, lay them, side by side, on a board or large dish ; sprinkle them with salt, and dredge them with flour. After a while turn them, and salt and dredge the other side. Put some lard or fresh beef-dripping into a frying-pan, and hold it over the fire. When the lard boils, put in the fish and fry them of a yellowish brown. Send to table with them in a boat, melted butter flavoured with soy or catchup.

Flounders or other small fish may be fried in the same manner. Also tutaug or porgies.

You may know when the lard or dripping is hot enough, by dipping in the tail of one of the fish. If it becomes crisp immediately, the lard is in a proper state for frying. Or you may try it with a piece of stale bread, which will become brown directly, if the lard is in order.

There should always be enough of lard to cover the fish entirely. After they have fried five minutes on one side, turn them and fry them five minutes on the other. Skim the lard or dripping always before you put in the fish.

TO FRY TROUT.

HAVING cleaned the fish, and cut off the fins, dredge them with flour. Have ready some beaten yolk of egg, and in a separate dish some grated bread crumbs. Dip each fish into the egg, and then strew them with bread crumbs. Put some butter or fresh beef-dripping into a frying-pan, and hold it over the fire till it is boiling hot; then, (having skimmed it,) put in the fish and fry them.

Prepare some melted butter with a spoonful of mushroom-catchup and a spoonful of lemon-pickle stirred into it. Send it to table in a sauce-boat to eat with the fish.

You may fry carp and flounders in the same manner.

TO BOIL TROUT.

Put a handful of salt into the water. When it boils put in the trout. Boil them fast about twenty minutes, according to their size.

For sauce, send with them melted butter, and put some soy into it; or flavour it with catchup.

FRIED SEA BASS.

Score the fish on the back with a knife, and season them with salt and cayenne pepper. Cut some small onions in round slices, and chop fine a bunch of parsley. Put some butter into a frying-pan over the fire, and when it is boiling hot lay in the fish. When they are about half done put the onions and parsley into the pan. Keep turning the fish that the onions and parsley may adhere to both sides. When quite done, put them into the dish in which they are to go to table, and garnish the edge of the dish with hard boiled eggs cut in round slices.

Make in the pan in which they have been fried, a gravy, by adding some butter rolled in flour, and a small quantity of vinegar. Pour it into the dish with the fish.

STURGEON CUTLETS OR STEAKS.

This is the most approved way of dressing sturgeon. Carefully take off the skin, as its oiliness will give the fish a strong and disagreeable taste when cooked. Cut from the tail-piece slices about half an inch thick, rub them with salt, and broil them over a clear fire of bright coals. Butter them, sprinkle them with cayenne pepper, and send them to table hot, garnished with sliced lemon, as lemon-juice is generally squeezed over them when eaten.

Another way is to make a seasoning of bread crumbs, sweet herbs, pepper and salt. First dip the slices of sturgeon in beaten yolk of egg, then cover them with seasoning, wrap them up closely in sheets of white paper well buttered, broil them over a clear fire, and send them to table either with or without the papers.

STEWED CARP.

HAVING cut off the head, tail, and fins, season the carp with salt, pepper, and powdered mace, both inside and out. Rub the seasoning on very well, and let them lay in it an hour Then put them into a stew-pan with a little parsley shred fine, a whole onion, a little sweet marjoram, a tea-cup of thick cream or very rich milk, and a lump of butter rolled in flour. Pour in sufficient water to cover the carp, and let it stew half an hour. Some port wine will improve it.

Perch may be done in the same way.

You may dress a piece of sturgeon in this manner, but you must first boil it for twenty minutes to extract the oil. Take off the skin before you proceed to stew the fish.

CHOWDER.

TAKE half a pound of salt pork, and having half boiled it, cut it into slips, and with some of them cover the bottom of a pot. Then strew on some sliced onion. Have ready a large fresh cod, or an equal quantity of haddock, tutaug, or any other firm fish Cut the fish into large pieces, and lay part of it on the pork and onions. Season it with pepper. Then cover it with a layer of biscuit, or crackers that have been previously soaked in milk or water. You may add also a layer of sliced potatoes.

Next proceed with a second layer of pork, onions, fish, &c and continue as before till the pot is nearly full ; finishing with soaked crackers. Pour in about a pint and a half of cold water. Cover it close, set it on hot coals, and let it simmer about an hour. Then skim it, and turn it out into a deep dish Leave the gravy in the pot till you have thickened it with a bit of butter rolled in flour, and some chopped parsley. Then give it one boil up, and pour it hot into the dish.

Chowder may be made of clams, first cutting off the hard part.

TO KEEP FRESH SHAD.

HAVING cleaned the fish, split it down the back, and lay it (with the skin side downward) upon a large dish. Mix together a large table-spoonful of brown sugar, a small tea-spoonful of salt, and a tea-spoonful of cayenne pepper. Cover the shad with this mixture, spread on evenly, and let it rest in it till next day, (unless you want it the same evening,) keeping it in a cold place.

Immediately before cooking, wipe the seasoning *entirely off*, and dry the shad in a clean cloth. Then broil it in the usual manner.

This way of keeping shad a day or two is much better than to salt or corn it. Prepared as above it will look and taste as if perfectly fresh. Any other fish may be kept in this manner.

SHELL FISH.

PICKLED OYSTERS.

Take a hundred and fifty fine large oysters, and pick off carefully the bits of shell that may be sticking to them. Lay the oysters in a deep dish, and then strain the liquor over them. Put them into an iron skillet that is lined with porcelain, and add salt to your taste. Without salt they will not be firm enough. Set the skillet on hot coals, and allow the oysters to simmer till they are heated all through, but not till they boil. Then take out the oysters and put them into a stone jar, leaving the liquor in the skillet. Add to it a pint of clear cider vinegar, a large tea-spoonful of blades of mace, three dozen whole cloves, and three dozen whole pepper corns. Let it come to a boil, and when the oysters are quite cold in the jar, pour the liquor on them.

They are fit for use immediately, but are better the next day. In cold weather they will keep a week.

If you intend sending them a considerable distance you must allow the oysters to boil, and double the proportions of the pickle and spice.

FRIED OYSTERS.

Get the largest and finest oysters. After they are taken from the shell wipe each of them quite dry with a cloth. Then beat up in a pan yolk of egg and milk, (in the proportion of two yolks to half a jill or a wine glass of milk,) and have some stale bread grated very fine in a large flat dish. Cut up at least half a pound of fresh butter in the frying-pan, and hold it over the fire till it is boiling hot. Dip the oysters all over lightly in the mixture of egg and milk, and then roll them up and down in the grated bread, making as many crumbs stick to them as you can.

Put them into the frying-pan of hot butter, and keep it over a hot fire. Fry them brown, turning them that they may be equally browned on both sides. If properly done they will be crisp, and not greasy.

Serve them dry in a hot dish, and do not pour over them the butter that may be left in the pan when they are fried.

Instead of grated bread you may use crackers finely powdered.

SCOLLOPED OYSTERS.

HAVING grated a sufficiency of stale bread, butter a deep dish, and line the sides and bottom thickly with bread crumbs. Then put in a layer of seasoned oysters, with a few very small bits of butter on them. Cover them thickly with crumbs, and put in another layer of oysters and butter, till the dish is filled up, having a thick layer of crumbs on the top. Put the dish into an oven, and bake them a very short time, or they will shrivel. Serve them up hot.

You may bake them in large clam shells, or in the tin scollop shells made for the purpose. Butter the bottom of each shell; sprinkle it with bread crumbs; lay on the oysters seasoned with cayenne and nutmeg, and put a morsel of butter on each. Fill up the shells with a little of the oyster liquor thickened with bread crumbs, and set them on a gridiron over coals, browning them afterwards with a red-hot shovel. Oysters are very nice taken whole out of the shells, and broiled.

STEWED OYSTERS.

PUT the oysters into a sieve, and set it on a pan to drain the liquor from them. Then cut off the hard part, and put the oysters into a stew-pan with some whole pepper, a few blades of mace, and some grated nutmeg. Add a small piece of butter rolled in flour. Then pour over them about half of the liquor, or a little more. Set the pan on hot coals, and simmer them gently about five minutes. Try one, and if it tastes raw cook them a little longer. Make some thin slices of toast, having cut off all the crust. Butter the toast and lay it in the bottom of a deep dish. Put the oysters upon it with the liquor in which they were stewed.

The liquor of oysters should never be thickened by stirring in flour. It spoils the taste, and gives them a sodden and disagreeable appearance, and is no longer practised by good cooks. A little cream is a fine improvement to stewed oysters.

OYSTER FRITTERS.

HAVE ready some of the finest and largest oysters; drain them from the liquor and wipe them dry.

Beat six eggs very light, and stir into them gradually six table-spoonfuls of fine sifted flour. Add by degrees a pint and a half of rich milk and some grated nutmeg, and beat it to a smooth batter.

Make your frying-pan very hot, and put into it a piece of butter or lard. When it has melted and begins to froth, put in a small ladle-full of the batter, drop an oyster in the middle of it, and fry it of a light brown. Send them to table hot.

If you find your batter too thin, so that it spreads too much in the frying-pan, add a little more flour beaten well into it. of it is too thick, thin it with some additional milk.

OYSTER PIE.

MAKE a puff-paste, in the proportion of a pound and a half of fresh butter to two pounds of sifted flour. Roll it out rather thick, into two sheets. Butter a deep dish, and line the bottom and sides of it with paste. Fill it up with crusts of bread for the purpose of supporting the lid while it is baking, as the oysters will be too much done if they are cooked in the pie. Cover it with the other sheet of paste, having first buttered the flat rim of the dish. Notch the edges of the pie handsomely, or ornament them with leaves of paste which you may form with tin cutters made for the purpose. Make a little slit in the middle of the lid, and stick firmly into it a paste tulip or other flower. Put the dish into a moderate oven, and while the paste is baking prepare the oysters, which should be large and fresh. Put them into a stew-pan with half their liquor thickened with yolk of egg boiled hard and grated, enriched with pieces of butter rolled in bread crumbs, and seasoned with mace and nutmeg. Stew the oysters five minutes. When the paste is baked, carefully take off the lid, remove the pieces of bread, and put in the oysters and gravy. Replace the lid, and send the pie to table warm.

TO BOIL A LOBSTER.

PUT a handful of salt into a large kettle or pot of boiling water. When the water boils very hard put in the lobster, having first brushed it, and tied the claws together with a bit of twine. Keep it boiling from half an hour to an hour in proportion to its size. If boiled too long the meat will be hard and stringy. When it is done, take it out, lay it on its claws to drain, and then wipe it dry. Send it to table cold, with the body and tail split open, and the claws taken off. Lay the large claws next to the body, and the small ones outside. Garnish with double parsley.

It is scarcely necessary to mention that the head of a lobster, and what are called the lady-fingers are not to be eaten.

TO DRESS LOBSTER COLD

PUT a table-spoonful of cold water on a clean plate, and with the back of a wooden spoon mash into it the coral or scarlet meat of the lobster, adding a salt-spoonful of salt, and about the same quantity of cayenne. On another part of the plate mix well together with the back of the spoon two table-spoonfuls of sweet oil, and a tea-spoonful of made mustard. Then mix the whole till they are well incorporated and perfectly smooth, adding, at the last, one table-spoonful of vinegar, and two more of oil.

This quantity of seasoning is for a small lobster. For a large one, more of course will be required. Many persons add a tea-spoonful of powdered white sugar, thinking that it gives a mellowness to the whole.

The meat of the body and claws of the lobster must be carefully extracted from the shell and minced very small.

When the dressing is smoothly and thoroughly amalgamated mix the meat with it, and let it be handed round to the company.

The vinegar from a jar of Indian pickle is by some preferred for lobster dressing.

You may dress the lobster *immediately before* you send it to table. When the dressing and meat are mixed together, pile it in a deep dish, and smooth it with the back of a spoon. Stick a bunch of the small claws in the top, and garnish with curled parsley.

Very large lobsters are not the best, the meat being coarse and tough.

STEWED LOBSTER.

Having boiled the lobster, extract the meat from the shell, and cut it into very small pieces. Season it with a powdered nutmeg, a few blades of mace, and cayenne and salt to your taste. Mix with it a quarter of a pound of fresh butter cut small, and two glasses of white wine or of vinegar. Put it into a stew-pan, and set it on hot coals. Stew it about twenty minutes, keeping the pan closely covered lest the flavour should evaporate. Serve it up hot.

If you choose, you can send it to table in the shell, which must first be nicely cleaned. Strew the meat over with sifted bread-crumbs, and brown the top with a salamander, or a red hot shovel held over it.

FRICASSEED LOBSTER.

Put the lobster into boiling salt and water, and let it boil according to its size from a quarter of an hour to half an hour.

The intention is to have it parboiled only, as it is afterwards to be fricasseed. Extract the meat from the shell, and cut it into small pieces. Season it with red pepper, salt, and nutmeg; and put it into a stew-pan with as much cream as will cover it. Keep the lid close; set the pan on hot coals, and stew it slowly for about as long a time as it was previously boiled. Just before you take it from the fire, stir in the beaten yolk of an egg. Send it to table in a small dish placed on a larger one, and arrange the small claws nicely round it on the large dish.

POTTED LOBSTER.

PARBOIL the lobster in boiling water well salted. Then pick out all the meat from the body and claws, and beat it in a mortar with nutmeg, mace, cayenne, and salt, to your taste. Beat the coral separately. Then put the pounded meat into a large potting can of block tin with a cover. Press it down hard, having arranged it in alternate layers of white meat and coral to give it a marbled or variegated appearance. Cover it with fresh butter, and put it into a slow oven for half an hour. When cold, take off the butter and clarify it, by putting it into a jar, which must be set in a pan of boiling water. Watch it well, and when it melts, carefully skim off the buttermilk which will rise to the top. When no more seum rises, take it off and let it stand for a few minutes to settle, and then strain it through a sieve.

Put the lobster into small potting-cans, pressing it down very hard. Pour the clarified butter over it, and secure the covers tightly.

Potted lobster is used to lay between thin slices of bread

as sandwiches. The clarified butter that accompanies it is excellent for fish sauce.

Prawns and crabs may be potted in a similar manner.

LOBSTER PIE.

PUT two middle-sized lobsters into boiling salt and water When they are half boiled, take the meat from the shell, cut it into very small pieces, and put it into a pie dish. Break up the shells, and stew them in a very little water with half a dozen blades of mace and a grated nutmeg. Then strain off the liquid. Beat the coral in a mortar, and thicken the liquid with it. Pour this into the dish of lobster to make the gravy. Season it with cayenne, salt, and mushroom catchup, and add bits of butter. Cover it with a lid of paste, made in the proportion of ten ounces of butter to a pound of flour, notched handsomely, and ornamented with paste leaves. Do not send it to table till it has cooled.

TO BOIL PRAWNS.

THROW a handful of salt into a pot of boiling water. When it boils very hard, put in the prawns. Let them boil a quarter of an hour, and when you take them out lay them on a sieve to drain, and then wipe them on a dry cloth, and put them aside till quite cold.

Lay a handful of curled parsley in the middle of a dish. Put one prawn on the top of it, and lay the others all round, as close as you can, with the tails outside. Garnish with parsley.

Eat them with salt, cayenne, sweet oil, mustard and vinegar, mixed together as for lobsters.

CRABS.

CRABS are boiled in the same manner, and in serving up may be arranged like prawns.

HOT CRABS.

HAVING boiled the crabs, extract all the meat from the shell, cut it fine, and season it to your taste with nutmeg, salt, and cayenne pepper. Add a bit of butter, some grated bread crumbs, and sufficient vinegar to moisten it. Fill the back-shells of the crab with the mixture; set it before the fire, and brown it by holding a red-hot shovel or a salamander a little above it.

Cover a large dish with small slices of dry toast with the crust cut off. Lay on each slice a shell filled with the crab. The shell of one crab will contain the meat of two.

COLD CRABS.

HAVING taken all the meat out of the shells, make a dressing with sweet oil, salt, cayenne pepper, mustard and vinegar, as for lobster. You may add to it some hard-boiled yolk of egg, mashed in the oil. Put the mixture into the back-shells of the crabs, and serve it up. Garnish with the small claws laid nicely round.

SOFT CRABS.

THESE crabs must be cooked directly, as they will not keep till next day.

Remove the spongy substance from each side of the crab, and also the little sand-bag. Put some lard into a pan, and when it is boiling hot, fry the crabs in it. After you take them out, throw in a handful of parsley, and let it crisp; but withdraw it before it loses its colour. Strew it over the crabs when you dish them.

Make the gravy by adding cream or rich milk to the lard, with some chopped parsley, pepper and salt. Let them all boil together for a few minutes, and then serve it up in a sauce-boat.

TERRAPINS.

HAVE ready a pot of boiling water. When it is boiling very hard put in the terrapins, and let them remain in it till quite dead. Then take them out, pull off the outer skin and the toe-nails, wash the terrapins in warm water and boil them again, allowing a tea-spoonful of salt to two terrapins. When the flesh becomes quite tender so that you can pinch it off, take them out off the shell, remove the sand-bag, and the gall, which you must be careful not to break, as it will make the terrapin so bitter as to be uneatable. Cut up all the other parts of the inside with the meat, and season it to your taste with cayenne pepper, nutmeg, and mace. Put all into a stew-pan with the juice or liquor that it has given out in cutting up, but not any water. To every two terrapins allow a quarter of a pound of butter divided into pieces and rolled in flour, one glass of Madeira, and the yolks of two eggs. The eggs must be beaten, and not stirred in till a moment before it goes to table. Keep it closely covered. Stew it gently till every thing is tender, and serve it up hot in a deep dish. The entrails are no longer cooked with terrapins.

Terrapins, after being boiled by the cook, may be brought to table plain, with all the condiments separate, that the company may dress them according to taste.

For this purpose heaters or chafing-dishes must be provided for each plate.

PICKLED LOBSTER.

TAKE half a dozen fine lobsters. Put them into boiling salt and water, and when they are all done, take them out and extract all the meat from the shells, leaving that of the claws as whole as possible, and cutting the flesh of the body into large pieces nearly of the same size. Season a sufficient quantity of vinegar very highly with whole pepper-corns, whole cloves, and whole blades of mace. Put the pieces of lobster into a stew-pan, and pour on just sufficient vinegar to keep them well covered. Set it over a moderate fire ; and when it has boiled hard about five minutes, take out the lobster, and let the pickle boil by itself for a quarter of an hour. When the pickle and lobster are both cold, put them together into a broad flat stone jar. Cover it closely, and set it away in a cool place.

Eat the pickled lobster with oil, mustard, and vinegar, and have bread and butter with it.

DIRECTIONS FOR COOKING MEAT.

BEEF.

GENERAL REMARKS.

WHEN beef is good, it will have a fine smooth open grain, and it will feel tender when squeezed or pinched in your fingers. The lean should be of a bright carnation red, and the fat white rather than yellow—the suet should be perfectly white. If the lean looks dark or purplish, and the fat very yellow, do not buy the meat.

See that the butcher has properly jointed the meat before it goes home. For good tables, the pieces generally roasted are the sirloin and the fore and middle ribs. In genteel houses other parts are seldom served up as *roast-beef*. In small fami-.ies the ribs are the most convenient pieces. A whole sirloin is too large, except for a numerous company, but it is the piece most esteemed.

The best beef-steaks are those cut from the ribs, or from the inner part of the sirloin. All other pieces are, for this purpose, comparatively hard and tough.

The round is generally corned or salted, and boiled. It is also used for the dish called beef à-la-mode.

The legs make excellent soup; the head and tail are also used for that purpose.

The tongue when fresh is never cooked except for mince-pies. Corned or salted it is seldom liked, as in that state it has a faint sickly taste that few persons can relish. But when pickled and afterwards smoked (the only good way of preparing a tongue) it is highly and deservedly esteemed.

The other pieces of the animal are generally salted and boiled. Or when fresh they may be used for soup or stews, if not too fat.

If the state of the weather will allow you to keep fresh beef two or three days, rub it with salt, and wrap it in a cloth.

In summer do not attempt to keep it more than twenty-four hours; and not then unless you can conveniently lay it in ice, or in a spring-house.

In winter if the beef is brought from market frozen, do not cook it that day unless you dine very late, as it will be im-possible to get it sufficiently done—meat that has been frozen requiring double the usual time. To thaw it, lay it in cold water, which is the only way to extract the frost without injuring the meat. It should remain in the water three hours or more.

TO ROAST BEEF.

THE fire should be prepared at least half an hour before the beef is put down, and it should be large, steady, clear, and bright, with plenty of fine hot coals at the bottom.

The best apparatus for the purpose is the well-known roaster frequently called a tin-kitchen.

Wash the meat in cold water, and then wipe it dry, and rub it with salt. Take care not to run the spit through the best parts of it. It is customary with some cooks to tie blank paper over the fat, to prevent it from melting and wasting too fast.

Put it evenly into the roaster, and do not set it too near the fire, lest the outside of the meat should be burned before the inside is heated.

Put some nice beef-dripping or some lard into the pan or bottom of the roaster, and as soon as it melts begin to baste the beef with it; taking up the liquid with a long spoon, and pouring it over the meat so as to let it trickle down again into the pan. Repeat this frequently while it is roasting; after a while you can baste it with its own fat. Turn the spit often, so that the meat may be equally done on all sides.

Once or twice draw back the roaster, and improve the fire by clearing away the ashes, bringing forward the hot coals, and putting on fresh fuel at the back. Should a coal fall into the dripping-pan take it out immediately.

An allowance of about half an hour to each pound of meat is the time commonly given for roasting; but this rule, like most others, admits of exceptions according to circumstances. Also, some persons like their meat very much done; others prefer it rare, as it is called. In summer, meat will roast in a shorter time than in winter.

When the beef is nearly done, and the steam draws towards the fire, remove the paper that has covered the fat part, sprinkle on a little salt, and having basted the meat well with the dripping, pour off nicely (through the spout of the roaster) all the liquid fat from the top of the gravy.

Lastly, dredge the meat very lightly with a little flour, and baste it with fresh butter. This will give it a delicate froth. To the gravy that is now running from the meat add nothing but a tea-cup of boiling water. Skim it, and send it to table in a boat. Serve up with the beef in a small deep plate, scraped horseradish moistened with vinegar.

Fat meat requires more roasting than lean, and meat that has been frozen will take nearly double the usual time.

Basting the meat continually with flour and water is a bad

practice, as it gives it a coddled par-boiled appearance, and diminishes the flavour.

These directions for roasting beef will apply equally to mutton.

Pickles are generally eaten with roast beef. French mustard is an excellent condiment for it. In carving begin by cutting a slice from the side.

TO SAVE BEEF-DRIPPING.

POUR off through the spout of the roaster or tin-kitchen, all the fat from the top of the gravy, after you have done basting the meat with it. Hold a little sieve under the spout, and strain the dripping through it into a pan. Set it away in a cool place; and next day when it is cold and congealed, turn the cake of fat, and scrape with a knife the sediment from the bottom. Put the dripping into a jar; cover it tightly, and set it away in the refrigerator, or in the coldest place you have. It will be found useful for frying, and for many other purposes.

Mutton-dripping cannot be used for any sort of cooking. as it communicates to every thing the taste of tallow.

BAKED BEEF.

THIS is a plain family dish, and is never provided for company.

Take a nice but not a fat piece of fresh beef. Wash it, rub it with salt, and place it on a trivet in a deep block tin or iron pan. Pour a little water into the bottom, and put under and round the trivet a sufficiency of pared potatoes, either white or sweet ones. Put it into a hot oven, and let it bake till thoroughly done, basting it frequently with its own gravy. Then transfer it to a hot dish, and serve up the potatoes in another. Skim the gravy, and send it to table in a boat.

Or you may boil the potatoes, mash them with milk, and put them into the bottom of the pan about half an hour before the meat is done baking. Press down the mashed potatoes hard with the back of a spoon, score them in cross lines over the top, and let them brown under the meat, serving them up laid round it.

Instead of potatoes, you may put in the bottom of the pan what is called a Yorkshire pudding, to be baked under the meat.

To make this pudding,—stir gradually four table-spoonfuls of flour into a pint of milk, adding a salt-spoon of salt. Beat four eggs very light, and mix them gradually with the milk and flour. See that the batter is not lumpy. Do not put the pudding under the meat at first, as if baked too long it will be hard and solid. After the meat has baked till the pan is quite hot and well greased with the drippings, you may put in the batter; having continued stirring it till the last moment.

If the pudding is so spread over the pan as to be but an inch thick, it will require about two hours baking, and need not be turned. If it is thicker than an inch, you must (after it is brown on the top) loosen it in the pan, by inserting a knife beneath it, and having cut it across into four pieces, turn them all nicely that the other side may be equally done.

But this pudding is lighter and better if laid so thin as not to require turning.

When you serve up the beef lay the pieces of pudding round it, to be eaten with the meat.

Veal may be baked in this manner with potatoes or a pudding. Also fresh pork.

TO BOIL CORNED OR SALTED BEEF.

THE best piece is the round. You may either boil it whole, or divide it into two, or even three pieces if it is large, taking care that each piece shall have a portion of the fat. Wash it well ; and, if very salt, soak it in two waters. Skewer it up tightly and in a good compact shape, wrapping the flap piece firmly round it. Tie it round with broad strong tape, or with a strip of coarse linen. Put it into a large pot, and cover it well with water. It will be found a convenience to lay it on a fish drainer.

Hang it over a moderate fire that it may heat gradually all through. Carefully take off the scum as it rises, and when no more appears, keep the pot closely covered, and let it boil slowly and regularly, with the fire at an equal temperature. Allow at least four hours to a piece weighing about twelve pounds, and from that to five or six hours in proportion to the size. Turn the meat twice in the pot while it is boiling. Put in some carrots and turnips about two hours after the meat. Many persons boil cabbage in the same pot with the beef, but it is a much nicer way to do the greens in a separate vessel, lest they become saturated with the liquid fat. Cauliflower or brocoli (which are frequent accompaniments to corned beef should never be boiled with it

Wash the cabbage in cold water, removing the outside leaves, and cutting the stalk close. Examine all the leaves carefully, lest insects should be lodged among them. If the cabbage is large, divide it into quarters. Put it into a pot of boiling water with a handful of salt, and boil it till the stalk is quite tender. Half an hour will generally be sufficient for a small young cabbage ; an hour for a large full-grown one

Drain it well before you dish it. If boiled separately from the meat, have ready some melted butter to eat with it.

Should you find the beef under-done, you may reboil it next day; putting it into boiling water and letting it simmer for half an hour or more, according to its size.

Cold corned beef will keep very well for some days wrapped in several folds of a thick linen cloth, and set away in a cool dry place.

In carving a round of beef, slice it horizontally and very thin. Do not help any one to the outside pieces, as they are generally too hard and salt. French mustard is very nice with corned beef.*

This receipt will apply equally to any piece of corned beef, except that being less solid than the round, they will, in proportion to their weight, require rather less time to boil.

In dishing the meat, remove the wooden skewers and substitute plated or silver ones.

Many persons think it best (and they are most probably right) to stew corned beef rather than to boil it. If you intend to stew it, put no more water in the pot than will barely cover the meat, and keep it gently simmering over a slow fire for four, five, or six hours, according to the size of the piece.

TO BROIL BEEF-STEAKS.

THE best beef steaks are those cut from the ribs or from the inside of the sirloin. All other parts are for this purpose comparatively hard and tough.

They should be cut about three quarters of an inch thick,

---

* French mustard is made of the very best mustard powder, diluted with tarragon vinegar mixed with an equal portion of sweet oil, adding a few drops of garlic vinegar. Use a wooden spoon.

and, unless the beef is remarkably fine and tender, the steaks will be much improved by beating them on both sides with a steak mallet, or with a rolling-pin. Do not season them till you take them from the fire.

Have ready on your hearth a fine bed of clear bright coals, entirely free from smoke and ashes. Set the gridiron over the coals in a slanting direction, that the meat may not be smoked by the fat dropping into the fire directly under it. When the gridiron is quite hot, rub the bars with suet, sprinkle a little salt over the coals, and lay on the steaks. Turn them frequently with a pair of steak-tongs, or with a knife and fork. A quarter of an hour is generally sufficient time to broil a beef-steak. For those who like them underdone or rare, ten or twelve minutes will be enough.

When the fat blazes and smokes very much as it drips into the fire, quickly remove the gridiron for a moment, till the blaze has subsided. After they are browned, cover the upper side of the steaks with an inverted plate or dish to prevent the flavour from evaporating. Rub a dish with a shalot, or small onion, and place it near the gridiron and close to the fire, that it may be well heated. In turning the steak drop the gravy that may be standing on it into this dish, to save it from being lost. When the steaks are done, sprinkle them with a little salt and pepper, and lay them in a hot dish, putting on each a piece of fresh butter. Then, if it is liked, season them with a very little raw shalot, minced as finely as possible, and moistened with a spoonful of water; and stir a tea-spoonful of catchup into the gravy. Send the steaks to table very hot, in a covered dish. You may serve up with them onion sauce in a small tureen.

Pickles are frequently eaten with beef-steaks.

Mutton chops may be broiled in the same manner.

TO FRY BEEF-STEAKS.

BEEF-STEAKS for frying should be cut thinner than for broil-ing. Take them from the ribs or sirloin, and remove the bone. Beat them to make them tender. Season them with salt and pepper.

Put some fresh butter, or nice beef-dripping into a frying-pan, and hold it over a clear bright fire till it boils and has done hissing. Then put in the steaks, and (if you like them) some sliced onions. Fry them about a quarter of an hour, turning them frequently. Steaks, when fried, should be thoroughly done. After they are browned, cover them with a large plate to keep in the juices.

Have ready a hot dish, and when they are done, take out the steaks and onions and lay them in it with another dish on the top, to keep them hot while you give the gravy in the pan another boil up over the fire. You may add to it a spoonful of mushroom catchup. Pour the gravy over the steaks, and send them to table as hot as possible.

Mutton chops may be fried in this manner.

BEEF-STEAK PUDDING.

FOR a small pudding take a pound of fresh beef suet. Clear it from the skin and the stringy fibres, and mince it as finely as possible. Sift into a large pan two pounds of fine flour, and add the suet gradually, rubbing it fine with your hands and mixing it thoroughly. Then pour in, by degrees, enough of cold water to make a stiff dough. Roll it out into a large even sheet. Have ready about a pound and a half of the best beef-steak, omitting the bone and fat which should be all cut off. Divide the steak into small thin pieces, and beat them well to make them tender. Season them with pepper and salt, and, if convenient, add some mushrooms. Lay the beef in the middle of the sheet of paste, and put on the top a bit of butter rolled in flour. Close the paste nicely over the meat as if you were making a large dumpling. Dredge with flour a thick square cloth, and tie the pudding up in it, leaving space for it to swell. Fasten the string very firmly, and stop up with flour the little gap at the tying-place so that no water can get in. Have ready a large pot of boiling water. Put the pudding into it, and let it boil fast three hours or more. Keep up a good fire under it, as if it stops boiling a minute the crust will be heavy. Have a kettle of boiling water at the fire to replenish the pot if it wastes too much. Do not take up the pudding till the moment before it goes to table. Mix some catchup with the gravy on your plate.

For a large pudding you must have two pounds of suet, three pounds of flour, and two pounds and a half of meat. It must boil at least five hours.

All the fat must be removed from the meat before it goes into the pudding, as the gravy cannot be skimmed when enclosed in the crust.

You may boil in the pudding some potatoes cut into slices.

A pudding of the lean of mutton chops may be made in the same manner; also of venison steaks.

A BEEF-STEAK PIE.

MAKE a good paste in the proportion of a pound of butter to two pounds of sifted flour. Divide it in half, and line with one sheet of it the bottom and sides of a deep dish, which must first be well buttered. Have ready two pounds of the best beef-steak, cut thin, and well beaten; the bone and fat being omitted. Season it with pepper and salt. Spread a layer of the steak at the bottom of the pie, and on it a layer of sliced potato, and a few small bits of butter rolled in flour. Then another layer of meat, potato, &c., till the dish is full. You may greatly improve the flavour by adding mushrooms, or chopped clams or oysters, leaving out the hard parts. If you use clams or oysters, moisten the other ingredients with a little of their liquor. If not, pour in, at the last, half a pint of cold water, or less if the pie is small. Cover the pie with the other sheet of paste as a lid, and notch the edges handsomely, having reserved a little of the paste to make a flower or tulip to stick in the slit at the top. Bake it in a quick oven an hour and a quarter, or longer, in proportion to its size. Send it to table hot.

You may make a similar pie of mutton chops, or veal cutlets, or venison steaks, always leaving out the bone and fat.

Many persons in making pies stew the meat slowly in a little water till about half done, and they then put it with its gravy into the paste and finish by baking. In this case add no water to the pie, as there will be already sufficient liquid. If you half-stew the meat, do the potatoes with it.

A-LA-MODE BEEF.

TAKE the bone out of a round of fresh beef, and beat the meat well all over to make it tender. Chop and mix together equal quantities of sweet marjoram and sweet basil, the leaves picked from the stalks and rubbed fine. Chop also some small onions or shalots, and some parsley ; the marrow from the bone of the beef; and a quarter of a pound, or more of suet. Add two penny rolls of stale bread grated ; and pepper, mace, and nutmeg to your taste. Mix all these ingredients well, and bind them together with the beaten yolks of four eggs. Fill with this seasoning the place from whence you took out the bone ; and rub what is left of it all over the out-side of the meat. You must, of course, proportion the quantity of stuffing to the size of the round of beef. Fasten it well with skewers, and tie it round firmly with a piece of tape, so as to keep it compact and in good shape. It is best to prepare the meat the day before it is to be cooked.

Cover the bottom of a stew-pan with slices of ham. Lay the beef upon them, and cover the top of the meat with more slices of ham. Place round it four large onions, four carrots, and four turnips, all cut in thick slices. Pour in from half a pint to a pint of water, and if convenient, add two calves' feet cut in half. Cover the pan closely, set it in an oven and let it bake for at least six hours ; or seven or eight, according to the size.

When it is thoroughly done, take out the beef and lay it on a dish with the vegetables round it. Remove the bacon and calves' feet, and (having skimmed the fat from the gravy carefully) strain it into a small sauce-pan ; set it on hot coals, and stir into it a teacup-full of port wine, and the same quantity of pickled mushrooms. Let it just come to a boil, and then send it to table in a sauce-tureen.

If the beef is to be eaten cold, you may ornament it as follows :—Glaze it all over with beaten white of egg. Then cover it with a coat of boiled potato grated finely. Have ready some slices of cold boiled carrot, and also of beet-root. Cut them into the form of stars or flowers, and arrange them handsomely over the top of the meat by sticking them on the grated potato. In the centre place a large bunch of double parsley, interspersed with flowers cut out of raw turnips, beets, and carrots, somewhat in imitation of white and red roses, and marygolds. Fix the flowers on wooden skewers concealed with parsley.

Cold à-la-mode beef prepared in this manner will at a little distance look like a large iced cake decorated with sugar flowers.

You may dress a fillet of veal according to this receipt. Of course it will require less time to stew.

TO STEW BEEF.

TAKE a good piece of fresh beef. It must not be too fat. Wash it, rub it with salt, and put it into a pot with barely sufficient water to cover it. Set it over a slow fire, and after it has stewed an hour, put in some potatoes pared and cut in half, and some parsnips, scraped and split. Let them stew with the beef till quite tender. Turn the meat several times in the pot. When all is done, serve up the meat and vegetables together, and the gravy in a boat, having first skimmed it.

This is a good family dish.

You may add turnips (pared and sliced) to the other vegetables.

Fresh pork may be stewed in this manner, or with sweet potatoes.

TO STEW A ROUND OF BEEF.

TRIM off some pieces from a round of fresh beef—take out the bone and break it. Put the bone and the trimmings into a pan with some cold water, and add an onion, a carrot, and a turnip all cut in pieces, and a bunch of sweet herbs. Simmer them for an hour, and having skimmed it well, strain off the liquid. Season the meat highly with what is called kitchen pepper, that is, a mixture, in equal quantities, of black pepper, or of cayenne, cinnamon, cloves, ginger and nutmeg, all finely powdered. Fasten it with skewers, and tie it firmly round with tape. Lay skewers in the bottom of the stewpan; place the beef upon them, and then pour over it the gravy you have prepared from the bone and trimmings. Simmer it about an hour and a half, and then turn the meat over, and add to it three carrots, three turnips, and two onions all sliced, and a dozen tomatas sliced. Keep the lid close, except when you are skimming off the fat. Let the meat stew till it is thoroughly done and tender throughout. The time will depend on the size of the round. It may require from five or six to eight hours.

Just before you take it up, stir into the gravy a table-spoonful or two of mushroom catchup, a little made mustard, and a piece of butter rolled in flour.

Send it to table hot, with the gravy poured round it.

ANOTHER WAY TO STEW A ROUND OF BEEF.

Take a round of fresh beef (or the half of one if it is very large) and remove the bone. The day before you cook it, lay it in a pickle made of equal proportions of water and vinegar with salt to your taste. Next morning take it out of the pickle, put it into a large pot or stew-pan, and just cover it with water. Put in with it two or three large onions, a few cloves, a little whole black pepper, and a large glass of port or claret.   If it is a whole round of beef allow two glasses of wine.   Stew it slowly for at least four hours or more, in proportion to its size.   It must be thoroughly done, and tender all through.   An hour before you send it to table take the meat out of the pot, and pour the gravy into a pan. Put a large lump of butter into the pot, dredge the beef with flour, and return it to the pot to brown, turning it often to prevent its burning.   Or it will be better to put it into a Dutch oven.   Cover the lid with hot coals, renewing them as they go out.   Take the gravy that you poured from the meat, and skim off all the fat.   Put it into a sauce-pan, and mix with it a little butter rolled in flour, and add some more cloves and wine.   Give it a boil up.   If it is not well browned, burn some sugar on a hot shovel, and stir it in.

If you like it stuffed, have ready when you take the meat out of the pickle, a force-meat of grated bread crumbs, sweet herbs, butter, spice, pepper and salt, and minced parsley, mixed with beaten yolk of egg.   Fill with this the opening from whence you took the bone, and bind a tape firmly round the meat.

BEEF BOUILLI.

TAKE part of a round of fresh beef (or if you prefer it a piece of the flank or brisket) and rub it with salt.   Place skewers in the bottom of the stew-pot, and lay the meat upon them with barely water enough to cover it.   To enrich the gravy you may add the necks and other trimmings of whatever poultry you may happen to have; also the root of a tongue, if convenient.   Cover the pot, and set it over a quick fire.   When it boils and the scum has risen, skim it well, and then diminish the fire so that the meat shall only simmer;

or you may set the pot on hot coals. Then put in four or five carrots sliced thin, a head of celery cut up, and four or five sliced turnips. Add a bunch of sweet herbs, and a small table-spoonful of black peppercorns tied in a thin muslin rag. Let it stew slowly for four or five hours, and then add a dozen very small onions roasted and peeled, and a large table-spoonful of capers or nasturtians. You may, if you choose, stick a clove in each onion. Simmer it half an hour longer, then take up the meat, and place it in a dish, laying the vegetables round it. Skim and strain the gravy ; season it with catchup, and made mustard, and serve it up in a boat.

Mutton may be cooked in this manner.

HASHED BEEF.

Take some roast beef that has been rather under-done, and having cut off the fat and skin, put the trimmings with the bones broken up into a stew-pan with two large onions sliced, a few sliced potatoes, and a bunch of sweet herbs. Add about a pint of warm water, or broth if you have it. This is to make the gravy. Cover it closely, and let it simmer for about an hour. Then skim and strain it, carefully removing every particle of fat.

Take another stew-pot, and melt in it a piece of butter, about the size of a large walnut. When it has melted, shake in a spoonful of flour. Stir it a few minutes, and then add to it the strained gravy. Let it come to a boil, and then put to it a table-spoonful of catchup, and the beef cut either in thin small slices or in mouthfuls. Let it simmer from five to ten minutes, but do not allow it to boil, lest (having beef cooked already) it should become tasteless and insipid

Serve it up in a deep dish with thin slices of toast cut into triangular or pointed pieces, the crust omitted. Dip the toast in the gravy, and lay the pieces in regular order round the sides of the dish.

You may hash mutton or veal in the same manner, adding sliced carrots, turnips, potatoes, or any vegetables you please. Tomatas are an improvement.

To hash cold meat is an economical way of using it; but there is little or no nutriment in it after being twice cooked, and the natural flavour is much impaired by the process.

Hashed meat would always be much better if the slices were cut from the joint or large piece as soon as it leaves the table, and soaked in the gravy till next day.

BEEF CAKES.

Take some cold roast beef that has been under-done, and mince it very fine. Mix with it grated bread crumbs, and a little chopped onion and parsley. Season it with pepper and salt, and moisten it with some beef-dripping and a little walnut or onion pickle. Some scraped cold tongue or ham will be found an improvement. Make it into broad flat cakes, and spread a coat of mashed potato thinly on the top and bottom of each. Lay a small bit of butter on the top of every cake, and set them in an oven to warm and brown.

Beef cakes are frequently a breakfast dish.

Any other cold fresh meat may be prepared in the same manner.

Cold roast beef may be cut into slices, seasoned with salt and pepper, broiled a few minutes over a clear fire, and served up hot with a little butter spread on them.

TO ROAST A BEEF'S HEART.

Cut open the heart, and (having removed the ventricles) soak it in cold water to free it from the blood. Parboil it about ten minutes. Prepare a force-meat of grated bread crumbs, butter or minced suet, sweet marjoram and parsley chopped fine, a little grated lemon-peel, nutmeg, pepper, and salt to your taste, and some yolk of egg to bind the ingredients. Stuff the heart with the force-meat, and secure the opening by tying a string around it. Put it on a spit, and roast it till it is tender throughout.

Add to the gravy a piece of butter rolled in flour, and a glass of red wine. Serve up the heart very hot in a covered dish. It chills immediately.

Eat currant jelly with it.

Boiled beef's heart is frequently used in mince pies.

TO STEW A BEEF'S HEART.

Clean the heart, and cut it lengthways into large pieces. Put them into a pot with a little salt and pepper, and cover them with cold water. Parboil them for a quarter of an hour, carefully skimming off the blood that rises to the top. Then take them out, cut them into mouthfuls, and having strained the liquid, return them to it, adding a head or two of chopped celery, a few sliced onions, a dozen potatoes pared and quartered, and a piece of butter rolled in flour. Season with whole pepper, and a few cloves if you like. Let it stew slowly till all the pieces of heart and the vegetables are quite tender.

You may stew a beef's kidney in the same manner.

The heart and liver of a calf make a good dish cooked as above.

TO DRESS BEEF KIDNEY.

HAVING soaked a fresh kidney in cold water and dried it in a cloth, cut it into mouthfuls, and then mince it fine. Dust it with flour. Put some butter into a stew-pan over a moderate fire, and when it boils put in the minced kidney. When you have browned it in the butter, sprinkle on a little salt and cayenne pepper, and pour in a very little boiling water. Add a glass of champagne or other wine, or a large tea-spoonful of mushroom catchup, or of walnut pickle. Cover the pan closely, and let it stew till the kidney is tender. Send it to table hot in a covered dish. It is eaten generally at breakfast.

TO BOIL TRIPE.

WASH it well in warm water, and trim it nicely, taking off all the fat. Cut it into small pieces, and put it on to boil five hours before dinner, in water enough to cover it very well. After it has boiled four hours, pour off the water, season the tripe with pepper and salt, and put it into a pot with milk and water mixed in equal quantities. Boil it an hour in the milk and water.

Boil in a sauce-pan ten or a dozen onions. When they are quite soft, drain them in a cullender, and mash them. Wipe out your sauce-pan and put them on again, with a bit of butter rolled in flour, and a wine-glass of cream or milk. Let them boil up, and add them to the tripe just before you send it to table. Eat it with pepper, vinegar, and mustard.

It is best to give tripe its first and longest boiling the day before it is wanted.

TRIPE AND OYSTERS.

Having boiled the tripe in milk and water, for four or five nours till it is quite tender, cut it up into small pieces. Pu it into a stew-pan with just milk enough to cover it, and a few blades of mace. Let it stew about five minutes, and then put in the oysters, adding a large piece of butter rolled in flour, and salt and cayenne pepper to your taste. Let it stew five minutes longer, and then send it to table in a tureen; first skimming off whatever fat may float on the surface.

TO FRY TRIPE.

Boil the tripe the day before, till it is quite tender, which it will not be in less than four or five hours. Then cover it and set it away. Next day cut it into long slips, and dip each piece into beaten yolk of egg, and afterwards roll them in grated bread crumbs. Have ready in a frying-pan over the fire, some good beef-dripping. When it is boiling hot put in the tripe, and fry it about ten minutes, till of a light brown.

You may serve it up with onion sauce.

Boiled tripe that has been left from the dinner of the preceding day may be fried in this manner.

PEPPER POT.

Take four pounds of tripe, and four ox feet. Put them into a large pot with as much water as will cover them, some whole pepper, and a little salt. Hang them over the fire early in the morning. Let them boil slowly, keeping the pot closely covered. When the tripe is quite tender, and the ox feet boiled to pieces, take them out, and skim the liquid and strain it. Then cut the tripe into small pieces; put it back into the pot, and pour the soup or liquor over it. Have ready some sweet herbs chopped fine, some sliced onions, and some sliced potatoes. Make some small dumplings with flour and butter. Season the vegetables well with pepper and salt, and put them into the pot. Have ready a kettle of boiling water, and pour on as much as will keep the ingredients covered while boiling, but take care not to weaken the taste by putting too much water. Add a large piece of butter rolled in flour, and lastly put in the dumplings. Let it boil till all the things are thoroughly done, and then serve it up in the tureen.

TO BOIL A SMOKED TONGUE.

In buying dried tongues, choose those that are thick and plump, and that have the smoothest skins. They are the most likely to be young and tender.

A smoked tongue should soak in cold water at least all night. One that is very hard and dry will require twenty-four hours' soaking. When you boil it put it into a pot full of cold water. Set it over a slow fire that it may heat gradually for an hour before it comes to a boil. Then keep it simmering from three and a half to four hours, according to its size and age. Probe it with a fork, and do not take it up till it is tender throughout. Send it to table with mashed potato laid round it, and garnish with parsley. Do not split it in half when you dish it, as is the practice with some cooks Cutting it lengthways spoils the flavour, and renders it comparatively insipid.

If you wish to serve up the tongue very handsomely, rub it

with yolk of egg after you take it from the pot, and strew over it grated bread crumbs; baste it with butter, and set it before the fire till it becomes of a light brown. Cover the root (which is always an unsightly object) with thick sprigs of double parsley; and (instead of mashed potato) lay slices of currant jelly all round the tongue.

TO BOIL A SALTED OR PICKLED TONGUE.

PUT it into boiling water, and let it boil three hours or more, according to its size. When you take it out peel and trim it, and send it to table surrounded with mashed potato, and garnished with sliced carrot.

TO CORN BEEF.

WASH the beef well, after it has lain awhile in cold water. Then drain and examine it, take out all the kernels, and rub it plentifully with salt. It will imbibe the salt more readily after being washed. In cold weather warm the salt by placing it before the fire. This will cause it to penetrate the meat more thoroughly.

In summer do not attempt to corn any beef that has not been fresh killed, and even then it will not keep more than a day and a half or two days. Wash and dry it, and rub a great deal of salt well into it. Cover it carefully, and keep it in a cold dry cellar.

Pork is corned in the same manner.

TO PICKLE BEEF OR TONGUES.

The beef must be fresh killed, and of the best kind. You must wipe every piece well, to dry it from the blood and moisture. To fifty pounds of meat allow two pounds and a quarter of coarse salt, two pounds and a quarter of fine salt, one ounce and a half of saltpetre, two pounds of good brown sugar, and two quarts of molasses. Mix all these ingredients well together, boil and skim it for about twenty minutes, and when no more scum rises, take it from the fire. Have ready the beef in a large tub, or in a barrel; pour the brine gradually upon it with a ladle, and as it cools rub it well into every part of the meat. A molasses hogshead sawed in two is a good receptacle for pickled meat. Cover it well with a thick cloth, and look at it frequently, skimming off whatever may float on the top, and basting the meat with the brine. In about a fortnight the beef will be fit for use.

Tongues may be put into the same cask with the beef, one or two at a time, as you procure them from the butcher. None of them will be ready for smoking in less than six weeks; but they had best remain in pickle seven or eight months They should not be sent to the smoke-house later than March. If you do them at home, they will require three weeks' smoking over a wood fire. Hang them with the root or large end upwards. When done, sew up each tongue tightly in coarse linen, and hang them up in a dark dry cellar.

Pickled tongues without smoking are seldom liked.

The last of October is a good time for putting meat into pickle. If the weather is too warm or too cold, it will not take the salt well.

In the course of the winter the pickle may probably require a second boiling with additional ingredients.

Half an ounce of pearl-ash added to the other articles will make the meat more tender, but many persons thinks it injures the taste.

The meat must always be kept completely immersed in the brine. To effect this a heavy board should be laid upon it.

DRIED OR SMOKED BEEF.

THE best part for this purpose is the round, which you must desire the butcher to cut into four pieces. Wash the meat and dry it well in a cloth. Grind or beat to powder an equal quantity of cloves and mace, and having mixed them together, rub them well into the beef with your hand. The spice will be found a great improvement both to the taste and smell of the meat. Have ready a pickle made precisely as that in the preceding article. Boil and skim it, and (the meat having been thoroughly rubbed all over with the spice) pour on the pickle as before directed. Keep the beef in the pickle at least six weeks, and then smoke it about three weeks. Corn cobs make a good fire for smoking meat.

Smoked beef is brought on the tea-table either shaved into thin chips without cooking, or chipped and fried in a skillet with some butter and beaten egg.

This receipt for dried or smoked beef will answer equally well for venison ham, which is also used as a relish at the tea-table.

Mutton hams may be prepared in the same way.

POTTED BEEF.

TAKE a good piece of a round of beef, and cut off all the fat. Rub the lean well with salt, and let it lie two days. Then put it into a jar, and add to it a little water in the proportion of half a pint to three pounds of meat. Cover the ja as closely as possible, (the best cover will be a coarse past or dough) and set it in a slow oven, or in a vessel of boiling water for about four hours. Then drain off all the gravy and set the meat before the fire that all the moisture may be drawn out. Pull or cut it to pieces and pound it for a long time in a mortar with black pepper, cloves, mace, nutmeg, and oiled fresh butter, adding these ingredients gradually, and moistening it with a little of the gravy. You must pound it to a fine paste, or till it becomes of the consistence of cream cheese.

Put it into potting cans, and cover it an inch thick with fresh butter that has been melted, skimmed, and strained. Tie a leather over each pot, and keep them closely covered. Set them in a dry place.

Game and poultry may be potted in this manner.

VEAL.

GENERAL REMARKS.

THE fore-quarter of a calf comprises the neck, breast, and shoulder: the hind-quarter consists of the loin, fillet, and knuckle. Separate dishes are made of the head, heart, liver, and sweetbread. The flesh of good veal is firm and dry, and the joints stiff. The lean is of a very light delicate red, and the fat quite white. In buying the head see that the eyes look full, plump, and lively; if they are dull and sunk the calf has been killed too long. In buying calves' feet for jelly or soup, endeavour to get those that have been singed only, and not skinned; as a great deal of gelatinous substance is contained in the skin. Veal should always be thoroughly cooked, and never brought to table rare or under-done, like beef or mutton. The least redness in the meat or gravy is disgusting.

Veal suet may be used as a substitute for that of beef; also veal-dripping.

TO ROAST A LOIN OF VEAL.

THE loin is the best part of the calf. It is always roasted. See that your fire is clear and hot, and broad enough to brown both ends. Cover the fat of the kidney and the back with paper to prevent it from scorching. A large loin of veal will require *at least* four hours and a half to roast it sufficiently. At first set the roaster at a tolerable distance from the fire that the meat may heat gradually in the beginning; afterwards place it nearer. Put a little salt and water into the dripping-pan and baste the meat with it till the gravy begins to drop. Then baste with the gravy. When the meat is nearly done, move it close to the fire, dredge it with a very little flour, and baste it with butter. Skim the fat from the gravy, which should be thickened by shaking in a very small quantity of flour. Put it into a small sauce-pan, and set it on hot coals. Let it just come to a boil, and then send it to table in a boat. If the gravy is not in sufficient quantity, add to it about half a jill or a large wine-glass of boiling water.

In carving a loin of veal help every one to a piece of the kidney as far as it will go.

TO ROAST A BREAST OF VEAL.

A BREAST of veal will require about three hours and a half to roast. In preparing it for the spit, cover it with the caul, and skewer the sweetbread to the back. Take off the caul when the meat is nearly done. The breast, being comparatively tough and coarse, is less esteemed than the loin and the fillet.

TO ROAST A FILLET OF VEAL.

TAKE out the bone, and secure with skewers the fat flap to the outside of the meat. Prepare a stuffing of fresh butter or suet minced fine, and an equal quantity of grated bread-crumbs, a large table-spoonful of grated lemon-peel, a table-spoonful of sweet marjoram chopped or rubbed to powder, a nutmeg grated. and a little pepper and salt, with a sprig of chopped parsley. Mix all these ingredients with beaten yolk of egg, and stuff the place from whence the bone was taken. Make deep cuts or incisions all over the top of the veal, and fill them with some of the stuffing. You may stick into each hole an inch of fat ham or bacon, cut very thin.

Having papered the fat, spit the veal and put it into the roaster, keeping it at first not too near the fire. Put a little salt and water into the dripping-pan, and for awhile baste the meat with it. Then baste it with its own gravy. A fillet of veal will require four hours roasting. As it proceeds, place it nearer to the fire. Half an hour before it is done, remove the paper, and baste the meat with butter, having first dredged it very lightly with flour. Having skimmed the gravy, mix some thin melted butter with it.

If convenient, you may in making the stuffing, use a large proportion of chopped mushrooms that have been preserved in sweet oil, or of chopped pickled oysters. Cold ham shred fine will improve it.

You may stuff a fillet of veal entirely with sausage meat.

To accompany a fillet of veal, the usual dish is boiled ham or bacon.

A shoulder of veal may be stuffed and roasted in a similar manner.

TO STEW A BREAST OF VEAL.

DIVIDE the breast into pieces according to the position of the bones. Put them into a stew-pan with a few slices of ham, some whole pepper, a bunch of sweet herbs, and a sliced onion. Add sufficient water to keep it from burning, and let it stew slowly till the meat is quite tender. Then put to it a quart or more of green peas that have boiled twenty minutes in another pot, and a piece of butter rolled in flour. Let all stew together a quarter of an hour longer. Serve it up, with the veal in the middle, the peas round it, and the ham laid on the peas.

You may stew a breast of veal with tomatas.

~~~~~~~~~~

TO STEW A FILLET OF VEAL.

Take a fillet of veal, wipe it well, and then with a sharp knife make deep incisions all over the surface, the bottom as well as the top and sides. Make a stuffing of grated stale bread, butter, chopped sweet marjoram, grated lemon-peel, nutmeg, pepper and salt, mixed up with beaten yolk of egg to bind and give it consistency. Fill the holes or incisions with the stuffing, pressing it down well with your fingers. Reserve some of the stuffing to rub all over the outside of the meat. Have ready some very thin slices of cold boiled ham, the fatter the better. Cover the veal with them, fastening them on with skewers. Put it into a pot, and stew it slowly in a very little water, just enough to cover it. It will take at least five hours to stew; or more, in proportion to its size. When done, take off the ham, and lay it round the veal in a dish.

You may stew with it a quart or three pints of young green peas, put in about an hour before dinner; add to them a little butter and pepper while they are stewing. Serve them up in the dish with the veal, laying the slices of ham upon them.

If you omit the ham, stew the veal entirely in lard.

~~~~~~~~~~

TO STEW A KNUCKLE OF VEAL.

Lay four wooden skewers across the bottom of your stewpan, and place the meat upon them; having first carefully washed it, and rubbed it with salt. Add a table-spoonful of

whole pepper, tne leaves from a bunch of sweet marjoram, a
sprig of parsley leaves chopped, two onions peeled and sliced,
and a piece of butter rolled in flour. Pour in two quarts of
water. Cover it closely, and after it has come to a boil, lessen
the fire, and let the meat only simmer for two hours or more.
Before you serve it up, pour the liquid over it.

This dish will be greatly improved by stewing with it
a few slices of ham, or the remains of a cold ham.

Veal when simply boiled is too insipid. To stew it is
much better.

VEAL CUTLETS.

THE best cutlets are those taken from the leg or fillet. Cut
them about half an inch thick, and as large as the palm of
your hand. Season them with pepper and salt. Grate some
stale bread, and rub it through a cullender, adding to it
chopped sweet marjoram, grated lemon-peel, and some pow
dered mace or nutmeg. Spread the mixture on a large flat
dish. Have ready in a pan some beaten egg. First dip each
cutlet into the egg, and then into the seasoning on the dish,
seeing that a sufficient quantity adheres to both sides of the
meat. Melt in your frying-pan, over a quick fire, some beef
dripping, lard, or fresh butter, and when it boils lay your cutlets in it, and fry them thoroughly; turning them on both
sides, and taking care that they do not burn. Place them in
a covered dish near the fire, while you finish the gravy in the
pan, by first skimming it, and then shaking in a little flour
and stirring it round. Pour the gravy hot round the cutlers,
and garnish with little bunches of curled parsley.

You may mix with the bread crumbs a little saffron

VEAL STEAKS.

Cut a neck of veal into thin steaks, and beat them to make them tender. For seasoning, mix together some finely chopped onion sprinkled with pepper and salt, and a little chopped parsley. Add some butter, and put it with the parsley and onion into a small sauce-pan, and set it on hot coals to stew till brown. In the mean time, put the steaks on a hot gridiron (the bars of which have been rubbed with suet) and broil them well, over a bed of bright clear coals. When sufficiently done on one side turn them on the other. After the last turning, cover each steak with some of the seasoning from the sauce-pan, and let all broil together till thoroughly done.

Instead of the onions and parsley, you may season the veal steaks with chopped mushrooms, or with chopped oysters, browned in butter.

Have ready a gravy made of the scraps and trimmings of the veal, seasoned with pepper and salt, and boiled in a little hot water in the same sauce-pan in which the parsley and onions have been previously stewed. Strain the gravy when it has boiled long enough, and flavour it with catchup.

MINCED VEAL.

Take some cold veal, cut it into slices, and mince it very finely with a chopping-knife. Season it to your taste with pepper, salt, sweet marjoram rubbed fine, grated lemon-peel and nutmeg. Put the bones and trimmings into a sauce-pan with a little water, and simmer them over hot coals to extract the gravy from them. Then put the minced veal into a stewpan, strain the gravy over it, add a piece of butter rolled in flour, and a little milk or cream. Let it all simmer together till thoroughly warmed, but do not allow it to boil lest the meat having been once cooked already, should become tasteless. When you serve it up, have ready some three-cornered pieces of bread toasted and buttered; place them all round the inside of the dish.

Or you may cover the mince with a thick layer of grated bread, moistened with a little butter, and browned on the top with a salamander, or a red hot shovel.

VEAL PATTIES.

MINCE very fine a pound of the lean of cold roast veal, and half a pound of cold boiled ham, (fat and lean equally mixed.) Put it into a stew-pan with three ounces of butter divided into bits and rolled in flour, a jill of cream, and a jill of veal gravy. Season it to your taste with cayenne pepper and nutmeg, grated lemon-peel, and lemon-juice. Set the pan on hot coals, and let the ingredients simmer till well warmed, stirring them well to prevent their burning.

Have, ready baked, some small shells of puff-paste. Fill them with the mixture, and eat the patties either warm or cold.

VEAL PIE.

TAKE two pounds of veal cut from the loin, fillet, or the best end of the neck. Remove the bone, fat, and skin, and put them into a sauce-pan with half a pint of water to stew for the gravy. Make a good paste, allowing a pound of butter to two pounds of flour. Divide it into two pieces, roll it out rather thick, and cover with one piece the sides and bottom of a deep dish.   Put in a layer of veal, seasoned with black pepper, then a layer of cold ham sliced thin, then more veal, more ham, and so on till the dish is full; interspersing the meat with yolks of eggs boiled hard.   If you can procure some small button mushrooms they will be found an improvement.   Pour in, at the last, the gravy you have drawn from the trimmings, and put on the lid of the pie, notching the edge handsomely, and ornamenting the centre with a flower made of paste.   Bake the pie at least two hours and a half.

You may make a very plain veal pie simply of veal chops, sliced onions, and potatoes pared and quartered.   Season with pepper and salt, and fill up the dish with water.

CALF'S HEAD DREST PLAIN.

Wash the head in warm water.   Then lay it in clean hot water and let it soak awhile.   This will blanch it.   Take out the brains and the black part of the eyes.   Tie the head in a cloth, and put it into a large fish-kettle, with plenty of cold water, and add some salt to throw up the scum, which must be taken off as it rises.   Let the head boil gently about three hours.

Put eight or ten sage leaves, and as much parsley, into a small sauce-pan with a little water, and boil them half an hour.   Then chop them fine, and set them ready on a plate. Wash the brains well in two warm waters, and then soak them for an hour in a basin of cold water with a little salt in it.   Remove the skin and strings, and then put the brains into a stew-pan with plenty of cold water, and let them boil gently for a quarter of an hour, skimming them well.   Take them out, chop them, and mix them with the sage and parsley leaves, two table-spoonfuls of melted butter, and the yolks of four hard-boiled eggs, and pepper and salt to your taste. Then put the mixture into a sauce-pan and set it on coals to warm.

Take up the head when it is sufficiently boiled, score it in diamonds, brush it all over with beaten egg, and strew it with a mixture of grated bread-crumbs, and chopped sage and parsley. Stick a few bits of butter over it, and set it in a Dutch oven to brown. Serve it up with the brains laid round it. Or you may send to table the brains and the tongue in a small separate dish, having first trimmed the tongue and cut off the roots. Have also parsley-sauce in a boat. You may garnish with very thin small slices of broiled ham, curled up.

If you get a calf's head with the hair on, sprinkle it all over with pounded rosin, and dip it into boiling water. This will make the hairs scrape off easily.

CALF'S HEAD HASHED.

TAKE a calf's head and a set of feet, and boil them until tender, having first removed the brains. Then cut the flesh off the head and feet in slices from the bone, and put both meat and bones into a stew-pan with a bunch of sweet herbs, some sliced onions, and pepper and salt to your taste; also a large piece of butter rolled in flour, and a little water. After it has stewed awhile slowly till the flavour is well extracted from the herbs and onions, take out the meat, season it a little with cayenne pepper, and lay it in a dish. Strain the gravy in which it was stewed, and stir into it two glasses of madeira, and the juice and grated peel of a lemon. Having poured some of the gravy over the meat, lay a piece of butter on the top, set it in an oven and bake it brown.

In the mean time, having cleaned and washed the brains (skinning them and removing the strings) parboil them in a sauce-pan, and then make them into balls with chopped sweet herbs, grated bread-crumbs, grated lemon-peel, nutmeg, and beaten yolk of egg. Fry them in lard and butter mixed; and send them to table laid round the meat (which should have the tongue placed on the top) and garnish with sliced lemon. Warm the remaining gravy in a small sauce-pan on hot coals, and stir into it the beaten yolk of an egg a minute before you take it from the fire. Send it to table in a boat.

CHITTERLINGS OR CALF'S TRIPE.

SEE that the chitterlings are very nice and white. Wash them, cut them into pieces, and put them into a stew-pan with pepper and salt to your taste, and about two quarts of water. Boil them two hours or more. In the mean time, peel eight or ten white onions, and throw them whole into a sauce-pan with plenty of water. Boil them slowly till quite soft; then drain them in a cullender, and mash them. Wipe out your sauce-pan, and put in the mashed onions with a piece of butter, two table-spoonfuls of cream or rich milk, some nutmeg, and a very little salt. Sprinkle in a little flour, set the pan on hot coals (keeping it well covered) and give it one boil up.

When the chitterlings are quite tender all through, take them up and drain them. Place in the bottom of a dish a slice or two of buttered toast with all the crust cut off. Lay the chitterlings on the toast, and send them to table with the stewed onions in a sauce-boat. When you take the chitterlings on your plate season them with pepper and vinegar.

This, if properly prepared, is a very nice dish.

TO FRY CALF'S FEET.

HAVING first boiled them till tender, cut them in two, and (having taken out the large bones) season the feet with pepper and salt, and dredge them well with flour. Strew some chopped parsley or sweet marjoram over them, and fry them of a light brown in lard or butter. Serve them up with parsley-sauce.

TO FRY CALF'S LIVER.

CUT the liver into thin slices. Season it with pepper, salt, chopped sweet herbs, and parsley. Dredge it with flour, and fry it brown in lard or dripping. See that it is thoroughly done before you send it to table. Serve it up with its own gravy.

Some slices of cold boiled ham fried with it will be found an improvement. If you use ham, add no salt.

You may dress a calf's heart in the same manner.

LARDED CALF'S LIVER.

TAKE a calf's liver and wash it well. Cut into long slips the fat of some bacon or old ham, and insert it all through the surface of the liver by means of a larding-pin. Put the liver into a pot with a table-spoonful of lard, a few sliced tomatas, or some tomata catchup; adding one large or two small onions minced fine, and some sweet marjoram leaves rubbed very fine. The sweet marjoram will crumble more easily if you first dry it before the fire on a plate.

Having put in all these ingredients, set the pot on hot coals in the corner of the fire-place, and keep it stewing, regularly and slowly, for four hours. Send the liver to table with the gravy round it.

TO ROAST SWEET-BREADS.

TAKE four fine sweet-breads, and having trimmed them nicely, parboil them, and then lay them in a pan of cold water till they become cool. Afterwards dry them in a cloth. Put some butter into a sauce-pan, set it on hot coals, and melt and skim it. When it is quite clear, take it off. Have ready some beaten egg in one dish, and some grated bread-crumbs in another. Skewer each sweet-bread, and fasten them on a spit. Then glaze them all over with egg, and sprinkle them with bread-crumbs. Spread on some of the clarified butter, and then another coat of crumbs. Roast them before a clear fire, at least a quarter of an hour. Have ready some nice veal gravy flavoured with lemon-juice, and pour it round the sweet-breads before you send them to table.

LARDED SWEET-BREADS.

PARBOIL four or five of the largest sweet-breads you can get. This should be done as soon as they are brought in, as few things spoil more rapidly if not cooked at once. When half boiled, lay them in cold water. Prepare a force-meat of grated bread, lemon-peel, butter, cayenne, and nutmeg mixed with beaten yolk of egg Cut open the sweet-breads and stuff them with it, fastening them afterwards with a skewer, or tying them round with packthread. Have ready some slips of bacon-fat, and some slips of lemon-peel cut about the thickness of very small straws. Lard the sweet-breads with them in alternate rows of bacon and lemon-peel, drawing them through with a larding-needle. Do it regularly and handsomely. Then put the sweet-breads into a Dutch oven, and bake them brown. Serve them up with veal gravy flavoured with a glass of Madeira, and enriched with beaten yolk of egg stirred in at the last.

MARBLED VEAL.

HAVING boiled and skinned two fine smoked tongues, cut them to pieces and pound them to a paste in a mortar, moistening them with plenty of butter as you proceed. Have ready an equal quantity of the lean of veal stewed and cut into very small pieces. Pound the veal also in a mortar, adding butter to it by degrees. The tongue and veal must be kept separate till both have been pounded. Then fill your potting cans with lumps of the veal and tongue, pressed down hard, and so placed, that when cut, the mixture will look variegated or marbled. Close the cans with veal; again press it down very hard, and finish by pouring on clarified butter. Cover the cans closely, and keep them in a dry place. It may be eaten at tea or supper. Send it to table cut in slices.

You may use it for sandwiches.

To clarify butter, cut it up, melt it in a sauce-pan over the fire, and skim it well.

MUTTON AND LAMB.

GENERAL REMARKS.

THE fore-quarter of a sheep contains the neck, breast, and shoulder; and the hind-quarter the loin and leg. The two loins together are called the chine or saddle. The flesh of good mutton is of a bright red, and a close grain, and the fat firm and quite white. The meat will feel tender and springy when you squeeze it with your fingers. The vein in the neck of the fore-quarter should be of a fine blue.

Lamb is always roasted; generally a whole quarter at once. In carving lamb, the first thing done is to separate the shoulder from the breast, or the leg from the loin.

If the weather is cold enough to allow it, mutton is more tender after being kept a few days.

TO ROAST MUTTON.

MUTTON should be roasted with a quick brisk fire. Every part should be trimmed off that cannot be eaten. Wash the meat well. The skin should be taken off and skewered on again before the meat is put on the spit; this will make it more juicy. Otherwise tie paper over the fat, having soaked the twine in water to prevent the string from burning. Put a little salt and water into the dripping-pan, to baste the meat at first, then use its own gravy for that purpose. A quarter of an hour before you think it will be done, take off the skin or paper, dredge the meat very lightly with flour, and baste it with butter. Skim the gravy and send it to table in a boat.

A leg of mutton will require from two hours roasting to two hours and a half in proportion to its size. A chine or saddle, from two hours and a half, to three hours. A shoulder, from an hour and a half, to two hours. A loin, from an hour and three quarters, to two hours. A haunch (that is a leg with part of the loin) cannot be well roasted in less than four hours.

Always have some currant jelly on the table to eat with roast mutton. It should also be accompanied by mashed turnips.

Slices cut from a cold leg of mutton that has been under-done, are very nice broiled or warmed on a gridiron, and sent to the breakfast table covered with currant jelly.

Pickles are always eaten with mutton.

In preparing a leg of mutton for roasting, you may make deep incisions in it, and stuff them with chopped oysters, or with a force-meat made in the usual manner; or with chest-nuts parboiled and peeled. The gravy will be improved by stirring into it a glass of port wine.

TO BOIL MUTTON.

To prepare a leg of mutton for boiling, wash it clean, cut a small piece off the shank bone, and trim the knuckle. Put it into a pot with water enough to cover it, and boil it gently for three hours, skimming it well. Then take it from the fire, and keeping the pot well covered, let it finish by remaining in the steam for ten or fifteen minutes. Serve it up with a sauce-boat of melted butter into which a tea-cup full of capers or nasturtians have been stirred.

Have mashed turnips to eat with it.

A few small onions boiled in the water with the mutton are thought by some to improve the flavour of the meat.   It is much better when sufficient time is allowed to boil or simmer it slowly; for instance, four hours.

A neck or a loin of mutton will require also about three hours slow boiling.   These pieces should on no account be sent to table the least under-done.   Serve up with them carrots and whole turnips.   You may add a dish of suet dumplings to eat with the meat, made of finely chopped suet mixed with double its quantity of flour, and a little cold water.

MUTTON CHOPS.

TAKE chops or steaks from a loin of mutton, cut off the bone close to the meat, and trim off the skin, and part of the fat. Beat them to make them tender, and season them with pepper and salt.   Make your gridiron hot over a bed of clear bright coals; rub the bars with suet, and lay on the chops.   Turn them frequently; and if the fat that falls from them causes a blaze and smoke, remove the gridiron for a moment till it is over.   When they are thoroughly done, put them into a warm dish and butter them.   Keep them covered till a moment before they are to be eaten.

When the chops have been turned for the last time, you may strew over them some finely minced onion moistened with boiling water, and seasoned with pepper.

Some like them flavoured with mushroom catchup.

Another way of dressing mutton chops is, after trimming them nicely and seasoning them with pepper and salt, to lay them for awhile in melted butter.   When they have imbibed a sufficient quantity, take them out, and cover them all over with grated bread-crumbs. Broil them over a clear fire, and see that the bread does not burn.

~~~~~~~~~~~~~~~~~

CUTLETS À LA MAINTENON.

Cut a neck of mutton into steaks with a bone in each ; trim them nicely, and scrape clean the end of the bone. Flatten them with a rolling pin, or a meat beetle, and lay them in oiled butter. Make a seasoning of hard-boiled yolk of egg and sweet-herbs minced small, grated bread, pepper, salt, and nutmeg; and, if you choose, a little minced onion. Take the chops out of the butter, and cover them with the seasoning. Butter some half sheets of white paper, and put the cutlets into them, so as to be entirely covered, securing the paper with pins or strings ; and twisting them nicely round the bone. Heat your gridiron over some bright lively coals. Lay the cutlets on it, and broil them about twenty minutes. The custom of sending them to table in the papers had best be omitted, as (unless managed by a French cook) these envelopes, after being on the gridiron, make a very bad appearance.

Serve them up hot, with mushroom sauce in a boat, or with a brown gravy, flavoured with red wine. You may make the gravy of the bones and trimmings, stewed in a little water, skimmed well, and strained when sufficiently stewed. Thicken it with flour browned in a Dutch oven, and add a glass of red wine.

You may bake these cutlets in a Dutch oven without the papers. Moisten them frequently with a little oiled butter.

STEWED MUTTON CHOPS.

CUT a loin or neck of mutton into chops, and trim away the fat and bones. Beat and flatten them. Season them with pepper and salt, and put them into a stew-pan with barely sufficient water to cover them, and some sliced carrots, turnips, onions, potatoes, and a bunch of sweet herbs, or a few tomatas. Let the whole stew slowly about three hours, or till every thing is tender. Keep the pan closely covered, except when you are skimming it.

Send it to table with sippets or three-cornered pieces of toasted bread, laid all round the dish.

HASHED MUTTON.

CUT into small pieces the lean of some cold mutton that has been underdone, and season it with pepper and salt. Take the bones and other trimmings, put them into a sauce-pan with as much water as will cover them, and some sliced onions, and let them stew till you have drawn from them a good gravy. Having skimmed it well, strain the gravy into a stew-pan, and put the mutton into it. Have ready-boiled some carrots, turnips, potatoes and onions. Slice them, and add them to the meat and gravy. Set the pan on hot coals, and let it simmer till the meat is warmed through, but do not allow it to boil, as it has been once cooked already. Cover the bottom of a dish with slices of buttered toast. Lay the meat and vegetables upon it, and pour over them the gravy.

Tomatas will be found an improvement.

If green peas, or Lima beans are in season, you may boil them, and put them to the hashed mutton; leaving out the other vegetables, or serving them up separately.

A CASEROLE OF MUTTON.

Butter a deep dish or mould, and line it with potatoes mashed with milk or butter, and seasoned with pepper and salt. Fill it with slices of the lean of cold mutton, or lamb, seasoned also. Cover the whole with more mashed potatoes. Put it into an oven, and bake it till the meat is thoroughly warmed, and the potatoes brown. Then carefully turn it out on a large dish; or you may, if more convenient, send it to table in the dish it was baked in.

MUTTON HARICO.

Take a neck of mutton, cut it into chops, and fry them brown. Then put them into a stew-pan with a bunch of sweet herbs, two or three cloves, a little mace, and pepper and salt to your taste. Cover them with boiling water, and let them stew slowly for about an hour. Then cut some carrots and turnips into dice; slice some onions, and cut up a head of celery; put them all into the stew-pan, and keep it closely covered except when you are skimming off the fat. Let the whole stew gently for an hour longer, and then send it to table in a deep dish, with the gravy about it.

You may make a similar harico of veal steaks, or of beef cut very thin.

STEWED LEG OF MUTTON

Take a leg of mutton and trim it nicely. Put it into a pot with three pints of water; or with two pints of water and one quart of gravy drawn from bones, trimmings, and coarse pieces

of meat.   Add some slices of carrots, and a little salt.   Stew
it slowly three hours.   Then put in small onions, small tur
nips, tomatas or tomata catchup, and shred or powdered swee
marjoram to your taste, and let it stew three hours longer. A
large leg will require from first to last from six hours and a
half to seven hours stewing.   But though it must be tender
and well done all through, do not allow it to stew to rags.
Serve it up with the vegetables and gravy round it.

Have mashed potatoes in another dish.

TO ROAST LAMB.

The best way of cooking lamb is to roast it; when drest
otherwise it is insipid, and not so good as mutton.   A hind
quarter of eight pounds will be done in about two hours; a
fore-quarter of ten pounds, in two hours and a half; a leg of
five pounds will take from an hour and a quarter to an hour
and a half; a loin about an hour and a half.   Lamb, like veal
and pork, is not eatable unless thoroughly done; no one
preferring it rare, as is frequently the case with beef and
mutton.

Wash the meat, wipe it dry, spit it, and cover the fat with
paper.   Place it before a clear brisk fire.   Baste it at first
with a little salt and water, and then with its own drippings.
Remove the paper when the meat is nearly done, and dredge
the lamb with a little flour.   Afterwards baste it with butter.
Do not take it off the spit till you see it drop white gravy.

Prepare some mint-sauce by stripping from the stalks the
leaves of young green mint, mincing them very fine, and
mixing them with vinegar and sugar.   There must be just
sufficient vinegar to moisten the mint, but not enough to make

the sauce liquid. Send it to table in a boat, and the gravy in another boat. Garnish with sliced lemon.

In carving a quarter of lamb, separate the shoulder from the breast, or the leg from the ribs, sprinkle a little salt and pepper, and squeeze on some lemon juice.

It should be accompanied by asparagus, green peas, and lettuce.

MUTTON HAMS.

TAKE large fine legs of mutton freshly killed, and wipe them dry with a clean towel. Allow to each ham half a pound of salt, and an ounce of saltpetre, and half a pound of brown sugar, all mixed together, slightly heated over the fire, and then well rubbed into the meat. Put the hams into a salting-tub, and keep them there two or three days, turning and rubbing them frequently. Then make a mixture, (allowing to each ham half a pound more of brown sugar, the same of salt, and an ounce of saltpetre, pounded fine, with an ounce of black pepper, and an ounce of cloves,) and heat this mixture a few minutes. Take the hams out of the tub, wipe them dry, and then rub into them this second mixture. Clean the salting-tub, and return the hams to it. Cover them, and let them lie for a fortnight, turning them several times, and basting them with the liquid. Then smoke them a fortnight, using for the fire green birch, oak, hickory, or corn-cobs.

Sow them up in new cloths and white-wash the outside of the covers.

PORK, HAM, &c.

~~~~~~~

GENERAL REMARKS.

IN cutting up pork, you have the spare-rib, shoulder, griskin or chine, the loin, middlings and leg; the head. feet, heart and liver. On the spare-rib and chine there is but little meat, and the pieces called middlings consist almost entirely of fat. The best parts are the loin, and the leg or hind quarter. Hogs make the best pork when from two and a half to four years old. They should be kept up and fed with corn at least six weeks before they are killed, or their flesh will acquire a disagreeable taste from the trash and offal which they eat when running at large. The Portuguese pork, which is fed on chestnuts, is perhaps the finest in the world.

If the meat is young, the lean will break on being pinched, and the skin will dent by nipping it with the fingers; the fat will be white, soft, and pulpy. If the skin or rind is rough, and cannot be nipped, it is old.

Hams that have short shank-bones, are generally preferred. If you put a knife under the bone of a ham, and it comes out clean, the meat is good; but quite the contrary if the knife appears smeared and slimy. In good bacon the fat is white, and the lean sticks close to the bone; if it is streaked with yellow, the meat is rusty, and unfit to eat.

Pork in every form should be thoroughly cooked. If the least under-done, it is disgusting and unwholesome.

TO ROAST A PIG.

BEGIN your preparations by making the stuffing. Take a sufficient quantity of grated stale bread, and mix it with sage and sweet marjoram rubbed fine or powdered; also some grated lemon-peel. Season it with pepper, salt, powdered nutmeg and mace; mix in butter enough to moisten it, and some beaten yolk of egg to bind it. Let the whole be very well incorporated.

The pig should be newly killed, (that morning if possible,) nicely cleaned, fat, and not too large. Wash it well in cold water, and cut off the feet close to the joints, leaving some skin all round to fold over the ends. Take out the liver and heart, and reserve them, with the feet, to make the gravy. Truss back the legs. Fill the body with the stuffing (it must be quite full) and then sew it up, or tie it round with a buttered twine. Put the pig on the spit, and place it before a clear brisk fire, but not too near lest it scorch. The fire should be largest at the ends, that the middle of the pig may not be done before the extremities. If you find the heat too great in the centre, you may diminish it by placing a flat-iron before the fire. When you first put it down, wash the pig all over with salt and water; afterwards rub it frequently with a feather dipped in sweet oil, or with fresh butter tied in a rag. If you baste it with any thing else, or with its own dripping, the skin will not be crisp. Take care not to blister or burn the outside by keeping it too near the fire. A good sized pig will require at least three hours' roasting.

Unless a pig is very small it is seldom sent to table whole Take the spit from the fire, and place it across a large dish: then, having cut off the head with a sharp knife, and cut down the back, slip the spit out. Lay the two halves of the body close together in the dish, and place half the head **on** each side. Garnish with sliced lemon.

For the gravy,—take that from the dripping-pan and skim it well. Having boiled the heart, liver, and feet, with some minced sage in a very little water, cut the meat from the feet, and chop it. Chop also the liver and heart. Put all into a small sauce-pan, adding a little of the water that they were boiled in, and some bits of butter rolled in flour. Flavour it with a glass of Madeira, and some grated nutmeg. Give it a boil up, and send it to table in a gravy-boat.

You may serve up with the pig, apple-sauce, cranberry-sauce, or bread-sauce in a small tureen; or currant jelly.

If you bake the pig instead of roasting it, rub it from time to time with fresh butter tied in a rag.

TO ROAST A LEG OF PORK.

TAKE a sharp knife and score the skin across in narrow stripes (you may cross it again so as to form diamonds) and rub in some powdered sage. Raise the skin at the knuckle, and put in a stuffing of minced onion and sage, bread-crumbs, pepper, salt, and beaten yolk of egg. Fasten it down with a buttered string, or with skewers. You may make deep incisions in the meat of the large end of the leg, and stuff them also; pressing in the filling very hard. Rub a little sweet oil all over the skin with a brush or a goose-feather, to make it crisp and of a handsome brown. Do not place the spit too near the fire, lest the skin should burn and blister. A leg of pork will require from three to four hours to roast. Moisten 't all the time by brushing it with sweet oil, or with fresh butter tied in a rag. To baste it with its own dripping will make the skin tough and hard. Skim the fat carefully from the gravy, which should be thickened with a little flour.

A roast leg of pork should always be accompanied by apple-sauce, and by mashed potato and mashed turnips.

TO ROAST A LOIN OF PORK.

SCORE the skin in narrow strips, and rub it all over with a mixture of powdered sage-leaves, pepper and salt. Have ready a force-meat or stuffing of sage and marjoram, mixed with a little grated bread and beaten yolk of egg, and seasoned with pepper and salt. Make deep incisions between the ribs and fill them with this stuffing. Put it on the spit before a clear fire and moisten it with butter or sweet oil, rubbed lightly over it. It will require three hours to roast.

Having skimmed the gravy well, thicken it with a little flour, and serve it up in a boat. Have ready some apple-sauce to eat with the pork. Also mashed turnips and mashed potatoes.

You may roast in the same manner, a shoulder, spare-rib, or chine of pork; seasoning it with sage and marjoram.

TO ROAST A MIDDLING OR SPRING PIECE OF PORK.

MAKE a force-meat of grated bread, and minced onion and sage, pepper, salt, and beaten yolk of egg; mix it well, and spread it all over the inside of the pork. Then roll up the meat, and with a sharp knife score it round in circles, rubbing powdered sage into the cuts. Tie a buttered twine round the roll of meat so as to keep it together in every direction. Put a hook through one end, and roast the pork before a clear brisk fire, moistening the skin occasionally with butter. Or you may bake it in a Dutch oven. It is a good side dish. Thicken the gravy with a little flour, and flavour it with a glass of wine. Have currant jelly to eat with it.

It should be delicate young pork.

TO STEW PORK.

TAKE a nice piece of the fillet or leg of fresh pork; rub it with a little salt, and score the skin. Put it into a pot with sufficient water to cover it, and stew it gently for two hours or more, in proportion to its size. Then put into the same pot a dozen or more sweet potatoes, scraped, split, and cut in pieces. Let the whole stew gently together for an hour and a half, or till all is thoroughly done, skimming it frequently. Serve up all together in a large dish.

This stew will be found very good. For sweet potatoes you may substitute white ones mixed with sliced turnips, or parsnips scraped and split.

TO BOIL CORNED PORK.

TAKE a nice piece of fresh pork, (the leg is the best,) rub it with salt, and let it lie in the salt two days. Boil it slowly in plenty of water, skimming it well. When the meat is about half done, you may put into the same pot a fine cabbage, washed clean and quartered. The pork and the cabbage should be thoroughly done, and tender throughout. Send them to table in separate dishes, having drained and squeezed all the water out of the cabbage. Take off the skin of the pork, and touch the outside at intervals with spots of cayenne pepper. Eat mustard with it.

Pork is never boiled unless corned or salted.

~~~~~~~~~~~~~~~

PICKLED PORK AND PEASE PUDDING.

Soak the pork all night in cold water, and wash and scrape it clean. Put it on early in the day, as it will take a long time to boil, and must boil slowly. Skim it frequently. Boil in a separate pot greens or cabbage to eat with it; also parsnips and potatoes.

Pease pudding is a frequent accompaniment to pickled pork, and is very generally liked. To make a small pudding, you must have ready a quart of dried split pease, which have been soaked all night in cold water. Tie them in a cloth, (leaving room for them to swell,) and boil them slowly till they are tender. Drain them, and rub them through a cullender or a sieve into a deep dish; season them with pepper and salt, and mix with them an ounce of butter, and two beaten eggs. Beat all well together till thoroughly mixed. Dip a clean cloth in hot water, sprinkle it with flour. and put the pudding into it. Tie it up very tightly, leaving a small space between the mixture and the tying, (as the pudding will still swell a little,) and boil it an hour longer. Send it to table and eat it with the pork.

You may make a pease pudding in a plain and less delicate way, by simply seasoning the pease with black pepper, (having first soaked them well,) tying them in a cloth, and putting them to boil in the same pot with the pork, taking care to make the string very tight, so that the water may not get in. When all is done, and you turn out the pudding, cut it into thick slices and lay it round the pork.

Pickled pork is frequently accompanied by dried beans and hominy.

PORK AND BEANS.

ALLOW two pounds of pickled pork to two quarts of dried beans. Soak the meat all night in a pan of cold water. Put the beans into a pot with cold water, and let them hang all night over the embers of the fire, or set them in the chimney corner, that they may warm as well as soak. Early in the morning rinse them through a cullender. Having scored the rind of the pork, (which should not be a very fat piece,) put it into a pot with cold water, and boil it till tender, carefully skimming off the liquid fat. *In another pot* boil the beans till they have all bursted. When soft, take them up; lay the pork in a tin pan; and cover it with the beans, adding a very little water. Then bake them in an oven till brown, but not longer.

This is a homely dish, but is by many persons much liked. It is customary to bring it to table in the pan in which it is baked. The chine is the proper piece for this purpose

PORK STEAKS.

PORK steaks or chops should be taken from the neck, or the loin. Cut them about half an inch thick, remove the skin, trim them neatly, and beat them. Season them with pepper, salt, and powdered sage-leaves or sweet marjoram, and broil them over a clear fire till quite done all through, turning them once. They require much longer broiling than beef-steaks or mutton chops. When you think they are nearly done, take up one on a plate and try it. If it is the least red inside, return it to the gridiron. Have ready a gravy made of the trimmings, or any coarse pieces of pork stewed in a little water with chopped onions and sage, and skimmed carefully. When all the essence is extracted, take out the bits of meat, &c, and serve up the gravy in a boat to eat with the steaks.

They should be accompanied with apple-sauce.

PORK CUTLETS.

Cut them from the leg, and remove the skin; trim them and beat them, and sprinkle on salt and pepper. Prepare some beaten egg in a pan; and on a flat dish a mixture of bread-crumbs, minced onion, and sage. Put some lard or drippings into a frying-pan over the fire; and when it boils put in the cutlets; having dipped every one first in the egg, and then in the seasoning. Fry them twenty or thirty minutes, turning them often. After you have taken them out of the frying-pan, skim the gravy, dredge in a little flour, give it one boil, and then pour it on the dish round the cutlets.

Have apple-sauce to eat with them.

Pork cutlets prepared in this manner may be stewed instead of being fried. Add to them a little water, and stew them slowly till thoroughly done, keeping them closely covered, except when you remove the lid to skim them.

PORK PIE.

TAKE the lean of a leg or loin of fresh pork, and season it with pepper, salt, and nutmeg. Cover the bottom and sides of a deep dish with a good paste, made with a pound of butter to two pounds of flour, and rolled out thick. Put in a layer of pork, and then a layer of pippin apples, pared, cored, and cut small. Strew over the apples sufficient sugar to make them very sweet. Then place another layer of pork, and so on till the dish is full. Pour in half a pint or more of sweet cider. Cover the pie with a thick lid of paste, and notch and ornament it according to your taste.

Set it in a brisk oven, and bake it well.

HAM PIE.

COVER the sides and bottom of a dish with a good paste rolled out thick. Have ready some slices of cold boiled ham, about half an inch thick, some eggs boiled hard and sliced, and a large young fowl cleaned and cut up. Put a layer of ham at the bottom, then the fowl, then the eggs, and then another layer of ham. Shake on some pepper, and pour in some water, or what will be much better, some veal gravy. Cover the pie with a crust, notch and ornament it, and bake it well.

Some mushrooms will greatly improve it.

Small button mushrooms will keep very well in a bottle of sweet oil—first peeling the skin, and cutting off the stalks.

HAM SANDWICHES.

Cut some thin slices of bread very neatly, having slightly buttered them; and, if you choose, spread on a very little mustard. Have ready some very thin slices of cold boiled ham, and lay one between two slices of bread. You may either roll them up, or lay them flat on the plates. They are used at supper, or at luncheon.

You may substitute for the ham, cold smoked tongue, shred or grated.

BROILED HAM.

Cut the ham into very thin slices, (the thinner the better.) Soak them in hot water at least half an hour, (a whole hour is better,) to draw out some of the salt; changing the water several times, and always pouring it on scalding hot. This process will not only extract the superfluous salt (which would otherwise ooze out in broiling and remain sticking about the surface of the meat) but it makes the ham more tender and mellow. After soaking, dry the slices in a cloth, and then heat your gridiron, and broil them over a clear fire.

If you have cold boiled ham, it is better for broiling than that which is raw; and being boiled, will require no soaking before you put it on the gridiron.

If you wish to serve up eggs with the ham, put some lard into a very clean frying-pan, and make it boiling hot. Break the eggs separately into a saucer, that in case a bad one should be among them it may not mix with the rest. Slip each egg gently into the frying-pan. Do not turn them while they are frying, but keep pouring some of the hot lard over them with an iron spoon; this will do them sufficiently on the upper

side. They will be done enough in about three minutes; th
white must retain its transparency so that the yolk will be
seen through it. When done, take them up with a tin slice,
drain off the lard, and if any part of the white is discoloured
or ragged, trim it off. Lay a fried egg upon each slice of the
broiled ham, and send them to table hot.

This is a much nicer way than the common practice of frying the ham or bacon with the eggs. Some persons bioil or
fry the ham without eggs, and send it to table cut into little
slips or mouthfuls.

To curl small pieces of ham for garnishing, slice as thin as
possible some that has been boiled or parboiled. The pieces
should be about two inches square. Roll it up round little
wooden skewers, and put it into a cheese toaster, or into a
tin oven, and set it before the fire for eight or ten minutes.
When it is done, slip out the skewers.

TO BOIL A HAM.

HAMS should always be soaked in water previous to boiling, to draw out a portion of the salt, and to make them
tender. They will soften more easily if soaked in lukewarm
water. If it is a new ham, and not very salt or hard, you
need not put it in water till the evening before you intend to
cook it. An older one will require twenty-four hours' soaking; and one that is very old and hard should be kept in soak
two or three days, frequently changing the water, which must
be soft. Soak it in a tub, and keep it well covered. When
you take it out of the water to prepare it for boiling, scrape
and trim it nicely, and pare off all the rough-looking parts.

Early in the morning put it into a large pot or kettle with

plenty of cold water. Place it over a slow fire that it may heat gradually ; it should not come to a boil in less than an hour and a half, or two hours. When it boils, quicken the fire, and skim the pot carefully. Then simmer it gently four or five hours or more, according to its size. A ham weighing fifteen pounds should simmer five hours after it has come to a boil. Keep the pot well skimmed.

When it is done, take it up, carefully strip off the skin, and reserve it to cover the ham when it is put away cold. Rub the ham all over with some beaten egg and strew on it fine bread-raspings shaken through the lid of a dredging box. Then place it in an oven to brown and crisp, or on a hot dish set over the pot before the fire. Cut some writing paper into a handsome fringe, and twist it round the shank-bone before you send the ham to table. Garnish the edge of the dish with little piles or spots of rasped crust of bread.

In carving a ham, begin not quite in the centre, but a little nearer to the hock. Cut the slices very thin. It is not only a most ungenteel practice to cut ham in thick slices, but it much impairs the flavour.

When you put it away after dinner, skewer on again the skin. This will make it keep the better.

Ham should always be accompanied by green vegetables, such as asparagus, peas, beans, spinach, cauliflower, brocoli, &c.

Bacon also should be well soaked before it is cooked ; and it should be boiled very slowly, and for a long time. The greens may be boiled with the meat. Take care to skim the pot carefully, and to drain and squeeze the greens very well before you send them to table. If there are yellow streaks in the lean of the bacon, it is rusty, and unfit to eat.

TO ROAST A HAM.

TAKE a very fine ham (a Westphalia one if you can procure it) and soak it in lukewarm water for a day or two, changing the water frequently.   The day before you intend cooking it, take the ham out of the water, and (having removed the skin) trim it nicely, and pour over it a bottle of Madeira or sherry. Let it steep till next morning; frequently during the day washing the wine over it.   Put it on the spit in time to allow at least six hours for slowly roasting it.   Baste it continually with hot water.   When it is done, dredge it all over with fine bread-raspings shaken on through the top of the dredging box ; and set it before the fire to brown.

For gravy, take the wine in which the ham was steeped, and add to it the essence or juice which flowed from the meat when taken from the spit.   Squeeze in the juice of two lemons.   Put it into a sauce-pan, and boil and skim it.   Send it to table in a boat.   Cover the shank of the ham (which should have been sawed short) with bunches of double parsley, and ornament it with a cluster of flowers cut out with a penknife from raw carrots, beets, and turnips; and made to imitate marygolds, and red and white roses.

DIRECTIONS FOR CURING HAM OR BACON.

HAM or bacon, however well cured, will never be good unless the pork of which it is made has been properly fed. The hogs should be well fattened on corn, and fed with it about eight weeks, allowing ten bushels to each hog.   They are best for curing when from two to four years old, and should not weigh more than one hundred and fifty or one hundred and sixty pounds. The first four weeks they may be fed on mush, or on Indian meal moistened with water; the remaining four on corn unground; giving them always as much as they will eat. Soap-suds may be given to them three or four times a week; or oftener if convenient.

When killed and cut up, begin immediately to salt them. Rub the outside of each ham with a tea-spoonful of powdered saltpetre, and the inside with a tea-spoonful of cayenne pepper. Having mixed together two pounds brown sugar and fine salt, in the proportion of a pound and a half of brown sugar to a pint of salt, rub the pork well with it. This quantity of sugar and salt will be sufficient for fifty pounds of meat. Have ready some large tubs, the bottoms sprinkled with salt, and lay the meat in the tubs with the skin downward. Put plenty of salt between each layer of meat. After it has lain eight days, take it out and wipe off all the salt, and wash the tubs. Make a pickle of soft water, equal quantities of salt and molasses, and a little saltpetre; allowing four ounces of saltpetre to two quarts of molasses and two quarts of salt, which is the proportion for fifty pounds of meat. The pickle must be strong enough to bear up an egg. Boil and skim it; and when it is cold, pour it over the meat, which must be turned every day and basted with the pickle. The hams should remain in the pickle at least four weeks; the shoulders and middlings of the bacon three weeks; and the jowls two weeks. They should then be taken out and smoked. Having washed off the pickle, before you smoke the meat, bury it, while wet, in a tub of bran. This will form a crust over it, and prevent evaporation of the juices. Let the smoke-house be ready to receive the meat immediately. Take it out of the tub after it has lain half an hour, and rub the bran evenly ove it. Then hang it up to smoke with the small end downwards. The smoke-house should be dark and cool, and should stand alone, for the heat occasioned by an adjoining building may spoil the meat, or produce insects. Keep up a good smoke all day, but have no blaze. Hickory is the best wood for a smoke-house fire. In three or four weeks the meat will be sufficiently smoked, and fit for use. During the process it should be occasionally taken down, examined, and hung up again. The best way of keeping hams is to sew them in coarse cloths, which should be white-washed. If they are to go to sea, pack them in pounded charcoal.

An old ham will require longer to soak, and longer to boil than a new one.

Tongues may be cured in the above manner.

LIVER PUDDINGS.

Boil some pigs' livers. When cold, mince them, and season them with pepper, salt, and some sage and sweet marjoram rubbed fine. You may add some powdered cloves. Have ready some large skins nicely cleaned, and fill them with the mixture, tying up the ends securely. Prick them with a fork to prevent their bursting; put them into hot water, and boil them slowly for about an hour. They will require no farther cooking before you eat them. Keep them in stone jars closely covered. They are eaten cold at breakfast or supper, cut into slices an inch thick or more; or they may be cut into large pieces, and broiled or fried.

The best liver puddings are made of boiled pigs-feet and livers, mixed together in equal portions.

COMMON SAUSAGE-MEAT.

HAVING cleared it from the skin, sinews, and gristle, take six pounds of the lean of young fresh pork, and three pounds of the fat, and mince it all as fine as possible. Take some dried sage, pick off the leaves and rub them to powder, allowing three tea-spoonfuls to each pound of meat. Having mixed the fat and lean well together, and seasoned it with six tea-spoonfuls of pepper, and the same quantity of salt, strew on the powdered sage, and mix the whole very well with your hands. Put it away in a stone jar, packing it down hard; and keep it closely covered. Set the jar in a cool dry place.

When you wish to use the sausage-meat, make it into flat cakes about an inch thick and the size of a dollar; dredge them with flour, and fry them in nothing, over rather a slow fire, till they are well browned on both sides, and thoroughly done. Their own fat will cook them.

Sausages are seldom eaten except at breakfast.

FINE SAUSAGES.

TAKE some fresh pork, (the leg is best,) and clear it from the skin, sinews, and gristle. Allow two pounds of fat to three pounds of lean. Mince it all very fine, and season it with two ounces and a half of salt, half an ounce of pepper, twelve cloves, and a dozen blades of mace powdered, three grated nutmegs, six table-spoonfuls of powdered sage, and two tea-spoonfuls of powdered rosemary. Mix all well together. Put it into a stone jar, and press it down very hard. Cover it closely, and keep it in a dry cool place.

When you use this sausage-meat, mix with it some beaten yolk of egg, and make it into balls or cakes. Dredge them with flour, and fry them in butter.

BOLOGNA SAUSAGES.

TAKE ten pounds of beef, and four pounds of pork; two-thirds of the meat should be lean, and only one third fat. Chop it very fine, and mix it well together. Then season it with six ounces of fine salt, one ounce of black pepper, half an ounce of cayenne, one table-spoonful of powdered cloves; and one clove or garlic minced very fine.

Have ready some large skins nicely cleaned and prepared, (they should be beef-skins,) and wash them in salt and vinegar. Fill them with the above mixture, and secure the ends by tying them with packthread or fine twine. Make a brine of salt and water strong enough to bear up an egg. Put the sausages into it, and let them lie for three weeks, turning them daily. Then take them out, wipe them dry, hang them up and smoke them. Before you put them away rub them all over with sweet oil.

Keep them in ashes. That of vine-twigs is best for them. You may fry them or not before you eat them.

PORK CHEESE.

TAKE the heads, tongues, and feet of young fresh pork, or any other pieces that are convenient. Having removed the skin, boil them till all the meat is quite tender, and can be easily stripped from the bones. Then chop it small, and season it with salt and black pepper to your taste, and if you choose, some beaten cloves. Add sage-leaves and sweet marjoram, minced fine, or rubbed to powder. Mix the whole very well together, with your hands. Put it into deep pans, with straight sides, (the shape of a cheese,) press it down hard and closely with a plate that will fit the pan; putting the under side of the plate next to the meat, and placing a heavy weight on it. In two or three days it will be fit for use, and you may turn it out of the pan. Send it to table cut in slices, and use mustard and vinegar with it. It is generally eaten at supper or breakfast.

PIG'S FEET AND EARS SOUSED.

HAVING cleaned them properly, and removed the skin, boil them slowly till they are quite tender, and then split the feet and put them with the ears into salt and vinegar, flavoured with a little mace. Cover the jar closely, and set it away. When you use them, dry each piece well with a cloth; dip them first in beaten yolk of egg, and then in bread-crumbs, and fry them nicely in butter or lard. Or you may eat them cold, just out of the vinegar.

If you intend keeping them some time, you must make a fresh pickle for them every other day

TO IMITATE WESTPHALIA HAM.

THE very finest pork must be used for these hams. Mix together an equal quantity of powdered saltpetre and brown sugar, and rub it well into the hams. Next day make a pickle in sufficient quantity to cover them very well. The proportions of the ingredients are a pound of fine salt, mixed with a pound of brown sugar, an ounce of black pepper and an ounce of cloves pounded to powder, a small bit of sal prunella, and a quart of stale strong beer or porter. Boil them all together, so as to make a pickle that will bear up an egg. Pour it boiling hot over the meat, and let it lie in the pickle two weeks, turning it two or three times every day, and basting or washing it with the liquid. Then take out the hams, rub them with bran and smoke them for a fortnight. When done, keep them in a barrel of fine charcoal.

In cooking these hams simmer them slowly for seven or eight hours.

To imitate the shape of the real Westphalia hams, cut some of the meat off the under side of the thick part, so as to give them a flat appearance. Do this before you begin to cure them, first loosening the skin and afterwards sewing it on again.

The ashes in which you keep them must be changed frequently, wiping the hams when you take them out.

TO GLAZE A COLD HAM.

WITH a brush or quill feather go all over the ham with beaten yolk of egg. Then cover it thickly with pounded cracker, made as fine as flour, or with grated crumbs of stale bread. Lastly go over it with thick cream. Put it to brown in the oven of a stove, or brown it on the spit of a tin roaster set before the fire and turned frequently.

This glazing will be found delicious. It should be put on half an inch thick, so as to form a crust.

VENISON, &c.

TO ROAST A SADDLE OR HAUNCH OF VENISON.

Wipe it all over with a sponge dipped in warm water. Then rub the skin with lard or nice dripping. Cover the fat with sheets of paper two double, buttered, and tied on with packthread that has been soaked to keep it from burning. Or, what is still better, you may cover the first sheets of paper with a coarse paste of flour and water rolled out half an inch thick, and then cover the paste with the second sheets of paper, securing the whole well with the string to prevent its falling off. Place the venison on the spit before a strong clear fire, such as you would have for a sirloin of beef, and let the fire be well kept up all the time. Put some claret and butter into the dripping-pan and baste the meat with it frequently. If wrapped in paste, it will not be done in less than five hours. Half an hour before you take it up, remove the coverings carefully, place the meat nearer to the fire, baste it with fresh butter and dredge it very lightly with flour. Send it to table with fringed white paper wrapped round the bone, and its own gravy well skimmed. Have currant jelly to eat with it. As venison chills immediately, the plates should oe kept on heaters.

You may make another gravy with a pound and a half of scraps and trimmings or inferior pieces of venison, put into a sauce-pan with three pints of water, a few cloves, a few blades of mace, half a nutmeg; and salt and cayenne to your taste. Boil it down slowly to a pint. Then skim off the fat, and strain the gravy into a clean sauce-pan. Add to it half a pint of currant jelly, half a pint of claret, and near a quarter of a pound of butter divided into bits and rolled in flour. Send i to table in two small tureens or sauce-boats. This gravy will be found very fine.

Venison should never be roasted unless very fat. Th shoulder is a roasting piece, and may be done without the paper or paste.

Venison is best when quite fresh; but if it is expedient to keep it a week before you cook it, wash it well with milk and water, and then dry it perfectly with cloths till there is not the least damp remaining on it. Then mix together powdered ginger and pepper, and rub it well over every part of the meat. Do not, however, attempt to keep it unless the weather is quite cold.

TO HASH COLD VENISON.

Cut the meat in nice small slices, and put the trimmings and bones into a sauce-pan with barely water enough to cover them. Let them stew for an hour. Then strain the liquid into a stew-pan; add to it some bits of butter rolled in flour, and whatever gravy was left of the venison the day before. Stir in some currant jelly, and give it a boil up. Then put in the meat, and keep it over the fire just long enough to warm t through; but do not allow it to boil, as it has been once cooked already.

VENISON STEAKS.

Cut them from the neck or haunch. Season them with pepper and salt. When the gridiron has been well heated over a bed of bright coals, grease the bars, and lay the steaks upon it. Broil them well, turning them once, and taking care to save as much of the gravy as possible. Serve them up with some currant jelly laid on each steak. Have your plates set on heaters.

VENISON PASTY.

The neck, breast, and shoulder are the parts used for a venison pie or pasty. Cut the meat into pieces (fat and lean together) and put the bones and trimmings into a stew-pan with pepper and salt, and water or veal broth enough to cover it. Simmer it till you have drawn out a good gravy. Then strain it.

In the mean time make a good rich paste, and roll it rather thick. Cover the bottom and sides of a deep dish with one sheet of it, and put in your meat, having seasoned it with pepper, salt, nutmeg, and mace. Pour in the gravy which you have prepared from the trimmings, and two glasses of port or claret, and lay on the top some bits of butter rolled in flour. Cover the pie with a thick lid of paste, and ornament it handsomely with leaves and flowers formed with a tin cutter Bake it two hours or more, according to its size.

VENISON HAMS.

VENISON for hams must be newly killed, and in every respect as good as possible. Mix together equal quantities of salt and brown sugar, and rub it well into the hams. Put them into a tub, and let them lie seven days; turning them and rubbing them daily with the mixture of salt and sugar. Next mix together equal quantities of West India molasses and fine salt. Rub it over your hams, and let them lie in it a week longer. Then wipe them, rub them with bran, and smoke them a fortnight over hickory wood. Pack them in wood ashes; or in charcoal, if to go to sea.

Venison ham must not be cooked before it is eaten. It is used for the tea-table, chipped or shred like dried beef, to which it is considered very superior.

It will not keep as long as other smoked meat.

TO ROAST A KID.

A KID should be cooked the day it is killed, or the day after at farthest. They are best from three to four months old, and are only eaten while they live on milk.

Wash the kid well, wipe it dry, and truss it. Stuff the body with a force-meat of grated bread, butter or suet, sweet herbs, pepper, salt, nutmeg, grated lemon-peel, and beaten egg; and sew it up to keep the stuffing in its place. Put it on the spit and rub it over with lard, or sweet oil. Put a little salt and water into the dripping-pan, and baste the kid first with that, and afterwards with its own gravy. Or you may make it very nice by basting it with cream. It should roast about three hours. At the last, transfer the gravy to a small sauce-pan; thicken it with a little butter rolled in flour, give it a boil up, and send it to table in a boat. Garnish the kid with lumps of currant jelly laid round the edge of the dish.

A fawn (which should never be kept more than one day) may be roasted in the same manner; also, a hare, or a couple of rabbits.

You may send to table, to eat with the kid, a dish of chestnuts boiled or roasted, and divested of the shells.

TO ROAST A HARE.

IF a hare is old do not roast it, but make soup of it. Wash and soak it in water for an hour, and change the water several times having made a little slit in the neck to let out the blood Take out the heart and liver, and scald them. Drain, dry, and truss the hare. Make a force-meat richer and more moist than usual, and add to it the heart and liver minced fine. Soak the bread-crumbs in a little claret before you mix them with the other ingredients. Stuff the body of the hare with this force-meat, and sew it up. Put it on the spit, rub it with butter, and roast it before a brisk fire. For the first half hour baste it with butter; and afterwards with cream, or with milk thickened with beaten yolk of egg. At the last, dredge it lightly with flour. The hare will require about two hours roasting.

For sauce, take the drippings of the hare mixed with cream or with claret, and a little lemon-juice, a bit of butter, and some bread-crumbs. Give it a boil up, and send it to table in a boat. Garnish the hare with slices of currant jelly laid round it in the dish.

FRICASSEED RABBITS.

THE best way of cooking rabbits is to fricassee them. Take a couple of fine ones, and cut them up, or disjoint them. Put them into a stew-pan; season them with cayenne pepper and salt, some chopped parsley, and some powdered mace. Pour in a pint of warm water (or of veal broth, if you have it) and stew it over a slow fire till the rabbits are quite tender; adding (when they are about half done) some bits of butter rolled in flour. Just before you take it from the fire, enrich the gravy with a jill or more of thick cream with some nutmeg grated into it. Stir the gravy well, but take care not to let it boil after the cream is in, lest it curdle.

Put the pieces of rabbit on a hot dish, and pour the gravy over them.

TO STEW RABBITS.

HAVING trussed the rabbits, lay them in a pan of warm water for about fifteen minutes. Then put them into a pot with plenty of water and a little salt, and stew them slowly for about an hour, or till they are quite tender. In the mean time, peel and boil in a sauce-pan a dozen onions. When they are quite tender all through, take them out, and drain and slice them. Have ready some drawn butter, prepared by taking six ounces of butter, (cut into bits and rolled in about three tea-spoonfuls of flour,) and melting it in a jill of milk. After shaking it round over hot coals till it simmers, add to it the onions, and give it one boil up.

When the rabbits are done stewing lay them on a large

dish (having first cut off their heads, which should not be sent to table) and cover them all over with the onion-sauce, to which you may add some grated nutmeg.

TO FRY RABBITS.

HAVING washed the rabbits well, put them into a pan of cold water, and let them lie in it two or three hours. Then cut them into joints, dry them in a cloth, dredge them with flour, strew them with chopped parsley, and fry them in butter. After you take them out of the frying-pan, stir a wineglass of cream into the gravy, or the beaten yolk of an egg. Do not let it boil, but pour it at once into the dish with the rabbits.

Rabbits are very good baked in a pie. A boiled or pot-pie may be made of them.

They may be stuffed with force-meat and roasted, basting them with butter. Cut off their heads before you send them to table.

VENISON SAUSAGES.

To six pounds of fresh-killed venison, allow two pounds of fresh fat pork. Chop the meat and mince it very fine. Add six tea-spoonfuls of sage leaves, dried and powdered, the same quantity of salt, and the same of ground black peppei. Having mixed the whole thoroughly, pack it down hard in stone jars, and keep it well covered in a cool dry place.

When wanted for use, make it into small flat cakes, and fry them.

POULTRY, GAME, &c.

GENERAL REMARKS.

In buying poultry choose those that are fresh and fat. Half-grown poultry is comparatively insipid; it is best when full-grown but not old. Old poultry is tough and hard. An old goose is so tough as to be frequently uneatable. When poultry is young the skin is thin and tender, and can be easily ripped by trying it with a pin; the legs are smooth; the feet moist and limber; and the eyes full and bright. The body should be thick and the breast fat. The bill and feet of a young goose are yellow, and have but few hairs on them; when old they are red and hairy.

Poultry is best when killed over night, as if cooked too soon after killing, it is hard and does not taste well. It is not the custom in America, as in some parts of Europe, to keep game, or indeed any sort of eatable, till it begins to taint; all food when inclining to decomposition being regarded by us with disgust.

When poultry or game is frozen, it should be brought into the kitchen early in the morning of the day on which it is to be cooked. It may be thawed by laying it several hours in cold water. If it is not thawed it will require double the time to cook, and will be tough and tasteless when done.

In drawing poultry be very careful not to break the gall, lest its disagreeable bitterness should be communicated to the liver.

Poultry should be always scalded in hot water to make the

feathers come out easily. Before they are cooked they should be held for a moment over the blaze of the fire to singe off the hairs that are about the skin. The head, neck, and feet should be cut off, and the ends of the legs skewered in the bodies. A string should be tied tightly round.

TO BOIL A PAIR OF FOWLS.

MAKE a force-meat in the usual manner, of grated bread-crumbs, chopped sweet herbs, butter, pepper, salt, and yolk of egg. Fill the bodies of the fowls with the stuffing, and tie a string firmly round them. Skewer the livers and giz-zards to the sides, under the wings. Dredge them with flour, and put them into a pot with just enough of water to cook them; cover it closely, and put it over a moderate fire. As soon as the scum rises, take off the pot and skim it. Then cover it again, and boil it slowly half an hour. Afterwards diminish the fire, and let them stew slowly till quite tender. An hour altogether is generally sufficient to boil a pair of fowls, unless they are quite old. By doing them slowly (rather stewing than boiling) the skin will not break, and they will be whiter and more tender than if boiled fast.

Serve them up with egg-sauce in a boat.

Young chickens are better for being soaked two hours in skim milk, previous to boiling. You need not stuff them Boil or stew them slowly in the same manner as large fowls. Three quarters of an hour will cook them.

Serve them up with egg-sauce, and garnish with parsley.

Boiled fowls should be accompanied by ham or smoked tongue.

TO ROAST A PAIR OF FOWLS.

LEAVE out the livers, gizzards and hearts, to be chopped and put into the gravy.   Fill the crops and bodies of the fowls witn a force-meat, put them before a clear fire and roast them an hour, basting them with butter or with clarified dripping.

Having stewed the necks, gizzards, livers, and hearts in a very little water, strain it and mix it hot with the gravy that has dripped from the fowls, and which must be first skimmed. Thicken it with a little browned flour, add to it the livers, hearts, and gizzards chopped small.   Send the fowls to table with the gravy in a boat, and have cranberry-sauce to eat with them.

BROILED CHICKENS.

SPLIT a pair of chickens down the back, and beat them flat. Wipe the inside, season them with pepper and salt, and let them lie while you prepare some beaten yolk of egg and grated bread-crumbs.   Wash the outside of the chickens all over with the egg, and then strew on the bread-crumbs.   Have ready a hot gridiron over a bed of bright coals.   Lay the chickens on it with the inside downwards, or next the fire. Broil them about three quarters of an hour, keeping them covered with a plate.   Just before you take them up, lay some small pieces of butter on them.

In preparing chickens for broiling, you may parboil them about ten minutes, to ensure their being sufficiently cooked ; as it is difficult to broil the thick parts thoroughly without burning the rest.   None but fine plump chickens are worth broiling.

FRICASSEED CHICKENS.

HAVING cut up your chickens, lay them in cold water till all the blood is drawn out. Then wipe the pieces, season them with pepper and salt, and dredge them with flour. Fry them in lard or butter; they should be of a fine brown on both sides. When they are quite done, take them out of the frying-pan, cover them up, and set them by the fire to keep warm. Skim the gravy in the frying-pan and pour into it half a pint of cream; season it with nutmeg, mace, and cayenne, and thicken it with a small bit of butter rolled in flour. Give it a boil, and then pour it round the chickens, which must be kept hot. Put some lard into the pan, and fry some parsley in it to lay on the pieces of chicken; it must be done green and crisp.

To make a white fricassee of chickens, skin them, cut them in pieces, and having soaked out the blood, season them with salt, pepper, nutmeg and mace, and strew over them some sweet marjoram shred fine. Put them into a stew-pan, and pour over them half a pint of cream, or rich unskimmed milk. Add some butter rolled in flour, and (if you choose) some small force-meat balls. Set the stew-pan over hot coals. Keep it closely covered, and stew or simmer it gently till the chicken is quite tender, but do not allow it to boil.

You may improve it by a few small slices of cold ham.

CHICKEN CROQUETS AND RISSOLES.

TAKE some cold chicken, and having cut the flesh from the bones, mince it small with a little suet and parsley; adding sweet marjoram and grated lemon-peel. Season it wi h pepper, salt and nutmeg, and having mixed the whole very well, pound it to a paste in a marble mortar, putting in a little at a time, and moistening it frequently with yolk of egg that has been previously beaten. Then divide it into equal portions, and having floured your hands, make it up in the shape of pears, sticking the head of a clove into the bottom of each to represent the blossom end, and the stalk of a clove into the top to look like the stem. Dip them into beaten yolk of egg, and then into bread-crumbs grated finely and sifted. Fry them in butter, and when you take them out of the pan, fry some parsley in it. Having drained the parsley, cover the bottom of a dish with it, and lay the croquets upon it. Send it to table as a side dish.

Croquets may be made of cold sweet-breads, or of cold veal mixed with ham or tongue.

Rissoles are made of the same ingredients, well mixed, and beaten smooth in a mortar. Make a fine paste, roll it out, and cut it into round cakes. Then lay some of the mixture on one half of the cake, and fold over the other upon it, in the shape of a half-moon. Close and crimp the edges nicely, and fry the rissoles in butter. They should be of a light brown on both sides. Drain them and send them to table dry.

BAKED CHICKEN PIE.

COVER the bottom and sides of a deep dish with a thick paste. Having cut up your chickens, and seasoned them to your taste with salt, pepper, mace and nutmeg, put them in, and lay on the top several pieces of butter rolled in flour. Fill up the dish about two-thirds with cold water. Then lay on the top crust, notching it handsomely. Cut a slit in the top, and stick into it an ornament of paste made in the form of a tulip. Bake it in a moderate oven.

It will be much improved by the addition of a quarter of a hundred oysters ; or by interspersing the pieces of chicken with slices of cold boiled ham, in which case use no other salt.

You may add also some yolks of eggs boiled hard.

A duck pie may be made in the same manner. A rabbit pie also.

A POT PIE.

TAKE a pair of large fine fowls. Cut them up, wash the pieces, and season them with pepper only.   Make a good paste in the proportion of a pound and a half of minced suet to three pounds of flour.   Let there be plenty of paste, as it is always much liked by the eaters of pot pie.   Roll out the paste not very thin, and cut most of it into long squares. Butter the sides of a pot, and line them with paste nearly to the top.   Lay slices of cold ham at the bottom of the pot, and then the pieces of fowl, interspersed all through with squares of paste, and potatoes pared and quartered.   Pour in a quart of water.   Cover the whole with a lid of paste, having a slit in the centre, through which the gravy will bubble up.   Boil it steadily for two hours.   Half an hour before you take it up, put in through the hole in the centre of the crust, some bits of butter rolled in flour, to thicken the gravy.   When done, put the pie on a large dish, and pour the gravy over it.

You may intersperse it all through with cold ham.

A pot-pie may be made of ducks, rabbits, squirrels, or venison. Also of beef-steaks. A beef-steak, or some pork-steaks (the lean only) greatly improve a chicken pot-pie. If you use no ham, season with salt.

CHICKEN CURRY.

TAKE a pair of fine fowls, and having cut them in pieces lay them in salt and water till the seasoning is ready. Take two table-spoonfuls of powdered ginger, one table-spoonful of fresh turmeric, a tea-spoonful of ground black pepper; some mace, a few cloves, some cardamom seeds, and a little cayenne pepper with a small portion of salt. These last articles according to your taste. Put all into a mortar, and add to them eight large onions, chopped or cut small. Mix and beat all together, till the onions, spices, &c. form a paste.

Put the chickens into a pan with sufficient butter rolled in flour, and fry them till they are brown, but not till quite done. While this is proceeding, set over the fire a sauce-pan three parts full of water, or sufficient to cover the chickens when they are ready. As soon as the water boils, throw in the curry-paste. When the paste has all dissolved, and is thoroughly mixed with the water, put in the pieces of chicken to boil, or rather to simmer. When the chicken is quite done, put it into a large dish, and eat it with boiled rice. The rice may either be laid round on the same dish, or served up separately.

This is a genuine East India receipt for curry.

Lamb, veal, or rabbits may be curried in the same manner.

To boil Rice for the Curry.

PICK the rice carefully, to clear it from husks and motes. Then soak it in cold water for a quarter of an hour, or more. When you are ready to boil it, pour off the water in which it has soaked. Have ready a pot or sauce-pan of boiling water, into which you have put a little salt. Allow two quarts of water to a pound of rice. Sprinkle the rice gradually into the water. Boil it hard for twenty minutes, then take it off the fire, and pour off all the water that remains. Set the pot in the chimney corner with the lid off, while dinner is dishing, that it may have time to dry. You may toss it up lightly with two forks, to separate the grains while it is drying, but do not stir it with a spoon.

A PILAU.

TAKE a large fine fowl, and cover the breast with slices of fat bacon or ham, secured by skewers. Put it into a stewpan with two sliced onions. Season it to your taste with white pepper and mace. Have ready a pint of rice that has been well picked, washed, and soaked. Cover the fowl with it. Put in as much water as will well cover the whole. Stew it about half an hour, or till the fowl and rice are thoroughly done ; keeping the stew-pan closely covered. Dish it all together, either with the rice covering the fowl, or laid round it in little heaps.

You may make a pilau of beef or mutton with a larger quantity of rice ; which must not be put in at first, or it will be done too much, the meat requiring a longer time to stew.

CHICKEN SALAD.

THE fowls for this purpose should be young and fine. You may either boil or roast them. They must be quite cold. Having removed all the skin and fat, and disjointed the fowls cut the meat from the bones into very small pieces, not exceeding an inch. Wash and split two large fine heads of celery, and cut the white part into pieces also about an inch long; and having mixed the chicken and celery together, put them into a deep china dish, cover it and set it away.

It is best not to prepare the dressing till just before the salad is to be eaten, that it may be as fresh as possible. Have ready the yolks of eight hard-boiled eggs. Put them into a flat dish, and mash them to a paste with the back of a wooden spoon. Add to the egg a small tea-spoonful of fine salt, the same quantity of cayenne pepper, half a jill of made mustard, a jill or a wine-glass and a half of vinegar, and rather more than two wine-glasses of sweet oil. Mix all these ingredients thoroughly; stirring them a long time till they are quite smooth.

The dressing should not be put on till a few minutes before the salad is sent in; as by lying in it the chicken and celery will become tough and hard. After you pour it on, mix the the whole well together with a silver fork.

Chicken salad should be accompanied with plates of bread and butter, and a plate of biscuits. It is a supper dish, and is brought in with terrapin, oysters, &c.

Cold turkey is excellent prepared as above.

An inferior salad may be made with cold fillet of veal, instead of chickens.

Cold boiled lobster is very fine cut up and drest in this manner, only substituting for celery, lettuce cut up and mixed with the lobster.

TO ROAST A PAIR OF DUCKS.

AFTER the ducks are drawn, wipe out the inside with a clean cloth, and prepate your stuffing. Mince very fine some green sage leaves, and twice their quantity of onion, (which should first be parboiled,) and add a little butter, and a seasoning of pepper and salt. Mix the whole very well, and fill the crops and bodies of the ducks with it, leaving a little space for the stuffing to swell. Reserve the livers, gizzards, and hearts to put in the gravy. Tie the bodies of the ducks firmly round with strings, (which should be wetted or buttered to keep them from burning,) and put them on the spit before a clear brisk fire. Baste them first with a little salt and water, and then with their own gravy, dredging them lightly with flour at the last. They will be done in about an hour. After boiling the livers, gizzards and hearts, chop them, and put them into the gravy; having first skimmed it, and thickened it with a little browned flour.

Send to table with the ducks a small tureen of onion-sauce with chopped sage leaves in it. Accompany them also with stewed cranberries and green peas, if in season.

Canvas-back ducks are roasted in the same manner, omitting the stuffing. They will generally be done enough in three quarters of an hour. Send currant jelly to table with them, and have heaters to place under the plates. Add to the gravy a little cayenne, and a large wine-glass of claret or port.

Other wild ducks and teal may be roasted in about half an hour. Before roasting, parboil them with a large carrot inside their bodies. This will draw all the fishy or sedgy taste that may be about the ducks. Then throw away the carrot, and lay them in fresh water.

You may serve up with wild ducks, &c. orange-sauce, which is made by boiling in a little water two large sweet oranges cut into slices, having first removed the rind. When the pulp is all dissolved, strain and press it through a sieve and add to it the juice of two more oranges, and a little sugar. Send it to table either warm or cold.

STEWED DUCK.

HALF roast a large duck. Cut it up, and put it into a stew-pan with a pint of beef-gravy, or dripping of roast-beef. Have ready two boiled onions, half a handful of sage leaves, and two leaves of mint, all chopped very fine and seasoned with pepper and salt. Lay these ingredients over the duck. Stew it slowly for a quarter of an hour. Then put in a quart of young green peas. Cover it closely, and simmer it half an hour longer, till the peas are quite soft. Then add a piece of butter rolled in flour; quicken the fire, and give it one boil. Serve up all together.

A cold duck that has been under-done may be stewed in this manner.

TO HASH A DUCK.

CUT up the duck and season it with pepper and mixed spices. Have ready some thin slices of cold ham or bacon. Place a layer of them in a stew-pan; then put in the duck and cover it with ham. Add just water enough to moisten it, and pour over all a large glass of red wine. Cover the pan closely and let it stew for an hour.

Have ready a quart or more of green peas, boiled tender,

drained, and mixed with butter and pepper. Lay them round the hashed duck.

If you hash a cold duck in this manner, a quarter of an hour will be sufficient for stewing it; it having been cooked already.

TO ROAST A GOOSE.

HAVING drawn and singed the goose, wipe out the inside with a cloth, and sprinkle in some pepper and salt. Make a stuffing of four good sized onions minced fine, and half their quantity of green sage leaves minced also, a large tea-cupful of grated bread-crumbs, a piece of butter the size of a walnut, and the beaten yolks of two eggs, with a little pepper and salt. Mix the whole together, and incorporate them well. Put the stuffing into the goose, and press it in hard; but do not entirely fill up the cavity, as the mixture will swell in cooking. Tie the goose securely round with a greased or wetted string; and paper the breast to prevent it from scorching. Fasten the goose on the spit at both ends. The fire must be brisk and well kept up. It will require from two hours to two and a half to roast. Baste it at first with a little salt and water, and then with its own gravy. Take off the paper when the goose is about half done, and dredge it with a little flour towards the last. Having parboiled the liver and heart, chop them and put them into the gravy, which must be skimmed well and thickened with a little browned flour.

Send apple-sauce to table with the goose; also mashed potatoes.

A goose may be stuffed entirely with potatoes, boiled and mashed with milk, butter, pepper and salt.

You may make a gravy of the giblets, that is the neck,

pinions, liver, heart and gizzard, stewed in a little water, thickened with butter rolled in flour, and seasoned with pepper and salt. Add a glass of red wine. Before you send it to table, take out all but the liver and heart; mince them and leave them in the gravy. This gravy is by many preferred to that which comes from the goose in roasting. It is well to have both.

If a goose is old it is useless to cook it, as when hard and tough it cannot be eaten.

A GOOSE PIE.

Cut a fine large young goose into eight pieces, and season it with pepper. Reserve the giblets for gravy. Take a smoked tongue that has been all night in soak, parboil it, peel it, and cut it into thick slices, omitting the root, which you must divide into small pieces, and put into a sauce-pan with the giblets and sufficient water to stew them slowly.

Make a nice paste, allowing a pound and a half of butter to three pounds of flour. Roll it out thick, and line with it the bottom and sides of a deep dish. Fill it with the pieces of goose, and the slices of tongue. Skim the gravy you have drawn from the giblets, thicken it with a little browned flour, and pour it into the pie dish. Then put on the lid or upper crust. Notch and ornament it handsomely with leaves and flowers of paste. Bake the pie about three hours in a brisk oven.

In making a large goose pie you may add a fowl, or a pair of pigeons, or partridges,—all cut up.

A duck pie may be made in the same manner.

Small pies are sometimes made of goose giblets only.

A CHRISTMAS GOOSE PIE.

THESE pies are always made with a standing crust. Put
into a sauce-pan one pound of butter cut up, and a pint and a
half of water; stir it while it is melting, and let it come to a
boil. Then skim off whatever milk or impurity may rise to
the top. Have ready four pounds of flour sifted into a pan.
Make a hole in the middle of it, and pour in the melted
butter while hot. Mix it with a spoon to a stiff paste, (adding the beaten yolks of three or four eggs,) and then knead it
very well with your hands, on the pasteboard, keeping it
dredged with flour till it ceases to be sticky. Then set it
away to cool.

Split a large goose, and a fowl down the back, loosen the
flesh all over with a sharp knife, and take out all the bones.
Parboil a smoked tongue; peel it and cut off the root. Mix
together a powdered nutmeg, a quarter of an ounce of powdered mace, a tea-spoonful of pepper, and a tea-spoonful of
salt, and season with them the fowl and the goose.

Roll out the paste near an inch thick, and divide it into
three pieces. Cut out two of them of an oval form for the
top and bottom; and the other into a long straight piece for
the sides or walls of the pie. Brush the paste all over with
beaten white of egg, and set on the bottom the piece that is
to form the wall, pinching the edges together, and cementing
them with white of egg. The bottom piece must be large
enough to turn up a little round the lower edge of the wall
piece, to which it must be firmly joined all round. When you
have the crust properly fixed, so as to be baked standing alone
without a dish, put in first the goose, then the fowl, and then
the tongue. Fill up what space is left with pieces of the flesh
of pigeons, or of partridges, quails, or any game that is conve-

nient. There must be no bones in the pie. You may add also some bits of ham, or some force-meat balls. Lastly, cover the other ingredients with half a pound of butter, and put on the top crust, which, of course, must be also of an oval form to correspond with the bottom. The lid must be placed not quite on the top edge of the wall, but an inch and a half below it. Close it very well, and ornament the sides and top with festoons and leaves cut out of paste. Notch the edges handsomely, and put a paste flower in the centre. Glaze the whole with beaten yolk of egg, and bind the pie all round with a double fold of white paper. Set it in a regular oven, and bake it four hours.

This is one way of making the celebrated goose pies that it is customary in England to send as presents at Christmas. They are eaten at luncheon, and if the weather is cold, and they are kept carefully covered up from the air, they will be good for two or three weeks; the standing crust assisting to preserve them.

TO ROAST A TURKEY.

MAKE a force-meat of grated bread-crumbs, minced suet, sweet marjoram, grated lemon-peel, nutmeg, pepper, salt, and beaten yolk of egg. You may add some grated cold ham. Light some writing paper, and singe the hairs from the skin of the turkey. Reserve the neck, liver, and gizzard for the gravy. Stuff the craw of the turkey with the force-meat, of which there should be enough made to form into balls for frying, laying them round the turkey when it is dished. Dredge it with flour, and roast it before a clear brisk fire, basting it with cold lard. Towards the last, set the turkey nearer to the fire, dredge it again very lightly with flour, and baste it with butter. It will require, according to its size, from two to three hours roasting.

Make the gravy of the giblets cut in pieces, seasoned, and stewed for two hours in a very little water; thicken it with a spoonful of browned flour, and stir into it the gravy from the dripping-pan, having first skimmed off the fat.

A turkey should be accompanied by ham or tongue. Serve up with it mushroom-sauce. Have stewed cranberries on the table to eat with it. Do not help any one to the legs, or drum-sticks as they are called.

Turkeys are sometimes stuffed entirely with sausage-meat. Small cakes of this meat should then be fried, and laid round it.

To bone a turkey, you must begin with a very sharp knife at the top of the wings, and scrape the flesh loose from the bone without dividing or cutting it to pieces. It one carefully and dexterously, the whole mass of flesh may be separated from the bone, so that you can take hold of the head and draw out the entire skeleton at once. A large quantity of force-meat having been prepared, stuff it hard into the turkey, restoring it by doing so to its natural form, filling out the body, breast, wings and legs, so as to resemble their original shape when the bones were in. Roast or bake it; pouring a glass of port wine into the gravy. A boned turkey is frequently served up cold, covered with lumps of currant jelly; slices of which are laid round the dish.

Any sort of poultry or game may be boned and stuffed in the same manner.

A cold turkey that has not been boned is sometimes sent to table larded all over the breast with slips of fat bacon, drawn through the flesh with a larding needle, and arranged in regular form.

TO BOIL A TURKEY.

TAKE twenty-five large fine oysters, and chop them. Mix with them half a pint of grated bread-crumbs, a little sweet marjoram, a quarter of a pound of butter, two table-spoonfuls of cream or rich mllk, and the beaten yolks of three eggs. When it is thoroughly mixed, stuff the craw of the turkey with it, and sew up the skin. Then dredge it with flour, put it into a large pot or kettle, and cover it well with cold water. Place it over the fire, and let it boil slowly for half an hour, taking off the scum as it rises. Then remove the pot from over the fire, and set it on hot coals to stew slowly for two hours, or two hours and a half, according to its size. Just before you send it to table, place it again over the fire to get well heated. When you boil a turkey, skewer the liver and gizzard to the sides, under the wings.

Send it to table with oyster-sauce in a small tureen.

In making the stuffing, you may substitute for the grated bread, chestnuts boiled, peeled, and minced or mashed. Serve up chestnut-sauce, made by peeling some boiled chestnuts and putting them whole into melted butter.

Some persons, to make them white, boil their turkeys tied up in a large cloth sprinkled with flour.

With a turkey, there should be on the table a ham, or a smoked tongue.

TO ROAST PIGEONS.

DRAW and pick four pigeons immediately after they are killed, and let them be cooked soon, as they do not keep well. Wash the inside very clean, and wipe it dry. Stuff them with a mixture of parsley parboiled and chopped; grated bread-crumbs, and butter; seasoned with pepper, salt, and nutmeg. Dredge them with flour, and roast them before a good fire, basting them with butter. They will be done in about twenty-five or thirty minutes. Serve them up with parsley-sauce. Lay the pigeons on the dish in a row.

If asparagus is in season, it will be much better than parsley both for the stuffing and sauce. It must first be boiled. Chop the green heads for the stuffing, and cut them in two for the melted butter. Have cranberry-sauce on the table.

Pigeons may be split and broiled, like chickens; also stewed or fricasseed.

They are very good stewed with slices of cold ham and green peas, serving up all in the same dish.

PIGEON PIE.

TAKE four pigeons, and pick and clean them very nicely. Season them with pepper and salt, and put inside of every one a large piece of butter and the yolk of a hard-boiled egg. Have ready a good paste, allowing a pound of butter to two pounds of sifted flour. Roll it out rather thick, and line with it the bottom and sides of a large deep dish. Put in the pigeons, and lay on the top some bits of butter rolled in flour. Pour in nearly enough of water to fill the dish. Cover the pie with a lid of paste rolled out thick, and nicely notched, and ornamented with paste leaves and flowers.

You may make a similar pie of pheasants, partridges, or grouse.

In preparing pigeons, &c. for pies, loosen the joints with a knife, as in carving.

TO ROAST PHEASANTS, PARTRIDGES, QUAILS OR GROUSE.

PICK and draw the birds immediately after they are brought in. Before you roast them, fill the inside with pieces of a fine ripe orange, leaving out the rind and seeds. Or stuff them with grated cold ham, mixed with bread-crumbs, butter, and a little yolk of egg. Lard them with small slips of the fat of bacon drawn through the flesh with a larding needle. Roast them before a clear fire.

Make a fine rich gravy of the trimmings of meat or poultry, stewed in a little water, and thickened with a spoonful of browned flour. Strain it, and set it on the fire again, having added half a pint of claret, and the juice of two large oranges. Simmer it for a few minutes, pour some of it into the dish with the game, and serve the remainder in a boat.

If you stuff them with force-meat, you may, instead of larding, brush them all over with beaten yolk of egg, and then cover them with bread-crumbs grated finely and sifted.

ANOTHER WAY TO ROAST PHEASANTS, PARTRIDGES, &c.

CHOP some fine raw oysters, omitting the hard part; mix them with salt, and nutmeg, and add some beaten yolk of egg to bind the other ingredients. Cut some very thin slices of cold ham or bacon, and cover the birds with them; then wrap them closely .n sheets of white paper well buttered, put them on the spit, and roast them before a clear fire.

Send them to table with oyster-sauce in a boat.

Pies may be made of any of these birds in the same manner as a pigeon pie.

TO ROAST SNIPES, WOODCOCKS, OR PLOVERS.

PICK them immediately; wipe them, and season them slightly with pepper and salt. Cut as many slices of bread as you have birds. Toast them brown, butter them, and lay them in the dripping-pan. Dredge the birds with flour, and put them on a small spit before a clear brisk fire. Baste them with lard, or fresh butter. They will be done in twenty or thirty minutes. Serve them up laid on the toast, and garnished with sliced orange, or with orange jelly.

Have brown gravy in a boat.

TO ROAST REED-BIRDS, OR ORTOLANS.

PUT into every bird, an oyster, or a little butter mixed with some finely sifted bread-crumbs. Dredge them with flour. Run a small skewer through them, and tie them on the spit. Baste them with lard or with fresh butter. They will be done in about ten minutes.

A very nice way of cooking these birds is, (having greased them all over with lard or with fresh butter, and wrapped them in vine leaves secured closely with a string,) to lay them in a heated iron pan, and bury them in ashes hot enough to roast or bake them. Remove the vine leaves before you send the birds to table.

Reed birds are very fine made into little dumplings with a thin crust of flour and butter, and boiled about twenty minutes Each must be tied in a separate cloth. Or you may cook a dozen in one paste, like an apple pudding.

LARDING.

To lard meat or poultry is to introduce into the surface of the flesh, slips of the fat only of bacon, by means of a larding-pin or larding-needle, it being called by both names. It is a steel instrument about a foot long, sharp at one end, and cleft at the other into four divisions, which are near two inches in length, and resemble tweezers. It can be obtained at the hardware stores.

Cut the bacon into slips about two inches in length, half an inch in breadth, and half an inch in thickness. If intended for poultry, the slips of bacon should not be thicker than a straw. Put them, one at a time, into the cleft or split end of the larding-needle. Give each slip a slight twist, and press it down hard into the needle with your fingers. Then push the needle through the flesh, (avoiding the places where the bones are,) and when you draw it out it will have left behind it the slip of bacon sticking in the surface. Take care to have all the slips of the same size, and arranged in regular rows at equal distances. Every slip should stand up about an inch. If any are wrong, take them out and do them over again. To lard handsomely and neatly requires practice and dexterity.

Fowls and game are generally larded on the breast only. If cold, they can be done with the fat of cold boiled ham. Larding may be made to look very tastefully on any thing that is not to be cooked afterwards.

FORCE-MEAT BALLS.

To a pound of the lean of a leg of veal, allow a pound of beef suet. Mince them together very fine. Then season it to your taste with pepper, salt, mace, nutmeg, and chopped sage or sweet marjoram. Then chop a half-pint of oysters, and beat six eggs very well. Mix the whole together, and pound it to a paste in a marble mortar. If you do not want it immediately, put it away in a stone pot, strew a little flour on the top, and cover it closely.

When you wish to use the force-meat, divide into equal parts as much of it as you want; and having floured your hands, roll it into round balls, all of the same size. Either fry them in butter, or boil them.

This force-meat will be found a very good stuffing for meat or poultry.

FINE PARTRIDGE PIE.

HAVING trussed your partridges, loosen all the joints with a knife, but do not cut them apart. Scald, peel, and chop some fresh mushrooms, mix them with grated bread crumbs, moistened with cream and beaten yolk of egg, and with this stuff the partridges. Cover the sides and bottom of a deep dish with a rich paste, adding a layer of cold boiled ham sliced very thin. Add some whole button mushrooms, and some hard boiled yolks of eggs. Season with pepper only. Put in the partridges, laying on each a bit of butter rolled in flour. Cover the whole with a thick lid of paste handsomely notched, and ornamented with paste leaves.

Before you put on the cover, pour a little water into the pie

GRAVY AND SAUCES.

DRAWN OR MADE GRAVY.

For this purpose you may use coarse pieces of the lean of beef or veal, or the giblets and trimmings of poultry or game. If must be stewed for a long time, skimmed, strained, thickened, and flavoured with whatever condiments are supposed most suited to the dish it is to accompany.

In preparing meat to stew for gravy, beat it with a mallet or meat-beetle, score it, and cut it into small pieces; this makes it give out the juices. Season it with pepper and salt, and put it into a stew-pan with butter only. Heat it gradually, till it becomes brown. Shake the pan frequently, and see that it does not burn or stick to the bottom. It will generally be browned sufficiently in half an hour. Then put in some boiling water, allowing one pint to each pound of meat. Simmer it on coals by the side of the fire for near three hours, skimming it well, and keeping it closely covered. When done, remove it from the heat, let it stand awhile to settle, and then strain it.

If you wish to keep it two or three days, (which you may in winter,) put it into a stone vessel, cover it closely, and set it in a cool place.

Do not thicken this gravy till you go to use it.

Mutton is unfit for made gravy.

MELTED BUTTER,

SOMETIMES CALLED DRAWN BUTTER.

MELTED butter is the foundation of most of the common sauces. Have a covered sauce-pan for this purpose. One lined with porcelain will be best. Take a quarter of a pound of the best fresh butter, cut it up, and mix with it about two tea-spoonfuls of flour. When it is thoroughly mixed, put it into the sauce-pan, and add to it four table-spoonfuls of cold water. Cover the sauce-pan, and set it in a large tin pan of boiling water. Shake it round continually (always moving it the same way) till it is entirely melted and begins to simmer. Then let it rest till it boils up.

If you set it on hot coals, or over the fire, it will be oily.

If the butter and flour is not well mixed it will be lumpy.

If you put too much water, it will be thin and poor. All these defects are to be carefully avoided.

In melting butter for sweet or pudding sauce, you may use milk instead of water.

TO BROWN FLOUR.—Spread some fine flour on a plate, and set it in the oven, turning it up and stirring it frequently that it may brown equally all through.

Put it into a jar, cover it well, and keep it to stir into gravies to thicken and colour them.

TO BROWN BUTTER.—Put a lump of butter into a frying-pan, and toss it round over the fire till it becomes brown. Then dredge some browned flour over it, and stir it round with a spoon till it boils. It must be made quite smooth.

You may make this into a plain sauce for fish by adding cayenne and some flavoured vinegar.

PLAIN SAUCES.

~~~~~~~~

LOBSTER SAUCE.—Boil a dozen blades of mace and half a dozen pepper-corns in about a jill and a half (or three wine-glasses) of water, till all the strength of the spice is extracted. Then strain it, and having cut three quarters of a pound of butter into little bits, melt it in this water, dredging in a little flour as you hold it over the fire to boil. Toss it round, and let it just boil up and no more.

Take a cold boiled lobster,—pound the coral in a mortar, adding a little sweet oil. Then stir it into the melted butter.

Chop the meat of the body into very small pieces, and rub it through a cullender into the butter. Cut up the flesh of the claws and tail into dice, and stir it in. Give it another boil up, and it will be ready for table.

Serve it up with fresh salmon, or any boiled fish of the best kind.

Crab sauce is made in a similar manner; also prawn and shrimp sauce.

———

ANCHOVY SAUCE.—Soak eight anchovies for three or four hours, changing the water every hour. Then put them into a sauce-pan with a quart of cold water. Set them on hot coals and simmer them till they are entirely dissolved, and till the liquid is diminished two-thirds. Then strain it, stir two glasses of red wine, and add to it about half a pint of melted butter.

Heat it over again, and send it to table with salmon or fresh cod.

CELERY SAUCE.—Take a large bunch of young celery. Wash and pare it very clean. Cut it into pieces, and boil it gently in a small quantity of water, till it is quite tender. Then add a little powdered mace and nutmeg, and a very little pepper and salt. Take a tolerably large piece of butter, roll it well in flour, and stir it into the sauce. Boil it up again, and it is ready to send to table.

You may make it with cream, thus :—Prepare and boil your celery as above, adding some mace, nutmeg, a piece of butter the size of a walnut, rolled in flour; and half a pint of cream. Boil all together.

Celery sauce is eaten with boiled poultry.

When celery is out of season, you may use celery seed, boiled in the water which you afterwards use for the melted butter, but strained out after boiling.

———

NASTURTIAN SAUCE.—This is by many considered superior to caper sauce and is eaten with boiled mutton. It is made with the green seeds of nasturtians, pickled simply in cold vinegar.

Cut about six ounces of butter into small bits, and put them into a small sauce-pan. Mix with a wine-glass of water sufficient flour to make a thick batter, pour it on the butter, and hold the sauce-pan over hot coals, shaking it quickly round, till the butter is melted. Let it just boil up, and then take it from the fire. Thicken it with the pickled nasturtians and send it to table in a boat.

Never pour melted butter over any thing, but always send it to table in a sauce-tureen or boat.

WHITE ONION SAUCE.—Peel a dozen onions, and throw them into salt and water to keep them white. Then boil them tender. When done, squeeze the water from them, and chop them. Have ready some butter that has been melted rich and smooth with milk or cream instead of water. Put the onions into the melted butter, and boil them up at once If you wish to have them very mild, put in a turnip with them at the first boiling.

Young white onions, if very small, need not be chopped, but may be put whole into the butter.

Use this sauce for rabbits, tripe, boiled poultry, or any boiled fresh meat.

———

BROWN ONION SAUCE.—Slice some large mild Spanish onions. Cover them with butter, and set them over a slow fire to brown. Then add salt and cayenne pepper to your taste, and some good brown gravy of roast meat, poultry or game, thickened with a bit of butter rolled in flour that has first been browned by holding it in a hot pan or shovel over the fire. Give it a boil, skim it well, and just before you take it off, stir in a half glass of port or claret, and the same quantity of mushroom catchup.

Use this sauce for roasted poultry, game, or meat.

———

MUSHROOM SAUCE.—Wash a pint of small button mushrooms,—remove the stems and the outside skin. Stew them slowly in veal gravy or in milk or cream, seasoning them with pepper and salt, and adding a piece of butter rolled in a large proportion of flour. Stew them till quite tender, now and then shaking the pan round.

The flavour will be heightened by having salted a few the

night before in a covered dish, to extract the juice, and then stirring it into the sauce while stewing.

This sauce may be served up with poultry, game, or beef-steaks.

In gathering mushrooms take only those that are of a dull pearl colour on the outside, and that have the under part tinged with pale pink.

Boil an onion with them. If there is a poisonous one among them the onion will turn black. Then throw away the whole.

EGG SAUCE.—Boil four eggs ten minutes. Dip them into cold water to prevent their looking blue. Peel off the shell. Chop the yolks of all, and the whites of two, and stir them into melted butter. Serve this sauce with boiled poultry or fish.

BREAD SAUCE.—Put some grated crumbs of stale bread into a sauce-pan, and pour over them some of the liquor in which poultry or fresh meat has been boiled. Add some plums or dried currants that have been picked and washed. Having simmered them till the bread is quite soft, and the currants well plumped, add melted butter or cream.

This sauce is for a roast pig.

MINT SAUCE.—Take a large bunch of young green mint; if old the taste will be unpleasant. Wash it very clean. Pick all the leaves from the stalks. Chop the leaves very fine, and mix them with cold vinegar, and a large proportion of powdered sugar. There must be merely sufficient vinegar to moisten the mint well, but by no means enough to make the sauce liquid. It should be very sweet.

It is only eaten in the spring with roast lamb. Send it to table in a sauce-tureen.

CAPER SAUCE.—Take two large table-spoonfuls of capers and a little vinegar. Stir them for some time into half a pint of thick melted butter.

This sauce is for boiled mutton.

If you happen to have no capers, pickled cucumber chopped fine, or the pickled pods of radish seeds, may be stirred into the butter as a tolerable substitute, or nasturtians.

PARSLEY SAUCE.—Wash a bunch of parsley in cold water. Then boil it about six or seven minutes in salt and water. Drain it, cut the leaves from the stalks, and chop them fine. Have ready some melted butter, and stir in the parsley. Allow two small table-spoonfuls of leaves to half a pint of butter.

Serve it up with boiled fowls, rock-fish, sea-bass, and other boiled fresh fish. Also with knuckle of veal, and with calf's head boiled plain.

APPLE SAUCE.—Pare, core, and slice some fine apples. Put them into a sauce-pan with just sufficient water to keep them from burning, and some grated lemon-peel. Stew them till quite soft and tender. Then mash them to a paste, and make them very sweet with brown sugar, adding a small piece of butter and some nutmeg.

Apple sauce is eaten with roast pork, roast goose and roast ducks.

Be careful not to have it thin and watery.

CRANBERRY SAUCE.—Wash a quart of ripe cranberries, and put them into a pan with about a wine-glass of water. Stew them slowly, and stir them frequently, particularly after they begin to burst. They require a great deal of stewing, and should be like a marmalade when done.

After you take them from the fire, stir in a pound of brown sugar.

When they are thoroughly done, put them into a deep dish, and set them away to get cold.

You may strain the pulp through a cullender or sieve into a mould, and when it is in a firm shape send it to table on a glass dish. Taste it when it is cold, and if not sweet enough, add more sugar. Cranberries require more sugar than any other fruit, except plums.

Cranberry sauce is eaten with roast turkey, roast fowls, and roast ducks.

———

PEACH SAUCE.—Take a quart of dried peaches, (those are richest and best that are dried with the skins on,) and soak them in cold water till they are tender. Then drain them, and put them into a covered pan with a very little water. Set them on coals, and simmer them till they are entirely dissolved. Then mash them with brown sugar, and send them to table cold to eat with roast meat, game or poultry.

———

WINE SAUCE.—Have ready some rich thick melted or drawn butter, and the moment you take it from the fire, stir in two large glasses of white wine, two table-spoonfuls of powdered white sugar, and a powdered nutmeg. Serve it up with plum pudding, or any sort of boiled pudding that is made of a batter.

COLD SWEET SAUCE.—Stir together, as for a pound-cake, equal quantities of fresh butter and powdered white sugar. When quite light and creamy, add some powdered cinnamon or nutmeg, and the juice of a lemon. Send it to table in a small deep plate with a tea-spoon in it.

Eat it with batter pudding, bread pudding, Indian pudding, &c. whether baked or boiled. Also with boiled apple pudding or dumplings, and with fritters and pancakes.

———

CREAM SAUCE.—Boil a pint and a half of rich cream with four table-spoonfuls of powdered sugar, some powdered nutmeg, and a dozen bitter almonds or peach kernels slightly broken up, or a dozen fresh peach leaves. As soon as it has boiled up, take it off the fire and strain it. If it is to be eaten with boiled pudding or with dumplings send it to table hot, but let it get quite cold if you intend it as an accompaniment to fruit pies or tarts.

———

OYSTER SAUCE.—Take a pint of oysters, and save out a little of their liquor. Put them with their remaining liquor, and some mace and nutmeg, into a covered saucepan, and simmer them on hot coals about ten minutes. Then drain them. Oysters for sauce should be large.

Having prepared in another saucepan some drawn or melted butter, (mixed with oyster liquor instead of water,) pour it into a sauce-boat, add the oysters to it, and serve it up with boiled poultry, or with boiled fresh fish.

Celery, first boiled and then chopped, is an improvement to oyster sauce.

STORE FISH SAUCES.

GENERAL REMARKS.

STORE fish sauces if properly made will keep for many months. They may be brought to table in fish castors, but a customary mode is to send them round in the small black bottles in which they have been originally deposited. They are in great variety, and may be purchased of the grocers that sell oil, pickles, anchovies, &c. In making them at home, the few following receipts may be found useful.

The usual way of eating these sauces is to pour a little on your plate, and mix it with the melted butter. They give flavour to fish that would otherwise be insipid, and are in general use at genteel tables.

Two table-spoonfuls of any of these sauces may be added to the melted butter a minute before you take it from the fire. But if brought to table in bottles, the company can use it or omit it as they please.

SCOTCH SAUCE.—Take fifteen anchovies, chop them fine, and steep them in vinegar for a week, keeping the vessel closely covered. Then put them into a pint of claret or port wine. Scrape fine a large stick of horseradish, and chop two onions, a handful of parsley, a tea-spoonful of the leaves of lemon-thyme, and two large peach leaves. Add a nutmeg, six or eight blades of mace, nine cloves, and a tea-spoonful of black pepper, all slightly pounded in a mortar. Put all these ingredients into a silver or block tin sauce-pan, or into an earthen pipkin, and add a few grains of cochineal to colour it. Pour in a large half pint of the best vinegar, and simmer it slowly till the bones of the anchovies are entirely dissolved.

Strain the liquor through a sieve, and when quite cold put t away for use in small bottles ; the corks dipped in melted rosin, and well secured by pieces of leather tied closely over them. Fill each bottle quite full, as it will keep the better tor leaving no vacancy.

This sauce will give a fine flavour to melted butter.

QUIN'S SAUCE.—Pound in a mortar six large anchovies, moistening them with their own pickle. Then chop and pound six small onions. Mix them with a little black pepper and a little cayenne, half a glass of soy, four glasses of mushroom catchup, two glasses of claret, and two of black walnut pickle. Put the mixture into a small sauce-pan or earthen pipkin, and let it simmer slowly till all the bones of the anchovies are dissolved. Strain it, and when cold, bottle it for use ; dipping the cork in melted rosin, and tying leather over it. Fill the bottles quite full.

KITCHINER'S FISH SAUCE.—Mix together a pint of claret, a pint of mushroom catchup, and half a pint of walnut pickle, four ounces of pounded anchovy, an ounce of fresh lemon-peel pared thin, and the same quantity of shalot or small onion. Also an ounce of scraped horseradish, half an ounce of black pepper, and half an ounce of allspice mixed, and the same quantity of cayenne and celery-seed. Infuse these ingredients in a wide-mouthed bottle (closely stopped) for a fortnight, shaking the mixture every day. Then strain and bottle it tor use. Put it up in small bottles, filling them quite full.

HARVEY'S SAUCE.—Dissolve six anchovies in a pint of strong vinegar and| then add to them three table-spoonfuls of India soy, and three table-spoonfuls of mushroom catchup, two heads of garlic bruised small, and a quarter of an ounce of cayenne. Add sufficient cochineal powder to colour the mixture red. Let all these ingredients infuse in the vinegar for a fortnight, shaking it every day, and then strain and bottle it for use. Let the bottles be small, and cover the corks with leather.

GENERAL SAUCE.—Chop six shalots or small onions, a clove of garlic, two peach leaves, a few sprigs of lemon-thyme and of sweet basil, and a few bits of fresh orange-peel. Bruise in a mortar a quarter of an ounce of cloves, a quarter of an ounce of mace, and half an ounce of long pepper. Mix two ounces of salt, a jill of claret, the juice of two lemons, and a pint of Madeira. Put the whole of these ingredients together in a stone jar, very closely covered. Let it stand all night over embers by the side of the fire. In the morning pour off the liquid quickly and carefully from the lees or settlings, strain it and put it into small bottles, dipping the corks in melted rosin.

This sauce is intended to flavour melted butter or gravy, for every sort of fish and meat.

PINK SAUCE.—Mix together half a pint of port wine, half a pint of strong vinegar, the juice and grated peel of two large lemons, a quarter of an ounce of cayenne, a dozen blades of mace, and a quarter of an ounce of powdered cochineal. Let it infuse a fortnight, stirring it several times a day. Then boil it ten minutes, strain it, and bottle it for use.

Eat it with any sort of fish or game. It will give a fine pink tinge to melted butter.

CATCHUPS.

LOBSTER CATCHUP.—This catchup, warmed in melted butter, is an excellent substitute for fresh lobster sauce at seasons when the fish cannot be procured, as, if properly made, it will keep a year.

Take a fine lobster that weighs about three pounds. Put it into boiling water, and cook it thoroughly. When it is cold break it up, and extract all the flesh from the shell. Pound the red part or coral in a marble mortar, and when it is well bruised, add the white meat by degrees, and pound that also; seasoning it with a tea-spoonful of cayenne, and moistening it gradually with sherry wine. When it is beaten to a smooth paste, mix it well with the remainder of the bottle of sherry. Put it into wide-mouthed bottles, and on the top of each put a table-spoonful of sweet oil. Dip the corks in melted rosin, and secure them well by tying leather over them.

In using this catchup, allow four table-spoonfuls to a common-seized sauce-boat of melted butter. Put in the catchup at the last, and hold it over the fire just long enough to be thoroughly heated.

ANCHOVY CATCHUP.—Bone two dozen anchovies, and then chop them. Put to them ten shalots, or very small onions, cut fine, and a handful of scraped horseradish, with a quarter of an ounce of mace. Add a lemon, cut into slices, twelve cloves, and twelve pepper-corns. Then mix together a pint of port, a pint of madeira, and a pint of anchovy liquor. Put the other ingredients into the liquid, and boil it slowly till reduced one-half. Then strain it, and when cold put it into small bottles, securing the corks with leather.

OYSTER CATCHUP.—Take large salt oysters that have just been opened. Wash them in their own liquor, and pound them in a mortar, omitting the hard parts. To every pint of the pounded oysters, add a half pint of white wine or vinegar, in which you must give them a boil up, removing the scum as it rises. Then to each quart of the boiled oysters allow a tea-spoonful of beaten white pepper, a tea-spoonful of pounded mace, and cayenne pepper to your taste. Let it boil up for a few minutes, and then pass it through a sieve into an earthen pan. When cold, put it into small bottles, filling them quite full, as it will not keep so well if there is a vacancy at the top. Dip the corks in melted rosin, and tie leather over each.

WALNUT CATCHUP.—Take green walnuts that are young enough to be easily pierced through with a large needle. Having pricked them all in several places, throw them into an earthen pan with a large handful of salt, and barely sufficient water to cover them. Break up and mash them with a potato-beetle, or a rolling-pin. Keep them four days in the salt and water, stirring and mashing them every day. The rinds will now be quite soft. Then scald them with boiling-hot salt and water, and raising the pan on the edge, let the walnut liquor flow away from the shells into another pan. Put the shells into a mortar, and pound them with vinegar, which will extract from them all the remaining juice.

Put all the walnut liquor together, and boil and skim it

then to every quart allow an ounce of bruised ginger, an ounce of black pepper, half an ounce of cloves, and half an ounce of nutmeg, all slightly beaten. Boil the spice and walnut liquor in a closely covered vessel for three quarters of an hour. When cold, bottle it for use, putting equal proportions of the spice into each bottle. Secure the corks with leather.

MUSHROOM CATCHUP.—Take mushrooms that have been freshly gathered, and examine them carefully to ascertain that they are of the right sort. Pick them nicely, and wipe them clean, but do not wash them. Spread a layer of them at the bottom of a deep earthen pan, and then sprinkle them well with salt; then another layer of mushrooms, and another layer of salt, and so on alternately. Throw a folded cloth over the jar, and set it by the fire or in a very cool oven. Let it remain thus for twenty-four hours, and then mash them well with your hands. Next squeeze and strain them through a bag.

To every quart of strained liquor add an ounce and a half of whole black pepper, and boil it slowly in a covered vessel for half an hour. Then add a quarter of an ounce of allspice, half an ounce of sliced ginger, a few cloves, and three or four blades of mace. Boil it with the spice fifteen minutes longer. When it is done, take it off, and let it stand awhile to settle. Pour it carefully off from the sediment, and put it into small bottles, filling them to the top. Secure them well with corks dipped in melted rosin, and leather caps tied over them.

The longer catchup is boiled, the better it will keep.

You may add cayenne and nutmeg to the spices.

The bottles should be quite small, as it soon spoils after being opened.

TOMATA CATCHUP.—Take a peck of large ripe tomatas. Having cut a slit in each, put them into a large preserving-kettle, and boil them half an hour. Then take them
out, and press and strain the pulp through a hair sieve. Put
it back into the kettle, and add an ounce of salt, an ounce of
powdered mace, half an ounce of powdered cloves, a small tea-
spoonful of ground black pepper, the same of cayenne pepper,
and eight table-spoonfuls of ground mustard. Mix the season
ing with the tomata pulp; let it boil slowly during four hours.
Then take it out of the kettle, and let it stand till next day,
in an uncovered tureen. When cold, stir into it one pint of
the best cider vinegar. Put it into clean bottles, and seal the
corks. It will be found excellent for flavouring stews, hashes,
fish-sauce, &c.

LEMON CATCHUP.—Grate the peel of a dozen large
fresh lemons. Prepare, by pounding them in a mortar,
two ounces of mustard seed, half an ounce of black pepper,
half an ounce of nutmeg, a quarter of an ounce of mace,
and a quarter of an ounce of cloves. Slice thin two ounces
of horseradish. Put all these ingredients together. Strew
over them one ounce of fine salt. Add the juice of the lemons.

Boil the whole twenty minutes. Then put it warm into a
jar, and let it stand three weeks closely covered. Stir it up
daily.

Then strain it through a sieve, and put it up in small bottles
to flavour fish and other sauces.

This is sometimes called lemon pickle.

SEA CATCHUP.—Take a gallon of stale strong beer, a pound of anchovies washed from the pickle, a pound of peeled shalots or small onions, half an ounce of mace, half an ounce of cloves, a quarter of an ounce of whole pepper, three or four large pieces of ginger, and two quarts of large mushroom-flaps rubbed to pieces. Put the whole into a kettle closely covered, and let it simmer slowly till reduced to one half. Then strain it through a flannel bag, and let it stand till quite cold before you bottle it. Have small bottles and fill them quite full of the catchup. Dip the corks in melted rosin.

This catchup keeps well at sea, and may be carried into any part of the world. A spoonful of it mixed in melted butter will make a fine fish sauce. It may also be used to flavour gravy.

FLAVOURED VINEGARS.

THESE vinegars will be found very useful, at times when the articles with which they are flavoured cannot be conveniently procured. Care should be taken to have the bottles that contain them accurately labelled, very tightly corked, and kept in a dry place. The vinegar used for these purposes should be of the very best sort.

TARRAGON VINEGAR.—Tarragon should be gathered on a dry day, just before the plant flowers Pick the green leaves from the stalks, and dry them a little before the fire. Then put them into a wide-mouthed stone jar, and cover them with the best vinegar, filling up the jar. Let it steep fourteen days, and then strain it into wide-mouthed bottles, in each of which put a large quantity of fresh tarragon leaves, and let them remain in the vinegar.

SWEET BASIL VINEGAR—Is made precisely in the same manner; also those of green mint, and sweet marjoram.

CELERY VINEGAR.—Pound two ounces of celery seed in a mortar, and steep it for a fortnight in a quart of vinegar. Then strain and bottle it.

BURNET VINEGAR.—Nearly fill a wide-mouthed bottle with the fresh green leaves of burnet, cover them with vinegar, and let them steep two weeks. Then strain off the vinegar, wash the bottle, put in a fresh supply of burnet leaves, pour the same vinegar over them, and let it infuse a fortnight longer. Then strain it again and it will be fit for use. The flavour will exactly resemble that of cucumbers.

HORSERADISH VINEGAR.—Make a quart of the best vinegar boiling hot, and pour it on four ounces of scraped horseradish. Let it stand a week, then strain it off, renew the horseradish, adding the same vinegar cold, and let it infuse a week longer, straining it again at the last.

SHALOT VINEGAR.—Peel and chop fine four ounces of shalots, or small button onions. Pour on them a quart of the best vinegar, and let them steep a fortnight; then strain and bottle it.

Make garlic vinegar in the same manner; using but one ounce of garlic to a quart of vinegar. Two or three drops will be sufficient to impart a garlic taste to a pint of gravy or sauce. More will be offensive. The cook should be cautioned to use it very sparingly, as to many persons it is extremely disagreeable.

CHILLI VINEGAR.—Take a hundred red chillies or capsicums, fresh gathered; cut them into small pieces and infuse them for a fortnight in a quart of the best vinegar shaking the bottle every day. Then strain it.

RASPBERRY VINEGAR.—Put two quarts of ripe fresh-gathered raspberries into a stone or china vessel, and pour on them a quart of vinegar. Let it stand twenty-four hours, and then strain it through a sieve. Pour the liquid over two quarts of fresh raspberries, and let it again infuse for a day and a night. Then strain it a second time. Allow a pound of loaf sugar to every pint of juice. Break up the sugar, and let it melt in the liquor.   Then put the whole into a stone jar, cover it closely, and set it in a kettle of boiling water, which must be kept on a quick boil for an hour.   Take off all the scum, and when cold, bottle the vinegar for use.

Raspberry vinegar mixed with water is a pleasant and cooling beverage in warm weather; also in fevers.

MUSTARD AND PEPPER.

COMMON MUSTARD—Is best when fresh made.   Take good flour of mustard; put it in a plate, add to it a little salt, and mix it by degrees with boiling water to the usual consistence, rubbing it for a long time with a broad-bladed knife or a wooden spoon.   It should be perfectly smooth.   The less that is made at a time the better it will be.   If you wish it very mild, use sugar instead of salt, and boiling milk instead of water.

KEEPING MUSTARD.—Dissolve three ounces of salt in a quart of boiling vinegar, and pour it hot upon two ounces of scraped horseradish.   Cover the jar closely and let it stand twenty-four hours.   Strain it and then mix it by degrees with the best flour of mustard.   Make it of the usual thickness, and beat it till quite smooth.   Then put it into wide-mouthed bottles and stop it closely.

FRENCH MUSTARD.—Mix together four ounces of the very best mustard powder, four salt-spoons of salt, a large table-spoonful of minced tarragon leaves, and two cloves of garlic chopped fine. Dilute it to the proper consistence by adding alternately equal portions of vinegar and salad oil. It will probably require about four wine-glassfuls or half a pint. Mix it well, using for the purpose a wooden spoon. When done, put it into a wide-mouthed bottle or into little white jars. Cork it very closely, and keep it in a dry place. It will not be fit for use in less than two days.

This (used as the common mustard) is a very agreeable condiment for beef or mutton.

If you cannot procure tarragon leaves, buy at a grocer's a bottle of tarragon vinegar. Mix it with an equal portion of sweet oil, adding a few drops of garlic vinegar. Then stir in mustard powder till sufficiently thick.

TO MAKE CAYENNE PEPPER.—Take ripe chillies and dry them a whole day before the fire, turning them frequently. When quite dry, trim off the stalks and pound the pods in a mortar till they become a fine powder, mixing in about one sixth of their weight in salt. Or you may grind them in a very fine mill. While pounding the chillies, wear glasses to save your eyes from being incommoded by them. Put the powder into small bottles, and secure the corks closely.

KITCHEN PEPPER.—Mix together two ounces of the best white ginger, an ounce of black pepper, an ounce of white pepper, an ounce of cinnamon, an ounce of nutmeg, and two dozen cloves. They must all be ground or pounded to a fine powder, and thoroughly mixed. Keep the mixture in a bottle, labelled and well corked. It will be found useful in seasoning many dishes; and being ready prepared will save much trouble.

VEGETABLES.

GENERAL REMARKS.

ALL vegetables should be well picked and washed. A very little salt should always be thrown into the water in which they are boiled. A steady regular fire should be kept up, and they should never for a moment be allowed to stop boiling or simmering till they are thoroughly done. Every sort of vegetable should be cooked till tender, as if the least hard or under-done they are both unpalatable and unwholesome. The practice of putting pearl-ash in the pot to improve the colour of green vegetables should be strictly forbidden, as it destroys the flavour, and either renders them flat and insipid, or communicates a very disagreeable taste of its own.

Every sort of culinary vegetable is infinitely best when fresh from the garden, and gathered as short a time as possible before it is cooked. They should all be laid in a pan of cold water for a while previous to boiling.

When done, they should be carefully drained before they go to table, or they will be washy all through, and leave puddles of discoloured water in the bottoms of the dishes, to the disgust of the company and the discredit of the cook.

TO BOIL POTATOES.

POTATOES that are boiled together, should be as nearly as possible of the same size. Wash, but do not pare them. Put them into a pot with water enough to cover them about an inch, and do not put on the pot-lid. When the water is very near boiling, pour it off, and replace it with the same quantity of cold water, into which throw a good portion of salt. The cold water sends the heat from the surface to the heart, and makes the potatoes mealy. Potatoes of a moderate size will require about half an hour boiling; large ones an hour. Try them with a fork. When done, pour off the water, cover the pot with a folded napkin, or flannel, and let them stand by the fire about a quarter of an hour to dry.

Peel them and send them to table.

Potatoes are often served up with the skins on. It has a coarse, slovenly look, and disfigures the appearance of the dinner; besides the trouble and inconvenience of peeling them at table. But many prefer them thus.

When the skins crack in boiling, it is no proof that they are done, as too much fire under the pot will cause the skins of some potatoes to break while the inside is hard.

After March, when potatoes are old, it is best to pare them before boiling and to cut out all the blemishes. It is then better to mash them always before they are sent to table. Mash them when quite hot, using a potato-beetle for the purpose; add to them a piece of fresh butter, and a little salt, and, if convenient, some milk, which will greatly improve them. You may score and brown them on the top.

A very nice way of serving up potatoes is, after they are peeled, to pour over them some hot cream in which a very little butter has been melted, and sprinkle them with pepper. This is frequently done in country houses where cream is plenty. New potatoes (as they are called when quite young) require no peeling, but should be well washed and brushed before they are boiled.

FRIED POTATOES.—Take cold potatoes that have been boiled, grate them, make them into flat cakes, and fry them in butter. They are nice at breakfast. You may mix some beaten yolk of egg with them.

Cold potatoes may be fried in slices or quarters, or broiled on a gridiron.

Raw potatoes, when fried, are generally hard, tough, and strong.

———

POTATO SNOW.—For this purpose use potatoes that are very white, mealy, and smooth. Boil them very carefully, and when they are done, peel them, pour off the water, and set them on a trivet before the fire till they are quite dry and powdery. Then rub them through a coarse wire sieve into the dish on which they are to go to table. Do not disturb the heap of potatoes before it is served up, or the flakes will fall and it will flatten. This preparation looks well; but many think that it renders the potato insipid.

———

ROASTED POTATOES.—Take large fine potatoes, wash and dry them, and either lay them on the hearth and keep them buried in hot wood ashes, or bake them slowly in a Dutch oven. They will not be done in less than two hours. It will save time to half-boil them before they are roasted. Send them to table with the skins on, and eat them with cold butter and salt. They are introduced with cold meat at supper.

Potatoes keep best buried in sand or earth. They should never be wetted till they are washed for cooking. If you have them in the cellar, see that they are well covered with matting or old carpet, as the frost injures them greatly.

SWEET POTATOES BOILED.

If among your sweet potatoes there should be any that are very large and thick, split them, and cut them in four, that they may not require longer time to cook than the others. Boil them with the skins on in plenty of water, but without any salt. You may set the pot on coals in the corner. Try them with a fork, and see that they are done all through ; they will take at least an hour. Then drain off the water, and set them for a few minutes in a tin pan before the fire, or in the stove, that they may be well dried. Peel them before they are sent to table. When very large, and all of a size, you may roast them.

FRIED SWEET POTATOES.—Choose them of the largest size. Half boil them, and then having taken off the skins, cut the potatoes in slices, and fry them in butter, or in nice dripping.

Sweet potatoes are very good stewed with fresh pork, veal, or beef.

The best way to keep them through the cold weather, is to bury them in earth or sand ; otherwise they will be scarcely eatable after October.

CABBAGE.

All vegetables of the cabbage kind should be carefully washed, and examined in case of insects lurking among the leaves. To prepare a cabbage for boiling, remove the outer leaves, and pare and trim the stalk, cutting it close and short. If the cabbage is large, quarter it; if small, cut it in half; and let it stand for a while in a deep pan of cold water with the large end downwards. Put it into a pot with plenty of water, (having first tied it together to keep it whole while boiling,) and, taking off the scum, boil it two hours, or till the stalk is quite tender. When done, drain and squeeze it well. Before you send it to table introduce a little fresh butter between the leaves; or have melted butter in a boat. If it has been boiled with meat add no butter to it.

A young cabbage will boil in an hour or an hour and a half.

CALE-CANNON.—Boil separately some potatoes and cabbage. When done, drain and squeeze the cabbage, and chop or mince it very small. Mash the potatoes, and mix them gradually but thoroughly with the chopped cabbage, adding butter, pepper and salt. There should be twice as much potato as cabbage.

Cale-cannon is eaten with corned beef, boiled pork, or bacon.

Cabbages may be kept good all winter by burying them in a hole dug in the ground.

CAULIFLOWER.

REMOVE the green leaves that surround the head or white part, and peel off the outside skin of the small piece of stalk that is left on. Cut the cauliflower in four, and lay it for an hour in a pan of cold water. Then tie it together before it goes into the pot. Put it into boiling water and simmer i till the stalk is thoroughly tender, keeping it well covered with water, and carefully removing the scum. It will take about two hours.

Take it up as soon as it is done; remaining in the water

will discolour it. Drain it well, and send it to table with melted butter.

It will be much whiter if put on in boiling milk and water.

BROCOLI.—Prepare brocoli for boiling in the same manner as cauliflower, leaving the stalks rather longer, and splitting the head in half only. Tie it together again, before it goes into the pot. Put it on in hot water, and let it simmer till the stalk is perfectly tender.

As soon as it is done take it out of the water and drain it. Send melted butter to table with it.

SPINACH.

SPINACH requires close examination and picking, as insects are frequently found among it, and it is often gritty. Wash it through three or four waters. Then drain it, and put it on in boiling water. Ten minutes is generally sufficient time to boil spinach. Be careful to remove the scum. When it is quite tender, take it up, and drain and squeeze it well. Chop it fine, and put it into a sauce-pan with a piece of butter and a little pepper and salt. Set it on hot coals, and let it stew five minutes, stirring it all the time.

SPINACH AND EGGS.—Boil the spinach as above, and drain and press it, but do not chop it. Have ready some eggs poached as follows. Boil in a sauce-pan, and skim some clear spring water, adding to it a table-spoonful of vinegar. Break the eggs separately, and having taken the sauce-pan off the fire, slip the eggs one at a time into it with as much dexterity as you can. Let the sauce-pan stand by the side of the fire till the white is set, and then put it over the fire for two minutes. The yolk should be thinly covered by the white. Take them up with an egg slice, and having trimmed the edges of the whites, lay the eggs on the top of the spinach, which should first be seasoned with pepper and salt and a little butter, and must be sent to table hot.

TURNIPS.

TAKE off a thick paring from the outside, and boil the turnips gently for an hour and a half. Try them with a fork, and when quite tender, take them up, drain them on a sieve, and either send them to table whole with melted butter, or mash them in a cullender, (pressing and squeezing them well;) season with a little pepper and salt, and mix with them a very small quantity of butter. Setting in the sun after they are cooked, or on a part of the table upon which the sun may happen to shine, will give to turnips a singularly unpleasant taste, and should therefore be avoided.

When turnips are very young, it is customary to serve them up with about two inches of the green top left on them.

If stewed with meat, they should be sliced or quartered.

Mutton, either boiled or roasted, should always be accompanied by turnips.

CARROTS.

WASH and scrape them well. If large cut them into two, three, o four pieces. Put them into boiling water with a little salt in it. Full grown carrots will require three hours' boiling; smaller ones two hours, and young ones an hour. Try them with a fork, and when they are tender throughout, take them up and dry them in a cloth. Divide them in pieces and split them, or cut them into slices.

Eat them with melted butter. They should accompany boiled beef or mutton.

PARSNIPS.

Wash, scrape and split them. Put them into a pot of boiling water; add a little salt, and boil them till quite tender, which will be in from two to three hours, according to their size. Dry them in a cloth when done, and pour melted butter over them in the dish. Serve them up with any sort of boiled meat, or with salt cod.

Parsnips are very good baked or stewed with meat.

RUSSIAN OR SWEDISH TURNIPS.

This turnip (the Ruta Baga) is very large and of a reddish yellow colour; they are generally much liked. Take off a thick paring, cut the turnips into large pieces, or thick slices, and lay them awhile in cold water. Then boil them gently about two hours, or till they are quite soft. When done, strain, squeeze and mash them, and season them with pepper and salt, and a very little butter. Take care not to set them in a part of the table where the sun comes, as it will spoil the taste.

Russian turnips should always be mashed.

SQUASHES OR CYMLINGS.

THE green or summer squash is best when the outside is beginning to turn yellow, as it is then less watery and insipid than when younger. Wash them, cut them into pieces, and take out the seeds. Boil them about three quarters of an hour, or till quite tender. When done, drain and squeeze them well till you have pressed out all the water; mash them with a little butter, pepper and salt. Then put the squash thus prepared into a stew-pan, set it on hot coals, and stir it very frequently till it becomes dry. Take care not to let it burn.

WINTER SQUASH, OR CASHAW.

THIS is much finer than the summer squash. It is fit to eat in August, and, in a dry warm place, can be kept well all winter. The colour is a very bright yellow. Pare it, take out the seeds, cut it in pieces, and stew it slowly till quite soft, in a very little water. Afterwards drain, squeeze, and press it well, and mash it with a very little butter, pepper and salt.

PUMPKIN.

DEEP coloured pumpkins are generally the best. In a dry warm place they can be kept perfectly good all winter. When you prepare to stew a pumpkin, cut it in half and take out all the seeds. Then cut it in thick slices, and pare them. Put it into a pot with a very little water, and stew it gently for an hour, or till soft enough to mash. Then take it out, drain, and squeeze it till it is as dry as you can get it

Afterwards mash it, adding a little pepper and salt, and a very little butter.

Pumpkin is frequently stewed with fresh beef or fresh pork.

The water in which pumpkin has been boiled, is said to be very good to mix bread with, it having a tendency to improve it in sweetness and to keep it moist.

HOMINY.

Wash the hominy very clean through three or four waters. Then put it into a pot (allowing two quarts of water to one quart of hominy) and boil it slowly five hours. When done, take it up, and drain the liquid from it through a cullender. Put the hominy into a deep dish, and stir into it a small piece of fresh butter.

The small grained hominy is boiled in rather less water, and generally eaten with butter and sugar.

INDIAN CORN.

Corn for boiling should be full grown but young and tender. When the grains become yellow it is too old. Strip it of the outside leaves and the silk, but let the inner leaves remain, as they will keep in the sweetness. Put it into a large pot with plenty of water, and boil it rather fast for half an hour. When done, drain off the water, and remove the leaves.

You may either lay the ears on a large flat dish and send them to table whole, or broken in half; or you may cut all the corn off the cob, and serve it up in a deep dish, mixed with butter, pepper and salt.

MOCK OYSTERS OF CORN.

TAKE a dozen and a half ears of large young corn, and grate all the grains off the cob as fine as possible. MIX with the grated corn three large table-spoonfuls of sifted flour, the yolks of six eggs well beaten. Let all be well incorporated by hard beating.

Have ready in a frying-pan an equal proportion of lard and fresh butter. Hold it over the fire till it is boiling hot, and then put in portions of the mixture as nearly as possible in shape and size like fried oysters. Fry them brown, and send them to table hot. They should be near an inch thick.

This is an excellent relish at breakfast, and may be introduced as a side dish at dinner. In taste it has a singular resemblance to fried oysters. The corn *must* be young.

STEWED EGG PLANT.

THE purple egg plants are better than the white ones. Put them whole into a pot with plenty of water, and simmer them till quite tender. Then take them out, drain them, and (having peeled off the skins) cut them up, and mash them smooth in a deep dish. Mix with them some grated bread, some powdered sweet marjoram, and a large piece of butter, adding a pounded nutmeg. Grate a layer of bread over the top, and put the dish into the oven and brown it. You must send it to table in the same dish.

Egg plant is sometimes eaten at dinner, but generally at breakfast.

TO FRY EGG PLANT.—Do not pare your egg plants if they are to be fried, but slice them about half an inch thick and lay them an hour or two in salt and water to remove their strong taste, which to most persons is very unpleasant. Then take them out, wipe them, and season them with pepper only. Beat some yolk of egg; and in another dish grate a sufficiency of bread-crumbs. Have ready in a frying-pan some lard and butter mixed, and make it boil. Then dip each slice of egg plant first in the egg, and then in the crumbs, till both sides are well covered; and fry them brown, taking care to have them done all through, as the least rawness renders them very unpalatable.

STUFFED EGG PLANTS.—Parboil them to take off their bitterness. Then slit each one down the side, and extract the seeds. Have ready a stuffing made of grated bread-crumbs, butter, minced sweet herbs, salt, pepper, nutmeg, and beaten yolk of egg. Fill with it the cavity from whence you took the seeds, and bake the egg plants in a Dutch oven. Serve them up with a made gravy poured into the dish.

FRIED CUCUMBERS.

Having pared your cucumbers, cut them lengthways into pieces about as thick as a dollar. Then dry them in a cloth. Season them with pepper and salt, and sprinkle them thick with flour. Melt some butter in a frying-pan, and when it boils, put in the slices of cucumber, and fry them of a light brown. Send them to table hot.

They make a breakfast dish.

TO DRESS CUCUMBERS RAW.—They should be as fresh from the vine as possible, few vegetables being more unwholesome when long gathered. As soon as they are brought in lay them in cold water. Just before they are to go to table take them out, pare them and slice them into a pan of fresh cold water. When they are all sliced, transfer them to a deep dish, season them with a little salt and black pepper, and pour over them some of the best vinegar, to which you may add a little salad oil. You may mix with them a small quantity of sliced onion; not to be eaten, but to communicate a slight flavour of onion to the vinegar.

SALSIFY.

HAVING scraped the salsify roots, and washed them in cold water, parboil them. Then take them out, drain them, cut them into large pieces and fry them in butter.

Salsify is frequently stewed slowly till quite tender, and then served up with melted butter. Or it may be first boiled, then grated, and made into cakes to be fried in butter.

Salsify must not be left exposed to the air, or it will turn blackish.

ARTICHOKES.

STRIP off the coarse outer leaves, and cut off the stalks close to the bottom. Wash the artichokes well, and let them lie two or three hours in cold water. Put them with their heads downward into a pot of boiling water, keeping them down by a plate floated over them. They must boil steadily from two to three hours; take care to replenish the pot with additional boiling water as it is wanted. When they are tender all through, drain them, and serve them up with melted butter.

BEETS.

WASH the beets, but do not scrape or cut them while they are raw ; for if a knife enters them before they are boiled they will lose their colour.   Boil them from two to three hours, according to their size.   When they are tender all through, take them up, and scrape off all the outside.   If they are young beets they are best split down and cut into long pieces, seasoned with pepper, and sent to table with melted butter.   Otherwise you may slice them thin, after they are quite cold, and pour vinegar over them.

TO STEW BEETS.—Boil them first, and then scrape and slice them.   Put them into a stew-pan with a piece of butter rolled in flour, some boiled onion and parsley chopped fine, and a little vinegar, salt and pepper.   Set the pan on hot coals, and let the beets stew for a quarter of an hour.

TO BOIL GREEN OR FRENCH BEANS.

THESE beans should be young, tender, and fresh gathered. Remove the strings with a knife, and take off both ends of the bean.   Then cut them in two or three pieces only ; for if split or cut very small, they become watery and lose much of their taste; and cannot be well drained.   As you cut them, throw them into a pan of cold water, and let them lay awhile   Boil them an hour and a half.   They must be perfectly tender before you take them up.   Then drain and press them well, season them with pepper and mix into them a piece of butter.   You may boil with the beans a little bit of nice bacon, to give them a bacon taste—take it out afterwards.

SCARLET BEANS —It is not generally known that the pod of the scarlet bean, if green and young, is extremely nice when cut into two or three pieces and boiled. They will require near two hours, and must be drained well, and mixed as before mentioned with butter and pepper. If gathered at the proper time, when the seed is just perceptible, they are superior to any of the common beans.

LIMA BEANS.

THESE are generally considered the finest of all beans, and should be gathered young. Shell them, lay them in a pan of cold water, and then boil them about two hours, or till they are quite soft. Drain them well, and add to them some butter and a little pepper.

They are destroyed by the first frost, but can be kept during the winter, by gathering them on a dry day when full grown but not the least hard, and putting them in their pods into a keg. Throw some salt into the bottom of the keg, and cover it with a layer of the bean-pods; then add more salt, and then another layer of beans, till the keg is full. Press them down with a heavy weight, cover the keg closely, and keep it in a cool dry place. Before you use them, soak the pods all night in cold water; the next day shell them. and soak the beans till you are ready to boil them.

DRIED BEANS.

WASH them and lay them in soak over night. Early in the morning put them into a pot with plenty of water, and boil them slowly till dinner time. They will require seven or eight hours to be sufficiently done. Then take them off, put them into a sieve, and strain off the liquid.

Send the beans to table in a deep dish, seasoned with pepper, and having a piece of butter mixed with them.

GREEN PEAS.

GREEN peas are unfit for eating after they become hard and yellowish; but they are better when nearly full grown than when very small and young. They should be gathered as short a time as possible before they are cooked, and laid in cold water as soon as they are shelled. They will require about an hour to boil soft. When quite done, drain them, mix with them a piece of butter, and add a little pepper.

Peas may be greatly improved by boiling with them two or three lumps of loaf-sugar, and a sprig of mint to be taken out before they are dished. This is an English way of cooking green peas, and is to most tastes a very good one.

TO BOIL ONIONS.

TAKE off the tops and tails, and the thin outer skin; but no more lest the onions should go to pieces. Lay them on the bottom of a pan which is broad enough to contain them without piling one on another; just cover them with water, and let them simmer slowly till they are tender all through, but not till they break.

Serve them up with melted butter.

TO ROAST ONIONS.—Onions are best when parboiled before roasting. Take large onions, place them on a ho hearth and roast them before the fire in their skins, turning them as they require it. Then peel them, send them to table whole, and eat them with butter and salt.

TO FRY ONIONS.—Peel, slice them, and fry them brown in butter or nice dripping.

Onions should be kept in a very dry place, as dampness injures them.

TO BOIL ASPARAGUS.

LARGE or full grown asparagus is the best. Before you begin to prepare it for cooking, set on the fire a pot with plenty of water, and sprinkle into it a spoonful of salt. Your asparagus should be all of the same size. Scrape the stalks till they are perfectly nice and white; cut them all of equal length, and short, so as to leave them but two or three inches below the green part. To serve up asparagus with long stalks is now becoming obsolete. As you scrape them, throw them into a pan of cold water. Then tie them up in small bundles with bass or tape, as twine will cut them to pieces. When the water is boiling fast, put in the asparagus, and boil it an hour; if old it will require an hour and a quarter. When it is nearly done boiling, toast a large slice of bread sufficient to cover the dish (first cutting off the crust) and dip it into the asparagus water in the pot. Lay it in a dish, and, having drained the asparagus, place it on the toast with all the heads pointed inwards towards the centre, and the stalks spreading outwards. Serve up melted butter with it.

SEA KALE.—Sea kale is prepared, boiled, and served up in the same manner as asparagus.

POKE.—The young stalks and leaves of the poke-berry plant when quite small and first beginning to sprout up from the ground in the spring, are by most persons considered very nice, and are frequently brought to market. If the least too old they acquire a strong taste, and should not be eaten, as they then become unwholesome. They are in a proper state when the part of the stalk nearest to the ground is not thicker than small asparagus. Scrape the stalks, (letting the leaves remain on them,) and throw them into cold water. Then tie up the poke in bundles, put it into a pot that has plenty of boiling water, and let it boil fast an hour at least Serve it up with or without toast, and send melted butter with it in a boat.

STEWED TOMATAS.

Peel your tomatas, cut them in half and squeeze out the seeds. Then put them into a stew-pan without any water, and add to them cayenne and salt to your taste, some grated bread, a little minced onion, and some powdered mace. Stew them slowly till they are first dissolved and then dry.

BAKED TOMATAS.—Peel some large fine tomatas, cut them up, and take out the seeds. Then put them into a deep dish in alternate layers with grated bread-crumbs, and a very little butter in small bits. There must be a large proportion of bread-crumbs. Season the whole with a little salt, and cayenne pepper. Set it in an oven, and bake it. In cooking tomatas, take care not to have them too liquid. They will not lose their raw taste in less than three hours' cooking.

MUSHROOMS.

Good mushrooms are only found in clear open fields where the air is pure and unconfined. Those that grow in low damp ground, or in shady places, are always poisonous. Mushrooms of the proper sort generally appear in August and September, after a heavy dew or a misty night. They may be known by their being of a pale pink or salmon colour on the gills or under side, while the top is of a dull pearl-coloured white; and by their growing only in open places. When they are a day old, or a few hours after they are gathered, the reddish colour changes to brown.

The poisonous or false mushrooms are of various colours, sometimes of a bright yellow or scarlet all over; sometimes entirely of a chalky white, stalk, top, and gills.

It is easy to detect a bad mushroom if all are quite fresh; but after being gathered a few hours the colours change, so that unpractised persons frequently mistake them.

It is said that if you boil an onion among mushrooms the onion will turn of a bluish black when there 's a bad one among them. Of course, the whole should then be thrown into the fire. If in stirring mushrooms, the colour of the silver spoon is changed, it is also most prudent to destroy them all.

———

TO STEW MUSHROOMS.—For this purpose the small button mushrooms are best. Wash them clean, peel off the skin, and cut off the stalks. Put the trimmings into a small sauce-pan with just enough water to keep them from burning, and covering them closely, let them stew a quarter of an hour. Then strain the liquor, and having put the mushrooms into a clean sauce-pan, (a silver one, or one lined with porce lain,) add the liquid to them with a little nutmeg, pepper and salt, and a piece of butter rolled in flour. Stew them fifteen minutes, and just before you take them up, stir in a very little cream or rich milk and some beaten yolk of egg. Serve them hot. While they are cooking, keep the pan as closely covered as possible; shaking it round frequently.

If you wish to have the full taste of the mushroom only, after washing, trimming, and peeling them, put them into a stew-pan with a little salt and no water. Set them on coals, and stew them slowly till tender, adding nothing to them but a little butter rolled in flour, or else a little cream. Be sure to keep the pan well covered.

BROILED MUSHROOMS.—For this purpose take large mushrooms, and be careful to have them freshly gathered. Peel them, score the under side, and cut off the stems. Lay them one by one in an earthen pan, brushing them over with sweet oil or oiled butter, and sprinkling each with a little pepper and salt. Cover them closely, and let them set for about an hour and a half. Then place them on a gridiron over clear hot coals, and broil them on both sides.

Make a gravy for them of their trimmings stewed in a very little milk, strained and thickened with a beaten egg stirred in just before it goes to table.

BOILED RICE.

Pick your rice clean, and wash it in two cold waters, not draining off the last water till you are ready to put the rice on the fire. Prepare a sauce-pan of water with a little salt in it, and when it boils, sprinkle in the rice. Boil it hard twenty minutes, keeping it covered. Then take it from the fire, and pour off the water. Afterwards set the sauce-pan in the chimney corner with the lid off, while you are dishing your dinner, to allow the rice to dry, and the grains to separate.

Rice, if properly boiled, should be soft and white, and every grain ought to stand alone. If badly managed, it will, when brought to table, be a grayish watery mass.

In most southern families, rice is boiled every day for the dinner table, and eaten with the meat and poultry.

The above is a Carolina receipt.

~~~~~~~~~

TO DRESS LETTUCE AS SALAD.

STRIP off the outer leaves, wash the lettuce, split it in half, and lay it in cold water till dinner time. Then drain it and put it into a salad dish. Have ready two eggs boiled hard, (which they will be in ten minutes,) and laid in a basin of cold water for five minutes to prevent the whites from turning blue. Cut them in half and lay them on the lettuce.

Put the yolks of the eggs on a large plate, and with a wooden spoon mash them smooth, mixing with them a table-spoonful of water, and two table-spoonfuls of sweet oil. Then add, by degrees, a salt-spoonful of salt, a tea-spoonful of mustard, and a tea-spoonful of powdered loaf-sugar. When these are all smoothly united, add very gradually three table-spoonfuls of vinegar. The lettuce having been cut up fine on another plate, put it to the dressing, and mix it well.

If you have the dressing for salad made before dinner, put it into the bottom of the salad dish; then (having cut it up) lay the salad upon it, and let it rest till it is to be eaten, as stirring it will injure it.

You may decorate the top of the salad with slices of red beet, and with the hard white of the eggs cut into rings.

CELERY.—Scrape and wash it well, and let it lie in cold water till shortly before it goes to table; then dry it in a cloth, trim it, and split down the stalks almost to the bottom, leaving on a few green leaves. Send it to table in a celery glass, and eat it with salt only; or chop it fine, and make a salad dressing for it.

RADISHES.—To prepare radishes for eating, wash them and lay them in clean cold water as soon as they are brought in. Shortly before they go to table, scrape off the thin outside skin, trim the sharp end, cut off the leaves at the top, leaving the stalks about an inch long, and put them on a small dish. Eat them with salt.

Radishes should not be eaten the day after they are pulled, as they are extremely unwholesome if not quite fresh.

The thick white radishes, after being scraped and trimmed, should be split or cleft in four, half way down from the top.

TO ROAST CHESTNUTS.

THE large Spanish chestnuts are the best for roasting. Cut a slit in the shell of every one to prevent their bursting when hot. Put them into a pan, and set them over a charcoal furnace till they are thoroughly roasted; stirring them up frequently and taking care not to let them burn. When

₋hey are done, peel off the shells, and send the chestnuts to table wrapped up in a napkin to keep them warm.

Chestnuts should always be roasted or boiled before they are eaten.

GROUND-NUTS.—These nuts are never eaten raw. Put them, with their shells on, into an iron pan, and set them in an oven; or you may do them in a skillet on hot coals. A large quantity may be roasted in an iron pot over the fire. Stir them frequently, taking one out from time to time, and breaking it to try if they are done.

CORN AND BEANS WITH PORK.

TAKE a good piece of pork, either salt or fresh. Boil it by itself till quite tender. Boil also the corn and beans separately. Either dried or green beans will do. If string-beans, they must be cut in three. When the corn is well boiled, cut it from the cob, and mix it with the boiled beans. Put it into a pot with the boiled pork, and barely sufficient water to cover it. Season with pepper, and stew the whole together till nearly dry.

TO KEEP OCHRAS AND TOMATOS.—Take ochras when they first come in season; slice them thin; with a large needle run a strong thread through the slices, and hang them up in your store-room in festoons. In winter, use them for soup; boiling them till quite dissolved.

Having filled a jar two-thirds with whole tomatos, fill it quite up with good lard; covering it closely. When wanted for use, take them out from under the lard, and wash them in hot water.

EGGS, &c.

TO KEEP EGGS.

THERE is no infallible mode of ascertaining the freshness of an egg before you break it, but unless an egg is perfectly good, it is unfit for any purpose whatever, and will spoil whatever it is mixed with. You may judge with tolerable accuracy of the state of an egg by holding it against the sun or the candle, and if the yolk, as you see it through the shell, appears round, and the white thin and clear, it is most probably a good one; but if the yolk looks broken, and the white thick and cloudy, the egg is certainly bad. You may try the freshness of eggs by putting them into a pan of cold water. Those that sink the soonest are the freshest; those that are stale or addled will float on the surface.

There are various ways of preserving eggs. To keep them merely for plain boiling, you may parboil them for one minute, and then bury them in powdered charcoal with their small ends downward. They will keep a few days in a jar of salt; but do not afterwards use the salt in which they have been immersed.

They are frequently preserved for two or three months by greasing them all over, when quite fresh, with melted mutton suet, and then wedging them close together (the small end downwards) in a box of bran, layer above layer; the box must be closely covered. Charcoal is better than bran.

Another way (and a very good one) is to put some lime in a large vessel, and slack it with boiling water, till it is of the consistence of thin cream; you may allow a gallon of water to a pound of lime. When it is cold, pour it off into a large stone jar, put in the eggs, and cover the jar closely. See that the eggs are always well covered with the lime-water, and lest they should break, avoid moving the jar. If you have hens of your own, keep a jar of lime-water always ready, and put in the eggs as they are brought in from the nests. Jars that hold about six quarts are the most convenient.

It will be well to renew the lime-water occasionally.

TO BOIL EGGS FOR BREAKFAST.

THE fresher they are the longer time they will require for boiling. If you wish them quite soft, put them into a sauce-pan of water that is boiling hard at the moment, and let them remain in it five minutes. The longer they boil the harder they will be. In ten minutes' fast boiling they will be hard enough for salad.

If you use one of the tin egg-boilers that are placed on the table, see that the water is boiling hard at the time you put in the eggs. When they have been in about four or five minutes, take them out, pour off the water, and replace it by some more that is boiling hard; as, from the coldness of the eggs having chilled the first water, they will not otherwise be done enough. The boiler may then be placed on the table, (keeping the lid closed,) and in a few minutes more they will be sufficiently cooked to be wholesome.

TO POACH EGGS.

POUR some boiling water out of a tea-kettle through a clean cloth spread over the top of a broad stew-pan; for by observing this process the eggs will be nicer and more easily done than when its impurities remain in the water. Set the pan with the strained water on hot coals, and when it boils, break each egg separately into a saucer. Remove the pan from the fire, and slip the eggs one by one into the surface of the water. Let the pan stand till the white of the eggs is set; then place it again on the coals, and as soon as the water boils again, the eggs will be sufficiently done. Take them out carefully with an egg-slice, and trim off all the ragged edges from the white, which should thinly cover the yolk. Have ready some thin slices of buttered toast with the crust cut off. Lay them in the bottom of the dish, with a poached egg on each slice of toast, and send them to the break fast table.

FRICASSEED EGGS.

TAKE a dozen eggs, and boil them six or seven minutes, or till they are just hard enough to peel and slice without breaking. Then put them into a pan of cold water while you prepare some grated bread-crumbs, (seasoned with pepper, salt and nutmeg,) and beat the yolks of two or three raw eggs very light. Take the boiled eggs out of the water, and having peeled off the shells, slice the eggs, dust a little flour over them, and dip them first into the beaten egg, and then into the bread-crumbs so as to cover them well on both sides. Have ready in a frying-pan some boiling lard; put the sliced eggs into it, and fry them on both sides. Serve them up at the breakfast table, garnished with small sprigs of parsley that has been fried in the same lard after the eggs were taken out.

PLAIN OMELET.

TAKE six eggs, leaving out the whites of two. Beat them very light, and strain them through a sieve. Add pepper and salt to your taste. Divide two ounces of fresh butter into little bits, and put it into the egg. Have ready a quarter of a pound of butter in a frying-pan, or a flat stew-pan. Place it on hot coals, and have the butter boiling when you put in the beaten egg. Fry it gently till of a light brown on the under side. Do not turn it while cooking as it will do better without. You may brown the top by holding a hot shovel over it. When done, lay it in the dish, double it in half, and stick sprigs of curled parsley over it.

You may flavour the omelet by mixing with the beaten egg some parsley or sweet herbs minced fine, some chopped celery, or chopped onion, allowing two moderate sized onions to an omelet of six eggs. Or what is still better, it may be seasoned with veal kidney or sweet-bread minced; with cold ham shred as fine as possible; or with minced oysters, (the hard part omitted,) with tops of asparagus (that has been previously boiled) cut into small pieces.

You should have one of the pans that are made purposely for omelets.

AN OMELETTE SOUFFLÉ.

BREAK eight eggs, separate the whites from the yolks, and strain them. Put the whites into one pan, and the yolks into another, and beat them separately with rods till the yolks are very thick and smooth, and the whites a stiff froth that will stand alone. Then add gradually to the yolks, three quarters of a pound of the finest powdered loaf-sugar, and orange-flower water or lemon-juice to your taste. Next stir the whites lightly into the yolks. Butter a deep pan or dish (that has been previously heated) and pour the mixture rapidly into it. Set it in a Dutch oven with coals under it, and on the top, and bake it five minutes. If properly beaten and mixed, and carefully baked, it will rise very high. Send it immediately to table, or it will fall and flatten.

Do not begin to make an omelette soufflé till the company at table have commenced their dinner, that it may be ready to serve up just in time, immediately on the removal of the meats. The whole must be accomplished as quickly as pos sible. Send it round with a spoon.

If you live in a large town, the safest way of avoiding a failure in an omelette souffie is to hire a French cook to come to your kitchen with his own utensils and ingredients, and make and bake it himself, while the first part of the dinner is progressing in the dining-room.

An omelette soufflé is a very nice and delicate thing when properly managed; but if flat and heavy, it should not be brought to table. If well made, you may turn it out on a dish.

TO DRESS MACCARONI.

Have ready a pot of boiling water. Throw a little salt into it, and then by slow degrees put in a pound of the maccaroni, a little at a time. Keep stirring it gently, and continue to do so very often while boiling. Take care to keep it well covered with water. Have ready a kettle of boiling water to replenish the maccaroni pot if it should be in danger of getting too dry. In about twenty minutes it will be done. It must be quite soft, but it must not boil long enough to break.

When the maccaroni has boiled sufficiently, pour in immediately a little cold water, and let it stand a few minutes, keeping it covered.

Grate half a pound of Parmesan cheese into a deep dish and scatter over it a few small bits of butter. Then with a skimmer that is perforated with holes, commence taking up the maccaroni, (draining it well,) and spread a layer of it over the cheese and butter. Spread over it another layer of grated cheese and butter, and then a layer of maccaroni, and so on till your dish is full; having a layer of maccaroni or the top, over which spread some butter without cheese. Cover the dish, and set it in an oven for half an hour. It will then be ready to send to table.

You may grate some nutmeg over each layer of maccaroni.

Allow half a pound of butter to a pound of maccaroni and half a pound of cheese.

ANOTHER WAY.

First put on the maccaroni in a very little water. Let it come to a hard boil, and then drain off the water. Put it on again with milk instead of water, and a large lump of butter. Boil it till quite tender all through. Then, while hot, mix in a little cream, and add some sugar and nutmeg, or powdered cinnamon.

PICKLING.

~~~~~~~~

GENERAL REMARKS.

NEVER on any consideration use brass, copper, or bell-metal kettles for pickling; the verdigris produced in them by the vinegar being of a most poisonous nature. Kettles lined with porcelain are the best, but if you cannot procure them, block tin may be substituted. Iron is apt to discolour any acid that is boiled in it.

Vinegar for pickles should always be of the best cider kind. In putting away pickles, use stone or glass jars. The lead which is an ingredient in the glazing of common earthenware, is rendered very pernicious by the action of the vinegar. Have a large wooden spoon and a fork, for the express purpose of taking pickles out of the jar when you want them for the table. See that, while in the jar, they are always completely covered with vinegar. If you discern in them any symptoms of not keeping well, do them over again in fresh vinegar and spice.

Vinegar for pickles should only boil five or six minutes.

The jars should be stopped with large flat corks, fitting closely, and having a leather or a round piece of oil-cloth tied over the cork.

It is a good rule to have two-thirds of the jar filled with pickles, and one-third with vinegar.

Alum is very useful in extracting the salt taste from pickles, and in making them firm and crisp. A very small quantity is sufficient Too much will spoil them.

In greening pickles keep them very closely covered, so that none of the steam may escape; as its retention promotes their greenness and prevents the flavour from evaporating.

Vinegar and spice for pickles should be boiled but a few minutes. Too much boiling takes away the strength.

TO PICKLE CUCUMBERS.

CUCUMBERS for pickling should be very small, and as free from spots as possible. Make a brine of salt and water strong enough to bear an egg. Pour it over your cucumbers, cover them with fresh cabbage leaves, and let them stand for a week, or till they are quite yellow, stirring them at least twice a day. When they are perfectly yellow, pour off the water. Take a porcelain kettle, and cover the bottom and sides with fresh vine leaves. Put in the cucumbers (with a small piece of alum) and cover them closely with vine leaves all over the top, and then with a dish or cloth to keep in the steam. Fill up the kettle with clear water, and hang it over the fire when dinner is done, but not where there is a blaze. The fire under the kettle must be kept very moderate. The water must not boil, or be too hot to bear your hand in. Keep them over the fire in a slow heat till next morning. If they are not then of a fine green, repeat the process. When they are well greened, take them out of the kettle, drain them on a sieve, and put them into a clean stone jar. Boil for five or six minutes sufficient of the best vinegar to cover the cucumbers well; putting into the kettle a thin muslin bag filled with cloves, mace, and mustard seed. Pour the vinegar scalding hot into the jar of pickles, which should be secured with a large flat cork, and an oil-cloth or leather cover tied over it.

Another way to green pickles is to cover them with vine leaves or cabbage leaves, and to keep them on a warm hearth, pouring boiling water on them five or six times a day ; renewing the water as soon as it becomes cold.

In proportioning the spice to the vinegar, allow to every two quarts, an ounce of mace, two dozen cloves, and two ounces of mustard seed. You may leave the muslin bag, with the spice, for about a week in the pickle jar to heighten the flavour, if you think it necessary.

GREEN PEPPERS—May be done in the same manner as cucumbers, only extracting the seeds before you put the pickles into the salt and water. Do not put peppers into the same jar with cucumbers, as the former will destroy the latter.

GHERKINS.—The gherkin is a small thick oval-shaped species of cucumber with a hairy or prickly surface, and is cultivated solely for pickling. It is customary to let the stems remain on them. Wipe them dry, put them into a broad stone jar, and scald them five or six times in the course of the day with salt and water strong enough to bear an egg, and let them set all night. This will make them yellow. Next day, having drained them from the salt and water, throw it out, wipe them dry, put them into a clean vessel (with a little piece of alum,) and scald them with boiling vinegar and water, (half and half of each,) repeating it frequently during the day till they are green. Keep them as closely covered as possible. Then put them away in stone jars, mixing among them whole mace and sliced ginger to your taste. Fill up with cold vinegar, and add a little alum, allowing to every hundred gherkins a piece about the size of a shelled almond.

The alum will make them firm and crisp.

RADISH PODS.—Gather sprigs or bunches of radish pods while they are young and tender, but let the pods remain on the sprigs; it not being the custom to pick them off Put them into strong salt and water, and let them stand two days. Then drain and wipe them and put them into a clean stone jar. Boil an equal quantity of vinegar and water. Pour it over the radish pods while hot, and cover them closely to keep in the steam. Repeat this frequently through the day till they are very green. Then pour off the vinegar and water, and boil for five minutes some very good vinegar, with a little bit of alum, and pour it over them. Put them into a stone jar, (and having added some whole mace, whole pepper, a little tumeric and a little sweet oil,) cork it closely, and tie over it a leather or oil-cloth.

———

GREEN BEANS.—Take young green or French beans; string them, but do not cut them in pieces. Put them in salt and water for two days, stirring them frequently. Then put them into a kettle with vine or cabbage leaves under, over, and all round them, (adding a little piece of alum.) Cover them closely to keep in the steam, and let them hang over a slow fire till they are a fine green.

Having drained them in a sieve, make for them a pickle of cider vinegar, and boil in it for five minutes, some mace, whole pepper, and sliced ginger tied up in a thin muslin bag. Pour it hot upon the beans, put them into a stone jar, and tie them up.

———

PARSLEY.—Make a brine of salt and water strong enough to bear an egg, and throw into it a large quantity of curled parsley tied up in little bunches with a thread. After it has stood three days (stirring it frequently) take it out drain it well, and lay it for three days in cold spring or pump-water, changing the water daily. Then scald it in hard water, and hang it, well covered, over a slow fire till it becomes green. Afterwards take it out, and drain and press it till quite dry.

Boil for five minutes a quart of cider vinegar with a small bit of alum, a few blades of mace, a sliced nutmeg, and a few slips of horseradish. Pour it on the parsley, and put it away in a stone jar.

MANGOES.

TAKE very young oval shaped musk-melons. Cut a round piece out of the top or side of each, (saving the piece to put on again,) and extract the seeds. Then (having tied on the pieces with packthread) put them into strong salt and water for two days. Afterwards drain and wipe them, put them into a kettle with vine leaves or cabbage leaves under and over them, and a little piece of alum, and hang them on a slow fire to green; keeping them closely covered to retain the steam, which will greatly accelerate the greening. When they are quite green, have ready the stuffing, which must be a mixture of scraped horseradish, white mustard seed, mace and nutmeg pounded, race ginger cut small, pepper, tumeric and sweet oil. Fill your mangoes with this mixture, putting a small clove of garlic into each, and replacing the pieces at the openings; tie them with a packthread crossing backwards and forwards round the mango. Put them into stone jars, pour boiling vinegar over them, and cover them well. Before you put them on the table remove the packthread.

NASTURTIANS.—Have ready a stone or glass jar of the best cold vinegar. Take the green seeds of the nasturtian after the flower has gone off. They should be full-grown but not old. Pick off the stems, and put the seeds into the vinegar. No other preparation is necessary, and they will keep a year with nothing more than sufficient cold vinegar to cover them. With boiled mutton they are an excellent substitute for capers.

MORELLA CHERRIES.—See that all your cherries are perfect. Remove the stems, and put the cherries into a jar or glass with sufficient vinegar to cover them well. They will keep perfectly in a cool dry place.

They are very good, always retaining the taste of the cherry. If you cannot procure morellas, the large red pie-cherries may be substituted.

PEACHES.—Take fine large peaches (either cling or free stones) that are not too ripe. Wipe off the down with a clean flannel, and put the peaches whole into a stone jar. Cover them with cold vinegar, and lay among them little muslin bags containing mace, nutmeg, and cinnamon, broken small. Put a cork in the jar and tie leather or oil cloth over it.

Plums and grapes may be pickled thus in cold vinegar, with bags of spice.

BARBERRIES.—Have ready a jar of cold vinegar, and put into it ripe barberries in bunches. They make a pretty garnish for the edges of dishes.

TO PICKLE GREEN PEPPERS.

THE bell pepper is the best for pickling, and should be gathered when quite young. Slit one side, and carefully take out the core, so as not to injure the shell of the pepper. Then put them into boiling salt and water, changing the water every day for one week, and keeping them closely covered in a warm place near the fire. Stir them several times a day. They will first become yellow, and then green. When they are a fine green put them into a jar, and pour cold vinegar over them, adding a small piece of alum.

They require no spice.

You may stuff the peppers as you do mangoes.

TO PICKLE BUTTERNUTS.

THESE nuts are in the best state for pickling when the shell is soft, and when they are so young that the outer skin can be penetrated by the head of a pin. They should be gathered when the sun is hot upon them.

If you have a large quantity, the easiest way to prepare them for pickling is to put them into a tub with sufficient lye to cover them, and to stir and rub them about with a hickory broom till they are clean and smooth on the outside. This is much less trouble than scraping them, and is not so likely to injure the nuts. Another method is to scald them, and then to rub off the outer skin. Put the nuts into strong salt and water for one week; changing the water every other day, and keeping them closely covered from the air. Then drain and wipe them, (piercing each nut through in several places with a large needle,) and prepare the pickle as follows:—For a hundred large nuts, take of black pepper

and ginger root of each an ounce; and of cloves, mace and
nutmeg of each a half ounce.   Pound all the spices to powder, and mix them well together, adding two large spoonfuls
of mustard seed.   Put the nuts into jars, (having first stuck
each of them through in several places with a large needle,)
strewing the powdered seasoning between every layer of nuts.
Boil for five minutes a gallon of the very best cider vinegar,
and pour it boiling hot upon the nuts.   Secure the jars closely
with corks and leathers.   You may begin to eat the nuts in
a fortnight.

Walnuts may be pickled in the same manner.

TO PICKLE WALNUTS BLACK.

THE walnuts should be gathered while young and soft, (so
that you can easily run a pin through them,) and when the
sun is upon them.   Rub them with a coarse flannel or tow
cloth to get off the fur of the outside.   Mix salt and water
strong enough to bear an egg, and let them lie in it a week,
(changing it every two days,) and stirring them frequently.
Then take them out, drain them, spread them on large dishes,
and expose them to the air about ten minutes, which will
cause them to blacken the sooner.   Scald them in boiling
water, (but do not let them lie in it,) and then rub them with
a coarse woollen cloth, and pierce every one through in several
places with a large needle, (that the pickle may penetrate
them thoroughly.)   Put them into stone jars, and prepare the
spice and vinegar.   To a hundred walnuts allow a gallon of
vinegar, an ounce of cloves, an ounce of allspice, an ounce of
black pepper, half an ounce of mace, and half an ounce of
nutmeg.   Boil the spice in the vinegar   or fifteen minutes,

then strain the vinegar, and pour it boiling hot over the walnuts. Tie up in a thin muslin rag, a tea-cupful of mustard seed, and a large table-spoonful of scraped horse-radish, and put it into the jars with the walnuts. Cover them closely with corks and leathers.

Another way of pickling walnuts black, is (after preparing them as above) to put them into jars with the spices pounded and strewed among them, and then to pour over them strong cold vinegar.

———

WALNUTS PICKLED WHITE.—Take large young walnuts while their shells are quite soft so that you can stick the head of a pin into them. Pare them very thin till the white appears; and as you do them, throw them into spring or pump water in which some salt has been dissolved. Let them stand in that water six hours, with a thin board upon them to keep them down under the water. Fill a porcelain kettle with fresh spring water, and set it over a clear fire, or on a charcoal furnace. Put the walnuts into the kettle, cover it, and let them simmer (but not boil) for about ten minutes. Then have ready a vessel with cold spring water and salt, and put your nuts into it, taking them out of the kettle with a wooden ladle. Let them stand in the cold salt and water for a quarter of an hour, with the board keeping them down as before; for if they rise above the liquor, or are exposed to the air, they will be discoloured. Then take them out, and lay them on a cloth covered with another, till they are quite dry. Afterwards rub them carefully with a soft flannel, and put them into a stone jar; laying among them blades of mace, and sliced nutmeg, but no dark-coloured spice. Pour over them the very best vinegar, and put on the top a table-spoonful of sweet oil.

WALNUTS PICKLED GREEN.—Gather them while the shells are very soft, and rub them all with a flannel. Then wrap them singly in vine leaves, lay a few vine leaves in the bottom of a large stone jar, put in the walnuts, (seeing that each of them is well wrapped up so as not to touch one another,) and cover them with a thick layer of leaves. Fill up the jar with strong vinegar, cover it closely, and let it stand three weeks. Then pour off the vinegar, take out the walnuts, renew all the vine leaves, fill up with fresh vinegar, and let them stand three weeks longer. Then again pour off the vinegar, and renew the vine leaves. This time take the best cider vinegar; put salt in it till it will bear an egg, and add to it mace, sliced nutmeg, and scraped horse-radish, in the proportion of an ounce of each and a gallon of vinegar to a hundred walnuts. Boil the spice and vinegar about ten minutes, and then pour it hot on the walnuts. Cover the jar closely with a cork and leather, and set it away, leaving the vine leaves with the walnuts. When you take any out for use, disturb the others as little as possible, and do not put back again any that may be left.

You may pickle butternuts green in the same manner.

TO PICKLE ONIONS.

TAKE very small onions, and with a sharp knife cut off the stems as close as possible, and peel off the outer skin. Then put them into salt and water, and let them stand in the brine for six days; stirring them daily, and changing the salt and water every two days. See that they are closely covered. Then put the onions into jars, and give them a scald in boiling salt and water. Let them stand till they are cold; then drain them on a sieve, wipe them, stick a clove in the top of each, and put them into wide-mouthed bottles; dispersing among them some blades of mace and slices of ginger or nutmeg. Fill up the bottles with the best cider vinegar, and put at the top a large spoonful of salad oil. Cork the bottles well.

ONIONS PICKLED WHITE.—Peel some very small white onions, and lay them for three days in salt and water, changing the water every day. Then wipe them, and put them into a porcelain kettle with equal quantities of milk and water, sufficient to cover them well. Simmer them over a slow fire, but when just ready to boil take them off, and drain and dry them, and put them into wide-mouthed glass bottles; interspersing them with blades of mace. Boil a sufficient quantity of the best cider vinegar to cover them and nll up the bottles, adding to it a little salt; and when it is cold, pour it into the bottles of onions. At the top of each bottle put a spoonful of sweet oil. Set them away closely corked.

TO PICKLE MUSHROOMS WHITE.

Take small fresh-gathered button mushrooms, peel them carefully with a penknife, and cut off the stems; throwing the mushrooms into salt and water as you do them. Then put them into a porcelain skillet of fresh water, cover it closely, and set it over a quick fire. Boil it as fast as possible for seven or eight minutes, not more. Take out the mushrooms, drain them, and spread them on a clean board, with the bottom or hollow side of each mushroom turned downwards. Do this as quickly as possible, and immediately, while they are hot, sprinkle them over with salt. When they are cold, put them into a glass jar with slight layers of mace and sliced ginger. Fill up the jar with cold cider vinegar. Put a spoonful of sweet oil on the top of each jar, and cork it closely.

MUSHROOMS PICKLED BROWN.—Take a quart of large mushrooms and (having trimmed off the stalks) rub them with a flannel cloth dipped in salt. Then lay them in a pan of allegar or ale vinegar, for a quarter of an hour, and wash them about in it. Then put them into a sauce-pan with a quart of allegar, a quarter of an ounce of cloves, the same of allspice and whole pepper, and a tea-spoonful of salt. Set the pan over coals, and let the mushrooms stew slowly for ten minutes; keeping the pan well covered. Then take them off, let them get cold by degrees, and put them into small bottles with the allegar strained from the spice and poured upon them.

It will be prudent to boil an onion with the mushrooms, and if it turns black or blueish, you may infer that there is a poisonous one among them; and they should therefore be thrown away. Stir them for the same reason, with a silver spoon.

TO PICKLE TOMATAS.

TAKE a peck of tomatas, (the small round ones are best for pickling,) and prick every one with a fork. Put them into a broad stone or earthen vessel, and sprinkle salt between every layer of tomatas. Cover them, and let them remain two days in the salt. Then put them into vinegar and water mixed in equal quantities, half and half, and keep them in it twenty-four hours to draw out the saltness. There must be sufficient of the liquid to cover the tomatas well.

To a peck of tomatas allow a bottle of mustard, half an ounce of cloves, and half an ounce of pepper, with a dozen onions sliced thin. Pack the tomatas in a stone jar, placing the spices and onions alternately with the layers of tomatas. Put them in till the jar is two-thirds full. Then fill it up with strong cold vinegar, and stop it closely. The pickles will be fit to eat in a fortnight.

If you do not like onions, substitute for them a larger quantity of spice.

———

TOMATA SOY.—For this purpose you must have the best and ripest tomatas, and they must be gathered on a dry day. Do not peel them, but merely cut them into slices. Having strewed some salt over the bottom of a tub, put in the tomatas in layers; sprinkling between each layer (which should be about two inches in thickness) a handful of salt. Repeat this till you have put in eight quarts or one peck of tomatas. Cover the tub and let it set for three days. Then early in the morning, put the tomatas into a large porcelain kettle, and boil it slowly and steadily till ten at night, frequently mashing and stirring the tomatas. Then put it out to cool. Next morning strain and press it through a sieve, and when no more liquid will pass through, put it into a clean kettle with two ounces of cloves, one ounce of mace, two ounces of black pepper, and two table-spoonfuls of cayenne, all powdered.

Again let it boil slowly and steadily all day, and put it to cool in the evening in a large pan. Cover it, and let it set all night. Next day put it into small bottles, securing the corks by dipping them in melted rosin, and tying leathers over them.

If made exactly according to these directions, and slowly

and thoroughly boiled, it will keep for years in a cool dry place, and may be used for many purposes when fresh tomatas are not to be had.

TO PICKLE CAULIFLOWERS.

TAKE the whitest and closest full-grown cauliflowers; cut off the thick stalk, and split the blossom or flower part into eight or ten pieces. Spread them on a large dish, sprinkle them with salt, and let them stand twenty-four hours. Then wash off the salt, drain them, put them into a broad flat jar or pan, scald them with salt and water, (allowing a quarter of a pound of salt to a quart of water,) cover them closely and let them stand in the brine till next day. Afterwards drain them in a hair sieve, and spread them on a cloth in a warm place to dry for a day and a night. Then put them carefully, piece by piece, into clean broad jars and pour over them a pickle which has been prepared as follows :—Mix together three ounces of coriander seed, three ounces of turmeric, one ounce of mustard seed, and one ounce of ginger. Pound the whole in a mortar to a fine powder. Put it into three quarts of the very best cider vinegar, set it by the side of the fire in a stone jar, and let it infuse three days. These are the proportions, but the quantity of the whole pickle must depend on the quantity of cauliflower, which must be kept well covered by the liquid. Pour it over the cauliflower, and secure the jars closely from the air.

You may pickle brocoli in the same manner. Also the green tops of asparagus.

TO PICKLE RED CABBAGE.

TAKE a fine firm cabbage of a deep red or purple colour. Strip off the outer leaves, and cut out the stalk. Quarter the cabbage lengthways, and then slice it crossways. Lay it in a deep dish, sprinkle a handful of salt over it, cover it with another dish, and let it lie twenty-four hours. Then drain it in a cullender from the salt, and wipe it dry. Make a pickle of sufficient cider vinegar to cover the cabbage well, adding to it equal quantities of cloves and allspice, with some mace. The spices must be put in whole, with a little cochineal to give it a good red colour. Boil the vinegar and spices hard for five minutes, and having put the cabbage into a stone jar, pour the vinegar over it boiling hot. Cover the jar with a cloth till it gets cold; and then put in a large cork, and tie a leather over it.

EXCELLENT COLD SLAW.

TAKE a nice fresh white cabbage, wash, and drain it, and cut off the stalk. Shave down the head evenly and nicely into very small shreds, with a cabbage-cutter, or a sharp knife. Put it into a deep china dish, and prepare for it the following dressing. Take a large half-pint of the best cider vinegar, and mix with it a quarter of a pound of fresh butter, divided into four bits, and rolled in flour; a small salt-spoon of salt, and the same quantity of cayenne. Stir all this well together, and boil it in a small saucepan. Have ready the yolks of four eggs well beaten. As soon as the mixture has come to a hard boil, take it off the fire, and stir in the beaten egg. Then pour it boiling hot over the shred cabbage, and mix it well, all through, with a spoon. Set it to cool on ice or snow, or in the open air. It must be quite cold before it goes to table.

_____

WARM SLAW.—Take a red cabbage; wash, drain, and shred it finely. Put it into a deep dish. Cover it closely, and set it on the top of a stove, or in a bake oven, till it is warm all through. Then make a dressing as in the receipt for cold slaw. Pour it hot over the cabbage. Cover the dish, and send it to table as warm as possible.

~~~~~~~~~~~

EAST INDIA PICKLE.

This is a mixture of various things pickled together, and put into the same jar.

Have ready a small white cabbage, sliced, and the stalk removed; a cauliflower cut into neat branches, leaving out the large stalk; sliced cucumbers; sliced carrots; sliced beets, (all nicked round the edges;) button-onions; string-beans; radish pods; barberries; cherries; green grapes; nasturtians; capsicums; bell-peppers, &c. Sprinkle all these things with salt, put them promiscuously into a large earthen pan, and pour scalding salt and water over them. Let them lie in the brine for four days, turning them all over every day. Then take them out, wash each thing separately in vinegar, and wipe them carefully in a cloth. Afterwards lay them on sieves before the fire, and dry them thoroughly.

For the pickle liquor.—To every two quarts of the best vinegar, put an ounce and a half of white ginger root, scraped and sliced; the same of long pepper; two ounces of peeled shalots, or little button-onions, cut in pieces; half an ounce of peeled garlic; an ounce of turmeric; and two ounces of mustard seed bruised, or of mustard powder. Let all these ingredients, mixed with the vinegar, infuse in a close jar for a week, setting in a warm place, or by the fire. Then (after the vegetables have been properly prepared, and dried from the brine) put them all into one large stone jar, or into smaller jars, and strain the pickle over them. The liquid must be in a large quantity, so as to keep the vegetables well covered with it, or they will spoil. Put a table-spoonful of sweet oil on the top of each jar, and secure them well with a large cork and a leather.

If you find that after awhile the vegetables have absorbed the liquor, so that there is danger of their not having a sufficiency, prepare some more seasoned vinegar and pour it over them.

East India pickle is very convenient, and will keep two years. As different vegetables come into season, you can prepare them with the salt and water process, and add them to the things already in the jar. You may put small mangoes into this pickle; also plums, peaches and apricots.

TO PICKLE OYSTERS FOR KEEPING.

For this purpose take none but the finest and largest oysters. After they are opened, separate them from their liquor, and put them into a bucket or a large pan, and pour boiling water upon them to take out the slime. Stir them about in it, and then take them out, and rinse them well in cold water. Then put them into a large kettle with fresh water, barely enough to cover them, (mixing with it a table-spoonful of salt to every hundred oysters,) and give them a boil up, just sufficient to plump them. Take them out, spread them on large dishes or on a clean table, and cover them with a cloth. Take the liquor of the oysters, and with every pint of it mix a quart of the best vinegar, a table-spoonful of salt, a table-spoonful of whole cloves, the same of whole black pepper, and a tea-spoonful of whole mace. Put the liquid over the fire in a kettle, and when it boils throw in the oysters, and let them remain in it five minutes. Then take the whole off the fire, stir it up well, and let it stand to get quite cold. Afterwards (if you have a large quantity) put it into a keg, which must first be well scalded, (a new keg is best,) and fill it as full as it can hold. Do not put a weight on the oysters to keep them down in the liquor, as it will crush them to pieces if the keg should be moved or conveyed to a distance. If you have not enough to fill a keg, put them into stone jars when they are perfectly cold, and cover them securely.

For pickling oysters and all other purposes use only the best cider vinegar. The sharp pungent vinegar made entirely of chemical substances will destroy the oysters, and is too unwholesome for any culinary purpose. No one should purchase it. It may be known by its excessive sharpness; being violently pungent without any pleasant flavour.

SWEETMEATS.

～～～～～

GENERAL REMARKS.

THE introduction of iron ware lined with porcelain has fortunately almost superseded the use of brass or bell-metal kettles for boiling sweetmeats; a practice by which the articles prepared in those pernicious utensils were always more or less imbued with the deleterious qualities of the verdigris that is produced in them by the action of acids.

Charcoal furnaces will be found very convenient for preserving; the kettles being set on the top. They can be used in the open air. Sweetmeats should be boiled rather quickly, that the watery particles may exhale at once, without being subjected to so long a process as to spoil the colour and diminish the flavour of the fruit. But on the other hand, if boiled too short a time they will not keep so well.

If you wish your sweetmeats to look bright and clear, use only the very best loaf-sugar. Fruit may be preserved for family use and for common purposes, in sugar of inferior quality, but it will never have a good appearance, and it is also more liable to spoil.

If too small a proportion of sugar is allowed to the fruit, it will *certainly* not keep well. When this experiment is tried it is generally found to be false economy; as sweetmeats, when they begin to spoil, can only be recovered and made eatable by boiling them over again with additional sugar; and even then, they are never so good as if done properly at first. If jellies have not sufficient sugar, they do not congeal, but will remain liquid.

Jelly bags should be made of white flannel. It is well to have a wooden stand or frame like a towel horse, to which the bag can be tied while it is dripping. The bag should first be dipped in hot water, for if dry it will absorb too much of the juice. After the liquor is all in, close the top of the bag, that none of the flavour may evaporate.

In putting away sweetmeats, it is best to place them in small jars, as the more frequently they are exposed to the air by opening, the more danger there is of their spoiling. The best vessels for this purpose are white queen's-ware pots, or glass jars. For jellies, jams, and for small fruit, common glass tumblers are very convenient, and may be covered simply with double tissue-paper, cut exactly to fit the inside of the top of the glass, laid lightly on the sweetmeat, and pressed down all round with the finger. This covering, if closely and nicely fitted, will be found to keep them perfectly well, and as it adheres so closely as to form a complete coat over the top, it is better for jellies or jams than writing-paper dipped in brandy, which is always somewhat shrivelled by the liquor with which it has been saturated.

If you find that your sweetmeats have become dry and candied, you may liquefy them again by setting the jars in water and making it boil round them.

In preserving fruit whole, it is best to put it first in a thin syrup. If boiled in a thick syrup at the beginning, the juice will be drawn out so as to shrink the fruit.

It is better to boil it but a short time at once, and then to take it out and let it get cold, afterwards returning it to the syrup, than to keep it boiling too long at a time, which will cause it to break and lose its shape.

Preserving kettles should be rather broad than deep, for the fruit cannot be done equally if it is too much heaped. They should all have covers belonging to them, to put on after the scum has done rising, that the flavour of the fruit may be kept in with the steam.

A perforated skimmer pierced all through with holes is a very necessary utensil in making sweetmeats.

The water used for melting the sugar should be very clear spring or pump water is best. But if you are obliged to use river water, let it first be filtered. Any turbidness or impurity in the water will injure the clearness of the sweetmeats.

If sweetmeats ferment in the jars, boil them over again with additional sugar.

CLARIFIED SUGAR SYRUP.

TAKE eight pounds of the best double-refined loaf-sugar and break it up or powder it. Then beat the whites of four eggs to a strong froth. Stir the white of egg gradually into two quarts of very clear spring or pump water. Put the sugar into a porcelain kettle, and mix with it the water and white of egg. While the sugar is melting, stir it frequently; and when it is entirely dissolved, put the kettle over a moderate fire, and let it boil, carefully taking off the scum as it comes to the top, and pouring in a little cold water when you find the syrup rising so as to run over the edge of the kettle. It will be well when it first boils hard to pour in half a pint of cold water to keep down the bubbles so that the scum may appear, and be easily removed. You must not however boil it to candy height, so that the bubbles will look like hard pearls, and the syrup will harden in the spoon and hang from it in strings; for though very thick and clear it must continue liquid When it is done, let it stand till it gets quite cold; and if you do not want it for immediate use, put it into bottles and seal the corks.

When you wish to use this syrup for preserving, you have only to put the fruit into it, and boil it till tender and clear, but not till it breaks. Large fruit that is done whole, should first be boiled tender in a very thin syrup that it may not shrink. Small fruit, such as raspberries, strawberries, grapes, currants, gooseberries, &c. may, if perfectly ripe, be put raw into strong cold sugar syrup; they will thus retain their form and colour, and their freshness and natural taste. They must be put into small glass jars, and kept well covered with the syrup. This, however, is an experiment which sometimes fails, and had best be tried on a small scale, or only for immediate use.

TO PRESERVE GINGER.

TAKE root of green ginger, and pare it neatly with a sharp knife, throwing it into a pan of cold water as you pare it. Then boil it till tender all through, changing the water three times. Each time put on the ginger in quite cold water to take out the excessive heat. When it is perfectly tender, throw it again into a pan of cold water, and let it lie an hour or more; this will make it crisp. In the mean time prepare the syrup.

For every six pounds of ginger root, clarify eight pounds of the best double-refined loaf-sugar. Break up the sugar. put it into a preserving kettle, and melt it in spring or pump water, (into which you have stirred gradually the beaten whites of four eggs,) and half a pint of water to each pound of sugar. Boil and skim it well. Then let the syrup stand till it is cold; and having drained the ginger, pour the syrup over it, cover it, and do not disturb it for two days. Then, having poured it from the ginger, boil the syrup over again. As soon as it is cold, pour it again on the ginger, and let it stand at least three days. Afterwards boil the syrup again, and pour it *hot* over the ginger. Proceed in this manner till you find that the syrup has thoroughly penetrated the ginger, (which you may ascertain by its taste and appearance when you cut a piece off,) and till the syrup becomes very thick and rich. Then put it all into jars, and cover it closely.

If you put the syrup hot to the ginger at first, it will shrink and shrivel. After the first time, you have only to boil and reboil the syrup; as it is not probable that it will require any further clarifying if carefully skimmed. It will be greatly improved by adding some lemon-juice at the close of the last boiling.

TO PRESERVE CITRONS.

PARE off the outer skin of some fine citrons, and cut them into quarters. Take out the middle. You may divid each quarter into several pieces. Lay them for four or five hours in salt and water. Take them out, and then soak them in spring or pump water (changing it frequently) till all the saltness is extracted, and till the last water tastes perfectly fresh. Boil a small lump of alum, and scald them in the alum-water. It must be very weak, or it will communicate an unpleasant taste to the citrons; a lump the size of a hickory nut will suffice for six pounds. Afterwards simmer them two hours with layers of green vine leaves. Then make a syrup, with half a pint of water to each pound of loaf-sugar; boil and skim it well. When it is quite clear, put in the citrons, and boil them slowly, till they are so soft that a straw will pierce through them without breaking. Afterwards put them into a large dish, and set them in the sun to harden.

Prepare some lemons, by paring off the yellow rind very

thin, and cutting it into slips of uniform size and shape. Lay the lemon-rind in scalding water, to extract the bitterness Then take the pared lemons, cut them into quarters, measure a half pint of water to each lemon, and boil them to a mash. Strain the boiled lemon through a sieve, and to each pint of liquid allow a pound of the best double-refined loaf-sugar, for the second syrup. Melt the sugar in the liquid, and stir into it gradually some beaten white of egg; allowing one white to four pounds of sugar. Then set it over the fire; put the lemon-peel into the syrup, and let it boil in it till quite soft.

Put the citrons cold into a glass jar, and pour the hot syrup over them. Let the lemon remain with the citrons, as it will improve their flavour.

If you wish the citrons to be candied, boil down the second syrup to candy height, (that is, till it hangs in strings from the spoon,) and pour it over the citrons. Keep them well covered.

You may, if you choose, after you take the citrons from the alum-water, give them a boil in very weak ginger tea, made of the roots of green ginger if you can procure it; if not, of race ginger. Powdered ginger will not do at all. This ginger tea will completely eradicate any remaining taste of the salt or the alum. Afterwards cover the sides and bottom of the pan with vine leaves, put a layer of leaves between each layer of citron, and cover the top with leaves. Simmer the citrons in this two hours to green them.

In the same manner you may preserve water-melon rind, or the rind of cantelopes. Cut these rinds into stars, dia-monds, crescents, circles, or into any fanciful shape you choose. Be sure to pare off the outside skin before you put the rinds into the salt and water.

Pumpkin cut into slips, may be preserved according to the above receipt.

CANTELOPES OR MUSK-MELONS.—Take very small cantelopes before they are ripe. Shave a thin paring off the whole outside. Cut out a small piece or plug about an inch square, and through it extract all the seeds, &c. from the middle. Then return the plugs to the hole from whence you took them, and secure them with a needle and thread, or by tying a small string round the cantelope.

Lay the cantelopes for four or five hours in salt and water. Then put them into spring water to extract the salt, changing the water till you find it salt no longer. Scald them in weak alum-water. Make a syrup in the proportion of a pint of water to a pound of loaf-sugar, and boil the cantelopes in it till a straw will go through them. Then take them out, and set them in the sun to harden.

Prepare some fine ripe oranges, paring off the yellow rind very thin, and cutting it into slips, and then laying it in scalding water to extract the bitterness. Cut the oranges into pieces; allow a pint of water to each orange, and boil them to a pulp. Afterwards strain them, and allow to each pint of the liquid, a pound of the best loaf-sugar, and stir in a little beaten white of egg; one white to two pounds of sugar. This is for the second syrup. Boil the peel in it, skimming it well. When the peel is soft, take it all out; for if left among the cantelopes, it will communicate to it too strong a taste of the orange.

Put the cantelopes into your jars, and pour over them the hot syrup. Cover them closely, and keep them in a dry cool place.

Large cantelopes may be prepared for preserving (after you have taken off the outer rind) by cutting them into pieces according to the natural divisions with which they are fluted.

This receipt for preserving cantelopes whole, will do very

well for green lemons or limes, substituting lemon-peel and lemon-juice for that of oranges in the second syrup.

You may use some of the first syrup to boil up the pulp of the orange or lemons that has been left. It will make a sort of marmalade, that is very good for colds.

———·

PRESERVED WATER-MELON RIND.—Having pared off the green skin, cut the rind of a water-melon into pieces of any shape you please; stars, diamonds, circles, crescents or leaves, using for the purpose a sharp penknife. Weigh the pieces, and allow to each pound a pound and a half of loaf sugar. Set the sugar aside, and put the pieces of melon-rind into a preserving kettle, the bottom and sides of which you have lined with green vine leaves. Put a layer of vine leaves between each layer of melon-rind, and cover the top with leaves. Disperse among the pieces some very small bits of alum, each about the bigness of a grain of corn, and allowing one bit to every pound of the melon-rind. Pour in just water enough to cover the whole, and place a thick double cloth (or some other covering) over the top of the kettle to keep in the steam, which will improve the greening. Let it simmer (but not boil) for two hours. Then take out the pieces of melon-rind and spread them on dishes to cool. Afterwards if you find that they taste of the alum, simmer them in very weak ginger tea for about three hours. Then proceed to make your syrup. Melt the sugar in clear spring or pump water, allow-ing a pint of water to a pound and a half of sugar, and mixing in with it some white of egg beaten to a stiff froth. The white of one egg will be enough for two pounds of sugar. Boil and skim it; and when the scum ceases to rise, put in the melon-rind, and let it simmer an hour. Take it out and spread it to cool on dishes, return it to the syrup, and simmer

it another hour. After this take it out, and put it into a tureen.
Boil up the syrup again, and pour it over the melon-rind.
Cover it, and let it stand all night. Next morning give the
syrup another boil ; adding to it some lemon-juice, allowing
the juice of one lemon to a quart of the syrup. When you
find it so thick as to hang in a drop on the point of the spoon,
it is sufficiently done. Then put the rind into glass jars,
pour in the syrup, and secure the sweetmeats closely from
the air with paper dipped in brandy, and a leather outer cover.

This, if carefully done and well greened, is a very nice
sweetmeat, and may be used to ornament the top of creams,
jellies, jams, &c. laying it round in rings or wreaths.

Citrons may be preserved green in the same manner, first
paring off the outer skin and cutting them into quarters. Also
green limes.

———

PRESERVED PEPPERS.—For this purpose take the
small round peppers while they are green. With a sharp
penknife extract the seeds and cores ; and then put the out-
sides into a kettle with vine leaves, and a little alum to give
them firmness, and assist in keeping them green. Proceed
precisely as directed for the water-melon rind, in the above
receipt.

———

PUMPKIN CHIPS.—It is best to defer making this
sweetmeat (which will be found very fine) till late in the season when lemons are ripe and are to be had in plenty. Pumpkins (as they keep well) can generally be procured at any
time through the winter.

Take a fine pumpkin of a rich deep colour, pare off the
outer rind ; remove the seeds; and having sliced the best
part, cut it into chips of equal size, and as thin as you can

do them.   They should be in long narrow pieces, two inches in breadth, and four in length.   It is best to prepare the pumpkin the day before; and having weighed the chips, allow to each pound of them a pound of the best loaf sugar.   You must have several dozen of fine ripe lemons sufficient to furnish a jill of lemon-juice to each pound of pumpkin.   Having rolled them under your hand on a table to make them yield as much juice as possible, grate off the yellow rind, and mix it with the sugar.   Then having cut the lemons, squeeze out all the juice into a pitcher. Lay the pumpkin chips in a large pan or tureen, strewing the sugar among them.   Then having measured the lemon-juice in a wine-glass, (two common wine-glasses making one jill,) pour it over the pumpkin and sugar, cover the vessel, and let it stand all night.

Next day transfer the pumpkin, sugar, and lemon-juice to a preserving kettle, and boil it slowly for an hour or more, or till the pumpkin becomes all through tender, crisp, and transparent; but it must not be over the fire long enough to break and lose its form.   You must skim it thoroughly. The chips should be so thin as to curl up at the ends. When you think it is done, take up the pumpkin chips in a perforated skimmer that the syrup may drain through the holes back into the kettle.   Spread the chips to cool on large dishes, and pass the syrup through a flannel bag that has been first dipped in hot water.   When the chips are cold, put them into glass jars or tumblers, pour in the syrup, and lay on the top white paper dipped in brandy.   Then tie up the jars with leather, or with covers of thick white paper.

If you find that when cold the chips are not perfectly clear, crisp, and tender, give them another boil in the syrup before you put them up.

This, if well made, is a handsome and excellent sweetmeat it need not be eaten with cream, the syrup being so delicious as to require nothing to improve it. Shells of puff-paste first baked empty, and then filled with pumpkin chips, will be fcund very nice.

Musk-melon chips may be done in the same manner.

———

TO PRESERVE PINE-APPLES.—Take fine large pine-apples; pare them, and cut off a small round piece from the bottom of each; let the freshest and best of the top leaves remain on. Have ready on a slow fire, a large preserving kettle with a thin syrup barely sufficient to cover the fruit. In making this syrup allow a pound of fine loaf-sugar to every quart of water, and half the white of a beaten egg; all to be mixed before it goes on the fire. Then boil and skim it, and when the scum ceases to rise, put in the pine-apples, and simmer them slowly an hour. Then take them out to cool, cover them carefully and put them away till next day; saving the syrup in another vessel. Next day, put them into the same syrup, and simmer them again an hour. On the third day, repeat the process. The fourth day, make a strong fresh syrup, allowing but a pint of water to each pound of sugar, and to every two pounds the beaten white of one egg. When this syrup has boiled, and is completely skimmed, put in the pine-apples, and simmer them half an hour. Then take them out to cool, and set them aside till next morning. Boil them again half an hour in the same syrup, and repeat this for seven or eight days, or till you can pierce through the pine-apple with a straw from a corn-broom. At the last of these boilings enrich the syrup by allowing to each pound of sugar a quarter of a pound more; and, having boiled and skimmed it, put in the pine apples for half an hour. Then take them out, and when quite cold put each into a separate glass jar, and fill up with the syrup.

Pine apples may be preserved in slices by a very simple process. Pare them, and cut them into round pieces near an inch thick, and take out the core from the centre of each slice. Allow a pound of loaf-sugar to every pound of the sliced pine-apple. Powder the sugar, and strew it in layers between the slices of pine-apple. Cover it and let it set all night. Next morning measure some clear spring or pump water, allowing half a pint to each pound of sugar. Beat some white of egg, (one white to two pounds of sugar,) and when it is a very stiff froth, stir it gradually into the water. Then mix with it the pine-apple and sugar, and put the whole into a preserving kettle. Boil and skim it well, till the pine-apple is tender and bright all through. Then take it out, and when cold, put it up in wide-mouthed glass jars, or in large tumblers.

TO PREPARE FRESH PINE-APPLES.—Cut off the top and bottom and pare off the rind. Then cut the pine-apples in round slices half an inch thick, and put them into a deep dish, sprinkling every slice with powdered loaf-sugar. Cover them, and let them lie in the sugar for an hour or two, before they are to be eaten.

PRESERVED LEMONS.—Take large fine ripe lemons, that have no blemishes. Choose those with thin, smooth rinds. With a sharp knife scoop a hole in the stalk end of each, large enough to admit the handle of a tea-spoon. This hole is to enable the syrup to penetrate the inside of the lemons. Put them into a preserving kettle with clear water, and boil them gently till you find them tender, keeping the kettle uncovered. Then take them out, drain, and cool them, and put them into a small tub. Prepare a thin syrup of a pound of loaf-sugar to a quart of water. When you have boiled and skimmed it, pour it over the lemons and cover them. Let them stand in the syrup till next day. Then pour the syrup from the lemons, and spread them on a large dish. Boil it a quarter of an hour, and pour it over them again, having first returned them to the tub. Cover them, and let them again stand till next day, when you must again boil the syrup and pour it over them. Repeat this process every day till you find that the lemons are quite clear, and that the syrup has penetrated them thoroughly. If you find the syrup becoming too weak, add a little more sugar to it. Finally, make a strong syrup in the proportion of half a pint of water to a pound of sugar, adding a jill of raw lemon-juice squeezed from fresh lemons, and allowing to every two pounds of sugar the beaten white of an egg. Mix all well together in the kettle. Boil and skim it, and when the scum ceases to rise, pour the syrup boiling hot over the lemons; and covering them closely, let them stand undisturbed for four days. Then look at them, and if you find that they have not sucked in enough of the syrup to make the inside very sweet, boil them gently in the syrup for a quarter of an hour. When they are cold, put them up in glass jars.

You may green lemons by burying them in a kettle of vine leaves when you give them the first boiling in the clear water.

Limes may be preserved by this receipt; also oranges.

To prepare fresh oranges for eating, peel and cut them in round slices and remove the seeds. Strew powdered loaf-sugar over them. Cover them and let them stand an hour before they are eaten.

ORANGE MARMALADE.—Take fine large ripe oranges, with thin deep-coloured skins. Weigh them, and allow to each pound of oranges a pound of loaf-sugar. Pare off the yellow outside of the rind from half the oranges, as thin as possible; and putting it into a pan with plenty of cold water, cover it closely (placing a double cloth beneath the tin cover) to keep in the steam, and boil it slowly till it is so soft that the head of a pin will pierce it. In the mean time grate the rind from the remaining oranges, and put it aside; quarter the oranges, and take out all the pulp and the juice; removing the seeds and core. Put the sugar into a preserving kettle, with a half pint of clear water to each pound, and mix it with some beaten white of egg, allowing one white of egg, to every two pounds of sugar. When the sugar is all dissolved, put it on the fire, and boil and skim it till it is quite clear and thick. Next take the boiled parings, and pound them to a paste in a mortar; put this paste into the sugar, and boil and stir it ten minutes. Then put it in the pulp and juice of the oranges, and the grated rind, (which will much improve the colour,) and boil all together for about half an nour, till it is a transparent mass. When cold, put it up in glass jars, laying brandy paper on the top.

Lemon marmalade may be made in a similar manner, but you must allow a pound and a half of sugar to each pound of lemons.

———

ORANGE JELLY.—Take twenty large ripe oranges, and grate the yellow rind from seven of them. Dissolve an ounce of isinglass in as much warm water as will cover it. Mix the juice with a pound of loaf-sugar broken up, and add the grated rind and the isinglass. Put it into a porcelain pan over hot coals, and stir it till it boils. Then skim it well.   Boil it ten minutes, and strain it (but do not squeeze it) through a jelly-bag till it is quite clear.   Put it into a mould to congeal, and when you want to turn it out dip the mould into luke-warm water.   Or you may put it into glasses at once.

You must have a pint of juice to a pound of sugar.

A few grains of saffron boiled with the jelly will improve the colour without affecting the taste.

PRESERVED PEACHES.

TAKE large juicy ripe peaches ; free-stones are the best, as they have a finer flavour than the cling-stones, and are much more manageable both to preserve, and to eat.   Pare them, and cut them in half, or in quarters, leaving out the stones, the half of which you must save.   To every pound of the peaches allow a pound of loaf-sugar.   Powder the sugar, and strew it among your peaches.   Cover them and let them stand all night.   Crack half the peach-stones, break them up, put them into a small sauce-pan and boil them slowly in as much water as will cover them.   Then when the water is well flavoured with the peach-kernels, strain them out, and set the water aside.   Take care not to use too much of the kernel-water ; a very little will suffice.   Put the peaches into a preserving kettle, and boil them in their juice over a quick fire, (adding the kernel-water,) and skimming them all the time. When they are quite clear, which should be in half an hour, take them off, and put them into a tureen.   Boil the syrup five minutes longer, and pour it hot over the peaches.   When they are cool, put them into glass jars, and tie them up with paper dipped in brandy laid next to them.

Apricots, nectarines, and large plums may be preserved in the same manner.

PEACHES FOR COMMON USE.—Take ripe free-stone peaches; pare, stone, and quarter them. To six pounds of the cut peaches allow three pounds of the best brown sugar. Strew the sugar among the peaches, and set them away. Next morning add a handful of the kernels, put the whole into a preserving kettle, and boil it slowly about an hour and three quarters, or two hours, skimming it well. When cold, put it up in jars, and keep it for pies, or for any common purpose.

BRANDY PEACHES.—Take large white or yellow free-stone peaches, the finest you can procure. They must not be too ripe. Rub off the down with a flannel, score them down the seam with a large needle, and prick every peach to the stone in several places. Scald them with boiling water, and let them remain in the water till it becomes cold, keeping them well covered. Repeat the scalding three times: it is to make them white. Then wipe them, and spread them on a soft table-cloth, covering them over with several folds. Let them remain in the cloth to dry. Afterwards put them into a tureen, or a large jar, and pour on as much white French brandy as will cover them well. Carefully keep the air from them, and let them remain in the brandy for a week. Then make a syrup in the usual manner, allowing to each pound of peaches a pound of loaf-sugar and half a pint of water mixed with a very little beaten white of egg; one white to every two pounds of sugar.

When the syrup has boiled, and been well skimmed put in the peaches and boil them slowly till they look clear; but do not keep them boiling more than half an hour. Then take them out, drain them, and put them into large glass jars. Mix the syrup, when it is cold, with the brandy in which you had the peaches, and pour it over them. Instead of scalding the peaches to whiten them, you may lay them for an hour in sufficient cold weak lye to cover them well. Turn them frequently while in the lye, and wipe them dry afterwards.

Pears and apricots may be preserved in brandy, according to the above receipt. The skin of the pears should be taken off, but the stems left on.

Large egg plums may be preserved in the same manner.

Another way of preparing brandy peaches is, after rubbing off the down and pricking them, to put them into a preserving kettle with cold water, and simmer them slowly till they become hot all through; but they must not be allowed to boil. Then dry them in a cloth, and let them lie till they are cold, covering them closely from the air. Dissolve loaf-sugar in the best white brandy, (a pound of sugar to a quart of brandy,) and having put the peaches into large glass jars, pour the brandy and sugar over them (without boiling) and cover the jars well with leather.

Pears, apricots, and egg plums may also be done in this manner.

PEACH MARMALADE.—Take ripe yellow free-stone peaches; pare, stone, and quarter them. To each pound of peaches, allow three quarters of a pound of powdered loaf sugar, and half an ounce of bitter almonds, or peach-kernels blanched in scalding water, and pounded smooth in a mortar. Scald the peaches in a very little water, mash them to a pulp, mix them with the sugar and pounded almonds, and put the whole into a preserving kettle. Let it boil to a smooth thick jam, skimming and stirring it well, and keeping the pan covered as much as possible. Fifteen minutes will generally suffice for boiling it. When cold, put it up in glass jars.

Plum marmalade may be made in this manner, flavouring it with pounded plum-kernels.

PEACH JELLY.—Take fine juicy free-stone peaches, and pare and quarter them. Scald them in a very little water, drain and mash them, and squeeze the juice through a jelly-bag. To every pint of juice allow a pound of loaf-sugar, and a few of the peach-kernels. Having broken up the kernels and boiled them by themselves for a quarter of an hour in just as much water as will cover them, strain off the kernel-water, and add it to the juice. Mix the juice with the sugar, and when it is melted, boil them together fifteen minutes, till it becomes a thick jelly. Skim it well when it boils. Try the jelly by taking a little in a spoon and holding it in the open air to see if it congeals. If you find, that after sufficient boiling, it still continues thin, you can make it congeal by stirring in an ounce or more of isinglass, dissolved and strained. When the jelly is done, put it into tumblers, and lay on the top double tissue paper cut exactly to fit the inside of the glass; pressing it down with your fingers.

You may make plum jelly in the same manner, allowing a pound and a half of sugar to a pint of juice.

TO PRESERVE APRICOTS.—Take ripe apricots; scald them, peel them, cut them in half, and extract the stones. Then weigh the apricots, and to each pound allow a pound of loaf-sugar. Put them into a tureen or large pan, in alternate layers of apricots and sugar; cover them, and let them stand all night. Next morning put all together into a preserving kettle, and boil them moderately a quarter of an hour

Then take them out, spread them on dishes, and let them stand till next day. Then boil them again in the same syrup another quarter of an hour. Afterwards, spread them out to cool, put them into glass jars, and pour the syrup over them.

Peaches may be preserved in the same manner. Also large plums or green gages; but to the plums you must allow additional sugar.

TO DRY PEACHES.—The best peaches for drying are juicy free-stones. They must be quite ripe. Cut them in half, and take out the stones. It is best not to pare them; as dried peaches are much richer with the skin on, and it dissolves and becomes imperceptible when they are cooked. Spread them out in a sunny balcony or on a scaffold, and let them dry gradually till they become somewhat like leather; always bringing them in at sunset, and not putting them out if the weather is damp or cloudy. They may also be dried in kilns or large ovens.

Apples are dried in the same manner, except that they must be pared and quartered.

Cherries also may be dried in the sun, first taking out all the stones. None but the largest and best cherries should be used for drying.

TO PRESERVE QUINCES.

TAKE large, yellow, ripe quinces, and having washed and wiped them, pare them, and extract the cores. Quarter the quinces, or cut them into slices half an inch thick, and lay them in scalding water (closely covered) and boil them till tender—lest they harden in the sugar. Put the parings, cores, and seeds into a preserving kettle.

cover them with the water in which you coddled the quinces, and boil them an hour, keeping them closely covered all the time. To every pint of this liquor allow a pound of loaf-sugar; and having dissolved the sugar in it, ut it over the fire in the preserving kettle. Boil it up nd skim it, and when the scum has ceased rising, put in the quinces, and boil them till they are red, tender, and clear all through, but not till they break. Keep the kettle closely covered while the quinces are in it, if you wish to have them bright coloured. You may improve the colour by boiling with them a little cochineal sifted through a muslin rag.

When they are done, take them out, spread them on large dishes to cool, and then put them into glasses. Give the syrup another boil up, and it will be like a fine jelly. Pour it hot over the quinces, and when cold, cover the jars, pasting paper round the covers.

———

TO PRESERVE QUINCES WHOLE.—Take those that are large, smooth, and yellow; pare them and extract the cores, carefully removing all the blemishes. Boil the quinces in a close kettle with the cores and parings, in sufficient water to cover them. In half an hour take them out, spread them to cool, and add to the cores and parings some small inferior quinces cut in quarters, but not pared or cored; and pour in some more water, just enough to boil them. Cover the pan, and let them simmer for an hour. Then take it off, strain the liquid, measure it, and to each quart allow a pound of loaf sugar. Put the sugar to melt in the liquid, and let it set all night. Next day boil the quinces in it for a quarter of an hour, and then take them out and cool them, saving the syrup. On the following day repeat the same; and the fourth day add a quarter of a pound more sugar to each pint of the syrup, and boil the quinces in it twelve minutes. If by this time they are not tender, bright, and transparent all through, repeat the boiling.

When they are quite done, put quince jelly or marmalade into the holes from whence you took the cores; put the quinces into glass jars and pour the syrup over them. If convenient, it is a very nice way to put up each quince in a separate tumbler.

QUINCE JELLY.—Take fine ripe yellow quinces, wash them and remove all the blemishes. Cut them in pieces, but do not pare or core them. Put them into a preserving-pan with clear spring water. If you are obliged to use river water, filter it first; allowing one pint to twelve large quinces. Boil them gently till they are all soft and broken. Then put them into a jelly-bag, and do not squeeze it till after the clear liquid has ceased running. Of this you must make the *best* jelly, allowing to each pint a pound of loaf-sugar. Having dissolved the sugar in the liquid, boil them together about twenty minutes, or till you have a thick jelly.

In the mean time squeeze out all that is left in the bag. It will not be clear, but you can make of it a very good jelly for common purposes.

QUINCE MARMALADE.—Take ten pounds of ripe yellow quinces; and having washed them clean, pare and core them, and cut them into small pieces. To each pound of the cut quinces allow half a pound of powdered loaf-sugar. Put the parings and cores into a kettle with water enough to cover them, and boil them slowly till they are all to pieces, and quite soft. Then having put the quinces with the sugar into a porcelain preserving kettle, strain over them, through a cloth, the liquid from the parings and cores. Add a little cochineal powdered, and sifted through thin muslin. Boil the whole over a quick fire till it becomes a thick smooth mass, keeping it covered except when you are skimming it; and always after skimming, stir it up well from the bottom.

When cold, put it up in glass jars. If you wish to use it soon, put it warm into moulds, and when it is cold, set the moulds in luke-warm water, and the marmalade will turn out easily.

QUINCE CHEESE.—Have fine ripe quinces, and pare and core them. Cut them into pieces, and weigh them; and to each pound of the cut quinces, allow half a pound of the best brown sugar. Put the cores and parings into a kettle with water enough to cover them, keeping the lid of the kettle closed. When you find that they are all boiled to pieces and quite soft, strain off the water over the sugar, and when it is entirely dissolved, put it over the fire and boil it to a thick syrup, skimming it well. When no more scum rises, put in the quinces, cover them closely, and boil them all day over a slow fire, stirring them and mashing them down with a spoon till they are a thick smooth paste. Then take it out, and put it into buttered tin pans or deep dishes. Let it set to get cold. It will then turn out so firm that you may cut it into slices like cheese. Keep it in a dry place in broad stone pots. It is intended for the tea-table.

PRESERVED APPLES.

Take fine ripe pippin or bell-flower apples. Pare and core them, and either leave them whole, or cut them into quarters

Weigh them, and to each pound of apples allow a pound of loaf-sugar. Put the apples into a stew-pan with just water enough to cover them, and let them boil slowly for about half an hour. They must be only parboiled. Then strain the apple water over the sugar into a preserving kettle, and when the sugar is melted put it on the fire with the yellow rind of some lemons pared thin, allowing two lemons to a dozen apples. Boil the syrup till clear and thick, skimming it carefully; then put in the apples, and after they have boiled slowly a quarter of an hour, add the juice of the lemons. Let it boil about fifteen minutes longer, or till the apples are tender and clear, but not till they break. When they are cold, put them into jars, and covering them closely, let them set a week. At the end of that time give them another boil in the same syrup; apples being more difficult to keep than any other fruit.

You may colour them red by adding, when you boil them in the syrup, a little cochineal.

BAKED APPLES.—Take a dozen fine large juicy apples, and pare and core them, but do not cut them in pieces. Put them side by side into a large baking-pan, and fill up with white sugar the holes from whence you have extracted the cores. Pour into each a little lemon-juice, or a few drops of essence of lemon, and stick in every one a long piece of lemon-peel evenly cut. Into the bottom of the pan put a very little water, just enough to prevent the apples from burning. Bake them about an hour, or till they are tender all through, but not till they break. When done, set them away to get cold.

If closely covered they will keep two days. They may be eaten at tea with cream. Or at dinner with a boiled custard poured over them. Or you may cover them with sweetened cream flavoured with a little essence of lemon, and whipped to a froth. Heap the froth over every apple so as to conceal them entirely.

———

APPLE JELLY.—Take twenty large ripe juicy pippins. Pare, core, and chop them to pieces. Put them into a jar with the yellow rind of four lemons, grated off with a grater. Cover the jar closely, and set it into a pot of hot water. Keep the water boiling hard all round it till the apples are dissolved. Then strain them through a jelly-bag, and mix with the liquid the juice of the lemons. To each pint of the mixed juice allow a pound of loaf-sugar. Put them into a porcelain kettle, and when the sugar is melted, set it on the fire, and boil and skim it for about twenty minutes, or till it becomes a thick jelly. Put it into tumblers, and cover it with double tissue paper nicely fitted to the inside of the top.

The red or Siberian crab apple makes a delicious jelly, prepared in the above manner.

———

APPLE BUTTER.—This is a compound of apples and cider boiled together till of the consistence of soft butter. It is a very good article on the tea-table, or at luncheon. It can only be made of sweet new cider fresh from the press, and not yet fermented.

Fill a very large kettle with cider, and boil it till reduced to one half the original quantity. Then have ready some fine juicy apples, pared, cored, and quartered; and put as many into the kettle as can be kept moist by the cider. Stir it frequently, and when the apples are stewed quite soft, take them out with a skimmer that has holes in it, and put them into a tub. Then add more app'es to the cider, and stew them soft in the same manner, stirring them nearly all the time with a stick. Have at hand some more cider ready boiled, to thin the apple butter in case you should find it too thick in the kettle.

If you make a large quantity, (and it is not worth while to prepare apple butter on a small scale,) it will take a day to stew the apples. At night leave them to cool in the tubs, (which must be covered with cloths,) and finish next day by boiling the apple and cider again till the consistence is that of soft marmalade, and the colour a very dark brown.

Twenty minutes or half an hour before you finally take it from the fire, add powdered cinnamon, cloves, and nutmeg to your taste. If the spice is boiled too long, it will lose its flavour.

When it is cold, put it into stone jars, and cover it closely. If it has been well made, and sufficiently boiled, it will keep a year or more.

It must not be boiled in a brass or bell-metal kettle, on account of the verdigris which the acid will collect in it, and which will render the apple butter extremely unwholesome, not to say poisonous.

TO PRESERVE GREEN CRAB APPLES.—Having washed your crab apples, (which should be full grown,) cover the bottom and sides of your preserving kettle with vine leaves, and put them in; spreading a thick layer of vine leaves over them. Fill up the kettle with cold water, and hang it over a slow fire early in the morning; simmer them slowly, but do not allow them to boil. When they are quite yellow, take them out, peel off the skin with a penknife, and extract the cores very neatly. Put them again into the kettle with fresh vine leaves and fresh water, and hang them again over a slow fire to simmer, but not to boil. When they have remained long enough in the second vine leaves to become green, take them out, weigh them, and allow a pound and a half of loaf-sugar to each pound of crab apples. Then after the kettle has been well washed and wiped, put them into it with a thick layer of sugar between each layer of apples, and about half a pint of water, for each pound and a half of sugar. Add the grated peel and the juice of some lemons. Boil them gently till they are quite clear and tender throughout. Skim them well, and keep the kettle covered when you are not skimming. When done, spread them on large dishes to cool, and then tie them up in glass jars with brandy papers.

TO PRESERVE RED CRAB APPLES.—Take red or Siberian crab apples when they are quite ripe and the seeds are black. Wash and wipe them, and put them into a kettle with sufficient water to cover them. Simmer them very slowly till you find that the skin will come off easily. Then take them out and peel and core them ; extract the cores carefully with a small knife, so as not to break the apples. Then weigh them, and to every pound of crab apples allow a pound and a half of loaf-sugar and a half pint of water. Put the sugar and water into a preserving kettle, and when they are melted together, set it over the fire and let it boil. After skimming it once, put in the crab apples, adding a little cochineal powder rubbed with a knife into a very small quantity of white brandy till it has dissolved. This will greatly improve the colour of the apples. Cover them and let them boil till clear and tender, skimming the syrup when necessary. Then spread them out on dishes, and when they are cold, put them into glass jars and pour the syrup over them.

The flavour will be greatly improved by boiling with them

in the syrup, a due proportion of lemon-juice and the peel of tne lemons grated so as to have the yellow rind only. If you use lemon-juice put a smaller quantity of water to the sugar. Allow one large lemon or two smaller ones to two pounds of crab apples.

If you find that after they have been kept awhile, the syrup inclines to become dry or candied, give it another boil with the crab apples in it, adding a tea-cup full of water to about three or four pounds of the sweetmeat.

TO PRESERVE GREEN GAGES.

TAKE large fine green gages that are all perfectly ripe. Weigh them, and to each pound of fruit allow a pound and a half of loaf-sugar. Put a layer of fresh vine leaves at the bottom of a porcelain preserving kettle, place on it a layer of gages, then cover them with a layer of vine leaves, and so on alternately, finishing with a layer of leaves at the top. Fill up the kettle with hard water, and set it over a slow fire. When the gages rise to the top, take them out and peel them, putting them on a sieve as you do so. Then replace them in the kettle with fresh vine leaves and water; cover them very closely, so that no steam can escape, and hang them up at some distance above the fire to green slowly for six hours. They should be warm all the time, but must not boil. When they are a fine green, take them carefully out, spread them on a hair sieve to drain, and make a syrup of the sugar, allow-ing a half pint of water to each pound and a half of sugar. When it has boiled and been skimmed, put in the green gages and boil them gently for a quarter of an hour. Then take them out and spread them to cool. Next day boil them in the same syrup for another quarter of an hour. When cold, put them into glass jars with the syrup, and tie them up with brandy paper.

You may green these, or any other sweetmeats, by substituting for the vine-leaves, layers of the fresh green husks tha inclose the ears of young indian corn.

TO PRESERVE PLUMS.—Take fine ripe plums: weigh them, and to each pound allow a pound and a half of loaf-sugar. Put them into a pan, and scald them in boiling water to make the skins come off easily. Peel them, and throw them as you do so into a large china pitcher. Let them set for an hour or two, and then take them out, saving all the juice that has exuded from them while in the pitcher. Spread the plums out on large dishes, and cover them with half the sugar you have allotted to them, (it must be previously powdered,) and let them lie in it all night. Next morning pour the juice out of the pitcher into a porcelain preserving kettle, add the last half of the sugar to it, and let it melt over the fire. When it has boiled skim it, and then put in the plums. Boil them over a moderate fire, for about half an hour. Then take them out one by one with a spoon, and spread them on large dishes to cool. If the syrup is not sufficiently thick and clear, boil and skim it a little longer till it is. Put the plums into glass jars and pour the syrup warm over them.

The flavour will be much improved by boiling in the syrup with the fruit a handful or more of the kernels of plums, blanched in scalding water and broken in half. Take the kernels out of the syrup before you pour it into the jars.

You may preserve plums whole, without peeling, by pricking them deeply at each end with a large needle.

Green gages and damsons may be preserved according to this receipt

PLUMS FOR COMMON USE.—Take fine ripe plums, and cut them in half. Extract all the stones, and spread out the plums on large dishes. Set the dishes on the sunny roof of a porch or shed, and let the plums have the full benefit of the sun for three or four days, taking them in as soon as it is off, or if the sky becomes cloudy. This will half dry them. Then pack them closely in stone jars with a thick layer of the best brown sugar between every layer of plums; putting plenty of sugar at the bottom and top of the jars. Cover them closely, and set them away in a dry place.

If they have been properly managed, they will keep a year; and are very good for pies and other purposes, in the winter and spring.

Peaches may be prepared for keeping in the same manner.

————

EGG PLUMS WHOLE.—Take large egg plums that are all quite ripe, and prick them all over with a small silver fork. Leave on the stems. To four pounds of plums allow four pounds and a half of loaf-sugar, broken small or powdered. Put the plums and sugar into a preserving kettle, and pour in one quart of clear hard water. Hang the kettle over a moderate fire, and boil and skim it. As soon as the skin begins to crack or shrivel, take out the plums one at a time, (leaving the syrup on the fire,) and spread them on large dishes to cool. Place them in the open air, and as soon as they are cool enough to be touched with your fingers, smooth the skin down where it is broken or ruffled. When quite cold, return them to the syrup, (which in the mean time must have been kept slowly simmering,) and boil the plums again till they are quite clear, but not till they break. Put them warm into large glass or queen's-ware jars, and pour the syrup over them.

TO PRESERVE PEARS.

TAKE large fine juicy pears that are all perfectly ripe, and pare them smoothly and thin; leaving on the stems, but cutting out the black top at the blossom end of the fruit. As you pare them, lay them in a pan of cold water. Make a thin syrup, allowing a quart of water to a pound of loaf-sugar. Simmer the pears in it for about half an hour. Then put them into a tureen, and let them lie in the syrup for two days. There must be syrup enough to cover them well. After two days, drain the syrup from the pears, and add to it more sugar. in the proportion of a pound to each pint of the thin syrup. Stir in a very little beaten white of egg, (not more than one white to three or four pounds of sugar,) add some fresh lemon-rind grated thin, and set the syrup over a brisk fire. Boil it for ten minutes, and skim it well. Then add sufficient lemon-juice to flavour it; and put in the pears. Simmer them in the strong syrup till they are quite transparent. Then take them out, spread them to cool, and stick a clove in the blossom end of each. Put them into glass jars; and having kept the syrup warm over the fire while the pears were cooling, pour it over them.

If you wish to have them red, add a little powdered cochineal to the strong syrup when you put in your pears.

BAKED PEARS.—The best for baking are the large late ones, commonly called pound pears. Pare them, cut them in half, and take out the cores. Lay them in a deep white dish, with a thin slip of fresh lemon-peel in the place from which each core was taken. Sprinkle them with sugar, and strew some whole cloves or some powdered cinnamon among them Pour into the dish some port wine. To a dozen large pears you may allow one pound of sugar, and a pint of wine. Cover the dish with a large sheet of brown paper tied on; set it in a moderate oven, and let them bake till tender all through, which you may ascertain by sticking a broom twig through them. They will be done in about an hour, or they may probably require more time; but you must not let them remain long enough in the oven to break or fall to pieces. When cool, put them up in a stone jar. In cold weather they will keep a week.

To bake smaller pears, pare them, but leave on the stems, and do not core them. Put them into a deep dish with fresh lemon or orange-peel; throw on them some brown sugar or molasses; pour in at the bottom a little water to keep them from burning; and bake them till tender throughout.

TO PRESERVE GOOSEBERRIES.

THE best way of preserving gooseberries is with jelly. They should be full grown but green. Take six quarts of gooseberries, and select three quarts of the largest and finest to preserve whole, reserving the others for the jelly. Put the whole ones into a pan with sufficient water to cover them, and simmer them slowly till they begin to be tender; but do not keep them on the fire till they are likely to burst. Take them out carefully with a perforated skimmer to drain the warm water from them, and lay them directly in a pan of cold water. Put those that you intend for the jelly into a stew-pan, allowing to each quart of gooseberries half a pint of water. Boil them fast till they go all to pieces, and stir and mash them with a spoon. Then put them into a jelly-bag that has been first dipped in hot water, and squeeze through it all the juice. Measure the juice, and to each pint allow a pound and a half of loaf-sugar. Break up the sugar, and put it into a preserving kettle ; pour the juice over it, and let it stand to melt, stirring it frequently. When it has all dissolved, set it over the fire, put the gooseberries into it, and let them boil twenty minutes, or till they are quite clear, and till the jelly is thick and congeals in the spoon when you hold it in the air. If the gooseberries seem likely to break, take them out carefully, and let the jelly boil by itself till it is finished. When all is done, put up the gooseberries and the jelly together in glass jars.

Strawberries, raspberries, grapes, currants or any small fruit may in a similar manner be preserved in jelly.

TO STEW GOOSEBERRIES.—Top and tail them. Pour some boiling water on the gooseberries, cover them up, and let them set about half an hour, or till the skin is quite tender, but not till it bursts, as that will make the juice run out into the water. Then pour off the water, and mix with the gooseberries an equal quantity of sugar. Put them into a porcelain stew-pan or skillet, and set it on hot coals, or on a charcoal furnace. In a few minutes you may begin to mash them against the side of the pan with a wooden spoon. Let them stew about half an hour, stirring them frequently. They must be quite cold before they are used for any thing.

GOOSEBERRY FOOL.—Having stewed two quarts of gooseberries in the above manner, stir them as soon as they are cold into a quart of rich boiling milk. Grate in a nutmeg, and covering the pan, let the gooseberries simmer in the milk for five minutes. Then stir in the beaten yolks of two or three eggs, and immediately remove it from the fire. Keep on the cover a few minutes longer ; then turn out the mixture into a deep dish or a glass bowl, and set it away to get cold, before it goes to table. Eat it with sponge-cake. It will probably require additional sugar, stirred in at the last.

Gooseberries prepared in this manner make a very good pudding, with the addition of a little grated bread. Use both whites and yolks of the eggs. Stir the mixture well, and bake it in a deep dish. Eat it cold, with sugar grated over it.

TO BOTTLE GOOSEBERRIES.—For this purpose the gooseberries must be large and full grown, but quite green. Top and tail them, and put them into wide-mouthed bottles as far up as the beginning of the neck. Cover the bottom of a large boiler or kettle with saw-dust or straw. Stand the bottles of gooseberries (slightly corked) upright in the boiler, and pour round them cold water to each, as far up as the fruit. Put a brisk fire under the boiler, and when the water boils up, instantly take out the bottles and fill them up to the mouth with boiling water, which you must have ready in a tea-kettle. Cork them again slightly, and when quite cold put in the corks very tight and seal them. Lay the bottles on their sides in a box of dry sand, and turn them every day for four or five weeks. If properly managed, the gooseberries will keep a year, and may be used at any time, by stewing them with sugar.

You may bottle damsons in the same manner; also grapes.

PRESERVED RASPBERRIES.

Take a quantity of ripe raspberries, and set aside the half, selecting for that purpose the largest and firmest. Then put the remainder into your preserving pan, mash them, and set them over the fire. As soon as they have come to a boil, take them out, let them cool, and then squeeze them through a bag.

While they are cooling, prepare your sugar, which must be fine loaf. Allow a pound of sugar to every quart of whole raspberries. Having washed the kettle clean, put the sugar into it, allowing half a pint of cold water to two pounds of sugar. When it has melted in the water, put it on the fire, and boil it till the scum ceases to rise, and it is a thick syrup; taking care to skim it well. Then put in the whole raspberries, and boil them rapidly a few minutes, but not long enough to cause them to burst. Take them out with a skimmer full of holes, and spread them on a large dish to cool. Then mix with the syrup the juice of those you boiled first, and let it boil about ten or fifteen minutes. Lastly, put in the whole fruit, and give it one more boil, seeing that it does not break.

Put it warm into glass jars or tumblers, and when quite cold cover it closely with paper dipped in brandy, tying another paper tightly over it.

Strawberries may be done in the same manner; blackberries also.

RASPBERRY JAM.—Take fine raspberries that are perfectly ripe. Weigh them, and to each pound of fruit allow three quarters of a pound of fine loaf-sugar. Mash the raspberries, and break up the sugar. Then mix them together. and put them into a preserving kettle over a good fire. Stir them frequently and skim them The jam will be done in half an hour. Put it warm into glasses. and lay on the top a white paper cut exactly to fit the inside and dipped in brandy Then tie on another cover of very thick white paper.

Make blackberry jam in the same manner.

TO PRESERVE CRANBERRIES.—The cranberries must be large and ripe. Wash them, and to six quarts of cranberries allow nine pounds of the best loaf sugar. Take three quarts of the cranberries, and put them into a stew-pan with a pint and a half of water. Cover the pan, and boil or stew them till they are all to pieces. Then squeeze the juice through a jelly-bag. Put the sugar into a preserving kettle, pour the cranberry juice over it and let it stand till it is all melted, stirring it up frequently. Then place the kettle over the fire, and put in the remaining three quarts of whole cranberries. Let them boil till they are tender, clear, and of a bright colour, skimming them frequently. When done, put them warm into jars with the syrup, which should be like a thick jelly.

RED CURRANT JELLY.—The currants should be perfectly ripe and gathered on a dry day. Strip them from the stalks, and put them into a stone jar. Cover the jar, and set it up to the neck in a kettle of boiling water. Keep the water boiling round the jar till the currants are all broken, stirring them up occasionally. Then put them into a jelly-bag, and squeeze out all the juice. To each pint of juice allow a pound and a quarter of the best loaf-sugar. Put the sugar into a porcelain kettle, pour the juice over it, and stir it frequently till i is all melted. Then set the kettle over a moderate fire, and let it boil twenty minutes, or till you find that the jelly congeals in the spoon when you hold it in the air; skim it carefully all the time. When the jelly is done, pour it warm into tumblers, and cover each with two rounds of white tissue paper, cut to fit exactly the inside of the glass.

Jelly of gooseberries, plums, raspberries, strawberries, barberries, blackberries, grapes, and other small fruit may all be made in this manner.

WHITE CURRANT JELLY.—The currants should be quite ripe, and gathered on a dry day. Having stripped them from the stalks, put them into a close stone jar, and set it in a kettle of boiling water. When all the currants are broken, take them out and strain them through a linen cloth. To each pint of juice allow a pound and a quarter of the best double refined loaf-sugar; break it small, and put it into a porcelain preserving pan with barely sufficient water to melt it; not quite half a pint to a pound and a quarter of sugar; it must be either clear spring water or river water filtered. Stir up the sugar while it is dissolving, and when all is melted, put it over a brisk fire, and boil and skim it till clear and thick. When the scum ceases to rise, put in the white currant juice and boil it fast for ten minutes. Then put it warm into tumblers, and when it is cold, cover it with double white tissue paper.

In making this jelly, use only a silver spoon, and carefully observe all the above precautions, that it may be transparent and delicate. If it is not quite clear and bright when done boiling, you may run it again through a jelly-bag.

White raspberry jelly may be prepared in the same manner. A very nice sweetmeat is made of white raspberries preserved whole, by putting them in white currant jelly during the ten minutes that you are boiling the juice with the syrup. You may also preserve red raspberries whole, by boiling them in red currant jelly.

BLACK CURRANT JELLY.—Take large ripe black currants; strip them from the stalks, and mash them with the back of a ladle. Then put them into a preserving kettle with a tumbler of water to each quart of currants; cover closely, set it over a moderate fire, and when the currants have come to a boil, take them out, and squeeze them through a jelly-bag. To each pint of juice you may allow about a pound of loaf-sugar, and (having washed the preserving kettle perfectly clean) put in the sugar with the juice; stir them together till well mixed and dissolved, and then boil it not longer than ten minutes; as the juice of black currants being very thick will come to a jelly very soon, and if boiled too long will be tough and ropy.

Black currant jelly is excellent for sore throats; and if eaten freely on the first symptoms of the disease, will frequently check it without any other remedy. It would be well for all families to keep it in the house.

GRAPE JELLY.—Take ripe juicy grapes, pick them from the stems; put them into a large earthen pan, and mash them with the back of a wooden ladle, or with a potato beetle. Put them into a kettle, (without any water,) cover them closely, and let them boil for a quarter of an hour; stirring them up occasionally from the bottom. Then squeeze them through a jelly-bag, and to each pint of juice allow a pound of loaf-sugar Dissolve the sugar in the grape juice; then put it over a quick fire in a preserving kettle, and boil and skim it twenty minutes When it is a clear thick jelly, take it off, put it warm into tumblers, and cover them with double tissue paper cut to fit the inside.

In the same manner you may make an excellent jelly for common use, of ripe fox grapes and the best brown sugar; mixing with the sugar before it goes on the fire, a little beaten white of egg; allowing two whites to two pounds of sugar.

BRANDY GRAPES.—Take some large close bunches of fine grapes, (they must be quite ripe,) and allow to each bunch a quarter of a pound of bruised sugar candy. Put the grapes and the sugar candy into large jars, (about two-thirds full,) and fill them up with French brandy. Tie them up closely, and keep them in a dry place. Morella cherries may be done in the same manner.

Foreign grapes are kept in bunches, laid lightly in earthen jars of dry saw-dust.

TO KEEP WILD GRAPES.—Gather the small black wild grapes late in the season, after they have been ripened by a frost. Pick them from the stems, and put them into stone jars, (two-thirds full,) with layers of brown sugar, and fill them up with cold molasses. They will keep all winter; and they make good common pies. If they incline to ferment in the jars, give them a boil with additional sugar.

ΓO PRESERVE STRAWBERRIES.

STRAWBERRIES for preserving should be large and ripe. They will keep best if gathered in dry weather, when there has been no rain for at least two days. Having hulled, or picked off the green, select the largest and firmest, and spread them out separately on flat dishes; having first weighed them, and allowed to each pound of strawberries a pound of powdered loaf-sugar. Sift half the sugar over them. Then take the inferior strawberries that were left, and those that are over-ripe; mix with them an equal quantity of powdered sugar, and mash them. Put them into a basin covered with a p'ate, and set them over the fire in a pan of boiling water, til he become a thick juice; then strain it through a bag.

and mix with it the other half of the sugar that you have allotted to the strawberries, which are to be done whole. Put it into a porcelain kettle, and boil and skim it till the scum ceases to rise; then put in the whole strawberries with the sugar in which they have been lying, and all the juice that may have exuded from them. Set them over the fire in the syrup, just long enough to heat them a little; and in a few minutes take them out, one by one, with a tea-spoon, and spread them on dishes to cool; not allowing them to touch each other. Then take off what scum may arise from the additional sugar. Repeat this several times, taking out the strawberries and cooling them till they become quite clear. They must not be allowed to boil; and if they seem likely to break, they should be instantly and finally taken from the fire. When quite cold, put them with the syrup into tumblers, or into white queen's-ware pots. If intended to keep a long time it will be well to put at the top a layer of apple jelly.

TO PRESERVE CHERRIES.

TAKE large ripe morella cherries; weigh them, and to each pound allow a pound of loaf-sugar. Stone the cherries, (opening them with a sharp quill,) and save the juice that comes from them in the process. As you stone them, throw them into a large pan or tureen, and strew about half the sugar over them, and let them lie in it an hour or two after they are all stoned. Then put them into a preserving kettle with the remainder of the sugar, and boil and skim them till the fruit is clear and the syrup thick.

CITRON MELON SLICES.—Take some fine citron melons; pare, core, and cut them into long broad slices. Weigh them, and to every six pounds of melon allow six pounds of fine loaf-sugar; the yellow rind grated off, and the juice of four lemons, and a quarter of a pound of root ginger. Put the slices of melon into a preserving-kettle; cover them with strong alum water, and boil them half an hour, or longer, till they are quite clear and tender. Then drain them, lay them in a broad vessel of cold water, cover them and let them stand all night. Next morning, tie up the race ginger in a piece of thin muslin, and boil it in three pints of clear spring or pump water, till the water is highly flavoured. Having broken up the sugar, put it into a clean preserving-kettle, and pour the ginger water over it. When the sugar is all melted, set it over the fire, add the lemon-grate, and boil and skim the sugar till no more scum rises, and the syrup is clear; stir in the juice, and put in the citron slices. Boil them in the syrup till they are transparent and soft, but not till they break. When done, put the citron slices and syrup into a large tureen, set it in a dry, cool, dark place, and leave it uncovered for two or three days. Then put the slices carefully into wide-mouthed glass jars, and gently pour in the syrup. Lay inside the top of each jar a double white tissue paper cut exactly to fit, and close the jars carefully with corks and cement. This will be found a delicious sweetmeat.

CHERRY JELLY.—Take fine juicy red cherries, and stone them. Save half the stones, crack them, and extract the kernels. Put the cherries and the kernels into a preserving kettle over a slow fire, and let them boil gently in their juice for half an hour. Then transfer them to a jelly-bag, and squeeze out the juice. Measure it, and to each pint allow a pound of fine loaf-sugar. Dissolve the sugar in the juice, and then boil and skim it for twenty or thirty minutes. Put it up in tumblers covered with tissue paper.

———

CHERRY JAM.—To each pound of cherries allow three quarters of a pound of the best white sugar. Stone them, and as you do so throw the sugar gradually into the pan with them. Cover them and let them set all night. Next day, boil them slowly till the cherries and sugar form a thick smooth mass. Put it up in queen's-ware jars.

———

TO DRY CHERRIES.—Choose the finest and largest red cherries for this purpose. Stone them, and spread them on large dishes in the sun, till they become quite dry, taking them in as soon as the sun is off, or if the sky becomes cloudy. Put them up in stone jars, strewing among them some of the best brown sugar.

The common practice of drying cherries with the stones in, (to save trouble,) renders them so inconvenient to eat, that they are of little use, when done in that manner.

With the stones extracted, dried cherries will be found very good for common pies.

———

BARBERRY JELLY.—Take ripe barberries, and having stripped them from the stalks, mash them, and boil them in their juice for a quarter of an hour. Then squeeze them through a bag; allow to each pint of juice, a pound of loaf-sugar; and having melted the sugar in the juice, boil them together twenty or twenty-five minutes, skimming carefully. Put it up in tumblers with tissue paper.

———

FROSTED FRUIT.—Take large ripe cherries, plums, apricots, or grapes, and cut off half the stalk. Have ready in one dish some beaten white of egg, and in another some fine loaf-sugar, powdered and sifted. Dip the fruit first into the white of egg, and then roll it one by one in the powdered sugar. Lay a sheet of white paper on the bottom of a reversed sieve, set it on a stove or in some other warm place, and spread the fruit on the paper till the icing is hardened.

PEACH LEATHER.—To six pounds of ripe peaches, (pared and quartered,) allow three pounds of the best brown sugar. Mix them together, and put them into a preserving kettle, with barely water enough to keep them from burning. Pound and mash them a while with a wooden beetle. Then boil and skim them for three hours or more, stirring them nearly all the time. When done, spread them thinly on large dishes, and set them in the sun for three or four days. Finish the drying by loosening the peach leather on the dishes, and setting them in the oven after the bread is taken out, letting them remain till the oven is cold. Roll up the peach leather and put it away in a box.

Apple leather may be made in the same manner.

RHUBARB JAM,—Peel the rhubarb stalks and cut them into small square pieces. Then weigh them, and to each pound allow three quarters of a pound of powdered loaf-sugar. Put the sugar and the rhubarb into a large, deep, white pan, in alternate layers, the top layer to be of sugar—cover it, and let it stand all night. In the morning, put it into a preserving kettle, and boil it slowly till the whole is dissolved into a thick mass, stirring it frequently, and skimming it before every stirring. Put it warm into glass jars, and tie it up with brandy paper.

PASTRY, PUDDINGS, ETC.

~~~~~~

THE BEST PLAIN PASTE.

ALL paste should be made in a very cool place, as heat ren
ders it heavy. It is far more difficult to get it light in summer
than in winter. A marble slab is much better to roll it on than
a paste-board. It will be improved in lightness by washing the
butter in very cold water, and squeezing and pressing out all
the salt, as salt is injurious to paste. In New York and in
the Eastern states, it is customary, in the dairies, to put more
salt in what is called fresh butter, than in New Jersey, Pennsylvania, and Delaware. This butter, therefore, should always undergo the process of washing and squeezing before it
is used for pastry or cakes. None but the very best butter
should be taken for those purposes; as any unpleasant taste
is always increased by baking. Potted butter never makes
good paste. As pastry is by no means an article of absolute
necessity, it is better not to have it at all, than to make it
badly, and of inferior ingredients; few things being more
unwholesome than hard, heavy dough. The flour for paste
should always be superfine.

You may bake paste in deep dishes or in soup plates. For
shells that are to be baked empty, and afterwards filled with
stewed fruit or sweetmeats, deep plates of block tin with
broad edges are best. If you use patty-pans, the more flat
they are the better. Paste always rises higher and is more
perfectly light and flaky, when unconfined at the sides while
baking. That it may be easily taken out, the dishes or tins
should be well buttered.

To make a nice plain paste,—sift three pints of superfine flour, by rubbing it through a sieve into a deep pan. Divide a pound of fresh butter into four quarters. Cut up one quarter into the flour, and rub it fine with your hands. Mix in, gradually, as much cold water as will make a tolerably stiff dough, and then knead it slightly. Use as little water as possible or the paste will be tough. Sprinkle a little flour on your paste-board, lay the lump of dough upon it, and knead it a very short time. Flour it, and roll it out into a very thin sheet, always rolling from you. Flour your rolling-pin to prevent its sticking. Take a second quarter of the butter, and with your thumb, spread it all over the sheet of paste. If your hand is warm, use a knife instead of your thumb; for if the butter oils, the paste will be heavy. When you have put on the layer of butter, sprinkle it with a very little flour, and with your hands roll up the paste as you would a sheet of paper. Then flatten it with a rolling-pin, and roll it out a second time into a thin sheet. Cover it with another layer of butter, as before, and again roll it up into a scroll. Flatten it again, put on the last layer of butter, flour it slightly, and again roll up the sheet. Then cut the scroll into as many pieces as you want sheets for your dishes or patty-pans. Roll out each piece almost an inch thick. Flour your dishes, lay the paste lightly on them, notch the edges, and bake it a light brown. The oven must be moderate. If it is too hot, the paste will bake before it has risen sufficiently. If too cold, it will scarcely rise at all, and will be white and clammy. When you begin to make paste in this manner, do not quit it till it is ready for the oven. It must always be baked in a close oven where no air can reach it.

The best rolling-pins, are those that are straight, and as thick at the ends as in the middle. They should be held by the handles, and the longer the handles the more convenient. The common rolling-pins that decrease in size towards the ends, are much less effective, and more tedious, as they can roll so little at a time; the extremities not pressing on the dough at all.

All pastry is best when fresh. After the first day it loses much of its lightness, and is therefore more unwholesome.

COMMON PIE CRUST.—Sift two quarts of superfine flour into a pan. Divide one pound of fresh butter into two equal parts, and cut up one half in the flour, rubbing it fine. Mix it with a very little cold water, and make it into a round lump; without kneading. Then flour your paste-board, and roll the dough out into a large thin sheet. Spread it all over with the remainder of the butter. Flour it, fold it up, and roll it out again. Then fold it again, or roll it into a scroll. Cut it into as many pieces as you want sheets of paste, and roll each not quite an inch thick. Butter your pie-dish.

This paste will do for family use, when covered pies are wanted. Also for apple dumplings, pot-pies, &c.; though all boiled paste is best when made of suet instead of butter. Short cakes may be made of this, cut out with the edge of a tumbler. It should always be eaten fresh.

SUET PASTE.—Having removed the skin and stringy fibres from a pound of beef suet, chop it as fine as possible. Sift two quarts of flour into a deep pan, and rub into it one half of the suet. Make it into a round lump of dough, with cold water; without kneading. Lay the dough on your paste-board, roll it out very thin, and cover it with the remaining half of the suet. Flour it, roll it out thin again, and then roll it into a scroll. Cut it into as many pieces as you want sheets of paste, and roll them out half an inch thick.

Suet paste should always be boiled. It is good for plain puddings that are made of apples, gooseberries, blackberr es or other fruit; and for dumplings. If you use it for pot-pie, roll it the last time rather thicker than if wanted for any other purpose. If properly made, it will be light and flaky, and the suet imperceptible. If the suet is minced very fine, and thoroughly incorporated with the flour, not the slightest lump will appear when the paste comes to table.

The suet must not be melted before it is used; but merely minced as fine as possible and mixed cold with the flour.

If for dumplings to eat with boiled mutton, the dough must be rolled out thick, and cut out of the size you want them, with a tin, or with the edge of a cup or tumbler.

DRIPPING PASTE.—To a pound of fresh beef-dripping, that has been nicely clarified, allow two pounds and a quarter of flour. Put the flour into a large pan, and mix the dripping with it, rubbing it into the flour with your hands till it is thoroughly incorporated. Then make it into a stiff dough with a little cold water, and roll it out twice. This may be used for common meat pies.

LARD PASTE.—Lard for paste should never be used without an equal quantity of butter. Take half a pound of nice lard, and half a pound of fresh butter; rub them together into two pounds and a quarter of flour, and mix it with a little cold water to a stiff dough. Roll it out twice. Use it for common pies. Lard should always be kept in tin.

POTATO PASTE.—To a pint and a half of flour, allow one pound of potatoes. Boil the potatoes till they are thoroughly done throughout. Then peel, and mash them very fine. Rub them through a cullender.

Having sifted the flour into a pan, add the potatoes gradually; rubbing them well into the flour with your hands Mix in sufficient cold water to make a stiff dough. Roll it out evenly, and you may use it for apple dumplings, boiled apple pudding, beef-steak pudding, &c.

Potato paste must be sent to table quite hot; as soon as it cools it becomes tough and heavy. It is unfit for baking; and even when boiled is less light than suet paste.

———

FINE PUFF PASTE.—To every pound of the best fresh butter allow a pound or a quart of superfine flour. Sift the flour into a deep pan, and then sift on a plate some additional flour to use for sprinkling and rolling. Wash the butter through two cold waters; squeezing out all the salt, and whatever milk may remain in it; and then make it up with your hands into a round lump, and put it in ice till you are ready to use it. Then divide the butter into four equal parts. Cut up one of the quarters into the pan of flour; and divide the remaining three quarters into six pieces,* cutting each quarter in half. Mix with a knife the flour and butter that is in the pan, adding by degrees a very little cold water till you have made it into a lump of stiff dough. Then sprinkle some flour on the paste-board, (you should have a marble slab,) take the dough from the pan by lifting it out with the knife, lay it on the board. and flouring your rolling-pin, roll out the paste into a large thin sheet. Then with the knife, put all over it, at

---

* Or into nine; and roll it in that number of times.

equal distances, one of the six pieces of butter divided into small bits. Fold up the sheet of paste, flour it, roll it out again, and add in the same manner another of the portions of butter. Repeat this process till the butter is all in. Then fold it once more, lay it on a plate, and set it in a cool place till you are ready to use it. Then divide it into as many pieces as you want sheets of paste; roll out each sheet, and put them into buttered plates or patty-pans. In using the rolling-pin, observe always to roll from you. Bake the paste in a moderate oven, but rather quick than slow. No air must be admitted to it while baking.

The edges of paste should always be notched before it goes into the oven. For this purpose, use a sharp penknife, dipping it frequently in flour as it becomes sticky. The notches should be even and regular. If you do them imperfectly at first, they cannot be mended by sticking on additional bits of paste; as, when baked, every patch will be doubly conspicuous. There are various ways of notching; one of the neatest is to fold over one corner of each notch; or you may arrange the notches to stand upright and lie flat, alternately, all round the edge. They should be made small and regular. You may form the edge into leaves with the little tin cutters made for the purpose.

If the above directions for puff paste are carefully followed, and if it is not spoiled in baking, it will rise to a great thickness and appear in flakes or leaves according to the number of times you have put in the butter.

It should be eaten the day it is baked.

———

SWEET PASTE.—Sift a pound and a quarter of the finest flour, and three ounces of powdered loaf-sugar into a deep dish. Cut up in it one pound of the best fresh butter,

and rub it fine with your hands. Make a hole in the middle,
pour in the yolks of two beaten eggs, and mix them with
the flour, &c. Then wet the whole to a stiff paste with
half a pint of rich milk. Knead it well, and roll it out.

This paste is intended for tarts of the finest sweetmeats
If used as shells, they should be baked empty, and filled when
cool. If made into covered tarts, they may be iced all over,
in the manner of cakes, with beaten white of egg and powdered loaf-sugar. To make puffs of it, roll it out and cut it
into round pieces with the edge of a large tumbler, or with a
tin cutter. Lay the sweetmeat on one half of the paste, fold
the other over it in the form of a half-moon, and unite the
edges by notching them together. Bake them in a brisk oven,
and when cool, send them to table handsomely arranged,
several on a dish.

Sweet paste is rarely used except for very handsome enter-
tainments. You may add some rose water in mixing it.

SHELLS.—Shells of paste are made of one sheet each,
rolled out in a circular form, and spread over the bottom,
sides, and edges of buttered dishes or patty-pans, and baked
empty ; to be filled, when cool, with stewed fruit, (which for
this purpose should be always cold,) or with sweetmeats.
They should be made either of fine puff paste, or of the best
plain paste, or of sweet paste. They are generally rolled out
rather thick, and will require about half an hour to bake. The
oven should be rather quick, and of equal heat throughout ; if
hotter in one part than in another, the paste will draw to one
side, and be warped and disfigured: The shells should be
baked of a light brown. When cool, they must be taken out
of the dishes on which they were baked, and transferred to
plates, and filled with the fruit.

Shells of puff paste will rise best if baked on flat patty-pans, or tin plates. When they are cool, pile the sweetmeats on them in a heap.

The thicker and higher the paste rises, and the more it flakes in layers or leaves, the finer it is considered.

Baking paste as empty shells, prevents it from being moist or clammy at the bottom.

Tarts are small shells with fruit in them.

PIES.—Pies may be made with any sort of paste. It is a fault to roll it out too thin; for if it has not sufficient substance, it will, when baked, be dry and tasteless. For a pie, divide the paste into two sheets; spread one of them over the bottom and sides of a deep dish well buttered. Next put in the fruit or other ingredients, (heaping it higher in the centre,) and then place the other sheet of paste on the top as a lid or cover; pressing the edges closely down, and afterwards crimping or notching them with a sharp small knife.

In making pies of juicy fruit, it is well to put on the centre of the under crust a common tea-cup, laying the fruit round it and over it. The juice will collect under the cup, and not be liable to run out from between the edges. There should be plenty of sugar strewed among the fruit as you put it into the pie.

Preserves should never be put into covered pies. The proper way is to lay them in baked shells.

All pies are best the day they are baked. If kept twenty four hours the paste falls and becomes comparatively hard heavy, and unwholesome. If the fruit is not ripe, it should be stewed, sweetened, and allowed to get cold before it is put into the pie. If put in warm it will make the paste heavy. With fruit pies always have a sugar dish on the table in case they should not be found sweet enough.

STANDING PIES.—Cut up half a pound of butter, and put it into a sauce-pan with three quarters of a pint of water; cover it, and set it on hot coals. Have ready in a pan two pounds of sifted flour; make a hole in the middle of it, pour in the melted butter as soon as it boils, and then with a spoon gradually mix in the flour. When it is well mixed, knead it with your hands into a stiff dough. Sprinkle your paste-board with flour, lay the dough upon it, and continue to knead it with your hands till it no longer sticks to them, and is quite light. Then let it stand an hour to cool. Cut off pieces for the bottom and top; roll them out thick, and roll out a long piece for the sides or walls of the pie, which you must fix on the bottom so as to stand up all round; cement them together with white of egg, pinching and closing them firmly. Then put in the ingredients of your pie, (which should be venison, game, or poultry,) and lay on the lid or top crust, pinching the edges closely together. You may ornament the sides and top with leaves or flowers of paste, shaped with a tin cutter, and notch or scollop the edges handsomely. Before you set it in the oven glaze it all over with white of egg. Bake it four hours. These pies are always eaten cold, and in winter will keep two or three weeks, if the air is carefully excluded from them; and they may be carried to a considerable distance.

A PYRAMID OF TARTS.—Roll out a sufficient quantity of the best puff paste, or sugar paste; and with oval or circular cutters, cut it out into seven or eight pieces of different sizes; stamping the middle of each with the cutter you intend using for the next. Bake them all separately, and when they are cool, place them on a dish in a pyramid, (gradually diminishing in size,) the largest piece at the bottom, and the smallest at the top. Take various preserved fruits, and lay some of the largest on the lower piece of paste; on the next place fruit that is rather smaller; and so on till you finish at the top with the smallest sweetmeats you have. The upper one may be not so large as a half-dollar, containing only a single raspberry or strawberry.

Notch all the edges handsomely. You may ornament the top or pinnacle of the pyramid with a sprig of orange blossom or myrtle.

APPLE AND OTHER PIES.

TAKE fine juicy acid apples; pare, core, and cut them into small pieces. Have ready a deep dish that has been lined with paste. Fill it with the apples; strewing among them layers of brown sugar, and adding the rind of a lemon grated, and also the juice squeezed in, or some essence of lemon. Put on another sheet of paste as a lid; close the edges well, and notch them. Bake the pie in a moderate oven, about three quarters of an hour. Eat it with cream and sugar, or with cold boiled custard.

If the pie is made of early green apples, they should first be stewed with a very little water, and then plenty of sugar stirred in while they are hot.

What are called sweet apples are entirely unfit for cooking, as they become tough and tasteless; and it is almost impossible to get them sufficiently done.

When you put stewed apples into baked shells, grate nutmeg over the top. You may cover them with cream whipped to a stiff froth, and heaped on them.

Cranberries and gooseberries should be stewed, and sweetened before they are put into paste ; peaches cut in half or quartered, and the stones removed. The stones of cherries and plums should also be extracted.

Raspberries or strawberries, mixed with cream and white sugar, may be put raw into baked shells.

RHUBARB TARTS.—Take the young green stalks of the rhubarb plant, or spring fruit as it is called in England ; and having peeled off the thin skin, cut the stalks into small pieces about an inch long, and put them into a sauce-pan with plenty of brown sugar, and its own juice. Cover it, and let it stew slowly till it is soft enough to mash to a marmalade. Then set it away to cool. Have ready some fresh baked shells ; fill them with the stewed rhubarb, and grate white sugar over the top.

For covered pies, cut the rhubarb very small ; mix a great deal of sugar with it, and put it in raw. Bake the pies about three quarters of an hour.

MINCE PIES.

THESE pies are always made with covers, and should be eaten warm. If baked the day before, heat them on the stove or before the fire.

Mince-meat made early in the winter, and packed closely in stone jars, will keep till spring, if it has a sufficiency of spice and liquor. Whenever you take out any for use, pour some additional brandy into the jar before you cover it again, and add some more sugar. No mince-meat, however, will keep well unless all the ingredients are of the best quality. The meat should always be boiled the day before you want to chop it.

GOOD MINCE-MEAT.—Take a bullock's heart and boil it, or two pounds of the lean of fresh beef. When it is quite cold, chop it very fine. Chop three pounds of beef suet (first removing the skin and strings) and six pounds of large juicy apples that have been pared and cored. Then stone six pounds of the best raisins, (or take sultana raisins that are without stones,) and chop them also. Wash and dry three pounds of currants. Mix all together; adding to them the grated peel and the juice of two or three large oranges. two table-spoonfuls of powdered cinnamon, two powdered nutmegs, and three dozen powdered cloves, a tea-spoonful of beaten mace, one pound of fine brown sugar, one quart of Madeira wine, one pint of French brandy, and half a pound of citron cut into large slips. Having thoroughly mixed the whole, put it into a stone jar, and tie it up with brandy paper.

THE BEST MINCE-MEAT.—Take a large fresh tongue rub it with a mixture, in equal proportions, of salt, brown sugar, and powdered cloves. Cover it, and let it lie two days, or at least twenty-four hours. Then boil it two hours. and when it is cold, skin it, and mince it very fine. Chop also three pounds of beef suet, six pounds of sultana raisins, and six pounds of the best pippin apples that have been previously pared and cored. Add three pounds of currants, picked, washed and dried; two large table-spoonfuls of powdered cinnamon; the juice and grated rinds of four large lemons; one pound of sweet almonds, one ounce of bitter almonds, blanched and pounded in a mortar with half a pint of rose water; also four powdered nutmegs; two dozen beaten cloves; and a dozen blades of mace powdered. Add a pound of powdered white sugar, and a pound of citron cut into slips. Mix all together, and moisten it with a quart of Madeira, and a pint of brandy. Put it up closely in a stone jar with brandy paper; and when you take any out, add some more sugar and brandy; and chop some fresh apples.

Bake this mince-meat in puff paste.

You may reserve the citron to put in when you make the pies. Do not cut the slips too small, or the taste will be almost imperceptible.

VERY PLAIN MINCE-MEAT.—Take a piece of fresh beef, consisting of about two pounds of lean, and one pound of fat. Boil it, and when it is quite cold, chop it fine. Or you may substitute cold roast beef. Pare and core some fine juicy apples, cut them in pieces, weigh three pounds, and chop them. Stone four pounds of raisins, and chop them also. Add a large table-spoonful of powdered cloves, and the same quantity of powdered cinnamon. Also a pound of brown sugar. Mix all thoroughly, moistening it with a quart of bottled or sweet cider. You may add the grated peel and the juice of an orange.

Bake it in good common paste.

This mince-meat will do very well for children or for family use, but is too plain to be set before a guest. Neither will it keep so long as that which is richer and more highly seasoned. It is best to make no more of it at once than you have immediate occasion for.

MINCE-MEAT FOR LENT.—Boil a dozen eggs quite hard, and chop the yolks very fine. Chop also a dozen pippins, and two pounds of sultana raisins. Add two pounds of currants, a pound of sugar, a table-spoonful of powdered cinnamon, a tea-spoonful of beaten mace, three powdered nutmegs, the juice and grated peel of three large lemons, and half a pound of citron cut in large strips. Mix these ingredients thoroughly, and moisten the whole with a pint of white wine, half a pint of rose-water, and half a pint of brandy Bake it in very nice paste.

These mince pies may be eaten by persons who refrain from meat in Lent.

ORANGE PUDDING.

GRATE the yellow part of the rind, and squeeze the juice of two large, smooth, deep-coloured oranges. Stir together to a cream, half a pound of butter, and half a pound of powdered white sugar, and add a wine-glass of mixed wine and brandy. Beat very light six eggs, and stir them gradually into the mixture. Put it into a buttered dish with a broad edge, round which lay a border of puff-paste neatly notched. Bake it half an hour, and when cool grate white sugar over it.

Send it to table quite cold.

LEMON PUDDING—May be made precisely in the same manner as the above; substituting lemons for oranges.

QUINCE PUDDING.—Take six large ripe quinces; pare them, and cut out all the blemishes. Then scrape them to a pulp, and mix the pulp with half a pint of cream, and half a pound of powdered sugar, stirring them together very hard. Beat the yolks of seven eggs, (omitting all the whites except two,) and stir them gradually into the mixture, adding two wine glasses of rose water. Stir the whole well together, and bake it in a buttered dish three quarters of an hour Grate sugar over it when cold.

If you cannot obtain cream, you may substitute a quarter ot a pound of fresh butter stirred with the sugar and quince.

A baked apple pudding may be made in the same manner.

ALMOND PUDDING.—Take half a pound of shelled sweet almonds, and three ounces of shelled bitter almonds, or peach-kernels. Scald and peel them; throwing them, as they are peeled, into cold water. Then pound them one at a time in a marble mortar, adding to each a few drops of rose water; otherwise they will be heavy and oily. Mix the sweet and bitter almonds together by pounding them alternately; and as you do them, take them out and lay them on a plate. They must each be beaten to a fine smooth paste, free from the smallest lumps. It is best to prepare them the day before you make the pudding.

Stir to a cream half a pound of fresh butter and half a pound of powdered white sugar; and by degrees pour into it a glass of mixed wine and brandy. Beat to a stiff froth, the whites only, of twelve eggs, (you may reserve the yolks for custards or other purposes,) and stir alternately into the butter and sugar the pounded almonds and the beaten white of egg. When the whole is well mixed, put it into a buttered dish and lay puff paste round the edge. Bake it about half an hour, and when cold grate sugar over it.

ANOTHER ALMOND PUDDING.—Blanch three quarters of a pound of shelled sweet almonds, and three ounces of shelled bitter almonds, and beat them in a mortar to a fine paste · mixing them well, and adding by degrees a tea-cup full, or more, of rose water. Boil in a pint of rich milk, a few sticks of cinnamon broken up, and a few blades of mace. When the milk has come to a boil, take it off the fire, strain

it into a pan, and soak in it two stale rusks cut into slices.
They must soak till quite dissolved. Stir to a cream three
quarters of a pound of fresh butter, mixed with the same quantity of powdered loaf-sugar. Beat ten eggs very light, yolks
and whites together, and then stir alternately into the butter
and sugar, the rusk, eggs, and almonds. Set it on a stove or a
chafing dish, and stir the whole together till very smooth and
thick. Put it into a buttered dish and bake it three quarters
of an hour. It must be eaten quite cold.

COCOA-NUT PUDDING.—Having opened a cocoa-nut,
pare off the brown skin from the pieces, and wash them all in
cold water. Then weigh three quarters of a pound, and grate
it into a dish. Cut up half a pound of butter into half a pound
of powdered loaf-sugar, and stir them together to a cream;
add to them a glass of wine and rose water mixed. Beat the
whites only, of twelve eggs, till they stand alone on the rods:
and then stir the grated cocoa-nut and the beaten white of egg
alternately into the butter and sugar; giving the whole a hard
stirring at the last. Put the mixture into a buttered dish, lay
puff paste round the flat edge, and bake it half an hour in a
moderate oven. When cold, grate powdered sugar over it.

ANOTHER COCOA-NUT PUDDING.—Peel and cut
up the cocoa-nut, and wash and wipe the pieces. Weigh one
pound, and grate it fine. Then mix with it two stale rusks
or small sponge-cakes, grated also. Stir together till very
light half a pound of butter and half a pound of powdered
white sugar, and add a glass of white wine. Beat six whole
eggs very light, and stir them gradually into the butter and sugar
in turn with the grated cocoa-nut. Having stirred the whole

very hard at the last, put it into a buttered dish and bake it half an hour.   Send it to table cold.

———

PUMPKIN PUDDING.—Take a pint of pumpkin that has been stewed soft, and pressed through a cullender.   Melt in half a pint of warm milk, a quarter of a pound of butter, and the same quantity of sugar, stirring them well together. If you can conveniently procure a pint of rich cream it will be better than the milk and butter.   Beat eight eggs very light, and add them gradually to the other ingredients, alternately with the pumpkin.   Then stir in a wine glass of rose water and a glass of wine mixed together; a large tea-spoonful of powdered mace and cinnamon mixed, and a grated nutmeg. Having stirred the whole very hard, put it into a buttered dish and bake it three quarters of an hour.   Eat it cold.

———

A SQUASH PUDDING.—Pare, cut in pieces, and stew in a very little water, a yellow winter squash.   When it is quite soft, drain it dry, and mash it in a cullender.   Then put it into a pan, and mix with it a quarter of a pound of butter. Prepare two pounded crackers, or an equal quantity of grated stale bread.   Stir gradually a quarter of a pound of powdered sugar into a quart of rich milk, and add by degrees, the squash, and the powdered biscuit.   Beat nine eggs very light, and stir them gradually into the mixture.   Add a glass of white wine, a glass of brandy, a glass of rose water, and a table-spoonful of mixed spice, nutmeg, mace, and cinnamon pow- dered.   Stir the whole very hard, till all the ingredients are thoroughly mixed.   Bake it three quarters of an hour in a buttered dish ; and when cold, grate white sugar over it.

YAM PUDDING.—Take one pound of roasted yam, and rub it through a cullender. Mix with it half a pound of white sugar, a pint of cream or half a pound of butter, a tea-spoonful of powdered cinnamon, a grated nutmeg, and a wine glass of rose water, and one of wine. Set it away to get cold. Then beat eight eggs very light, and add them by degrees to the mixture, alternately with half a pound of the mashed potato. Bake it three-quarters of an hour in a buttered dish.

CHESTNUT PUDDING—May be made in the above manner.

POTATO PUDDING.—Boil a pound of fine potatoes, peel them, mash them, and rub them through a cullender. Stir together to a cream, three quarters of a pound of sugar, and the same quantity of butter. Add to them gradually, a wine glass of rose water, a glass of wine, and a glass of brandy; a tea-spoonful of powdered mace and cinnamon, a grated nutmeg, and the juice and grated peel of a large lemon. Then beat six eggs very light, and add them by degrees to the mixture, alternately with the potato. Bake it three quarters of an hour in a buttered dish.

SWEET POTATO PUDDING.—Take half a pound of sweet potatoes, wash them, and put them into a pot with very little water, barely enough to keep them from burning. Let them simmer slowly for about half an hour; they must be only parboiled, otherwise they will be soft, and may make the pudding heavy. When they are half done, take them out, peel them, and when cold, grate them. Stir together to a cream, half a pound of butter and a quarter of a pound and two ounces of powdered sugar, add a grated nutmeg, a large tea-spoonful of powdered cinnamon, and half a tea-spoonful of beaten mace. Also the juice and grated peel of a lemon, a wine glass of rose water, a glass of wine, and a glass of brandy. Stir these ingredients well together. Beat eight eggs very light, and stir them into the mixture in turn with the sweet potato, a little at a time of each. Having stirred the whole very hard at the last, put it into a buttered dish and bake it three quarters of an hour. Eat it cold.

CARROT PUDDING—May be made in the above manner.

GREEN CORN PUDDING.—Take twelve ears of green corn, as it is called, (that is, Indian corn when full grown, but before it begins to harden and turn yellow,) and grate it. Have ready a quart of rich milk, and stir into it by degrees a quarter of a pound of fresh butter, and a quarter of a pound of sugar. Beat four eggs till quite light; and then stir them into the milk, &c. alternately with grated corn, a little of each at a time. Put the mixture into a large buttered dish and bake it four hours. It should be eaten quite warm. For sauce, beat together butter and white sugar in equal proportions, mixed with grated nutmeg.

To make this pudding,—you may if more convenient, boil the corn and cut it from the cob; but let it get quite cold before you stir it into the milk. If the corn has been previously boiled, the pudding will require but two hours to bake.

SAGO PUDDING.—Pick, wash, and dry half a pound of currants; and prepare a tea-spoonful of powdered cinnamon; a half tea-spoonful of powdered mace; and a grated nutmeg. Have ready six table-spoonfuls of sago, picked clean, and soaked for two hours in cold water. Boil the sago in a quart of milk till quite soft. Then stir alternately into the milk, a quarter of a pound of butter, and six ounces of powdered sugar, and set it away to cool. Beat eight eggs, and when they are quite light, stir them gradually into the milk, sago, &c. Add the spice, and lastly the currants; having dredges them well with flour to prevent their sinking. Stir the whole very hard, put it into a buttered dish, and bake it three quarters of an hour. Eat it cold.

ARROW ROOT PUDDING.—Take a large tea-cup of arrow root, and melt it in half a pint of rich milk. Then boil another half pint of milk with some cinnamon, and a few bitter almonds or peach-leaves. Strain the milk hot over the dissolved arrow root; stir it to a thick, smooth batter, and set it away to cool. Next, beat three eggs very light, and stir them into the batter, alternately with four large table-spoonsful of powdered sugar. Add some nutmeg, and some fresh lemon-peel, grated. Put the mixture into a buttered dish, and bake it half an hour. When cold, ornament the top handsomely, with slices of preserved quince or peach, or with whole strawberries or raspberries.

GROUND RICE PUDDING.—Mix a quarter of a pound of ground rice with a pint of cold milk, till it is a smooth batter and free from lumps. Boil one pint of milk; and when it has boiled, stir in gradually the rice batter, alternately with a quarter of a pound of butter. Keep it over the fire, stirring all the time, till the whole is well mixed, and has boiled hard. Then take it off, add a quarter of a pound of white sugar; stir it well, and set it away to cool. Beat eight eggs very light, and stir them into the mixture when it is quite cold. Then strain it through a sieve, (this will make it more light and delicate,) add a grated nutmeg, and a small tea-spoonful of powdered cinnamon. Stir in the juice and the grated peel of a lemon, or a small tea-spoonful of essence of lemon. Put it into a deep dish or dishes, and bake it an hour. As soon as it comes out of the oven, lay slips of citron over the top; and when cold, strew powdered sugar on it.

A RICE PLUM PUDDING.—Take three jills of whole rice; wash it, and boil it in a pint of milk. When it is soft, mix in a quarter of a pound of butter, and set it aside to cool; and when it is quite cold, stir it into another pint of milk. Prepare a pound and a half of raisins or currants; if currants, wash and dry them; if raisins, seed them and cut them in half. Dredge them well with flour, to prevent their sinking; and prepare also a powdered nutmeg; a table-spoonful of mixed mace and cinnamon powdered; a wine glass of rose water; and a wine glass of brandy or white wine. Beat six eggs very light, and stir them into the mixture, alternately with a quarter of a pound of sugar. Then add by degrees the spice and the liquor, and lastly, stir in, a few at a time, the raisins or currants. Put the pudding into a buttered dish and bake it an hour and a half. Send it to table cool.

You may make this pudding of ground rice, using but half a pint instead of three jills.

A PLAIN RICE PUDDING.—Pick, wash, and boil half a pint of rice. Then drain off the water, and let the rice dry, and get cold. Afterwards mix with it two ounces of butter, and four ounces of sugar, and stir it into a quart of rich milk. Beat four or five eggs very light, and add them gradually to the mixture. Stir in at the last a table-spoonful of grated nutmeg and cinnamon. Bake it an hour in a deep dish. Eat it cold. ———

A FARMER'S RICE PUDDING.—This pudding is made without eggs. Wash a common-sized tea-cup of rice through cold water. Stir it raw into a quart of rich milk, or of cream and milk mixed; adding a quarter of a pound of brown sugar, and a table-spooonful of powdered cinnamon. Put it into a deep pan, and bake it two hours or more. When done, the rice will be perfectly soft, which you may ascertain by dipping a tea-spoon into the edge of the pudding and taking out a little to try. Eat it cold.

———

RICE MILK.—Pick and wash half a pint of rice, and boil it in a quart of water till it is quite soft. Then drain it, and mix it with a quart of rich milk. You may add half a pound of whole raisins. Set it over hot coals, and stir it frequently till it boils. When it boils hard, stir in alternately two beaten eggs, and four large table-spoonfuls of brown sugar. Let it continue boiling five minutes longer; then take it off, and send it to table hot. If you put in raisins you must let it boil till they are quite soft.

———

A BOILED RICE PUDDING.—Mix a quarter of a pound of ground rice with a pint of milk, and simmer it over hot coals; stirring it all the time to prevent its being lumpy, or burning at the bottom. When it is thick and smooth, take it off, and pour it into an earthen pan. Mix a quarter of a pound of sugar, and a quarter of a pound of butter with half a pint of cream or very rich milk, and stir it into the rice; adding a powdered nutmeg, and the grated rind of two lemons; also squeeze in their juice. Beat the yolks of six eggs with the whites of two only. When the eggs are quite

light, mix them gradually with the other ingredients, and stir
the whole very hard. Butter a large bowl, or a pudding mould
Put in the mixture; tying a cloth tightly over the top,
(so that no water can get in,) and boil it two hours. When
done, turn it out into a dish. Send it to table warm, and eat
it with sweetened cream, flavoured with a glass of brandy
or white wine and a grated nutmeg.

A MARLBOROUGH PUDDING.—Pare, core and quar-
ter six large ripe pippin apples. Stew them in about a jill of
water. When they are soft but not broken, take them out,
drain them through a sieve, and mash them to a paste with
the back of a spoon. Mix with them six large table-spoon
fuls of sugar and a quarter of a pound of butter, and set
them away to get cold. Grate two milk biscuits or smal'
sponge cakes, or an equal quantity of stale bread, and
grate also the yellow peel, and squeeze the juice of a large
lemon. Beat six eggs light, and when the apple is cold stir
them gradually into it, adding the grated biscuit and the
lemon. Stir in a wine glass of rose water and a grated nutmeg. Put the mixture into a buttered dish or dishes; lay
round the edge a border of puff paste, and bake it three
quarters of an hour. When cold, grate white sugar over the
top, and ornament it with slips of citron handsomely arranged.

ALMOND CHEESE CAKE.

THIS though usually called a cheese cake, is in fact a
pudding

Cut a piece of rennet about two inches square, wash off
the salt in cold water, and wipe it dry. Put it into a tea-cup,

pour on it sufficient luke-warm water to cover it, and .et it soak all night, or at least several hours. Take a quart of milk, which must be made warm, but not boiling. Stir the rennet-water into it. Cover it, and set it in a warm place, When the curd has become quite firm, and the whey looks greenish, drain off the whey, and set the curd in a cool place. While the milk is turning, prepare the other ingredients. Wash and dry half a pound of currants, and dredge them well with flour. Blanch three ounces of sweet and one ounce of bitter almonds, by scalding and peeling them. Then cool them in cold water, wiping them dry before you put them into the mortar. If you cannot procure bitter almonds, peach kernels may be substituted. Beat them, one at a time, in the mortar to a smooth paste, pouring in with every one a few drops of rose water to prevent their being oily, dull-coloured, and heavy. If you put a sufficiency of rose water, the pounded almond paste will be light, creamy, and perfectly white Mix, as you do them, the sweet and bitter almonds together. Then beat the yolks of eight eggs, and when light, mix them gradually with the curd. Add five table-spoonfuls of cream, and a tea-spoonful of mixed spice. Lastly, stir in, by degrees, the pounded almonds, and the currants alternately. Stir the whole mixture very hard. Bake it in buttered dishes, laying puff paste round the edges. If accurately made, it will be found delicious. It must be put in the oven immediately.

COMMON CHEESE CAKE.—Boil a quart of rich milk Beat eight eggs, put them to the milk, and let the milk and eggs boil together till they become a curd. Then drain it through a very clean sieve, till all the whey is out. Put the curd into a deep dish, and mix with it half a pound of butter, working them well together. When it is cold, add to it the beaten yolks of four eggs, and four large table-spoonfuls of powdered white sugar; also a grated nutmeg. Lastly, stir in, by degrees, half a pound of currants that have been previously picked, washed, dried, and dredged with flour. Lay puff paste round the rim of the dish, and bake the cheese cake half an hour. Send it to table cold, dredged with sugar.

PRUNE PUDDING.—Scald a pound of prunes; cover them, and let them swell in the hot water till they are soft. Then drain them, and extract the stones; spread the prunes on a large dish, and dredge them with flour. Take one jill or eight large table-spoonfuls from a quart of rich milk, and stir into it, gradually, eight spoonfuls of sifted flour. Mix it to a smooth batter, pressing out all the lumps with the back of the spoon. _Beat eight eggs light, and stir them, by degrees, into the remainder of the milk, alternately with the batter that you have just mixed. Then add the prunes one at a time, stirring the whole very hard. Tie the pudding in a cloth that nas been previously dipped in boiling water and then dredged with flour. Leave room for it to swell, but secure it firmly, so that no water can get in. Put it into a pot of boiling water, and boil it two hours. Send it to table hot, (not taking it out of the pot till a moment before it is wanted,) and eat it with cream sauce; or with butter, sugar, and nutmeg beaten together, and served up in a little tureen.

A similar pudding may be made with whole raisins.

EVE'S PUDDING.—Pare, core, and quarter six large pippins, and chop them very fine. Grate stale bread till you have six ounces of crumbs, and roll fine six ounces of white sugar. Pick, wash, and dry six ounces of currants, and sprinkle them with flour. Mix all these ingredients together in a large pan, adding six ounces of butter cut small, and two table-spoonfuls of flour. Beat six eggs very light, and moisten the mixture with them. Add a grated nutmeg, and a tea-spoonful of powdered cinnamon. Stir the whole very well together. Have ready a pot of boiling water. Dip your pudding cloth into it, shake it out, and dredge it with flour. Then put in the mixture, and tie it very firmly; leaving space for the pudding to swell, and stopping up the tying place with a paste of wetted flour. Boil it three hours; keeping at the fire a kettle of boiling water, to replenish the pot, that the pudding may be always well covered. Send it to table hot, and eat it with sweetened cream flavoured with wine and nutmeg.

CINDERELLAS OR GERMAN PUFFS.—Sift half a pound of the finest flour. Cut up in a quart of rich milk, half a pound of fresh butter, and set it on the stove, or near the fire, till it has melted. Beat eight eggs very light, and stir them gradually into the milk and butter, alternately with the flour. Add a powdered nutmeg, and a tea-spoonful of powdered cinnamon. Mix the whole very well to a fine smooth batter, in which there must be no lumps. Butter some large common tea-cups, and divide the mixture among them till they are half full or a little more. Set them immediately in a quick oven, and bake them about a quarter of an hour. When done, turn them out into a dish, and grate white sugar over them. Serve them up hot, with a sauce of sweetened cream flavoured with wine and nutmeg; or you may eat them with molasses and butter; or with sugar and wine. Send them round whole, for they will fall almost as soon as cut.

A BOILED BREAD PUDDING.—Boil a quart of rich milk. While it is boiling, take a small loaf of baker's bread, such as is sold for five or six cents. It may be either fresh or stale. Pare off all the crust, and cut up the crumb into very small pieces. You should have baker's bread if you can procure it, as home-made bread may not make the pudding light enough. Put the bread into a pan; and when the milk boils, pour it scalding hot over the bread. Cover the pan closely, and let it steep in the hot steam for about three quarters of an hour. Then remove the cover, and allow the bread and milk to cool. In the mean time, beat four eggs till they are thick and smooth. Then beat into them a table-spoonful and a half of fine wheat flour. Next beat the egg and flour into the bread and milk, and continue to beat hard till the mixture is as light as possible; for on this the success of the pudding chiefly depends.

Have ready over the fire a pot of boiling water. Dip your pudding-cloth into it, and shake it out. Spread out the cloth in a deep dish or pan, and dredge it well with flour. Pour in the mixture, and tie up the cloth, leaving room for it to swell. Tie the string firmly and plaster up the opening (if there is any) with flour moistened with water. If any water gets into it the pudding will be spoiled.

See that the water boils when you put in the pudding, and keep it boiling hard. If the pot wants replenishing, do it with boiling water from a kettle. Should you put in cold water to supply the place of that which has boiled away, the pudding will chill, and become hard and heavy. Boil it an hour and a half.

Turn it out of the bag the minute before you send it to table. Eat it with wine sauce, or with sugar and butter, or molasses.

It will be much improved by adding to the mixture half a

pound of whole raisins, well floured to prevent their sinking.
Sultana raisins are best, as they have no seeds.

If these directions are exactly followed, this will be found
a remarkably good and wholesome plain pudding.

For all boiled puddings, a square pudding-cloth which can
be opened out, is much better than a bag. It should be very
thick.

A BAKED BREAD PUDDING.—Take a stale five cent
loaf of bread; cut off all the crust, and grate or rub the crumb
as fine as possible. Boil a quart of rich milk, and pour it hot
over the bread; then stir in a quarter of a pound of butter.
and the same quantity of sugar, a glass of wine and brandy
mixed, or a glass of rose water. Or you may omit the liquor
and substitute the grated peel of a large lemon. Add a table-
spoonful of mixed cinnamon and nutmeg powdered. Stir the
whole very well, cover it, and set it away for half an hour.
Then let it cool. Beat seven or eight eggs very light, and stir
them gradually into the mixture after it is cold. Then butter
a deep dish, and bake the pudding an hour. Send it to table
cool.

A BREAD AND BUTTER PUDDING.—Cut some
slices of bread and butter moderately thick, omitting the
crust; stale bread is best. Butter a deep dish, and cover the
bottom with slices of the buttered bread. Have ready a
pound of currants, picked, washed and dried. Spread one
third of them thickly over the bread and butter, and strew on
some brown sugar. Then put another layer of bread and
butter, and cover it also with currants and sugar. Finish
with a third layer of each, and pour over the whole four eggs
beaten very light and mixed with a pint of milk, and a wine

glass of rose water. Bake the pudding an hour, and grate nutmeg over it when done. Eat it warm, but not hot.

You may substitute for the currants, raisins seeded, and cut in half.

This pudding may be made also with layers of stewed gooseberries instead of the currants, or with pippin apples, pared, cored and minced fine.

———

A SUET PUDDING.—Mince very finely as much beef suet as will make two large table-spoonfuls. Grate two handfuls of bread-crumbs; boil a quart of milk and pour it hot on the bread. Cover it, and set it aside to steep for half an hour; then put it to cool. Beat eight eggs very light; stir the suet, and six table-spoonfuls of flour alternately into the bread and milk, and add, by degrees, the eggs. Lastly, stir in a table-spoonful of powdered nutmeg and cinnamon mixed, and a glass of mixed wine and brandy. Pour it into a square cloth dipped in hot water, and floured; tie it firmly, put it into a pot of boiling water, and boil it two hours. Do not take it up till immediately before it is wanted, and send it to table hot.

Eat it with wine sauce, or with molasses.

———

A CUSTARD PUDDING.—Take five table-spoonfuls out of a quart of cream or rich milk, and mix them with two large spoonfuls of fine flour. Set the rest of the milk to boil, flavouring it with half a dozen peach leaves, or with bitter almonds broken up. When it has boiled hard, take it off, strain it, and stir it in the cold milk and flour. Set it away to cool, and beat well eight yolks and four whites of eggs; add them to the milk, and stir in, at the last, a glass of brandy or white wine, a powdered nutmeg, and a quarter of a pound of

sug ar. Butter a large bowl or mould ; pour in the mixture;
tie a cloth tightly over it ; put it into a pot of boiling water,
and boil it two hours, replenishing the pot with hot water from
a tea-kettle. When the pudding is done, let it get cool before
you turn it out. Eat it with butter and sugar stirred together
to a cream, and flavoured with lemon juice or orange.

FLOUR HASTY PUDDING.—Tie together half a dozen
peach-leaves, put them into a quart of milk, and set it on the
fire to boil. When it has come to a hard boil, take out the
leaves, but let the pot remain boiling on the fire. Then with
a large wooden spoon in one hand, and some wheat flour in
the other, thicken and stir it till it is about the consistence of
a boiled custard. Afterwards throw in, one at a time, a dozen
small bits of butter rolled in a thick coat of flour. You may
enrich it by stirring in a beaten egg or two, a few minutes
before you take it from the fire. When done, pour it into a
deep dish, and strew brown sugar thickly over the top. Eat
it warm.

INDIAN MUSH.—Have ready on the fire a pot of boiling
water. Stir into it by degrees (a handful at a time) sufficient
Indian meal to make it very thick, and then add a very small
portion of salt. You must keep the pot boiling on the fire all
the time you are throwing in the meal ; and between every
handful, stir very hard with the mush-stick, (a round stick
flattened at one end;) that the mush may not be lumpy After
it is sufficiently thick, keep it boiling for an hour longer,
stirring it occasionally. Then cover the pot, and hang it
higher up the chimney, so as to simmer slowly or keep hot
for another hour. The goodness of mush depends greatly on its
being long and thoroughly boiled. If sufficienlty cooked, it is

wholesome and nutritious, but exactly the reverse, if made in haste. It is not too long to have it altogether three or four hours over the fire; on the contrary it will be much the better for it.

Eat it warm; either with milk, or cover your plate with mush, make a hole in the middle, put some butter in the hole and fill it up with molasses.

Cold mush that has been left, may be cut into slices and fried in butter.

Burgoo is made precisely in the same manner as mush, but with oatmeal instead of Indian.

A BAKED INDIAN PUDDING.—Cut up a quarter of a pound of butter in a pint of molasses, and warm them together till the butter is melted. Boil a quart of milk; and while scalding hot, pour it slowly over a pint of sifted Indian meal, and stir in the molasses and butter. Cover it, and let it steep for an hour. Then take off the cover, and set the mixture to cool. When it is cold, beat six eggs, and stir them gradually into it; add a table-spoonful of mixed cinnamon and nutmeg; and the grated peel of a lemon. Stir the whole very hard; put it into a buttered dish, and bake it two hours. Serve it up hot, and eat it with wine sauce, or with butter and molasses.

A BOILED INDIAN PUDDING.—Chop very fine a quarter of a pound of beef suet. Mix it with a quart of sifted Indian meal. Boil a quart of milk with some pieces of cinnamon broken up; strain it, and while it is hot, stir in gradually the meal and suet; add half a pint of molasses. Cover the mixture and set it away for an hour; then put it to cool. Beat six eggs, and stir them gradually into the mixture when it is cold; add a grated nutmeg, and the grated peel of a lemon. Tie the pudding in a cloth that has been dipped in hot water and floured; and leave plenty of room for it to swell. Secure it well at the tying place lest the water should get in, which will infallibly spoil it. Put it into a pot of boiling water, (which must be replenished as it boils away,) and boil it four hours at least; but five or six will be better. To have an Indian pudding *very good*, it should be mixed the night before, (all except the eggs,) and put on to boil early in the morning. Do not take it out of the pot till immediately before it is wanted. Eat it with wine sauce, or with molasses and butter. What is left may be boiled again next day.

INDIAN PUDDING WITHOUT EGGS.—Boil some cinnamon in a quart of milk, and then strain it. While the milk is hot, stir into it a pint of molasses, and then add by degrees a quart or more of Indian meal so as to make a thick batter. It will be much improved by the grated peel and juice of a large lemon or orange. Tie it very securely in a thick cloth, leaving room for it to swell, and pasting up the tying-place with a lump of flour and water. Put it into a pot of boiling water, (having ready a kettle to fill it up as it boils away,) hang it over a good fire, and keep it boiling hard for four or five hours. Eat it warm with molasses and butter.

This is a very economical, and not an unpalatable pudding; and may be found convenient when it is difficult to obtain eggs. The molasses should be West India.

A BAKED PLUM PUDDING.—Grate all the crumb of a stale six cent loaf; boil a quart of rich milk, and pour it boiling hot over the grated bread; cover it, and let it steep for an hour; then set it out to cool. In the mean time prepare half a pound of currants, picked, washed, and dried ; half a pound of raisins, stoned and cut in half; and a quarter of a pound of citron cut in large slips; also, two nutmegs beaten to a powder; and a table-spoonful of mace and cinnamon powdered and mixed together. Crush with a rolling-pin half a pound of sugar, and cut up half a pound of butter. When the bread and milk is uncovered to cool, mix with it the butter, sugar, spice and citron; adding a glass of brandy, and a glass of white wine. Beat eight eggs very light, and when the milk is quite cold, stir them gradually into the mixture. Then add, by degrees, the raisins and currants, (which must be previously dredged with flour,) and stir the whole very hard. Put it into a buttered dish, and bake it two hours. Send it to table warm, and eat it with wine sauce, or with wine and sugar only.

In making this pudding, you may substitute for the butter, half a pound of beef suet minced as fine as possible. It will be found best to prepare the ingredients the day before, covering them closely and putting them away.

A BOILED PLUM PUDDING.—Grate the crumb of a twelve cent loaf of bread, and boil a quart of rich milk with a small bunch of peach leaves in it, then strain it and set it out to cool. Pick, wash and dry a pound of currants, and stone and cut in half a pound of raisins; strew over them three large table-spoonfuls of flour. Roll fine a pound of brown sugar, and mince as fine as possible three quarters of a pound of beef suet. Prepare two beaten nutmegs, and a large table-spoontul of powdered mace and cinnamon; also the grated peel and the juice of two large lemons or oranges. Beat ten eggs very light, and (when it is cold) stir them gradually into the milk, alternately with the suet and grated bread.

Add, by degrees, the sugar, fruit, and spice, with a large glass of brandy, and one of white wine. Mix the whole very well, and stir it hard. Then put it into a thick cloth that has been scalded and floured ; leave room for it to swell, and tie it very firmly, pasting the tying-place with a small lump of moistened flour. Put the pudding into a large pot of boiling water, and boil it steadily six hours, replenishing the pot occasionally from a boiling kettle. Turn the pudding frequently in the pot. Prepare half a pound of citron cut in slips, and half a pound of almonds blanched and split in half lengthways. Stick the almonds and the citron all over the outside of the pudding as soon as you take it out of the cloth. Send it to table hot, and eat it with wine sauce, or with cold wine and sugar.

If there is much of the pudding left, tie it in a cloth and boil it again next day.

All the ingredients of this plum pudding (except the eggs) should be prepared the day before, otherwise it cannot be made in time to allow of its being sufficiently boiled.

We have known of a very rich plum pudding being mixed in England and sent to America in a covered bowl ; it arrived perfectly good after a month's voyage, the season being winter.

A BAKED APPLE PUDDING.—Take nine large pippin apples ; pare and core them whole. Set them in the bottom of a large deep dish, and pour round them a very little water, just enough to keep them from burning. Put them into an oven, and let them bake about half an hour. In the mean time, mix three table-spoonfuls of flour with a quart of milk, a quarter of a pound of white sugar, and a tea-spoonful of mixed spice. Beat seven eggs very light, and stir them gradually into the milk. Then take out the dish of apples, (which by this time should be half baked,) and fill up the holes from whence you extracted the cores, with white sugar; pressing down into each a slice of fresh lemon. Pour the batter round the apples; put the dish again into the oven, and let it bake another half hour; but not long enough for the apples to fall to pieces; as they should, when done, be soft throughout, but quite whole. Send it to table warm.

This is sometimes called a *Bird's Nest Pudding.*

It will be much improved by previously boiling in the milk a small handful of peach-leaves. Let it get cold before you stir in the eggs.

———

BOILED APPLE PUDDING.—Pare, core, and quarter as many fine juicy apples as will weigh two pounds wher done. Strew among them a quarter of a pound of browr sugar, and add a grated nutmeg, and the juice and yellow peel of a large lemon. Prepare a paste of suet and flour, in the proportion of a pound of chopped suet to two pounds of flour. Roll it out of moderate thickness; lay the apples in the centre, and close the paste nicely over them in the form of a large dumpling; tie it in a cloth and boil it three hours. Send it to table hot, and eat with it cream sauce, or with butter and sugar. The water must boil before the pudding goes in.

Any fruit pudding may be made in a similar manner.

———

AN EASTERN PUDDING.—Make a paste of a pound of flour and half a pound of minced suet; and roll it out thin into a square or oblong sheet; trim off the edges so as to make it an even shape. Spread thickly over it some marma-laae, or cold stewed fruit, (which must be made very sweet,) either apple, peach, plum, gooseberry or cranberry. Roll up the paste, with the fruit spread on it, into a scroll. Secure each end by putting on nicely a thin round piece rolled out from the trimmings that you cut off the edges of the sheet. Put the pudding into a cloth, and boil it at least three hours. Serve it up hot, and eat it with cream sauce, or with butter and sugar. The pudding must be put on in boiling water.

APPLE DUMPLINGS.

TAKE large fine juicy apples. Pare them, and extract the cores without dividing the apple. Fill each hole with brown sugar, and some chips of lemon-peel. Also squeeze in some lemon juice. Or you may fill the cavities with raspberry jam, or with any sort of marmalade. Have ready a paste, made in the proportion of a pound of suet, chopped as fine as possible, to two pounds and a half of sifted flour, well mixed, and wetted with as little water as possible. Roll out the paste to a moderate thickness, and cut it into circular pieces, allowing two pieces to each dumpling. Lay your apple on one piece, and put another piece on the top, closing the paste round the sides with your fingers, so as to cover the apple entirely. This is a better way than gathering up the paste at one end, as the dumpling is less liable to burst. Boil each dumpling in a small coarse cloth, which has first been dipped in hot water. There should always be a set of cloths kept for the purpose. Tie them tightly, leaving a small space for the dumpling to swell. Plaster a little flour on the inside of each tying place to prevent the water from getting in. Have ready a pot of boiling water. Put in the dumplings and boil them steadily for an hour. Send them to table hot in a covered dish. Do not take them up till a moment before they are wanted.

Eat them with cream and sugar, or with butter and sugar.

You may make the paste with butter instead of suet, allowing a pound of butter to two pounds and a quarter of flour. But when paste is to be boiled, suet will make it much lighter and finer than butter.

Apple dumplings may be made in a very plain manner with potato paste, and boiled without cloths, dredging the outside of each dumpling with flour. They should boil about three quarters of an hour when without cloths.

The apples for dumplings should always be whole, (except the cores;) for if quartered, the pieces will separate in boiling and break through the crust. The apples should never be sweet ones.

———

RICE DUMPLINGS.—Pick and wash a pound of rice, and boil it gently in two quarts of water till it becomes dry; keeping the pot well covered, and not stirring it. Then take it off the fire, and spread it out to cool on the bottom of an inverted sieve; loosening the grains lightly with a fork, that all the moisture may evaporate. Pare a dozen pippins or other large juicy apples, and scoop out the core. Then fill up the cavity with marmalade, or with lemon and sugar. Cover every apple all over with a thick coating of the boiled rice. Tie up each in a separate cloth,* and put them into a pot of cold water. They will require about an hour and a quarter after they begin to boil; perhaps longer.

Turn them out on a large dish, and be careful in doing so

———

* Your pudding and dumpling cloths should be squares of coarse thick linen, hemmed, and with tape strings sewed to them. After using, they should be washed, dried, and ironed; and kept in one of the kitchen drawers, that they may be always ready when wanted.

not to break the dumplings. Eat them with cream sauce, or with wine sauce, or with butter, sugar, and nutmeg beaten together.

PIGEON DUMPLINGS OR PUDDINGS.—Take six pigeons and stuff them with chopped oysters, seasoned with pepper, salt, mace, and nutmeg. Score the breasts, and loosen all the joints with a sharp knife, as if you were going to carve them for eating; but do not cut them quite apart. Make a sufficient quantity of nice suet paste, allowing a pound of suet to two pounds of flour; roll it out thick, and divide it into six. Lay one pigeon on each sheet of the paste with the back downwards, and put in the lower part of the breast a piece of butter rolled in flour. Close the paste over the pigeon in the form of a dumpling or small pudding; pouring in at the last a very little cold water to add to the gravy. Tie each dumpling in a cloth, put them into a pot of hot water, and boil them two hours. Send them to table with made gravy in a boat.

Partridges or quails may be cooked in this manner; also chickens, which must be accompanied by egg sauce.

These dumplings or puddings will be found very good.

FINE SUET DUMPLINGS.—Grate the crumb of a stale six cent loaf, and mix it with half as much beef suet, chopped as fine as possible. Add a grated nutmeg, and two large table-spoonfuls of sugar. Beat four eggs with four table-spoonfuls of white wine or brandy. Mix all well together to a stiff paste. Flour your hands, and make up the mixture into balls or dumplings about the size of turkey eggs. Have ready a pot of boiling water. Put the dumplings into cloths, and let them boil about half an hour. Serve them hot, and eat them with wine sauce.

PLAIN SUET DUMPLINGS.—Sift two pounds of flour into a pan, and add a salt-spoon of salt. Mince very fine one pound of beef suet, and rub it into the flour. Make it into a stiff dough with a little cold water. Then roll it out an inch thick or rather more. Cut it into dumplings with the edge of a tumbler. Put them into a pot of boiling water, and let them boil an hour and a half. Send them to table hot, to eat with boiled loin of mutton, or with molasses after the meat is removed.

INDIAN DUMPLINGS.—Take a pint of milk, and four eggs well beaten. Stir them together, and add a salt-spoon of salt. Then mix in as much sifted Indian meal as will make a stiff dough. Flour your hands; divide the dough into equal portions, and make it into balls about the size of a goose egg. Flatten each with the rolling-pin, tie them in cloths, and put them into a pot of boiling water. They will boil in a short time. Take care not to let them go to pieces by keeping them too long in the pot.

Serve them up hot, and eat them with corned pork, or with bacon. Or you may eat them with molasses and butter after the meat is removed.

If to be eaten without meat, you may mix in the dough a quarter of a pound of finely chopped suet.

LIVER DUMPLINGS.—Take a calf's liver, and chop it very fine. Mix with it half a pound of beef suet chopped fine also; half a pound of flour; one minced onion; a handful of bread crumbs; a table-spoonful of chopped parsley and sweet marjoram mixed; a few blades of mace and some grated nutmeg; and a little pepper and salt. Mix all well together. Wet the mixture with six eggs well beaten, and make it up into dumplings, with your hands well floured. Have ready a large pot of boiling water. Drop the dumplings into it with a ladle, and let them boil an hour. Have ready bread-crumbs browned in butter to pour over them before they go to table.

HAM DUMPLINGS.—Chop some cold ham, the fat and lean in equal proportions. Season it with pepper and minced sage. Make a crust, allowing half a pound of chopped suet, or half a pound of butter to a pound of flour. Roll it out thick, and divide it into equal portions. Put some minced ham into each, and close up the crust. Have ready a pot of boiling water, and put in the dumplings. Boil them about three quarters of an hour. You may use potatoe paste.

LIGHT DUMPLINGS.—Mix together as much grated bread, butter and beaten egg (seasoned with powdered cinnamon) as will make a stiff paste. Stir it well. Make the mixture into round dumplings, with your hands well floured. Tie up each in a separate cloth, and boil them a short time,—about fifteen minutes. Eat them with wine sauce, or with molasses and butter

PLAIN FRITTERS.

BEAT seven eggs very light, and stir them gradually into a quart of milk; add, by degrees, three quarters of a pound, or a pint and a half of sifted flour. Beat the whole very hard. Have ready in a frying-pan over the fire, a large quantity of lard. When the lard has come to a hard boil, begin to put in the fritters; allowing for each about a jill of batter, or half a large tea-cup full. They do not require turning, and will be done in a few minutes. Fry as many at a time as the pan will hold. Send them to table hot, and eat them with powdered cinnamon, sugar, and white wine. Let fresh hot ones be sent in as they are wanted; they chill and become heavy immediately.

Begin to fry the fritters as soon as the batter is mixed, as it will fall by setting. Near a pound and a half of lard will be required for the above quantity of fritters.

APPLE FRITTERS.—Pare, core, and parboil (in a very little water) some large juicy pippins. When half done, take them out, drain them, and mince them very fine. Make a batter according to the preceding receipt; adding some lemon juice and grated lemon-peel. Stir into the batter a sufficient quantity of the minced apple to make it very thick. Then fry the fritters in hot lard as before directed. Eat them with nutmeg and sugar.

PLAIN PANCAKES.—Sift half a pound or a pint of flour. Beat seven eggs very light, and stir them gradually into a quart of rich milk. Then add by degrees the flour, so as to make a thin batter. Mix it very smooth, pressing out all the lumps with the back of a spoon. Set the frying-pan over the fire, and when it is hot, grease it with a spoonful of lard. Then put in a ladle full of the batter, and fry it of a light brown, turning it with care to prevent its breaking. Make each pancake large enough to cover the bottom of a dessert plate; greasing the pan every time. Send them to table hot, accompanied by powdered sugar and nutmeg mixed in a small glass bowl. Have wine with them also.

SWEETMEAT PANCAKES.—Take a large red beet-root that has been boiled tender; cut it up and pound it in a mortar till you have sufficient juice for colouring the pancakes. Then make a batter as in the preceding receipt, and stir into it at the last enough of the beet juice to give it a fine pink colour. Or instead of the beet juice, you may use a little cochineal dissolved in a very small quantity of brandy. Fry the pancakes in a pan greased with lard or fresh butter; and as fast as they are done, spread thickly over them raspberry jam or any sort of marmalade. Then roll them up nicely, and trim off the ends. Lay them, side by side, on a large dish, and strew powdered sugar over them. Send them to table hot, and eat them with sweetened cream.

PLAIN CUSTARDS.

Tie together six or eight peach leaves, and boil them in a quart of milk with a large stick of cinnamon broken up. If you cannot procure peach leaves, substitute a handful of peach-kernels or bitter almonds, or a vanilla bean split in pieces. When it has boiled hard, strain the milk and set it away to cool. Beat very light eight eggs, and stir them by degrees into the milk when it is quite cold, (if warm, the eggs will curdle it, and cause whey at the bottom,) and add gradually a quarter of a pound of sugar. Fill your cups with it; set them in a Dutch oven, and pour round them boiling water sufficient to reach nearly to the tops of the cups. Put hot coals under the oven and on the lid, (which must be pre-viously heated by standing it up before a hot fire,) and bake the custards about fifteen minutes. Send them to table cold, with nutmeg grated over each. Or you may bake the whole in one large dish.

SOFT CUSTARDS—Are made in the above manner, except that to a quart of milk you must have twelve yolks of eggs, and no whites. You may devote to this purpose the yolks that are left when you have used the whites for cocoanut or almond puddings, or for lady cake or maccaroons.

BOILED CUSTARDS.—Beat eight eggs very light, omitting the whites of four. Mix them gradually with a quart of cold milk and a quarter of a pound of sugar. Put the mixture into a saucepan with a bunch of peach leaves, or a handful of broken up peach-kernels or bitter almonds; the yellow peel of a lemon, and a handful of broken cinnamon; or you may boil in it a vanilla bean. Set it on hot coals, and simmer it slowly, stirring it all the time. As soon as it comes to a boil, take it immediately off the fire, or it will curdle and be lumpy. Then strain it; add a table-spoonful of rosewater, and put it into glass cups. You may lay in the bottom of each cup a maccaroon soaked in wine. Grate nutmeg over the top, and send it to table cold. Eat it with tarts or sweetmeats.

RICE CUSTARD.—Boil some rice in milk till it is quite dry; then put it into small tea-cups, (pressing it down hard,) and when it is cold and has taken the shape of the cups, turn it out into a deep dish, and pour a boiled custard round it. Lay on the top of each lump of rice a piece of preserved quince or peach, or a piece of fruit jelly. In boiling the rice, you may mix with it raisins or currants; if so, omit the sweetmeats on the top. Ground rice is best.

Another way of boiling custard is to put the mixture into a pitcher, set it in a vessel of boiling water, place it on hot coals or in a stove, and let it boil slowly, stirring it all the time.

SNOWBALL CUSTARD.—Make a boiled custard as in the preceding receipts; and when it is done and quite cold, put it into a deep glass dish. Beat to a stiff froth the four whites of eggs that have been omitted in the custard, adding eight or ten drops of oil of lemon. Drop the froth in balls on the top of the dish of custard, heaping and forming them with a spoon into a regular size and shape. Do not let them touch each other. You may lay a fresh rose leaf on the top of every one.

—————

APPLE CUSTARD.—Pare, core, and quarter a dozen large juicy pippins. Strew among them the yellow peel of a large lemon grated very fine; and stew them till tender, in a very small portion of water. When done, mash them smooth with the back of a spoon; (you must have a pint and a half of the stewed apple;) mix a quarter of a pound of sugar with them, and set them away till cold. Beat six eggs very light, and stir them gradually into a quart of rich milk, alternately with the stewed apple. Put the mixture into cups, or into a deep dish, and bake it about twenty minutes. Send it to table cold, with nutmeg grated over the top.

—————

LEMON CUSTARD.—Take four large ripe lemons, and roll them under your hand on the table to increase the juice. Then squeeze them into a bowl, and mix with the juice a very small tea-cup full of cold water. Use none of the peel. Add gradually sufficient sugar to make it *very sweet*. Beat twelve eggs till quite light, and then stir the lemon juice gradually into them, beating very hard at the last. Put the mixture into cups, and bake it ten minutes. When done, grate nutmeg over the top of each, and set them among ice, or in a very cold place.

These custards being made without milk, can be prepared at a short notice; they will be found very fine.

Orange custards may be made in the same manner.

GOOSEBERRY CUSTARD.—Top and tail two quarts of green gooseberries. Stew them in a very little water; stirring and mashing them frequently. When they have stewed till entirely to pieces, take them out, and with a wooden spoon press the pulp through a cullender. Stir in (while the pulp is hot) a table-spoonful of butter, and sufficient sugar to make it very sweet. Beat six eggs very light. Simmer the gooseberry pulp over a gentle fire, and gradually stir the beaten eggs into it. When it comes to a boil, take it off immediately, stir it very hard, and set it out to cool. Serve it up cold in glasses or custard cups, grating some nutmeg over each.

ALMOND CUSTARD.—Scald and blanch half a pound of shelled sweet almonds, and three ounces of shelled bitter almonds; throwing them as you do them into a large bowl of cold water. Then pound them one at a time in a mortar; pouring in frequently a little rose water to prevent their oiling, and becoming dark-coloured and heavy. Melt a quarter of a pound of loaf-sugar in a quart of cream or rich milk, and stir in by degrees the pounded almonds. Beat ten eggs very light, and stir them gradually into the mixture; adding a powdered nutmeg, and a tea-spoonful of powdered mace and cinnamon mixed. Then put the whole into a pitcher, and place it in a kettle or pan of boiling water, the water coming up to the lower part of the neck of the pitcher. Set it over hot coals, and let it boil (stirring it all the time) till it is quite thick, but not till it curdles. Then take the pitcher out of the water; pour the custard into a large bowl, and stir it till it cools. Put it into glass cups, and send it to table cold. Sweeten some cream or white of egg. Beat it to stiff froth and pile it on the top of the custards.

BOILED COCOA-NUT CUSTARD.—To a pound of grated cocoa-nut allow a pint of unskimmed milk, and six ounces of white sugar. Beat very light the yolks of six eggs. Stir them gradually into the milk, alternately with the cocoa-nut and sugar. Put the mixture into a pitcher; set it in a vessel of boiling water; place it on hot coals, and simmer it till it is very smooth and thick; stirring it all the time. As soon as it comes to a hard boil, take it off the fire; pour it into a large bowl, and set it out to cool. When cold, put it into glass cups. Beat to a stiff froth the white of egg that was left, and pile it on the custards.

BAKED COCOA-NUT CUSTARD.—Grate as much cocoa-nut as will weigh a pound. Mix half a pound of powdered white sugar with the milk of the cocoa-nut, or with a pint of cream; adding two table-spoonfuls of rose water. Then stir in gradually a pint of rich milk. Beat to a stiff froth the whites of eight eggs, and stir them into the milk and sugar, a little at a time, alternately with the grated cocoa-nut: add a tea-spoonful of powdered nutmeg and cinnamon. Then put the mixture into cups, and bake them twenty minutes in a Dutch oven half filled with boiling water. When cold, grate loaf-sugar over them.

CHOCOLATE CUSTARD.—Scrape fine a quarter of a pound of chocolate, and pour on it a pint of boiling water. Cover it, and let it stand by the fire till it has dissolved, stirring it twice. Beat eight eggs very light, omitting the whites of two. Stir them by degrees into a quart of cream or rich milk, alternately with the melted chocolate, and three table-spoonfuls of powdered white sugar. Put the mixture into cups, and bake it about ten minutes. Send them to table cold, with sweetened cream, or white of egg beaten to a stiff froth, and heaped on the top of each custard. No chocolate is so good as Baker's prepared cocoa.

MACCAROON CUSTARDS.—These must be made in china custard cups. Put four maccaroons into each cup, and pour on them three spoonfuls of white wine. Mix together a pint of cream, and a pint of milk; and boil them with a large stick of cinnamon broken up, and a small bunch of peach leaves or a handful of broken bitter almonds. Then strain the milk; stir in a quarter of a pound of white sugar, and set it away to cool. Beat very light eight eggs, (omitting the whites of four,) and stir them gradually into the cream and milk when quite cold. Fill your cups with the mixture, (leaving the maccaroons at the bottom,) and set them in a Dutch oven or iron baking pan, which must be half full of boiling water. Heat the oven-lid first, by standing it up before a hot fire; then put it on, spreading coals over the top. Place sufficient coals under the oven, and bake the custards about ten minutes. When cold, heap beaten white of egg on the top of each. These custards are very fine.

SYLLABUB, OR WHIPT CREAM.

PARE off very thin the yellow rind of four large lemons, and lay it in the bottom of a deep dish. Squeeze the juice of the lemons into a large bowl containing a pint of white wine, and sweeten it with half a pound of powdered loaf-sugar. Then, by degrees, mix in a quart of cream. Pour the who.e into the dish in which you have laid the lemon-peel, and let the mixture stand untouched for three hours. Then beat it with rods to a stiff froth, (first taking out the lemon-peel,) and having put into each of your glasses a table-spoonful or more of fruit jelly, heap the syllabub upon it so as to stand up high at the top. This syllabub, if it can be kept in a cold place, may be made the day before you want to use it.

COUNTRY SYLLABUB.—Mix half a pound of white sugar with a pint of fine sweet cider, or of white wine; and grate in a nutmeg. Prepare them in a large bowl, just before milking time. Then let it be taken to the cow, and have about three pints milked into it; stirring it occasionally with a spoon. Let it be eaten before the froth subsides. If you use cider, a little brandy will improve it.

A TRIFLE.—Place half a pound of maccaroons or Naples biscuits at the bottom of a large glass bowl. Pour on them as much white wine as will cover and dissolve them. Make a rich custard, flavoured with bitter almonds or peach leaves: and pour it when cold on the maccaroons; the custard may be either baked or boiled. Then add a layer of marmalade or jam. Take a quart of cream, mix with it a quarter of a pound of sugar, and half a pint of white wine, and whip it with rods to a stiff froth; laying the froth (as you proceed) on an inverted sieve, with a dish under it to catch the cream that drips through; which must be saved and whipped over again. Instead of rods you may use a little tin churn. Pile the frothed cream upon the marmalade in a high pyramid. To ornament it,—take preserved water-melon rind that has been cut into leaves or flowers; split them nicely to make them thinner and lighter; place a circle or wreath of them round the heap of frothed cream, interspersing them with spots of stiff red currant jelly. Stick on the top of the pyramid a sprig of real flowers.

———

FLOATING ISLAND.—Take a quart of rich cream, and divide it in half. Sweeten one pint of it with loaf-sugar, and stir into it sufficient currant jelly to colour it of a fine pink Put it into a glass bowl, and place in the centre a pile of sliced almond-sponge cake, or of lady cake; every slice spread thickly with raspberry jam or marmalade, and laid evenly one on another. Have ready the other pint of cream, flavoured with the juice of two lemons, and beaten with rods to a stiff froth. Heap it all over the pile of cake, so as entirely to cover it. Both creams must be made very sweet.

———

A RASPBERRY CHARLOTTE.—Take a dozen of the square or oblong sponge-cakes that are commonly called Naples biscuits. They should be quite fresh. Spread over each a thick layer of raspberry jam, and place them in the bottom and round the sides of a glass bowl. Take the whites of six eggs, and mix with them six table-spoonfuls of raspberry or currant jelly. Beat the egg and jelly with rods till very light, and then fill up the bowl with it. For this purpose, cream (if you can conveniently procure it) is still better than white of egg.

You may make a charlotte with any sort of jam, marmalade, or fruit jelly. It can be prepared at a short notice, and is very generally liked. You may use ripe strawberries, mashed and sweetened.

A PLUM CHARLOTTE.—Stone a quart of ripe plums; first stew, and then sweeten them. Cut slices of bread and butter, and lay them in the bottom and round the sides of a large bowl or deep dish. Pour in the plums boiling hot, cover the bowl, and set it away to cool gradually. When quite cold, send it to table, and eat it with cream.

CLOTTED CREAM.—Mix together a jill of rich milk, a large wine glass of rose water, and four ounces of white sugar. Add to it the beaten yolks of two eggs. Stir the mixture into a quart of the best cream; set it over hot coals, and let it just come to a boil, stirring it all the time. Then take it off, pour it into a glass bowl, and set it away to get cold. Eat it with fresh strawberries, raspberries, or with any sort of sweetmeats.

LEMON CREAM.—Beat well together a quart of thick cream and the yolks of eight eggs. Then gradually beat in half a pound of powdered loaf-sugar, and the grated rind of three large lemons. Put the mixture into a porcelain skillet, and set it on hot coals till it comes to a boil; then take it off, and stir it till nearly cold. Squeeze the juice of the lemons into a bowl; pour the cream upon it, and continue to stir it till quite cold. You may serve it up in a glass bowl, in glass cups, or in jelly glasses. Eat it with tarts or sweetmeats.

ORANGE CREAM.—Beat very light six eggs, omitting the whites of two. Have ready a pint of orange juice, and stir it gradually into the beaten egg, alternately with a pound of powdered loaf-sugar. Put into a porcelain skillet the yellow rind of one orange, pared very thin; pour the mixture upon it, and set it over a slow fire. Simmer it steadily, stirring it all the time; but when nearly ready to boil, take off, remove the orange-peel, and put the mixture into glasses to get cold.

———

CURDS AND WHEY.—Take a piece of rennet about three inches square, and wash it in two or three cold waters to get off the salt; wipe it dry, and fasten a string to one corner of it. Have ready in a deep dish or pan, a quart of unskimmed milk that has been warmed but not boiled. Put the rennet into it, leaving the string hanging out over the side, that you may know where to find it. Cover the pan, and set it by the fire-side or in some other warm place. When the milk becomes a firm mass of curd, and the whey looks clear and greenish, remove the rennet as gently as possible, pulling it out by the string; and set the pan in ice, or in a very cold place. Send to table with it a small pitcher of white wine, sugar and nutmeg mixed together; or a bowl of sweetened cream, with nutmeg grated over it.

You may keep rennet in white wine; cutting it in small pieces, and putting it into a glass jar with wine enough to cover it well. Either the wine or the rennet will be found good for turning milk; but do not put in both together, or the curd will become so hard and tough as to be uneatable.

Rennets properly prepared and dried, are sold constantly in the Philadelphia markets. The cost is trifling; and it is well to have one always in the house, in case of being wanted to make whey for sick persons. They will keep a year or more.

———

LEMON ICE CREAM

HAVE ready two quarts of very rich thick cream, and take out a pint. Stir gradually into the pint, a pound of the best loaf-sugar powdered fine; and the grated rind and the juice of four ripe lemons of the largest size, or of five or six smaller ones. If you cannot procure the fruit, you may flavour the cream with essence or oil of-lemon; a tea-spoonful or more, according to its strength. The strongest and best essence of lemon is the white or whitish; when tinged with green, it is comparatively weak, having been diluted with water; if quite green, a large tea-spoonful will not communicate as much flavour as five or six drops of the white. After you have mixed the pint of cream with the sugar and lemon, beat it gradually and hard into the remaining cream, that is, the three pints. Cover it, and let it stand to infuse from half an hour to an hour. Then taste it, and if you think it necessary, stir in a little more lemon juice or a little more sugar. Strain it into the freezer through a fine strainer, (a tin one with small close holes is best,) to get rid of the grated lemon-peel, which if left in would prevent the cream from being smooth. Cover the freezer, and stand it in the ice cream tub, which should be filled with a mixture, in equal quantities, of coarse salt, and ice broken up as small as possible, that it may lie close and compact round the freezer, and thus add to its coldness. Snow, when it can be procured, is still better than ice to mix with the salt. It should be packed closely into the tub. and pressed down hard. While the cream is freezing, keep it always in motion, whirling the freezer round by the handle, and opening the lid frequently to stir and beat the cream, and to scrape it down from the sides with a long-handled tin spoon. Take care that no salt gets in, or the cream will be spoiled. When it is entirely frozen, take it out of the freezer and put it into your mould; set it again in the tub, (which must be filled with fresh ice and salt,) and leave it undisturbed till you want it for immediate use. This second freezing, however, should not continue longer than an hour, or the cream will become inconveniently and unpleasantly hard, and have much of the flavour frozen out of it. Place the mould in the ice tub, with the head downwards, and cover the tub with pieces of old carpet while the second freezing is going on. When it has arrived at the proper consistence, and it is time to serve it up, dip a cloth in cold water, and wash it round the mould for a few moments, to loosen the cream and make it come out easily; setting the mould on a glass or china dish. If a pyramid or obelisk mould, lift it carefully off the top. If the mould or form represents doves, dolphins, lap-dogs, fruit baskets, &c. it will open down the middle, and must be taken off in that manner. Serve it up immediately lest it begin to melt. Send round sponge-cake with it, and wine or cordials immediately after.

If you have no moulds, but intend serving it up in a large bowl or in glasses, it must still be frozen twice over; otherwise it can have no smoothness, delicacy, or consistence, but will be rough and coarse, and feel in the mouth like broken icicles. The second freezing (if you have no mould) must be done in the freezer, which should be washed out, and set again in the tub with fresh ice and salt. Cover it closely and let the cream stand in it untouched, but not less than two hours. When you put it into glasses, heap it high on the top.

Begin to make ice cream about four or five hours before it is wanted for use. If you commence it too early, it may probably be injured by having to remain too long in the second freezing, as it must not be turned out till a few moments before it is served up. In damp weather it requires a longer time to freeze.

If cream is scarce, mix with it an equal quantity of rich milk, and then add, for each quart, two table-spoonfuls of powdered arrow-root rubbed smooth in a little cold milk. Orange ice cream is made in the same manner as lemon.

STRAWBERRY ICE CREAM.—Take two quarts of ripe strawberries; hull them, and put them into a deep dish, strewing among them half a pound of powdered loaf-sugar. Cover them, and let them stand an hour or two. Then mash them through a sieve till you have pressed out all the juice, and stir into it half a pound more of powdered sugar, or enough to make it very sweet, and like a thick syrup. Then mix it by degrees with two quarts of rich cream, beating it in very hard. Put it into a freezer, and proceed as in the foregoing receipt. In two hours, remove it to a mould, or take it out and return it again to the freezer with fresh salt and ice, that it may be frozen a second time. In one hour more. It should be ready to turn out.

RASPBERRY ICE CREAM—Is made according to the preceding receipt.

PINE-APPLE ICE CREAM.—To each quart of cream allow a large ripe pine-apple, and a pound of powdered loaf-sugar. Pare the pine-apple, slice it very thin, and mince it small. Lay it in a deep dish and strew the sugar among it. Cover the dish, and let the pine-apple lie in the sugar for two or three hours. Then strain it through a sieve, mashing and pressing out all the juice. Stir the juice gradually into the cream, beating it hard. Put it into the freezer, and let it be twice frozen before it is served up.

VANILLA ICE CREAM.—Take a large vanilla bean, and boil it slowly in half a pint of milk till all the flavour is drawn out, which you may know by tasting it. Then mix into the milk half a pound of powdered loaf-sugar, and stir it very hard into a quart of rich cream. Put it into the freezer, and proceed as directed in the receipt for **Lemon Ice Cream;** freezing it twice.

___

ALMOND ICE CREAM.—Take six ounces of bitter almonds, (sweet ones will not do,) blanch them, and pound them in a mortar, adding by degrees a little rose water. Then boil them gently in a pint of cream till you find that it is highly flavoured with them. Then pour the cream into a bowl, stir in a pound of powdered loaf-sugar, cover it, and set it away to cool gradually; when it is cold, strain it, and then stir it gradually and hard into three pints of cream. Put it into the freezer, and proceed as directed in the first ice cream receipt. Freeze it twice. It will be found very fine.

Send round always with ice cream, sponge cake or Savoy biscuits. Afterwards wine, and cordials, or liqueurs as they are now generally called.

___

ICE ORANGEADE.—Take a pint and a half of orange juice, and mix it with half a pint of clear or filtered water. Stir in half a pound of powdered loaf-sugar. Pare very thin the yellow rind of six deep-coloured oranges, cut in pieces, and lay it at the bottom of a bowl or tureen. Pour the orange juice and sugar upon it; cover it, and let it infuse an hour. Then strain the liquid into a freezer, and proceed as for ice cream. When it is frozen, put it into a mould, (it will look best in the form of a pine-apple,) and freeze it a second time. Serve it in glass cups, with any sort of very nice sweet cakes.

___

ICE LEMONADE—May be made in the above manner, but with a larger proportion of sugar.

The juice of pine-apples, strawberries, raspberries, currants and cherries, may be prepared and frozen according to the above receipts. They will freeze in a shorter time than if mixed with cream, but are very inferior in richness.

~~~~~~~~~~~~~~~~~

BLANC-MANGE.

PUT into a pan an ounce of isinglass; (in warm weather you must take an ounce and a quarter;) pour on as much rose water as will cover the isinglass, and set it on hot coals to dissolve.* Blanch a quarter of a pound of shelled almonds, (half sweet and half bitter,) and beat them to a paste in a mortar, (one at a time,) moistening them all the while with a little rose water. Stir the almonds by degrees into a quart of cream, alternately with half a pound of powdered white sugar; add a large tea-spoonful of beaten mace. Put in the melted isinglass, and stir the whole very hard. Then put it into a porcelain skillet, and let it boil fast for a quarter of an hour. Then strain it into a pitcher, and pour it into your moulds, which must first be wetted with cold water. Let it stand in a cool place undisturbed, till it has entirely congealed, which will be in about five hours. Then wrap a cloth dipped in hot water round the moulds, loosen the blanc-mange round the edges with a knife, and turn it out into glass dishes. It is best to make it the day before it is wanted.

Instead of using a figure-mould, you may set it to congea. in tea-cups or wine glasses.

Blanc-mange may be coloured green by mixing with the

---

* You may make the stock for blanc-mange without isinglass, by boiling four calves' feet in two quarts of water till reduced one half, and till the meat is entirely to rags. Strain it, and set it away till next day. Then clear it from the fat and sediment; cut it into pieces, and boil it with the cream and the other ingredients. When you take it from the fire, and strain it into the pitcher, keep stirring it till it gets cold.

cream a little juice of spinage ; cochineal which has been infused in a little brandy for half an hour, will colour it red ; and saffron will give it a bright yellow tinge.

CARRAGEEN BLANC-MANGE.—This is made of a sea-weed resembling moss, that is found in large quantities on some parts of our coast, and is to be purchased in the cities at most of the druggists. Carrageen costs but little, and is considered extremely salutary for persons of delicate constitutions. Its glutinous nature when boiled, renders it very suitable for blanc-mange.

From a quart of rich unskimmed milk take half a pint. Add to the half pint two ounces of bitter almonds, blanched and pounded; half a nutmeg; and a large stick of cinnamon, broken up; also eight or nine blades of mace. Set it in a closed pan over hot coals, and boil it half an hour. In the mean time, wash through two or three *cold* waters half a handful of carrageen, (if you put in too much it will communicate an unpleasant taste to the blanc-mange,) and add it to the pint and a half of cold milk. Then when it is sufficiently flavoured, stir in the boiled milk, adding gradually half a pound of powdered sugar, and mix the whole very well. Set it over the fire, and keep it boiling hard five minutes from the time it has come to a boil. Then strain it into a pitcher; wet your moulds or cups with cold water, put the blanc-mange into them, and leave it undisturbed till it congeals.

After washing the sea-weed, you must drain it well, and shake the water from the sprigs. You may flavour the mixture (*after* it is boiled and strained) with rose-water or peach-water, stirred in at the last.

ARROW ROOT BLANC-MANGE.—Take a tea-cup full of arrow root, put it into a large bowl, and dissolve it in a little cold water. When it is melted, pour off the water, and let the arrow root remain undisturbed. Boil in half a pint of unskimmed milk, (made very sweet with white sugar,) a beaten nutmeg, and eight or nine blades of mace, mixed with the juice and grated peel of a lemon. When it has boiled long enough to be highly flavoured, strain it into a pint and a half of very rich milk or cream, and add a quarter of a pound of sugar. Boil the whole for ten minutes; then strain it, boiling hot, over the arrow root. Stir it well and frequently till cold; then put it into moulds and let it set to congeal.

JAUNE-MANGE.—Put two ounces of isinglass into a pint of water, and boil it till it has dissolved. Then strain it into a porcelain skillet, and add to it half a pint of white wine: the grated peel and juice of two large deep-coloured oranges: half a pound of loaf-sugar; and the yolks only of eight eggs that have been well beaten. Mix the whole thoroughly; place it on hot coals and simmer it, stirring it all the time till it boils hard. Then take it off directly, strain it, and put it into moulds to congeal.

CALVES' FOOT JELLY.

THE best calves' feet for jelly are those that have had the hair removed by scalding, but are not skinned; the skin containing a great deal of glutinous matter. In Philadelphia, unskinned calves' feet are generally to be met with in the lower or Jersey market.

Boil a set of feet in four quarts of cold water; (if the feet have been skinned allow but three quarts;) they should boil slowly till the liquid is reduced to two quarts or one half the original quantity, and the meat has dropped in rags from the bone. Then strain the liquid; measure and set it away in a large earthen pan to get cold; and let it rest till next morning. Then if you do not find it a firm cake of jelly, boil it over again with an ounce of isinglass, and again set it away till cold and congealed. Remove the sediment from the bottom of the cake of jelly, and carefully scrape off all the fat. The smallest bit of fat will eventually render it dull and cloudy. Press some clean blotting paper all over it to absorb what little grease may yet remain. Then cut the cake of jelly into pieces, and put it into a porcelain kettle to melt over the fire. To each quart allow a pound of broken up loaf-sugar, a pint of Madeira wine, and a large glass of brandy; three large sticks of the best Ceylon cinnamon broken up, (if common cinnamon, use four sticks,) the grated peel and juice of four large lemons; and lastly, the whites of four eggs strained, but not beaten. In breaking the eggs, take care to separate them so nicely that none of the yellow gets into the white; as the smallest portion of yolk of egg will prevent the jelly from being perfectly clear. Mix all the ingredients well together, and put them to the jelly in the kettle. Set it on the fire, and boil it hard for twenty minutes, but do not stir it. Then throw in a tea-cup of cold water, and boil it five minutes longer; then take the kettle off the fire, and set it aside, keeping it closely covered for half an hour; this will improve its clearness. Take a large white flannel jelly-bag; suspend it by the strings to a wooden frame made for such purposes, or to the legs of a table. Pour in the mixture boiling hot, and when it is all in, close up the mouth of the bag that none of the flavour may evaporate. Hang it over a deep white dish or bowl, and let it drip slowly, but on no account squeeze the bag, as that will certainly make the jelly dull and cloudy. If it is not clear the first time, empty the bag, wash it, put in the jelly that has dripped into the dish, and pass it through again. Repeat this till it is clear. You may put it into moulds to congeal, setting them in a cold place. When it is quite firm, wrap a cloth that has been dipped in hot water, round the mou'ds to make the jelly turn out easily. But it will look much better, and the taste will be more lively, if you break it up after it has congealed, and put it into a glass bowl, or heap it in jelly glasses Unless it is broken, its sparkling clearness shows to little advantage.

After the clear jelly has done dripping, you may return the ingredients to the kettle, and warm them over again for about five minutes. Then put them into the bag (which you may now squeeze hard) till all the liquid is pressed out of it into a second dish or bowl. This last jelly cannot, of course, be clear, but it will taste very well, and may be eaten in the family.

A pound of the best raisins picked and washed, and boiled with the other ingredients, is thought by many persons greatly to improve the richness and flavour of calves' feet jelly. They must be put in whole, and can be afterwards used for a pudding.

Similar jelly may be made of pigs' or sheep's feet: but it is not so nice and delicate as that of calves.

By boiling two sets, or eight calves' feet in five quarts of water, you may be sure of having the jelly very firm. In damp weather it is sometimes very difficult to get it to congeal if you use but one set of feet; there is the same risk if the weather is hot. In winter it may be made several days before it is to be eaten.   In summer it will keep in ice for two days; perhaps longer.

TO PRESERVE CREAM.—Take four quarts of new cream ; it must be of the richest quality, and have no milk mixed with it.   Put it into a preserving kettle, and simmer it gently over the fire ; carefully taking off whatever scum may rise to the top, till nothing more appears.   Then stir, gradually, into it four pounds of double-refined loaf-sugar that has been finely powdered and sifted.   Let the cream and sugar boil briskly together half an hour; skimming it, if necessary, and afterwards stirring it as long as it continues on the fire.   Put it into small bottles ; and when it is cold, cork it, and secure the corks with melted rosin.   This cream, if properly prepared, will keep perfectly good during a long sea voyage.

ITALIAN CREAM.—Put two pints of cream into two bowls.   With one bowl mix six ounces of powdered loaf-sugar, the juice of two large lemons, and two glasses of white wine.   Then add the other pint of cream, and stir the whole very hard.   Boil two ounces of isinglass with four small teacups full of water, till it is reduced to one half.   Then stir the isinglass lukewarm into the other ingredients, and put them into a glass dish to congeal.

CHOCOLATE CREAM.—Melt six ounces of scraped chocolate and four ounces of white sugar in one pint of boiling milk.   Stir in an ounce of dissolved isinglass.   When the whole has boiled, pour it into a mould.

COLOURING FOR CONFECTIONARY.

RED.—Take twenty grains of cochineal, and fifteen grains of cream of tartar finely powdered; add to them a piece of alum the size of a cherry stone, and boil them with a jill of soft water, in an earthen vessel, slowly, for half an hour. Then strain it through muslin, and keep it tightly corked in a phial.

COCHINEAL FOR PRESENT USE.—Take two cents' worth of cochineal. Lay it on a flat plate, and bruise it with the blade of a knife. Put it into half a tea-cup of alcohol. Let it stand a quarter of an hour, and then filter it through fine muslin.

YELLOW COLOURING.—Take a little saffron, put it into an earthen vessel with a very small quantity of cold soft water, and let it steep till the colour of the infusion is a bright yellow. Then strain it. The yellow seeds of lilies will answer nearly the same purpose.

GREEN.—Take fresh spinach or beet leaves, and pound them in a marble mortar. If you want it for immediate use, take off the green froth as it rises, and mix it with the article you intend to colour. If you wish to keep it a few days, take the juice when you have pressed out a tea-cup full, and adding to it a piece of alum the size of a pea, give it a boil in a saucepan.

WHITE.—Blanch some almonds, soak them in cold water, and then pound them to a smooth paste in a marble mortar; adding at intervals a little rose water.

Thick cream will communicate a white colour.

These preparations may be used for jellies, ice creams, blanc-mange, syllabubs, icing for cakes; and for various articles of confectionary.

CAKES, ETC.

~~~~~~~~

GENERAL OBSERVATIONS.

UNLESS you are provided with proper and convenient utensils and materials, the difficulty of preparing cakes will be great, and in most instances a failure; involving disappointment, waste of time, and useless expense. Accuracy in proportioning the ingredients is indispensable; and therefore scales and weights, and a set of tin measures (at least from a quart down to a jill) are of the utmost importance. A large sieve for flour is also necessary; and smaller ones for sugar and spice. There should be a marble mortar, or one of lignum vitæ, (the hardest of all wood;) those of iron (however well tinned) are apt to discolour the articles pounded in them. Spice may be ground in a mill kept exclusively for that purpose. Every kitchen should be provided with spice-boxes. You should have a large grater for lemon, cocoa-nut, &c., and a small one for nutmeg. Butter and sugar cannot be stirred together conveniently without a spaddle or spattle, which is a round stick flattened at one end; and a deep earthen pan with sides nearly straight. For beating eggs, you should have hickory rods or a wire whip, and broad shallow earthen pans. Neither the eggs, nor the butter and sugar should be beaten in tin, as the coldness of the metal will prevent them from becoming light.

For baking large cakes, the pans (whether of block tin or earthen) should have straight sides; if the sides slope inward, there will be much difficulty in icing the cake. Pans with a hollow tube going up from the centre, are supposed to diffuse the heat more equally through the middle of the cake. Buns and some other cakes should be baked in square shallow

pans of block tin or iron. Little tins for queen cakes, &c. are
most convenient when of a round or oval shape. All baking
pans, whether large or small, should be well greased with
fresh butter before the mixture is put into them, and should
be filled but little more than half. You should have at least
two dozen little tins, that a second supply may be ready for
the oven the moment the first is taken out. You will also
want tin cutters for cakes that are rolled out in dough.

All the utensils should be cleaned and put away as soon as
they are done with. They should be all kept together, and,
if possible, not used for any other purposes.*

As it is always desirable that cake-making should be commenced at an early hour, it is well on the day previous to
ascertain if all the materials are in the house; that there may
be no unnecessary delay from sending or waiting for them in
the morning. Wastefulness is to be avoided in every thing;
but it is utterly impossible that cakes can be good (or indeed
any thing else) without a liberal allowance of good materials.
Cakes are frequently rendered hard, heavy, and uneatable by
a misplaced economy in eggs and butter; or tasteless and
insipid for want of their due seasoning of spice, lemon; &c.

Use no flour but the best superfine ; if the flour is of inferior
quality, the cakes will be heavy, ill-coloured, and unfit to
eat. Even the best flour should always be sifted. No butter
that is not fresh and good, should ever be put into cakes; for
it will give them a disagreeable taste which can never be
disguised by the other ingredients. Even when of excellent
quality, the butter will be improved by washing it in cold

---

* Hickory rods, spaddles, etc. can be obtained by bespeaking them
at a turner's.

Apple-corers are sold by tinners.

water, and squeezing and pressing it. Except for gingerbread, use only white sugar, (for the finest cakes the best loaf,) and have it pulverized by pounding it in a mortar, or crushing it on the pasteboard with the rolling-pin. It should then be sifted. In mixing butter and sugar, sift the sugar into a deep pan, cut up the butter in it, set it in a warm place to soften, and then stir it very hard with the spaddle, till it becomes quite light, and of the consistence of cream. In preparing eggs, break them one at a time, into a saucer, that, in case there should be a bad one among them, it may not spoil the others. Put them into a broad shallow pan, and beat them with rods or with a wire whisk, not merely till they froth, but long afterwards, till the froth subsides, and they become thick and smooth like boiled custard. White of egg by itself may be beaten with small rods, or with a three-pronged fork, or a broad knife. It is a very easy process, and should be continued till the liquid is all converted into a stiff froth so firm that it will not drop from the rods when held up. In damp weather it is sometimes difficult to get the froth stiff.

The first thing to be done in making cake, is to weigh or measure all the ingredients. Next sift the flour, powder the sugar, pound or grind the spice, and prepare the fruit; afterwards mix and stir the butter and sugar, and lastly beat the eggs; as, if allowed to stand any time, they will fall and become heavy. When all the ingredients are mixed together, they should be stirred very hard at the last; and (unless there is yeast in the cake) the sooner it is put into the oven the better. While baking, no air should be admitted to it, except for a moment, now and then, when it is necessary to examine if it is baking properly. For baking cakes, the best guide is practice and experience; so much depending on the state of the fire, that it is impossible to lay down any infallible rules.

If you bake in a Dutch oven, let the lid be first heated by standing it up before the fire; and cover the inside of the bottom with sand or ashes, to temper the heat. For the same purpose, when you bake in a stove, place bricks under the pans. Sheets of iron without sides will be found very useful for baking small flat akes. For cakes of this description, the fire should be brisk; if baked slowly, they will spread, lose their shape, and run into each other. For all cakes, the heat should be regular and even; if one part of the oven is cooler than another, the cake will bake imperfectly, and have heavy streaks through it. Gingerbread (on account of the molasses) is more apt to scorch and burn than any other cake; therefore it should be baked with a moderate fire.

It is safest, when practicable, to send all large cakes to a professional baker's; provided they can be put immediately into the oven, as standing will spoil them. If you bake them at home, you will find that they are generally done when they cease to make a simmering noise; and when on probing them to the bottom with a twig from a broom, or with the blade of the knife, it comes out quite clean. The fire should then be withdrawn, and the cake allowed to get cold in the oven. Small cakes should be laid to cool on an inverted sieve. It may be recommended to novices in the art of baking, to do every thing in little tins or in very shallow pans; there being then less risk than with a large thick cake. In mixing batter that is to be baked in small cakes, use a less proportion of flour.

Small cakes should be kept closely covered in stone jars. For large ones, you should have broad stone pans with close lids, or else tin boxes. All cakes that are made with yeast, should be eaten quite fresh; so also should sponge cake. Some sorts may be kept a week; black cake much longer.

BLACK CAKE.

PREPARE two pounds of currants by picking them clean, washing and draining them through a cullender, and then spreading them out on a large dish to dry before the fire or in the sun, placing the dish in a slanting position. Pick and stone two pounds of the best raisins, and cut them in half. Dredge the currants (when they are dry) and the raisins thickly with flour to prevent them from sinking in the cake. Grind or powder as much cinnamon as will make a large gravy-spoonful when done; also a table-spoonful of mace and four nutmegs; sift these spices, and mix them all together in a cup. Mix together two large glasses of white wine, one of brandy and one of rose water, and cut a pound of citron into large slips. Sift a pound of flour into one pan, and a pound of powdered loaf-sugar into another. Cut up among the sugar a pound of the best fresh butter, and stir them to a cream. Beat twelve eggs till perfectly thick and smooth, and stir them gradually into the butter and sugar, alternately with the flour. Then add by degrees, the fruit, spice and liquor and stir the whole very hard at the last. Then put the mixture into a well-buttered tin pan with straight or perpendicular sides. Put it immediately into a moderate oven, and bake it at least six hours. When done, take it out and set it on an inverted sieve to cool gradually. Ice it next morning; first dredging the outside all over with flour, and then wiping it with a towel. This will make the icing stick.

———

ICING.—A quarter of a pound of finely-powdered loaf-sugar, of the whitest and best quality, is the usual allowance to one white of egg. For the cake in the preceding receipt, three quarters of a pound of sugar and the whites of three eggs will be about the proper quantity. Beat the white of egg by itself till it stands alone. Have ready the powdered sugar, and then beat it hard into the white of egg, till it becomes thick and smooth; flavouring it as you proceed with the juice of a lemon, or a little extract of roses. Spread it evenly over the cake with a broad knife or a feather; if you find it too thin, beat in a little more powdered sugar. Cover with it thickly the top and sides of the cake, taking care not to have it rough and streaky. When dry, put on a second coat; and when that is nearly dry, lay on the ornaments. You may flower it with coloured sugar-sand or nonparels; but a newer and more elegant mode is to decorate it with devices and borders in white sugar. These are put on with a syringe, moving it skilfully, so as to form the pattern. A little gum tragacanth should be mixed with this icing.

You may colour icing of a pale or deep yellow, by rubbing the lumps of loaf-sugar (before they are powdered) upon the outside of a large lemon or orange. This will also flavour it finely.

Almond icing, for a very fine cake, is made by mixing gradually with the white of egg and sugar, some almonds, half bitter and half sweet, that have been pounded in a mortar with rose water to a smooth paste. The whole must be well incorporated, and spread over the cake near half an inch thick. It must be set in a cool oven to dry, and then taken out and covered with a smooth plain icing of sugar and white of egg.

Whatever icing is left, may be used to make maccaroons or kisses.

POUND CAKE.—Prepare a table-spoonful of powdered cinnamon, a tea-spoonful of powdered mace, and two nutmegs grated or powdered. Mix together in a tumbler, a glass of white wine, a glass of brandy, and a glass of rose water. Sift a pound of the finest flour into a broad pan, and powder a pound of loaf-sugar. Put the sugar into a deep pan, and cut up in it a pound of fresh butter. Warm them by the fire till soft; and then stir them to a cream. When they are perfectly light, add gradually the spice and liquor, a little at a time. Beat ten eggs as light as possible, and stir them by degrees into the mixture alternately with the flour. Then add the juice of two lemons or three large oranges. Stir the whole very hard; put it into a deep tin pan with straight or upright sides, and bake it in a moderate oven from two to three hours. If baked in a Dutch oven, take off the lid when you have ascertained that the cake is quite done, and let it remain in the oven to cool gradually. If any part is burnt, scrape it off as soon as cold.

It may be iced either warm or cool; first dredging the cake with flour and then wiping it off. It will be best to put on two coats of icing; the second coat not till the first is entirely dry. Flavour the icing with essence of lemon, or with extract of roses.

This cake will be very delicate if made with a pound of rice flour instead of wheat.

———

INDIAN POUND CAKE.—Sift a pint of fine yellow Indian meal, and half a pint of wheat flour, and mix them well together. Prepare a nutmeg beaten, and mixed with a table-spoonful of powdered cinnamon. Stir together till very light, half a pound of powdered white sugar; and half a pound of fresh butter; adding the spice, with a glass of white wine, and a glass of brandy. Having beaten eight eggs as light as possible, stir them into the butter and sugar, a little at a time,

In turn with the meal. Give the whole a hard stirring at the last; put it into a well-buttered tin pan, and bake it about two hours.

This cake (like every thing else in which Indian meal is an ingredient) should be eaten quite fresh; it is then very nice. When stale, (even a day old,) it becomes dry and rough as if made with saw-dust.

QUEEN CAKE.—Sift fourteen ounces of the finest flour, being two ounces less than a pound. Cakes baked in little tins, should have a smaller proportion of flour than those that are done in large loaves. Prepare a table-spoonful of beaten cinnamon, a tea-spoonful of mace, and two beaten nutmegs; and mix them all together when powdered. Mix in a tumbler, half a glass of white wine, half a glass of brandy, and half a glass of rose water. Powder a pound of loaf-sugar, and sift it into a deep pan; cut up in it a pound of fresh butter; warm them by the fire, and stir them to a cream. Add gradually the spice and the liquor. Beat ten eggs very light, and stir them into the mixture in turn with the flour. Stir in the juice of two lemons, and beat the whole very hard. Butter some little tins; half fill them with the mixture; set them into a brisk oven, and bake them about a quarter of an hour. When done, they will shrink from the sides of the tins. After you turn them out, spread them on an inverted sieve to cool. If you have occasion to fill your tins a second time, scrape and wipe them well before they are used again.

Make an icing, flavoured with lemon juice or with extract of roses; and spread two coats of it on the queen cakes. Set them to dry in a warm place, but not near enough the fire to discolour the icing and cause it to crack.

Queen cakes are best the day they are baked.

FRUIT QUEEN CAKES.—Make them in the above manner, with the addition of a pound of currants, (picked, washed, dried, and floured,) and the juice and grated peel of two large lemons, stirred in gradually at the last. Instead of currants, you may put in sultana or seedless raisins, cut in half and floured. You may substitute oranges for lemons

You may make a fruit pound cake in this manner.

LADY CAKE.—Take a quarter of a pound of shelled bitter almonds, or peach-kernels. Put them into a bowl of boiling water, (renewing the water as it cools,) and let them lie in it till the skin peels off easily; then throw them, as they are blanched, into a bowl of cold water, which will much improve their whiteness. Pound them, one at a time, in a mortar; pouring in frequently a few drops of rose water to prevent them from oiling and being heavy. Cut up three quarters of a pound of fresh butter into a whole pound of powdered loaf-sugar. Having warmed it, stir it to a light cream, and then add very gradually the pounded almonds, beating them in very hard. Sift into a separate pan half a pound and two ounces of flour, and beat in another pan to a stiff froth, the whites only of seventeen eggs. Stir the flour and the white of egg alternately into the pan of butter, sugar and almonds, a very little at a time of each. Having beaten the whole as hard as possible, put it into a buttered tin pan, (a square one is best,) and set it immediately into a moderate oven. Bake it about an hour, more or less, according to its thickness. When cool, ice it, flavouring the icing with lemon juice. It is best the day it is baked, and should be eaten fresh. When you put it away wrap it in a thick cloth.

If you bake it in little tins, use two ounces less of flour.

SPANISH BUNS.—Cut up three quarters of a pound of butter into a jill and a half or three wine glasses of rich unskimmed milk, (cream will be still better,) and set the pan on a stove or near the fire, till the butter becomes soft enough to stir all through the milk with a knife; but do not let it get so hot as to oil of itself. Then set it away in a cold place. Sift into separate pans, a half pound and a quarter of a pound of the finest flour; and having beaten four eggs as light as possible, mix them with the milk and butter, and then pour the whole into the pan that contains the half pound of flour. Having previously prepared two grated nutmegs, and a tablespoonful of powdered cinnamon and mace, stir them into the mixture; adding six drops of extract of roses, or a large tablespoonful of rose water. Add a wine glass and a half of the best fresh yeast from a brewery. If you cannot procure yeast of the very best quality, an attempt to make these buns will most probably prove a failure, as the variety of other ingredients will prevent them from rising unless the yeast is as strong as possible. Before you put it in, skim off the thin liquid or beer from the top, and then stir up the bottom. After you have put in the yeast, add the sugar; stirring it well in, a very little at a time. If too much sugar is put in at once, the buns will be heavy. Lastly, sprinkle in the quarter of a pound of flour that was sifted separately; and stir the whole very hard. Put the mixture into a square pan well buttered. and (having covered it with a cloth) place it in a corner of the hearth to rise, which will require, perhaps, about five hours; therefore these buns should always be made early in the day. Do not bake it till the batter has risen to twice its original quantity, and is covered on the top with bubbles; then set the pan into a moderate oven, and bake it half an hour. Let it get cool in the pan; then cut it into squares, and either ice them, (flavouring the icing with essence of lemon or extract of roses,) or sift grated loaf-sugar thickly over them. These buns (like all other cakes made with yeast) should be eaten the day they are baked ; as when stale, they fall and become hard.

In mixing them, you may stir in at the last half a pound of raisins, stoned, chopped and floured ; or half a pound of currants. If you use fruit, put in half a wine glass more of the yeast.

————

BATH BUNS.—Boil a little saffron in sufficient water to cover it, till the liquid is of a bright yellow ; then strain it, and set it to cool. Rub half a pound of fresh butter into a pound of sifted flour, and make it into a paste with four eggs that have been well beaten, and a large wine glass of the best and strongest yeast ; adding the infusion of saffron to colour it yellow. Put the dough into a pan, cover it with a cloth, and set it before the fire to rise. When it is quite light, mix into it a quarter of a pound of powdered and sifted loaf-sugar ; a grated nutmeg ; and, if you choose, two or three spoonfuls of carraway seeds. Roll out the dough into a thick sheet, and divide it into round cakes with a cutter. Strew the top of each bun with carraway comfits, and bake them on flat tins buttered well. They should be eaten the day they are baked, as they are not good unless quite fresh.

————

JELLY CAKE.—Sift three quarters of a pound of flour. Stir to a cream a pound of butter and a pound of powdered white sugar, and mix in half a tea-cup of rose water, and a grated nutmeg, with a tea-spoonful of powdered cinnamon. Beat ten eggs very light, and add them gradually to the mixture, alternately with the flour; stirring the whole very hard. Put your griddle into the oven of a stove; and when it is quite hot, grease it with fresh butter tied in a clean rag, and set on it a tin cake-ring, (about the size of a large dinner plate,) greased also. Dip out two large table-spoonfuls and a half of the cake batter; put it within the tin ring, and bake it about five minutes (or a little longer) without turning it. When it is done, take it carefully off; place it on a large d sh to cool; wipe the griddle, grease it afresh, and put on another cake. Proceed thus till all the batter is baked. When the cakes are cool, spread every one thickly over with grape jelly, peach marmalade, or any other sweetmeat that is smooth and thick; currant jelly will be found too thin, and is liable to run off. Lay the cakes smoothly one on another, (each having a layer of jelly or marmalade between,) and either grate loaf-sugar over the top one, or ice it smoothly; marking the icing with cross lines of coloured sugar-sand, all the lines meeting at the centre so as to divide the cake, when cut, into triangular or wedge-shaped slices. If you ice it, add the juice of a lemon to the icing.

Jelly cake should be eaten fresh. It is best the day it is baked.

You may bake small jelly cakes in muffin rings.

SPONGE CAKE.—Sift half a pound of flour,* and powder a pound of the best loaf-sugar. Grate the yellow rind and squeeze into a saucer the juice of three lemons. Beat twelve eggs; and when they are as light as possible, beat into them gradually and very hard the sugar, adding the lemon, and beating the whole for a long time. Then by

---

* Sponge cake may be made with rice flour.

degrees, stir in the flour slowly and lightly; for if the flour is stirred hard and fast into sponge cake, it will make it porous and tough. Have ready buttered, a sufficient number of little square tins, (the thinner they are the better,) half fill them with the mixture; grate loaf-sugar over the top of each; put them immediately into a quick oven, and bake them about ten minutes; taking out one to try when you think they are done. Spread them on an inverted sieve to cool. When baked in small square cakes, they are generally called Naples biscuits.

If you are willing to take the trouble, they will bake much nicer in little square paper cases, which you must make of thick letter paper, turning up the sides all round, and pasting together or sewing up the corners.

If you bake the mixture in one large cake, (which is not advisable unless you have had much practice in baking,) put it into a buttered tin pan or mould, and set it directly into a hot Dutch oven, as it will fall and become heavy if allowed to stand. Keep plenty of live coals on the top, and under the bottom till the cake has risen very high, and is of a fine colour; then diminish the fire, and keep it moderate till the cake is done. It will take about an hour. When cool, ice it; adding a little lemon juice or extract of roses to the icing. Sponge cake is best the day it is baked.

Diet Bread is a foolish name for Sponge Cake.

ALMOND CAKE.—Blanch, and pound in a mortar four ounces of shelled sweet almonds and two ounces of shelled bitter ones; adding, as you proceed, sufficient rose-water to make them light and white. Sift half a pound of flour, and powder a pound of loaf-sugar. Beat thirteen eggs; and when they are as light as possible, stir into them alter-

nately the almonds, sugar, and flour; adding a grated nutmeg.
Butter a large square pan; put in the mixture, and bake it
in a brisk oven about half an hour, less or more, according to
its thickness. When cool, ice it. It is best when eaten
fresh.

COCOA-NUT CAKE.—Cut up and wash a cocoa-nut,
and grate as much of it as will weigh a pound. Powder a
pound of loaf-sugar. Beat fifteen eggs very light; and then
beat into them, gradually, the sugar. Then add by degrees
the cocoa-nut; and lastly, a handful of sifted flour. Stir the
whole very hard, and bake it either in a large tin pan, or in
little tins. The oven should be rather quick.

WASHINGTON CAKE.—Stir together a pound of butter
and a pound of sugar; and sift into another pan a pound of
flour. Beat six eggs very light, and stir them into the butter
and sugar, alternately with the flour and a pint of rich milk or
cream; if the milk is sour it will be no disadvantage. Add
a glass of wine, a glass of brandy, a powdered nutmeg, and a
table-spoonful of powdered cinnamon. Lastly, stir in a small
tea-spoonful of soda, or sal-aratus, that has been melted
in tepid water; take care not to put in too much soda,
lest it give the cake an unpleasant taste. Stir the whole very
hard; put it into a buttered tin pan, (or into little tins,) and
bake it in a brisk oven. Wrapped in a thick cloth, this cake
will keep soft for a week.

CIDER CAKE.—Pick, wash, and dry a pound of currants,
and sprinkle them well with flour; and prepare two nutmegs
and a large table-spoonful of powdered cinnamon. Sift half a
pound and two ounces of flour. Stir together till very light,

six ounces of fresh butter, and half a pound of powdered white sugar; and add gradually the spice, with two wine glasses of brandy, (or one of brandy and one of white wine.) Beat four eggs very light, and stir them into the mixture alternately with the flour. Add by degrees half a pint of brisk cider; and then stir in the currants, a few at a time. Lastly, a small tea-spoonful of pearl-ash or sal-aratus dissolved in a little cider. Having stirred the whole very hard, put it into a buttered tin pan, have the oven ready, and put in the cake immediately. Bake it in a brisk oven an hour or more, according to its thickness. Or you may bake it as little cakes, putting it into small tins; in which case use but half a pound of flour in mixing the batter.

ELECTION CAKE.—Make a sponge (as it is called) in the following manner :—Sift into a pan two pounds and a half of flour; and into a deep plate another pound. Take a second pan, and stir two table-spoonfuls of the best West India molasses into five jills or two tumblers and a half of strong fresh yeast; adding a jill of water, warm, but not hot. Then stir gradually into the yeast, &c. the pound of flour that you have sifted separately. Cover it, and let it set by the fire three hours to rise. While it is rising, prepare the other ingredients, by stirring in a deep pan two pounds of fresh butter and two pounds of powdered sugar, till they are quite light and creamy; adding to them a table-spoonful of powdered cinnamon; a tea-spoonful of powdered mace; and two powdered nutmegs. Stir in also half a pint of rich milk. Beat fourteen eggs till very smooth and thick, and stir them gradually into the mixture, alternately with the two pounds and a half of flour which you sifted first. When the sponge is quite light, mix the whole together, and bake it in buttered tin pans in a moderate oven. It should be eaten fresh, as no sweet cake made with yeast is so good after the first day. If it is not probable that the whole will come into use on the day it is baked, mix but half the above quantity.

MORAVIAN SUGAR CAKE.—Cut up a quarter of a pound of butter into a pint of rich milk, and warm it till the butter becomes soft; then stir it about in the milk so as to mix them well. Sift three quarters of a pound of flour (or a pint and a half) into a deep pan, and making a hole in the middle of it, stir in a large table-spoonful of the best brewer's yeast in which a salt-spoonful of salt has been dissolved; and then thin it with the milk and butter. Cover it, and set it near the fire to rise. If the yeast is sufficiently strong, it will most probably be light in two hours. When it is quite light, mix with the dough two beaten eggs and three quarters of a pound more of sifted flour; adding a tea-spoonful of oil of cinnamon, and stirring it very hard. Butter a large round baking pan, and put the mixture into it. Set it to rise again, as before. Mix together five ounces or a large coffee-cup of fine brown sugar; two ounces of butter; and two table-spoonfuls of powdered cinnamon. When the dough is thoroughly light, make deep incisions all over it, at equal distances, and fill them with the mixture of butter, sugar and cinnamon, pressing it hard down into the bottom of the holes, and closing the dough a little at the top to prevent the seasoning from running out. Strew some sugar over the top of the cake; set it immediately into the oven, and bake it from an hour and a half to two hours, or more, in a brisk oven in proportion to its thickness. When cool, cut it into squares This is a very good plain cake; but do not attempt it unless you have excellent yeast.

HUCKLEBERRY CAKE. — Spread a quart of ripe huckleberries on a large dish, and dredge them thickly with flour. Mix together half a pint of milk; half a pint of molasses; half a pint of powdered sugar; and half a pound of butter. Warm them by the fire till the butter is quite soft · then stir them all together, and set them away till cold. Prepare a large table-spoonful of powdered cloves and cinnamon mixed. Beat five eggs very light, and stir them gradually into the other ingredients; adding, by degrees, sufficient sifted flour to make a thick batter. Then stir in a small tea-spoonful of pearl-ash or dissolved sal-aratus. Lastly, add by degrees the huckleberries. Put the mixture into a buttered pan, or into little tins, and bake it in a moderate oven. It is best the second day.

BREAD CAKE.—When you are making wheat bread, and the dough is quite light and ready to bake, take out as much of it as would make a twelve cent loaf, and mix with it a tea-cup full of powdered sugar, and a tea-cup full of butter that has been softened and stirred about in a tea-cup of warm milk. Add also a beaten egg. Knead it very well, put it into a square pan, dredged with flour, cover it, and set it near the fire for half an hour. Then bake it in a moderate oven, and wrap it in a thick cloth as soon as it is done. It is best when fresh.

FEDERAL CAKES.

SIFT two pounds of flour into a deep pan, and cut up in it a pound of fresh butter; rub the butter into the flour with your hands, adding by degrees, half a pound of powdered white sugar; a tea-spoonful of powdered cinnamon; a beaten nutmeg; a glass of wine or brandy, and two glasses of rose water. Beat four eggs very light; and add them to the mixture with a salt-spoonful of soda melted in a little lukewarm water. Mix all well together; add, if necessary, sufficient cold water to make it into a dough just stiff enough to roll out; knead it slightly, and then roll it out into a sheet about half an inch thick. Cut it out into small cakes with a tin cutter, or with the edge of a tumbler; dipping the cutter frequently into flour, to prevent its sticking. Lay the cakes in shallow pans buttered, or on flat sheets of tin, (taking care not to let them touch, lest they should run into each other,) and bake them of a light brown in a brisk oven. They are best the second day.

SAVOY BISCUITS.—Take four eggs, and separate the whites from the yolks. Beat the whites by themselves, to a stiff froth; then add gradually the yolks, and beat them both together for a long time. Next add by degrees half a pound of the finest loaf-sugar, powdered and sifted, beating it in very hard; and the juice of a lemon or orange. Lastly, stir in a quarter of a pound of sifted flour, a little at a time. Stir the whole very hard, and then with a spoon lay it on sheets of white paper, forming it into thin cakes of an oblong or oval shape. Take care not to place them too close to each other, lest they run. Grate loaf-sugar over the top of each, to assist in keeping them in shape. Have the oven quite ready to put them in immediately. It should be rather brisk. They will bake in a few minutes, and should be but slightly coloured. They are sometimes called lady-fingers.

ALMOND MACCAROONS.—Take a pound of shelled sweet almonds, and a quarter of a pound of shelled bitter almonds. Blanch them in scalding water, mix them together and pound them, one or two at a time, in a mortar to a very smooth paste; adding frequently a little rose water to prevent them from oiling and becoming heavy. Prepare a pound of powdered loaf-sugar. Beat the whites of seven eggs to a stiff froth, and then beat into it gradually the powdered sugar, adding a table-spoonful of mixed spice, (nutmeg, mace, and cinnamon.) Then mix in the pounded almonds, (which it is best to prepare the day before,) and stir the whole very hard. Form the mixture with a spoon into little round or oval cakes, upon sheets of buttered white paper, and grate white sugar over each. Lay the paper in square shallow pans, or on iron sheets, and bake the maccaroons a few minutes in a brisk oven, till of a pale brown. When cold, take them off the papers.

It will be well to try two or three first, and if you find them likely to lose their shape and run into each other, you may omit the papers and make the mixture up into little balls with your hands well floured; baking them in shallow tin pans slightly buttered.

You may make maccaroons with icing that is left from a cake; adding pounded almonds &c.

COCOA-NUT MACCAROONS.—Beat to a stiff froth the whites of six eggs, and then beat into it very hard a pound of powdered loaf-sugar. Mix with it a pound of grated cocoa-nut, or sufficient to make a stiff paste. Then flour your hands, and make it up into little balls. Lay them on sheets of buttered white paper, and bake them in a brisk oven; first grating loaf-sugar over each. They will be done in a few minutes.

Maccaroons may be made in a similar manner of pounded cream-nuts, ground-nuts, filberts, or English walnuts.

WHITE COCOA-NUT CAKES.—Break up a cocoa-nut; peel, and wash the pieces in cold water, and grate them. Mix in the milk of the nut and some powdered loaf-sugar, and then form the grated cocoa-nut into little balls upon sheets of white paper. Make them all of a regular and handsome form, and touch the top of each with a spot of red sugar-sand. Do not bake them, but place them to dry for twenty-four hours, in a warm room where nothing is likely to disturb them.

COCOA-NUT JUMBLES.—Grate a large cocoa-nut. Rub half a pound of butter into a pound of sifted flour. and wet it with three beaten eggs, and a little rose water. Add by degrees the cocoa-nut, so as to form a stiff dough. Flour your hands and your paste-board, and dividing the dough into equal portions, make the jumbles with your hands into long rolls, and then curl them round and join the ends so as to form rings. Grate loaf-sugar over them; lay them in buttered pans, (not so near as to run into each other,) and bake them in a quick oven from five to ten minutes.

COMMON JUMBLES.—Sift a pound of flour into a large pan. Cut up a pound of butter into a pound of powdered white sugar, and stir them to a cream. Beat six eggs till very light, and then pour them all at once into the pan of flour; next add the butter and sugar, with a large table-spoonful of mixed mace and cinnamon, two grated nutmegs, and the juice of two lemons, or a wine glass of rose water. When all the ingredients are in, stir the mixture very hard with a broad knife. Having floured your hands and spread some flour on the paste-board, make the dough into long rolls, (all of equal size,) and form them into rings by joining the two ends very nicely. Lay them on buttered tins, and bake them in a quick oven from five to ten minutes. Grate sugar over them when cool.

APEES.—Rub a pound of fresh butter into two pounds of sifted flour, and mix in a pound of powdered white sugar, a grated nutmeg, a table-spoonful of powdered cinnamon, and four large table-spoonfuls of carraway seeds. Add a wine glass of rose water, and mix the whole with sufficient cold water to make it a stiff dough. Roll it out into a large sheet about a third of an inch in thickness, and cut it into round cakes with a tin cutter or with the edge of a tumbler. Lay them in buttered pans, and bake them in a quick oven, (rather hotter at the bottom than at the top,) till they are of a very pale brown.

WHITE CUP CAKE.—Measure one large coffee cup of cream or rich milk, (which, for this cake, is best when sour,) one cup of fresh butter; two cups of powdered white sugar; and four cups of sifted flour. Stir the butter and sugar together till quite light; then by degrees add the cream, alternately with half the flour. Beat five eggs as light as possible, and stir them into the mixture, alternately with the remainder of the flour. Add a grated nutmeg and a large tea-spoonful of powdered cinnamon, with rose water to your taste. Lastly, stir in a very small tea-spoonful of sal-aratus or pearl-ash, melted in a little tepid water. Having stirred the whole very hard, put it into little tins; set them in a moderate oven, and bake them about twenty minutes.

KISSES.—Powder a pound of the best loaf-sugar. Beat to a strong froth the whites of eight eggs, and when it is stiff

enough to stand alone, beat into it the powdered sugar, (a
tea-spoonful at a time,) adding the juice of two lemons, or of
two large oranges. Having beaten the whole very hard,
drop it in oval or egg-shaped heaps upon sheets of white
paper, smoothing them with a broad knife dipped in cold
water. Place them in a moderate oven, (if it is too cool
they will not rise, but will flatten and run into each other,)
and bake them till coloured of a very pale brown. Then take
them off the papers very carefully, place two bottoms (or
flat sides) together so as to unite them in an oval ball, and
lay them on their sides to cool. You may scoop out a little
from the under-surface of each, and put in some jelly. Then
stick the flat sides together.

MARMALADE CAKE.—Make a batter as for queen-cake.
and bake it in small tin rings on a griddle. Beat white or
egg, and powdered loaf-sugar according to the preceding receipt, flavouring it with lemon. When the batter is baked into
cakes, and they are quite cool, spread over each a thick layer
of marmalade, and then heap on with a spoon the icing or
white of egg and sugar. Pile it high, and set the cakes in a
moderate oven till the icing is coloured of a very pale brown.

Instead of small ones you may bake the whole in one large
cake.

SECRETS.—Take glazed paper of different colours, and
cut it into squares of equal size, fringing two sides of each.
Have ready, burnt almonds, chocolate nuts, and bonbons or
sugar-plums of various sorts; and put one in each paper
with a folded slip containing two lines of verse; or what will
be much more amusing, a conundrum with the answer. Twist

the coloured paper so as entirely to conceal their contents, leaving the fringe at each end. This is the most easy, but there are various ways of cutting and ornamenting these envelopes.

———

SCOTCH CAKE.—Rub three quarters of a pound of butter into a pound of sifted flour; mix in a pound of powdered sugar, and a large table-spoonful of powdered cinnamon. Mix it into a dough with three well beaten eggs. Roll it out into a sheet; cut it into round cakes, and bake them in a quick oven; they will require but a few minutes.

———

SCOTCH QUEEN CAKE.—Melt a pound of butter by putting it into a skillet on hot coals. Then set it away to cool. Sift two quarts of oatmeal into a deep pan, and mix with it a pound of powdered sugar and a table-spoonful of powdered cinnamon and mace. Make a hole in the middle, put in the melted butter, and mix it with a knife till you have formed of the whole a lump of dough. If it is too stiff, moisten it with a little rose water. Knead it well, and roll it out into a large oval sheet, an inch thick. Cut it down the middle, and then across, so as to divide it into four cakes. Prick them with a fork, and crimp or scollop the edges neatly. Lay them in shallow pans; set them in a quick oven and bake them of a light brown. This cake will keep a week or two.

You may mix in with the dough half a pound of currants, picked, washed, and dried.

———

HONEY CAKES.—Take a quart of strained honey, half a pound of fresh butter, and a small tea-spoonful of pearl-ash dissolved in a little sour milk. Add by degrees as much sifted flour as will make a stiff paste. Work the whole well together. Roll it out about half an inch thick. Cut it into cakes with the edge of a tumbler or with a tin cake-cutter. Lay them on buttered tins and bake them with rather a brisk fire, but see that they do not burn.

WAFER CAKES.

Mix together half a pound of powdered sugar, and a quarter of a pound of butter; and add to them six beaten eggs. Then beat the whole very light; stirring into it as much sifted flour as will make a stiff batter; a powdered nutmeg, and a tea-spoonful of cinnamon; and the juice of a lemon, or a table-spoonful of rose water. The batter must be very smooth when it is done, and without a single lump. Heat your wafer iron on both sides by turning it in the fire; but do not allow it to get too hot. Grease the inside with butter tied in a rag, (this must be repeated previous to the baking of every cake,) and put in the batter, allowing to each wafer two large table-spoonfuls, taking care not to stir up the batter. Close the iron, and when one side is baked, turn it on the other; open it occasionally to see if the wafer is doing well. They should be coloured of a light brown. Take them out carefully with a knife. Strew them with powdered sugar, and roll them up while warm, round a smooth stick, withdrawing it when they grow cold. They are best the day after they are baked.

If you are preparing for company, fill up the hollow of the wafers with whipt cream, and stop up the two ends with preserved strawberries, or with any other small sweetmeat.

WONDERS, OR CRULLERS.—Rub half a pound of butter into two pounds of sifted flour, mixing in three quarters of a pound of powdered sugar. Add a tea-spoonful of powdered cinnamon, and a grated nutmeg, with a large table-spoonful of rose water. Beat six eggs very light, and stir them into the mixture. Mix it with a knife into a soft paste. Then put it on the paste-board, and roll it out into a sheet an inch thick. If you find it too soft, knead in a little more flour, and roll it out over again. Cut it into long slips with a jagging iron, or with a sharp knife, and twist them into various fantastic shapes. Have ready on hot coals, a skillet of boiling lard ; put in the crullers and fry them of a light brown, turning them occasionally by means of a knife and fork. Take them out one by one on a perforated skimmer, that the lard may drain off through the holes. Spread them out on a large dish, and when cold grate white sugar over them.

They will keep a week or more.

DOUGH NUTS.—Take two deep dishes, and sift three quarters of a pound of flour into each. Make a hole in the centre of one of them, and pour in a wine glass of the best brewer's yeast; mix the flour gradually into it, wetting it with lukewarm milk ; cover it, and set it by the fire to rise for about two hours. This is setting a sponge. In the mean time, cut up five ounces of butter into the other dish of flour, and rub it fine with your hands ; add half a pound of powdered sugar, a tea-spoonful of powdered cinnamon, a grated nutmeg, a table-spoonful of rose water, and a half pint of milk. Beat three eggs very light, and stir them hard into the mixture. Then when the sponge is perfectly light, add it to the other ingredients, mixing them all thoroughly with a knife. Cover it, and set it again by the fire for another hour. When it is quite light, flour your paste-board, turn out the lump of dough, and cut it into thick diamond shaped cakes with a jagging iron. If you find the dough so soft as to be unmanageable, mix in a little more flour; but not else. Have ready a skillet of boiling lard; put the dough-nuts into it, aud fry them brown; and when cool grate loaf-sugar over them. They should be eaten quite fresh, as next day they will be tough and heavy; therefore it is best to make no more than you want for immediate use. The New York Oley Koeks are dough-nuts with currants and raisins in them.

WAFFLES.—Put two pints of rich milk into separate pans. Cut up and melt in one of them a quarter of a pound of butter, warming it slightly; then, when it is melted, stir it about, and set it away to cool. Beat eight eggs till very light, and mix them gradually into the other pan of milk, alternately with half a pound of flour. Then mix in by degrees the milk that has the butter in it. Lastly, stir in a large table-spoonful of strong fresh yeast. Cover the pan, and set it near the fire to rise. When the batter is quite light, heat your waffle-iron, by putting it among the coals of a clear bright fire; grease the inside with butter tied in a rag, and then put in some batter. Shut the iron closely, and when the waffle is done on one side, turn the iron on the other. Take the cake out by slipping a knife underneath; and then heat and grease the iron for another waffle. Send them to table quite hot, four or six on a plate; having buttered them and strewed over each a mixture of powdered cinnamon, and white sugar. Or you may send the sugar and cinnamon in a little glass bowl.

In buying waffle-irons, do not choose those broad shallow ones that are to hold four at a time; as the waffles baked in them are too small, too thin, and are never of a good shape

The common sort that bake but two at once are much the best. They should be of a deep well-cut pattern.

NEW YORK COOKIES.—Take a half-pint or a tumbler full of cold water, and mix it with half a pound of powdered white sugar. Sift three pounds of flour into a large pan, and cut up in it a pound of butter; rub the butter very fine into the flour. Add a grated nutmeg, and a tea-spoonful of powdered cinnamon, with a wine glass of rose water. Work in the sugar, and make the whole into a stiff dough, adding, if necessary, a little cold water. Dissolve a tea-spoonful of soda in just enough tepid water to cover it; and mix it in at the last. Take the lump of dough out of the pan, and knead it on the paste-board till it becomes quite light. Then roll it out rather more than half an inch thick, and cut it into square cakes with a jagging iron or with a sharp knife. Stamp the surface of each with a cake print. Lay them in buttered pans, and bake them of a light brown in a brisk oven.

They are similar to what are called New Year's cakes, and will keep two or three weeks.

In mixing the dough, you may add three table-spoonfuls of carraway seeds.

SUGAR BISCUIT.—Wet a pound of sugar with two large tea-cups full of milk; and rub a pound of butter into two pounds of flour; adding a table-spoonful of cinnamon, or a handful of carraway seeds. Mix in the sugar, add a tea-spoonful of soda dissolved, and make the whole into a stiff dough. Knead it, and then roll it out into a sheet about half an inch thick. Beat it on both sides with the rolling-pin, and then cut it out with the edge of a tumbler into round cakes. Prick them with a fork, lay them in buttered pans, and bake them light brown in a quick oven. You may colour them yellow by mixing in with the other ingredients a little of the infusion of saffron. These are the hard sugar-biscuits.

RUSKS.—Sift three pounds of flour into a large pan, and rub into it half a pound of butter, and half a pound of sugar. Beat two eggs very light, and stir them into a pint and a half of milk, adding two table-spoonfuls of rose water, and three table-spoonfuls of the best and strongest yeast. Make a hole in the middle of the flour, pour in the liquid, and gradually mix the flour into it till you have a thick batter. Cover it, and set it by the fire to rise. When it is quite light, put it on your paste-board and knead it well. Then divide it into small round cakes and knead each separately. Lay them very near each other in shallow iron pans that have been sprinkled with flour. Prick the top of each rusk with a fork, and set them by the fire to rise again for half an hour or more. When they are perfectly light, bake them in a moderate oven. They are best when fresh. The sugar-biscuits are made the same way.

You can convert them into what are called Hard Rusks, or Tops and Bottoms, by splitting them in half, and putting them again into the oven to harden and crisp.

MILK BISCUIT.—Cut up three quarters of a pound of butter in a quart of milk, and set it near the fire to warm, til. the butter becomes soft ; then with a knife, mix it thoroughly with the milk, and set it away to cool. Afterwards stir in two wine glasses of strong fresh yeast, and add by degrees as much sifted flour as will make a dough just stiff enough to roll out. As soon as it is mixed, roll it into a thick sheet. and cut it out into round cakes with the edge of a tumbler or a wine glass. Sprinkle a large iron pan with flour; lay the biscuits in it, cover it and set it to rise near the fire. When the biscuits are quite light, knead each one separately; prick them with a fork, and set them again in a warm place for about half an hour. When they are light again, bake them in a moderate oven. They should be eaten fresh, and pulled open with the fingers, as splitting them with a knife will make them heavy.

WHITE GINGERBREAD.

SIFT two pounds of flour into a deep pan, and rub into it three quarters of a pound of butter; then mix in a pound of common white sugar powdered; and three table-spoonfuls of the best white ginger. Having beaten four eggs very light, mix them gradually with the other ingredients in the pan, and add a small tea-spoonful of pearl-ash melted in a wine glass of sour milk. Stir the whole as hard as possible. Flour your paste-board; lay the lump of dough upon it, and roll it out into a sheet an inch thick; adding more flour if necessary. Butter a large shallow square pan. Lay the dough into it, and bake it in a moderate oven. When cold, cut it into squares. Or you may cut it out into separate cakes with a jagging iron, previous to baking. You must be careful not to lay them too close together in the pan, lest they run into each other.

COMMON GINGERBREAD.—Cut up a pound of butter in a quart of West India molasses, which must be perfectly sweet; sugar-house molasses will make it hard and heavy. Warm it slightly, just enough to melt the butter. Crush with the rolling-pin, on the paste-board, half a pound of brown sugar, and add it by degrees to the molasses and butter; then stir in three table-spoonfuls of ginger, a large

tea-spoonful of powdered cloves, and a tea-spoonful of pow
dered cinnamon. Add gradually sufficient flour to make a
dough stiff enough to roll out easily; and lastly, a small tea-
spoonful of pearl-ash melted in a little sour milk. Mix and
stir the dough very hard with a spaddle, or a wooden spoon;
but do not knead it. Then divide it with a knife into equal
portions; and, having floured your hands, roll it out on the
paste-board into long even strips. Place them in shallow
tin pans, that have been buttered; either laying tne strips
side by side in straight round sticks, (uniting them at both
ends,) or coil them into rings one within another, as you see
them at the cake shops. Bake them in a brisk oven, taking
care that they do not burn; gingerbread scorching sooner than
any other cake.

To save time and trouble, you may roll out the dough into
a sheet near an inch thick, and cut it into round flat cakes
with a tin cutter, or with the edge of a tumbler.

Ground ginger loses much of its strength by keeping.
Therefore it will be frequently found necessary to put in more
than the quantity given in the receipt.

GINGERBREAD NUTS.—Rub half a pound of butter
into a pound and a half of sifted flour; and mix in half a
pound of brown sugar, crushed fine with the rolling-pin. Add
three table-spoonfuls of ginger, a tea-spoonful of powdered
cloves, and a tea-spoonful of powdered cinnamon. Stir in a
pint of molasses, and the grated peel of a large lemon, but
not the juice, as you must add at the last a very small tea-
spoonful of pearl-ash dissolved in tepid water, and pearl-
ash entirely destroys the taste of lemon-juice and of every
other acid. Stir the whole mixture very hard with a spaddle
or with a wooden spoon, and make it into a lump of dough

just stiff enough to roll out into a sheet about half an inch thick. Cut it out into small cakes about the size of a quarter dollar; or make it up, with your hands well floured, into little round balls, flattening them on the top. Lay them in buttered pans, and bake them in a moderate oven. They will keep several weeks. Use West India molasses.

FRANKLIN CAKE.—Mix together a pint of molasses, and half a pint of milk, and cut up in it half a pound of butter. Warm them just enough to melt the butter, and then stir in six ounces of brown sugar; adding three table-spoonfuls of ginger, a table-spoonful of powdered cinnamon, a tea-spoonful of powdered cloves, and a grated nutmeg. Beat seven eggs very light, and stir them gradually into the mixture, in turn with a pound and two ounces of flour. Add. at the last, the grated peel and juice of two large lemons or oranges; the peel grated very fine. This gingerbread requires no pearl-ash. Stir the mixture very hard; put it into little queen-cake tins, well buttered; and bake it in a moderate oven. It is best the second day, and will keep soft a week. Use West India molasses.

GINGER PLUM CAKE.—Stone a pound and a half of raisins, and cut them in two. Wash and dry half a pound of currants. Sift into a pan two pounds of flour. Put into another pan a pound of brown sugar, (rolled fine,) and cut up in it a pound of fresh butter. Stir the butter and sugar to a cream, and add to it two table-spoonfuls of the best ginger, one table-spoonful of powdered cinnamon; and one of pow- dered cloves. Then beat six eggs very light, and add them gradually to the butter and sugar, in turn with the flour and a quart of molasses. Lastly, stir in a tea-spoonful of pearl-ash dissolved in lukewarm water and add by degrees the fruit, which must be well dredged with flour. Stir all very hard; put the mixture into a buttered pan, and bake it in a moderate oven. Use West India molasses.

MOLASSES CANDY.—Mix a pound of the best brown sugar with two quarts of West India molasses, (which must be perfectly sweet,) and boil it in a preserving kettle over a moderate fire for three hours, skimming it well, and stirring it frequently after the scum has ceased to rise; taking care that it does not burn. Have ready the grated rind and the juice of three lemons, and stir them into the molasses after it has boiled about two hours and a half; or you may substitute the juice and rind of three large oranges. The flavour of the lemon will all be boiled out if it is put in too soon. The mixture should boil at least three hours, that it may be crisp and brittle when cold. If it is taken off the fire too soon, or before it has boiled sufficiently, it will not congeal, but will be tough and ropy, and must be boiled over again. It will cease boiling of itself when it is thoroughly done. Then take it off the fire; have ready a square tin pan; put the mixture into it, and set it away to cool. The pan should be buttered.

You may make molasses candy with almonds blanched and slit into pieces; stir them in by degrees after the mixture has boiled two hours and a half. Or you may blanch a quart of ground-nuts and put them in instead of the almonds.

NOUGAT.—Blanch a pound of shelled sweet almonds; and with an almond-cutter, or a sharp penknife, split each almond into two slips. Spread them over a lage dish, and place them in a gentle oven. Powder two pounds of the best loaf-sugar, and put it into a preserving pan without a drop of water. Set it on a chafing-dish over a slow fire, or on a hot stove, and stir it with a wooden spoon till the heat has entirely dissolved it. Then take the almonds out of the oven, and mix with them the juice of two or three lemons. Put them into the sugar a few at a time, and let them simmer till it becomes a thick stiff paste, stirring it hard all the while. Have ready a mould, or a square tin pan, greased all over the inside with sweet oil; put the mixture into it; smooth it evenly, and set it in a cold place to harden. When almost hard cut it into long slips.

LEMON DROPS.—Squeeze some lemon-juice into a pan. Pound in a mortar some of the best loaf-sugar, and then sift it through a very fine sieve. Mix it with the lemon-juice, making it so thick that you can scarcely stir it. Put it into a porcelain saucepan, set it on hot coals, and stir it with a wooden spoon five minutes or more. Then take off the pan, and with the point of a knife drop the liquid on writing paper. When cold, the drops will easily come off.

Peppermint drops may be made as above, substituting for the lemon-juice essence of peppermint.

Orange drops may be made in the same manner.

WARM CAKES FOR BREAKFAST AND TEA.

~~~~~~

BUCKWHEAT CAKES.

TAKE a quart of buckwheat meal, mix with it a tea-spoonful of salt, and add a handful of Indian meal. Pour two table-spoonfuls of the best brewer's yeast into the centre of the meal. Then mix it with lukewarm water till it becomes a batter. Cover it, put it in a warm place and set it to rise; it will take about three hours. When it is quite light, and covered with bubbles, it is fit to bake. Put your griddle over the fire, and let it get quite hot before you begin. Grease it well with a piece of butter tied in a rag. Then dip out a large ladle full of the batter and bake it on the griddle; turning it with a broad wooden paddle. Let the cakes be of large size, and even at the edges. Ragged edges to batter cakes look very badly. Butter them as you take them off the griddle. Put several on a plate, and cut them across in six pieces.

Keep the griddle very clean.

If your batter has been mixed over night and is found to be sour in the morning, melt in warm water a piece of pearl-ash the size of a grain of corn, or a little larger; stir it into the batter; let it set half an hour, and then bake it. The pearl-ash will remove the sour taste, and increase the lightness of the cakes.

———

FLANNEL CAKES.—Put a table-spoonful of butter into a quart of milk, and warm them together till the butter has melted; then stir it well, and set it away too cool. Beat five eggs as light as possible, and stir them into the milk in turn with three pints of sifted flour; add a small tea-spoonful of salt, and a large table-spoonful and a half of the best fresh yeast. Set the pan of batter near the fire to rise; and if the yeast is good, it will be light in three hours. Then bake it on a griddle in the manner of buckwheat cakes. Send them to table hot, and cut across into four pieces. This batter may be baked in waffle-irons. If so, send to table with the cakes powdered white sugar and cinnamon.

INDIAN BATTER CAKES.—Mix together a quart of sifted Indian meal, (the yellow meal is best for all purposes,) and a handful of wheat flour. Warm a quart of milk, and stir into it a small tea-spoonful of salt, and two large table-spoonfuls of the best fresh yeast. Beat three eggs very light, and stir them gradually into the milk in turn with the meal. Cover it, and set it to rise for three or four hours. When quite light, bake it on a griddle in the manner of buckwheat cakes. Butter them, cut them across, and send them to table hot, with molasses in a sauce-boat.

If the batter should chance to become sour before it is baked, stir in about a salt-spoonful of pearl-ash dissolved in a little lukewarm water; and let it set half an hour longer before it is baked.

INDIAN MUSH CAKES.—Pour into a pan three pints of cold water, and stir gradually into it a quart of sifted Indian meal which has been mixed with half a pint of wheat flour, and a small tea-spoonful of salt. Give it a hard stirring at the last. Have ready a hot griddle, and bake the batter immediately, in cakes about the size of a saucer. Send them to table piled evenly, but not cut. Eat them with butter or molasses.

This is the most economical and expeditious way of making soft Indian cakes; but it cannot be recommended as the best. It will be some improvement to mix the meal with milk rather than water.

JOHNNY CAKE.—Sift a quart of Indian meal into a pan; make a hole in the middle, and pour in a pint of warm water. Mix the meal and water gradually into a batter, adding a small tea-spoonful of salt. Beat it very hard, and for a long time, till it becomes quite light. Then spread it thick and even on a stout piece of smooth board. Place it upright on the hearth before a clear fire, with a flat iron or something of the sort to support the board behind, and bake it well. Cut it into squares, and split and butter them hot.

INDIAN FLAPPERS.—Have ready a pint of sifted Indian meal, mixed with a handful of wheat flour, and a small tea-spoonful of salt. Beat four eggs very light, and stir them by degrees into a quart of milk, in turn with the meal. They can be made in a very short time, aud should be baked as soon as mixed, on a hot griddle; allow a large ladle full of batter to each cake, and make them all of the same size. Send them to table hot, buttered and cut in half.

INDIAN MUFFINS.—Sift and mix together a pint and a half of yellow Indian meal, and a handful of wheat flour. Melt a quarter of a pound of fresh butter in a quart of milk Beat four eggs very light, and stir into them alternately (a little at a time of each) the milk when it is quite cold, and the meal; adding a small tea-spoonful of salt. The whole must be beaten long and hard Then butter some muffin rings; set them on a hot griddle, and pour some of the batter into each.

Send the muffins to table hot, and split them by pulling them open with your fingers, as a knife will make them heavy. Eat them with butter, molasses or honey.

———

WATER MUFFINS.—Put four table-spoonfuls of fresh strong yeast into a pint of lukewarm water. Add a little salt; about a small tea-spoonful; then stir in gradually as much sifted flour as will make a thick batter. Cover the pan, and set it in a warm place to rise. When it is quite light, and your griddle is hot, grease and set your muffin rings on it · having first buttered them round the inside. Dip out a ladle full of the batter for each ring, and bake them over a quick fire. Send them to table hot, and split them by pulling them open with your hands.

———

COMMON MUFFINS.—Having melted three table-spoonfuls of fresh butter in three pints of warm milk, set it away to cool. Then beat three eggs as light as possible, and stir them gradually into the milk when it is quite cold; adding a tea-spoonful of salt. Stir in by degrees enough of sifted flour to make a batter as thick as you can conveniently beat it; and lastly, add two table-spoonfuls of strong fresh yeast from the brewery. Cover the batter and set it in a warm place to rise. It should be light in about three hours. Having heated your griddle, grease it with some butter tied in a rag; grease your muffin rings round the inside, and set them on the griddle. Take some batter out of the pan with a ladle or a large spoon, pour it lightly into the rings, and bake the muffins of a light brown. When done, break or split them open with your fingers; butter them and send them to table hot.

SODA BISCUITS.—Melt half a pound of butter in a pint of warm milk, adding a tea-spoonful of soda; and stir in by degrees half a pound of sugar. Then sift into a pan two pounds of flour; make a hole in the middle; pour in the milk, &c., and mix it with the flour into a dough. Put it on your paste-board, and knead it long and hard till it becomes very light. Roll it out into a sheet half an inch thick. Cut it into little round cakes with the top of a wine glass, or with a tin cutter of that size; prick the tops; lay them on tins sprinkled with flour, or in shallow iron pans; and bake them of a light brown in a quick oven; they will be done in a few minutes. These biscuits keep very well.

A SALLY LUNN.—This cake is called after the inventress. Sift into a pan a pound and a half of flour. Make a hole in the middle, and put in two ounces of butter warmed in a pint of milk, a salt-spoonful of salt, three well-beaten eggs, and two table-spoonfuls of the best fresh yeast. Mix the flour well into the other ingredients, and put the whole into a square tin pan that has been greased with butter. Cover it, set it in a warm place, and when it is quite light, bake it in a moderate oven. Send it to table hot, and eat it with butter.

Or, you may bake it on a griddle, in small muffin rings, pulling the cakes open and buttering them when brought to table.

SHORT CAKES.—Rub three quarters of a pound of fresh butter into a pound and a half of sifted flour; and make it into a dough with a little cold water. Roll it out into a sheet half an inch thick, and cut it into round cakes with the edge of a tumbler. Prick them with a fork; lay them in a shallow iron pan sprinkled with flour, and bake them in a moderate oven till they are brown. Send them to table hot; split and butter them.

TEA BISCUIT.—Melt a quarter of a pound of fresh butter in a quart of warm milk, and add a salt-spoonful of salt. Sift two pounds of flour into a pan, make a hole in the centre, and put in three table-spoonfuls of the best brewer's yeast. Add the milk and butter and mix it into a stiff paste. Cover it and set it by the fire to rise. When quite light, knead it well, roll it out an inch thick, and cut it into round cakes with the edge of a tumbler. Prick the top of each with a fork; lay them in buttered pans and bake them light brown. Send them to table warm, and split and butter them.

RICE CAKES.—Pick and wash half a pint of rice, and boil it very soft. Then drain it, and let it get cold. Sift a pint and a half of flour over the pan of rice, and mix in a quarter of a pound of butter that has been warmed by the fire, and a salt-spoonful of salt. Beat five eggs very light, and stir them gradually into a quart of milk. Beat the whole very hard, and bake it in muffin rings, or in waffle-irons. Send them to table hot, and eat them with butter, honey, or molasses.

You may make these cakes of rice flour instead of mixing together whole rice and wheat flour.

CREAM CAKES.—Having beaten three eggs very light, stir them into a quart of cream alternately with a quart of sifted flour; and add one wine glass of strong yeast, and a salt-spoon of salt. Cover the batter, and set it near the fire to rise When it is quite light, stir in a large table-spoonful of butter that has been warmed by the fire. Bake the cakes in muffin rings, and send them to table hot, split with your fingers, and buttered.

FRENCH ROLLS.—Sift a pound of flour into a pan, an rub into it two ounces of butter; mix in the whites only of three eggs, beaten to a stiff froth, and a table-spoonful of strong yeast; add sufficient milk to make a stiff dough, and a salt-spoonful of salt. Cover it and set it before the fire to rise. It should be light in an hour. Then put it on a paste-board, divide it into rolls, or round cakes; lay them in a floured square pan, and bake them about ten minutes in a quick oven.

COMMON ROLLS.—Sift two pounds of flour into a pan, and mix with it a tea-spoonful of salt. Warm together a jill of water and a jill of milk. Make a hole in the middle of the pan of flour; mix with the milk and water a jill of the best yeast, and pour it into the hole. Mix into the liquid enough of the surrounding flour to make a thin batter, which you must stir till quite smooth and free from lumps. Then strew a handful of flour over the top, and set it in a warm place to rise for two hours or more. When it is quite light, and has cracked on the top, make it into a dough with some more milk and water. Knead it well for ten minutes. Cover it, and set it again to rise for twenty minutes. Then make the dough into rolls or round balls. Bake them in a square pan, and send them to table hot, cut in three, buttered and put together again.

BREAD.

~~~~~~~~

T**AKE** one peck or two gallons of fine wheat flour, and sift
it into a kneading trough, or into a small clean tub, or a
large broad earthen pan; and make a deep hole in the middle
of the heap of flour, to begin the process by what is called
setting a sponge. Have ready half a pint of warm water,
which in summer should be only lukewarm, but even in
winter it must not be hot or boiling, and stir it well into half
a pint of strong fresh yeast; (if the yeast is home-made you
must use from three quarters to a whole pint;) then pour
it into the hole in the middle of the flour. With a spoon
work in the flour round the edges of the liquid, so as to bring
in by degrees sufficient flour to form a thin batter, which must
be well stirred about, for a minute or two. Then take a handful of flour, and scatter it thinly over the top of this batter, so
as to cover it entirely. Lay a warmed cloth over the whole,
and set it to rise in a warm place; in winter put it nearer the
fire than in summer. When the batter has risen so as to
make cracks in the flour on the top, scatter over it three or
four table-spoonfuls (not more) of fine salt, and begin to form
the whole mass into a dough; commencing round the hole
containing the batter, and pouring as much soft water as is
necessary to make the flour mix with the batter; the water
must never be more than lukewarm. When the whole is well
mixed, and the original batter which is to give fermentation
to the dough is completely incorporated with it, knead it hard,
turning it over, pressing it, folding it, and working it thoroughly
with your clenched hands for twenty minutes or half an hour:
or till it becomes perfectly light and stiff. The goodness of

bread depends much on the kneading, which to do well requires strength and practice. When it has been sufficiently worked, form the dough into a lump in the middle of the trough or pan, and scatter a little dry flour thinly over it: then cover it, and set it again in a warm place to undergo a farther fermentation; for which, if all has been done rightly, about twenty minutes or half an hour will be sufficient.

The oven should be hot by the time the dough has remained twenty minutes in the lump. If it is a brick oven it should be heated by faggots or small light wood, allowed to remain in till burnt down into coals. When the bread is ready, clear out the coals, and sweep and wipe the floor of the oven clean. Introduce nothing wet into the oven, as it may crack the bricks when they are hot. Try the heat of the bottom by throwing in some flour; and if it scorches and burns black, do not venture to put in the bread till the oven has had time to become cooler.

Put the dough on the paste-board, (which must be sprinkled with flour,) and divide it into loaves, forming them of a good shape. Place them in the oven, and close up the door, which you may open once or twice to see how the bread is going on. The loaves will bake in from two hours and a half to three hours, or more, according to their size. When the loaves are done, wrap each in a clean coarse towel, and stand them up on end to cool slowly. It is a good way to have the cloths previously made damp by sprinkling them plentifully with water, and letting them lie awhile rolled up tightly. This will make the crust of the bread less dry and hard. Bread should be kept always wrapped in a cloth, and covered from the air in a box or basket with a close lid. Unless you have other things to bake at the same time, it is not worth while to heat a brick oven for a small quantity of bread. Two or three loaves can be baked very well in a stove. (putting them into square iron pans,) or in a Dutch oven.*

If the bread has been mixed over night (which should never be done in warm weather) and is found, on tasting it, to be sour in the morning, melt a tea-spoonful of pearl-ash in a little milk-warm water, and sprinkle it over the dough; let it set half an hour, and then knead it. This will remove the acidity, and rather improve the bread in lightness. If dough is allowed to freeze it is totally spoiled. All bread that is sour, heavy or ill-baked is not only unpalatable, but extremely unwhole some, and should never be eaten. These accidents so fre- quently happen when bread is made at home by careless, unpractised or incompetent persons, that families who live in cities or towns will generally risk less and save more, by obtaining their bread from a professional baker.

If you like a little Indian in your wheat bread, prepare rather a larger quantity of warm water for setting the sponge; stirring into the water, while it is warming, enough of sifted Indian meal to make it like thin gruel. Warm water that has had pumpkin boiled in it is very good for bread.

Strong fresh yeast from the brewery should always be used in preference to any other. If the yeast is home-made, or not very strong and fresh, double or treble the quantity mentioned in the receipt will be necessary to raise the bread. On the other hand, if too much yeast is put in, the bread will be disagreeably bitter.†

---

* If you bake bread in a Dutch oven, take off the lid when the loaf is done, and let it remain in the oven uncovered for a quarter of an hour.

† If you are obliged from its want of strength to put in a large quantity of yeast, mix with it two or three handfuls of bran; add the warm water to it, and then strain it through a sieve or cloth, or you may correct the bitterness by putting in a few bits of charcoal and then straining it.

You may take off a portion of the dough that has been pre
pared for bread, make it up into little round cakes or rolls, and
bake them for breakfast or tea.

BRAN BREAD.—Sift into a pan three quarts of unbolted
wheat meal. Stir a jill of strong yeast, and a jill of molasses
into a quart of soft water, (which must be warm but not hot,)
and add a small tea-spoonful of pearl-ash, or sal-aratus. Make
a hole in the heap of flour, pour in the liquid, and proceed in
the usual manner of making bread. This quantity may be
made into two loaves. Bran bread is considered very whole
some; and is recommended to persons afflicted with dyspepsia.

RYE AND INDIAN BREAD.—Sift two quarts of rye,
and two quarts of Indian meal, and mix them well together.
Boil three pints of milk; pour it boiling hot upon the meal;
add two tea-spoonfuls of salt, and stir the whole very hard.
Let it stand till it becomes of only a lukewarm heat, and then
stir in half a pint of good fresh yeast; if from the brewery
and quite fresh, a smaller quantity will suffice. Knead the
mixture into a stiff dough, and set it to rise in a pan. Cover it
with a thick cloth that has been previously warmed, and set
it near the fire. When it is quite light, and has cracked
all over the top, make it into two loaves, put them into a
moderate oven, and bake them two hours and a half.

COMMON YEAST.—Put a large handful of hops into two
quarts of boiling water, which must then be set on the fire
again, and boiled twenty minutes with the hops. Have ready
in a pan three pints of sifted flour; strain the liquid, and pour
half of it on the flour. Let the other half stand till it becomes

cool, and then mix it gradually into the pan with the flour, &c Then stir into it half a pint of good strong yeast, fresh from the brewery if possible ; if not, use some that was left of the last making.   You may increase the strength by stirring into your yeast before you bottle it, four or five large tea-spoonfuls f brown sugar, or as many table-spoonfuls of molasses.

Put it into clean bottles, and cork them loosely till the fermentation is over.   Next morning put in the corks tightly, and set the bottles in a cold place.   When you are going to bottle the yeast it will be an improvement to place two or three raisins at the bottom of each bottle.   It is best to make yeast very frequently ; as, with every precaution, it will scarcely keep good a week, even in cold weather.   If you are apprehensive of its becoming sour, put into each bottle a lump of pearl-ash the size of a hazle-nut.

BRAN YEAST.—Mix a pint of wheat bran, and a handful of hops with a quart of water, and boil them together about twenty minutes.   Then strain it through a sieve into a pan ; when the liquid becomes only milk-warm, stir into it four table-spoonfuls of brewer's yeast, and two of brown sugar, or four of molasses.   Put it into a wooden bowl, cover it, and set it near the fire for four or five hours.   Then bottle it, and cork it tightly next day.

PUMPKIN YEAST.—Pare a fine ripe pumpkin, and cut it into pieces.   Put them into a kettle with a large handful of hops, and as much water as will cover them.   Boil them till the pumpkin is soft enough to pass through a cullender. Having done this, put the pulp into a stone jar, adding half a pint of good strong yeast to set it into a fermentation.   The yeast must be well stirred into the pumpkin.   Leave the jar

uncovered till next day ; then secure it tightly with a cork.
If pumpkin yeast is well made, and of a proper consistence,
neither too thick nor too thin, it will keep longer than any
other.

BAKER'S YEAST.—To a gallon of soft water put two
quarts of wheat bran, one quart of ground malt, (which may
be obtained from a brewery,) and two handfuls of hops. Boil
them together for half an hour. Then strain it through a
sieve, and let it stand till it is cold; after which put to it two
large tea-cups of molasses, and half a pint of strong yeast.
Pour it into a stone jug, and let it stand uncorked till next
morning. Then pour off the thin liquid from the top, and
cork the jug tightly. When you are going to use the yeast,
if it has been made two or three days, stir in a little pearl-ash
dissolved in warm water, allowing a lump the size of a hickory-
nut to a pint of yeast. This will correct any tendency to sour
ness, and make the yeast more brisk.

TO MAKE BUTTER.

Scald your milk pans every day after washing them ; and
let them set till the water gets cold. Then wipe them with a
clean cloth. Fill them all with cold water half an hour before
milking time, and do not pour it out till the moment before
you are ready to use the pans. Unless all the utensils are
kept perfectly sweet and nice, the cream and butter will never
be good. Empty milk-pans should stand all day in the sun.

When you have strained the milk into the pans, (which
should be broad and shallow,) place them in the spring-house
setting them down in the water. After the milk has stood

twenty-four hours, skim off the cream, and deposite it in a large deep earthen jar, commonly called a crock, which must be kept closely covered, and stirred up with a stick at least twice a day, and whenever you add fresh cream to it. This stirring is to prevent the butter from being injured by the skin that will gather over the top of the cream.

You should churn at least twice a week, for if the cream is allowed to stand too long, the butter will inevitably have a bad taste. Add to the cream the strippings of the milk.

Butter of only two or three days gathering is the best. With four or five good cows, you may easily manage to have a churning every three days. If your dairy is on a large scale, churn every two days.

Have your churn very clean, and rinse and cool it with cold water. A barrel churn is best; though a small upright one, worked by a staff or dash, will do very well where there are but one or two cows.

Strain the cream from the crock into the churn, and put on the lid. Move the handle slowly in warm weather, as churning too fast will make the butter soft. When you find that the handle moves heavily and with great difficulty, the butter has come ; that is, it has separated from the thin fluid and gathered into a lump, and it then is not necessary to churn any longer. Take it out with a wooden ladle, and put it into a small tub or pail. Squeeze and press it hard with the ladle, to get out all that remains of the milk. Add a little salt, and then squeeze and work it for a long time. If any of the milk is allowed to remain in, it will speedily turn sour and spoil the butter. Set it away in a cool place for three hours, and then work it over again.* Wash it in cold water; weigh

---

* A marble slab or table will be found of great advantage in working and making up butter

it; make it up into separate pounds, smoothing and shaping it; and clap each pound on your wooden butter print, dipping the print every time in cold water. Spread a clean linen cloth on a bench in the spring-house; place the butter on it, and let it set till it becomes perfectly hard. Then wrap each pound in a separate piece of linen that has been dipped in cold water.

Pour the buttermilk into a clean crock, and place it in the spring-house, with a saucer to dip it out with. Keep the pot covered. The buttermilk will be excellent the first day; but afterwards it will become too thick and sour. Winter buttermilk is never very palatable.

Before you put away the churn, wash and scald it well; and the day that you use it again, keep it for an hour or more filled with cold water.

In cold weather, churning is a much more tedious process than in summer, as the butter will be longer coming. It is best then to have the churn in a warm room, or near the fire.

If you wish to prepare the butter for keeping a long time, take it after it has been thoroughly well made, and pack it down tightly into a large jar. You need not in working it, add more salt than if the butter was to be eaten immediately. But preserve it by making a brine of fine salt, dissolved in water. The brine must be strong enough to bear up an egg on the surface without sinking. Strain the brine into the jar, so as to be about two inches above the butter. Keep the jar closely covered, and set it in a cool place.

When you want any of the butter for use, take it off evenly from the top; so that the brine may continue to cover it at a regular depth.

This receipt for making butter is according to the method in use at the best farm-houses in Pennsylvania, and if exactly followed will be found very good. The badness of butter is generally owing to carelessness or mismanagement; to keeping the cream too long without churning; to want of cleanliness in the utensils; to not taking the trouble to work it sufficiently; or to the practice of salting it so profusely as to render it unpleasant to the taste, and unfit for cakes or pastry. All these causes of bad butter are inexcusable, and can easily be avoided. Unless the cows have been allowed to feed where there are bitter weeds or garlic, the milk cannot naturally have any disagreeable taste, and therefore the fault of the butter must be the fault of the maker. Of course, the cream is much richer where the pasture is fine and luxuriant; and in winter, when the cows have only dry food, the butter must be consequently whiter and more insipid than in the grazing season. Still, if properly made, even winter butter cannot taste badly.

Many economical housekeepers always buy for cooking, butter of inferior quality. This is a foolish practice; as when it is bad, the taste will predominate through all attempts to disguise it, and render every thing unpalatable with which it is combined. As the use of butter is designed to improve and not to spoil the flavour of cookery, it is better to omit it altogether, and to substitute something else, unless you can procure that which is good. Lard, suet, beef-drippings, and sweet oil, may be used in the preparation of various dishes; and to eat with bread or warm cakes, honey, molasses, or stewed fruit, &c. are far superior to bad butter.

CHEESE.

In making *good* cheese, skim milk is never used. The milk should either be warm from the cow or heated to that temperature over the fire When the rennet is put in, the heat of the milk should be from 90° to 96°. Three quarts of milk will yield, on an average, about a pound of cheese. In infusing the rennet, allow a quart of lukewarm water, and a table-spoonful of salt to a piece about half the size of your hand. The rennet must soak all night in the water before it can be fit for use. In the morning (after taking as much of it as you want) put the rennet water into a bottle and cork it tightly. It will keep the better for adding to it a wine glass of brandy If too large a proportion of rennet is mixed with the milk, the cheese will be tough and leathery.

To make a very good cheese, take three buckets of milk warm from the cow, and strain it immediately into a large tub or kettle. Stir into it half a tea-cupful of infusion of rennet or rennet-water; and having covered it, set it in a warm place for about half an hour, or till it becomes a firm curd. Cut the curd into squares with a large knife, or rather with a wooden slitting-dish, and let it stand about fifteen minutes. Then break it up fine with your hands, and let it stand a quarter of an hour longer. Then pour off from the top as much of the whey as you can; tie up the curd in a linen cloth or bag, and hang it up to drain out the remainder of the whey; setting a pan under it to catch the droppings. After all the whey is drained out, put the curd into the cheese-tray, and cut it again into slices; chop it coarse; put a cloth about it; place it in the cheese-hoop or mould, and set it in the screw press for half an hour, pressing it hard.* Then take it out; chop the curd very fine; add salt to your taste; and put it again into

* If you are making cheese on a small scale, and have not a regular press, put the curd (after you have wrapped it in a cloth) into a small circular wooden box or tub with numerous holes bored in the bottom; and with a lid that fits the inside exactly. Lay heavy weights on the lid in such a manner as to press evenly all over.

the cheese-hoop with a cloth about it, and press it again. You must always wet the cloth all over to prevent its sticking to the cheese, and tearing the surface. Let it remain in the press till next morning, when you must take it out and turn it; then wrap it in a clean wet cloth, and replace it in the press, where it must remain all day. On the following morning again take out the cheese; turn it, renew the cloth, and put it again into the press. Three days pressing will be sufficient.

When you finally take it out of the press, grease the cheese all over with lard, and put it on a clean shelf in a dry dark room, or in a wire safe. Wipe, grease, and turn it carefully every day. If you omit this a single day the cheese will spoil Keep the shelf perfectly clean, and see that the cheese does not stick to it. When the cheese becomes firm, you may omit the greasing; but continue to rub it all over every day with a clean dry cloth. Continue this for five or six weeks; the cheese will then be fit to eat.

The best time for making cheese is when the pasture is in perfection.

You may enrich the colour of the cheese by a little anatto or arnotta; of which procure a small quantity from the druggist, powder it, tie it in a muslin rag, and hold it in the warm milk, (after it is strained,) pressing out the colouring matter with your fingers, as laundresses press their indigo or blue rag in the tub of water. Anatto is perfectly harmless.

After they begin to dry, (or ripen, as it is called,) it is the custom in some dairy-farms, to place the cheeses in the hay-stack, and keep them there among the hay for five or six weeks. This is said greatly to improve their consistence and flavour. Cheeses are sometimes ripened by putting them every day in fresh grass.

SAGE CHEESE.—Take some of the young top leaves of the sage plant, and pound them in a mortar till you have extracted the juice. Put the juice into a bowl, wipe out the mortar, put in some spinach leaves, and pound them till you have an equal quantity of spinach juice. Mix the two juices together, and stir them into the warm milk immediately after you have put in the rennet. You may use sage juice alone; but the spinach will greatly improve the colour; besides correcting the bitterness of the sage.

STILTON CHEESE.—Having strained the morning's milk, and skimmed the cream from the milk of the preceding evening, mix the cream and the new milk together while the latter is quite warm, and stir in the rennet-water. When the curd has formed, you must not break it up, (as is done with other cheese,) but take it out all at once with a wooden skimming dish, and place it on a sieve to drain gradually. While it is draining, keep pressing it gently till it becomes firm and dry. Then lay a clean cloth at the bottom of a wooden cheesehoop or mould, which should have a few small holes bored in the bottom. The cloth must be large enough for the end to turn over the top again, after the curd is put in. Place it in the press for two hours; turn it, (putting a clean cloth under it,) and press it again for six or eight hours. Then turn it again, rub the cheese all over with salt, and return it to the press for fourteen hours. Should the edges of the cheese project, they must be pared off.

When you take it finally out of the press, bind it round tightly with a cloth, (which must be changed every day when you turn the cheese,) and set it on a shelf or board. Continue the cloths till the cheese is firm enough to support tself: rubbing or brushing the outside every day when you turn it. After the cloths are left off, continue to brush the cheese every day for two or three months; during which time it may be improved by keeping it covered all round, under and over, with grass, which must be renewed every day, and gathered when quite dry after the dew is off. Keep the cheese and the grass between two large plates.

A Stilton cheese is generally made of a small size, seldom larger in circumference than a dinner plate, and about four or five inches thick. They are usually put up for keeping, in cases of sheet lead, fitting them exactly. There is no cheese superior to them in richness and mildness.

Cream cheeses (as they are generally called) may be made in this manner. They are always eaten quite fresh, while the inside is still somewhat soft. They are made small, and are sent to table whole, cut across into triangular slices like a pie or cake. After they become fit to eat, they will keep good but a day or two, but they are considered while fresh very delicious.

COTTAGE CHEESE.—This is that preparation of milk vulgarly called Smear Case. Take a pan of milk that has just began to turn sour; cover it, and set it by the fire till it becomes a curd. Pour off the whey from the top, and tie up the curd in a pointed linen bag, and hang it up to drain; setting something under it to catch the droppings. Do not squeeze it. Let it drain all night, and in the morning put the curd into a pan, (adding some rich cream,) and work it very fine with a spoon, chopping and pressing it till about the consistence of a soft bread pudding. To a soup plate of the fine curd put a tea-spoonful of salt, and a piece of butter about the size of a walnut; mixing all thoroughly together. Having prepared the whole in this manner, put it into a stone or china vessel; cover it closely, and set it in a cold place till tea time.

You may make it of milk that is entirely sweet by forming the curd with rennet.

A WELSH RABBIT. — Toast some slices of bread, (having cut off the crust,) butter them, and keep them hot. Grate or shave down with a knife some fine mellow cheese : and, if it is not very rich, mix with it a few small bits of butter. Put it into a cheese-toaster, or into a skillet, and add to it a tea-spoonful of made mustard ; a little cayenne pepper ; and if you choose, a wine glass of fresh porter or of red wine. Stir the mixture over hot coals, till it is completely dissolved ; and then brown it by holding over it a salamander, or a red-hot shovel. Lay the toast in the bottom and round the sides of a deep dish ; put the melted cheese upon it, and serve it up as hot as possible, with dry toast in a separate plate; and accompanied by porter or ale.

This preparation of cheese is for a plain supper.

Dry cheese is frequently grated on little plates for the tea-table.

TO MAKE CHOCOLATE.

To each square of a chocolate cake allow three jills, or a chocolate cup and a half of boiling water. Scrape down the chocolate with a knife, and mix it first to a paste with a small quantity of the hot water; just enough to melt it in. Then put it into a block tin pot with the remainder of the water, set it on hot coals; cover it, and let it boil (stirring it twice) till the liquid is one third reduced. Supply that third with cream or rich milk ; stir it again, and take it off the fire. Serve it up as hot as possible, with dry toast, or dry rusk It chills immediately. If you wish it frothed, pour it into the cup, and twirl round in it the little wooden instrument called a chocolate mill, till you have covered the top with foam.

TO MAKE TEA.—In buying tea, it is best to get it by the box, of an importer, that you may be sure of having it fresh, and unmixed with any that is old and of inferior quality. The box should be kept in a very dry place. If green tea is good, it will look green in the cup when poured out. Black tea should be dark coloured and have a fragrant flowery smell. The best pots for making tea are those of china. Metal and Wedgwood tea-pots by frequent use will often communicate a disagreeable taste to the tea. This disadvantage may be remedied in Wedgwood ware, by occasionally boiling the tea-pots in a vessel of hot water.

In preparing to make tea, let the pot be twice scalded from the tea-kettle, which must be boiling hard at the moment the water is poured on the tea; otherwise it will be weak and insipid, even when a large quantity is put in. The best way is to have a chafing dish, with a kettle always boiling on it, in the room where the tea is made. It is a good rule to allow two heaping tea-spoonfuls of tea to a large cup-full of water, or two tea-spoonfuls for each grown person that is to drink tea, and one spoonful extra. The pot being twice scalded, put in the tea, and pour on the water about ten minutes before you want to fill the cups, that it may have time to draw or infuse. Have hot water in another pot, to weaken the cups of those that like it so. That the second course of cups may be as strong as the first, put some tea into a cup just before you sit down to table, pour on it a very little boiling water, (just enough to cover it,) set a saucer over it to keep in the steam, and let it infuse till you have filled all the first cups; then add it to that already in the tea-pot, and pour in a little boiling water from the kettle. Except that it is less convenient for a large family, a kettle on a chafing dish is better than an urn, as the water may be kept longer boiling.

In making black tea, use a larger quantity than of green, as it is of a much weaker nature. The best black teas in general use are pekoe and pouchong; the best green teas are imperial, young hyson, and gunpowder.

TO MAKE COFFEE.—The manner in which coffee is roasted is of great importance to its flavour. If roasted too little, it will be weak and insipid; if too much, the taste will be bitter and unpleasant. To have it very good, it should be roasted immediately before it is made, doing no more than the quantity you want at that time. It loses much of its strength by keeping, even in twenty-four hours after roasting. It should on no consideration be ground till directly before it is made. Every family should be provided with a coffee roaster, which is an iron cylinder to stand before the fire, and is either turned by a handle, or wound up like a jack to go of itself. If roasted in an open pot or pan, much of the flavour evaporates n the process. Before the coffee is put into the roaster, it should be carefully examined and picked, lest there should be stones or bad grains among it. It should be roasted of a bright brown; and will be improved by putting among it a piece of butter when about half done.

Watch it carefully while roasting, looking at it frequently.

A coffee-mill affixed to the wall is far more convenient than one that must be held on the lap. It is best to grind the coffee while warm.

Allow half a pint of ground coffee to one quart of water. If the coffee is not freshly roasted, you should put in more. Put the water into the tin coffee-pot, and set it on hot coals;

when it boils, put in the coffee, a spoonful at a time, (stirring it between each spoonful,) and add two or three chips of isinglass, or the white of an egg. Stir it frequently, till it has risen up to the top in boiling; then set it a little farther from the fire, and boil it gently for ten minutes, or a quarter of an hour; after which pour in a tea-cup of cold water, and put it in the corner to settle for ten minutes. Scald your silver or china pot, and transfer the coffee to it; carefully pouring it off from the grounds, so as not to disturb them.

If coffee is allowed to boil too long, it will lose much of its strength, and also become sour.

FRENCH COFFEE.—To make coffee without boiling, you must have a biggin, the best sort of which is what in France is called a Grecque. They are to be had of various sizes and prices at the tin stores. Coffee made in this manner is much less troublesome than when boiled, and requires no white of egg or isinglass to clear it. The coffee should be freshly roasted and ground. Allow two cupfuls of ground coffee to six cupfuls of boiling water. Having first scalded the biggin, (which should have strainers of perforated tin, and not of linen,) put in the coffee, and pour on the water, which should be boiling hard at the time. Shut down the lid, place the pot near the fire, and the coffee will be ready as soon as it has all drained through the coarse and fine strainers into the receiver below the spout. Scald your china or silver pot, and pour the coffee into it. But it is best to have a biggin in the form of an urn, in which the coffee can both be made and brought to table.

For what is called milk coffee,—boil the milk or cream separately; bring it to table in a covered vessel, and pour it hot into the coffee, the flavour of which will be impaired if the milk is boiled with it.

DOMESTIC LIQUORS ETC.

SPRUCE BEER.

Put into a large kettle, ten gallons of water, a quarter of a pound of hops, and a tea-cupful of ginger. Boil them together till all the hops sink to the bottom. Then dip out a bucket full of the liquor, and stir into it six quarts of molasses. and three ounces and a half of the essence of spruce. When all is dissolved, mix it with the liquor in the kettle; strain it through a hair sieve into a cask; and stir well into it half a pint of good strong yeast. Let it ferment a day or two; then bung up the cask, and you may bottle the beer the next day. It will be fit for use in a week.

For the essence of spruce, you may substitute two pounds of the outer sprigs of the spruce fir, boiled ten minutes in the liquor.

To make spruce beer for present use, and in a smaller quantity, boil a handful of hops in two gallons and a half of water, till they fall to the bottom. Then strain the water, and when it is lukewarm, stir into it a table-spoonful of ground white ginger; a pint of molasses; a table-spoonful of essence of spruce; and half a pint of yeast. Mix the whole well together in a stone jug, and let it ferment for a day and a half, or two days. Then put it into bottles, with three or four raisins in the bottom of each, to prevent any further fermentation. It will then be fit for immediate use.

GINGER BEER.—Break up a pound and a half of loaf sugar, and mix with it three ounces of strong white ginger, and the grated peel of two lemons. Put these ingredients into a large stone jar, and pour over them two gallons of boiling water. When it becomes milkwarm strain it, and add the juice of the lemons and two large table-spoonfuls of strong yeast. Make this beer in the evening and let it stand all night. Next morning bottle it in little half pint stone bottles, tying down the corks with twine.

MOLASSES BEER.—To six quarts of water, add two quarts of West India molasses half a pint of the best brewer's yeast; two table-spoonfuls of ground ginger; and one table-spoonful of cream of tartar. Stir all together. Let it stand twelve hours, and then bottle it, putting three or four raisins into each bottle.

It will be much improved by substituting the juice and grated peel of a large lemon, for one of the spoonfuls of ginger.

Molasses beer keeps good but two or three days.

SASSAFRAS BEER.—Have ready two gallons of soft water; one quart of wheat bran; a large handful of dried apples; half a pint of molasses; a small handful of hops; half a pint of strong fresh yeast, and a piece of sassafras root the size of an egg.

Put all the ingredients (except the molasses and yeast) at once into a large kettle. Boil it till the apples are quite soft. Put the molasses into a small clean tub or a large pan. Set a hair sieve over the vessel, and strain the mixture through it. Let it stand till it becomes only milkwarm, and then stir in the yeast. Put the liquor immediately into the keg or jugs, and let it stand uncorked to ferment. Fill the jugs quite full, that the liquor in fermenting may run over. Set them in a large tub. When you see that the fermentation or working has subsided, cork it, and it will be fit for use next day.

Two large table-spoonfuls of ginger stirred into the molasses will be found an improvement.

If the yeast is stirred in while the liquor is too warm, it will be likely to turn sour.

If the liquor is not put immediately into the jugs, it wil. not ferment well.

Keep it in a cold place. It will not in warm weather be good more than two days. It is only made for present use

GOOSEBERRY WINE.

ALLOW three gallons of soft water (measured after it has boiled an hour) to six gallons of gooseberries, which must be full ripe. Top and tail the gooseberries; put them, a few at a time, into a wooden dish, and with a rolling-pin or beetle break and mash every one; transferring them, as they are done, into a large stone jar. Pour the boiling water upon the mashed gooseberries; cover the jar, and let them stand twelve hours. Then strain and measure the juice, and to each quart allow three-quarters of a pound of loaf-sugar; mix it with the liquid, and let it stand eight or nine hours to dissolve, stirring it several times.

Then pour it into a keg of proper size for containing it, and let it ferment at the bung-hole; filling it up as as it works out with some of the liquor reserved for that purpose. As soon as it ceases to hiss, stop it close with a cloth wrapped round the bung. A pint of white brandy for every gallon of the gooseberry wine may be added on bunging it up. At the end of four or five months it will probably be fine enough to bottle off. It is best to bottle it in cold frosty weather. You may refine it by allowing to every gallon of wine the whites of two eggs, beaten to a froth, with a very small tea-spoonful of salt. When the white of egg, &c. is a stiff froth, take out a quart of the wine, and mix them well together. Then pour it into the cask, and in a few days it will be fine and clear. You may begin to use it any time after it is bottled. Put two or three raisins in the bottom of each bottle. They will tend to keep the wine from any farther fermentation.

Fine gooseberry wine has frequently passed for champagne. Keep the bottles in saw-dust, lying on their sides.

CURRANT WINE.—Take four gallons of ripe currants; strip them from the stalks into a great stone jar that has a cover to it, and mash them with a long thick stick. Let them stand twenty-four hours; then put the currants into a large linen bag; wash out the jar, set it under the bag, and squeeze the juice into it. Boil together two gallons and a half of water, and five pounds and a half of the best loaf-sugar, skimming it well. When the scum ceases to rise, mix the syrup with the currant juice. Let it stand a fortnight or three weeks to settle; and then transfer it to another vessel, taking care not to disturb the lees or dregs. If it is not quite clear and bright, refine it by mixing with a quart of the wine, (taken out for the purpose,) the whites of two eggs beaten to a stiff froth, and half an ounce of cream of tartar. Pour this gradually into the vessel. Let it stand ten days, and then bottle it off. Place the bottles in saw-dust, laying them on their sides. Take care that the saw-dust is not from pine wood. The wine will be fit to drink in a year, but is better when three or four years old.

You may add a little brandy to it when you make it; allowing a quart of brandy to six gallons of wine.

RASPBERRY WINE.—Put four gallons of ripe rasp-berries into a stone jar, and mash them with a round stick. Take four gallons of soft water, (measured after it has boiled an hour,) and strain it warm over the raspberries. Stir it well and let it stand twelve hours. Then strain it through a bag, and to every gallon of liquor put three pounds of loaf-sugar. Set it over a clear fire, and boil and skim it till the scum ceases to rise. When it is cold bottle it. Open the bottles every day for a fortnight, closing them again in a few minutes. Then seal the corks, and lay the bottles on their sides in saw-dust, which must not be from pine wood.

ELDERBERRY WINE.—Gather the elderberries when quite ripe; put them into a stone jar, mash them with a round stick, and set them in a warm oven, or in a large kettle of boil-ing water till the jar is hot through, and the berries begin to simmer. Then take them out, and press and strain them through a sieve. To every quart of juice allow a pound of Havanna or Lisbon sugar, and two quarts of cold soft water. Put the sugar into a large kettle, pour the juice over it, and, when it has dissolved, stir in the water. Set the kettle over the fire, and boil and skim it till the scum ceases to rise. To four gallons of the liquor add a pint and a half of brandy. Put it into a keg, and let it stand with the bung put in loosely for four or five days, by which time it will have ceased to fer-ment. Then stop it closely, plastering the bung with clay. At the end of six months, draw off a little of it; and if it is not quite clear and bright, refine it with the whites and shells of three or four eggs, beaten to a stiff froth and stirred into a quart of the wine, taken out for the purpose and then returned to the cask; or you may refine it with an ounce or more of dis-solved isinglass. Let it stand a week or two, and then bottle it.

This is an excellent domestic wine, very common in England, and deserving to be better known in America, where the elderberry tree is found in great abundance. Elderberry wine is generally taken mulled with spice, and warm.

ELDER FLOWER WINE.—Take the flowers or blossoms of the elder tree, and strip them from the stalks. To every quart of flowers allow one gallon of water, and three pounds of white sugar. Boil and skim the sugar and water, and then pour it hot on the flowers. When cool, mix in with it some lemon juice and some yeast; allowing to six gallons of the liquor the juice of six lemons, and four or five tablespoonfuls of good yeast stirred in very hard. Let it ferment for three days in a tub covered with a double blanket. Then strain the wine through a sieve, (add six whites of eggs beaten to a stiff froth, or an ounce of melted isinglass,) and put it into a cask, in the bottom of which you have laid four or five pounds of the best raisins, stoned. Stop the cask closely, and in six months the wine will be fit to bottle. It will much resemble Frontiniac, the elder flowers imparting to it a very pleasant taste.

CIDER WINE.—Take sweet cider immediately from the press. Strain it through a flannel bag into a tub, and stir into it as much honey as will make it strong enough to bear up an egg. Then boil and skim it, and when the scum ceases to rise, strain it again. When cool, put it into a cask, and set it in a cool cellar till spring. Then bottle it off; and when ripe, it will be found a very pleasant beverage. The cider must be of the very best quality, made entirely from good sound apples.

MEAD.—To every gallon of water put five pounds of strained honey, (the water must be hot when you add the honey,) and boil it three quarters of an hour, skimming it well. Then put in some hops tied in a thin bag, (allowing an ounce or a handful to each gallon,) and let it boil half an hour longer. Strain it into a tub, and let it stand four days. Then put it into a cask, (or into a demijohn if the quantity is small,) adding for each gallon of mead a jill of brandy and a sliced lemon. If a large cask, do not bottle it till it has stood a year.

FOX GRAPE SHRUB.—Gather the grapes when they are full grown, but before they begin to purple. Pick from the stems a sufficient quantity to nearly fill a large preserving kettle, and pour on them as much boiling water as the kettle will hold. Set it over a brisk fire, and keep it scalding hot till all the grapes have burst. Then take them off, press out and strain the liquor, and allow to each quart a pound of sugar stirred well in. Dissolve the sugar in the juice; then put them together into a clean kettle, and boil and skim them for ten minutes, or till the scum ceases to rise. When cold, bottle it; first putting into each bottle a jill of brandy. Seal the bottles, and keep them in a warm closet.

You may make gooseberry shrub in this manner.

CURRANT SHRUB.—Your currants must be quite ripe. Pick them from the stalks, and squeeze them through a linen bag. To each quart of juice allow a pound of loaf-sugar. Put the sugar and juice into a preserving kettle, and let it melt before it goes on the fire. Boil it ten minutes, skimming it well. When cold, add a jill of the best white brandy to each quart of the juice. Bottle it, and set it away for use; sealing the corks. It improves by keeping.

Raspberry shrub may be made in this manner ; also straw berry.

CHERRY SHRUB.—Pick from the stalks, and stone a sufficient quantity of ripe morellas, or other red cherries of the best and most juicy description.   Put them with all their juice into a stone jar, and set it, closely covered, into a deep kettle of boiling water.   Keep it boiling hard for a quarter of an hour.   Then pour the cherries into a bag, and strain and press out all the juice.   Allow a pound of sugar to a quart of juice, boil them together ten minutes in a preserving kettle, skimming them well, and when cold, bottle the liquid ; first putting a jill of brandy into each bottle.

CHERRY BOUNCE.—Mix together six pounds of ripe morellas and six pounds of large black heart cherries.   Put them into a wooden bowl or tub, and with a pestle or mallet mash them so as to crack all the stones.   Mix with the cherries three pounds of loaf-sugar, or of sugar candy broken up, and put them into a demijohn, or into a large stone jar.   Pour on two gallons of the best double rectified whiskey.   Stop the vessel closely, and let it stand three months, shaking it every day during the first month.   At the end of the three months you may strain the liquor and bottle it off.   It improves by age.

LEMON SYRUP.—Break up into large pieces six pounds of fine loaf-sugar.   Take twelve large ripe lemons, and (without cutting them) grate the yellow rind upon the sugar.   Then put the sugar, with the lemon gratings and two quarts of water, into a preserving kettle, and let it dissolve.   When it is all melted, boil it till quite thick, skimming it till no more scum rises ; it will then be done.   Have ready the juice of all the lemons, stir it in, and boil it ten minutes more. Bottle it, and keep it in a cold place.

It makes a delicious drink in summer, in the proportion of one third lemon syrup and two thirds ice water.

LEMON CORDIAL.

PARE off very thin the yellow rind of a dozen large lemons; throw the parings into a gallon of white brandy, and let them steep till next day, or at least twelve hours. Break up four pounds of loaf-sugar into another vessel, and squeeze upon it the juice of the lemons. Let this too stand all night. Next day mix all together, boil two quarts of milk, and pour it boiling hot into the other ingredients. Cover the vessel, and let it stand eight days, stirring it daily. Then strain it through a flannel bag till the liquid is perfectly clear. Let it stand six weeks in a demijohn or glass jar, and then bottle it.

To make it still more clear, you may filter it through a piece of fine muslin pinned down to the bottom of a sieve, or through blotting paper, which must be frequently renewed. It should be white blotting paper. Orange cordial may be made in the same manner.

ROSE CORDIAL.— Put a pound of fresh rose leaves into a tureen, with a quart of lukewarm water. Cover the vessel, and let them infuse for twenty-four hours. Then squeeze them through a linen bag till all the liquid is pressed out. Put a fresh pound of rose leaves into the tureen, pour the liquid back into it, and let it infuse again for two days. You may repeat this till you obtain a very strong infusion. Then to a pint of the infusion add half a pound of loaf-sugar, half a pint of white brandy, an ounce of broken cinnamon, and an ounce of coriander seeds. Put it into a glass jar, cover it well, and let it stand for two weeks. Then filter it through a fine muslin or a blotting paper (which must be white) pinned on the bottom of a sieve; and bottle it for use.

STRAWBERRY CORDIAL.—Hull a sufficient quantity of ripe strawberries, and squeeze them through a linen bag. To each quart of the juice allow a pint of white brandy, and half a pound of powdered loaf-sugar. Put the liquid into a glass jar or a demijohn, and let it stand a fortnight. Then filter it through a sieve, to the bottom of which a piece of fine muslin or blotting paper has been fastened; and afterwards bottle it.

RASPBERRY CORDIAL—May be made in the above manner.

QUINCE CORDIAL.—Take the finest and ripest quinces you can procure, wipe them clean, and cut out all the defective parts. Then grate them into a tureen or some other large vessel, leaving out the seeds and cores. Let the grated pulp remain covered in the tureen for twenty-four hours. Then squeeze it through a jelly-bag or cloth. To six quarts of the juice allow a quart of cold water, three pounds of loaf-sugar, (broken up,) and a quart of white brandy. Mix the whole well together, and put it into a stone jar. Have ready three very small flannel or thick muslin bags, (not larger than two inches square,) fill one with grated nutmeg, another with powdered mace, and the third with powdered cloves; and put them into the jar that the spice may flavour the liquor without mixing with it. Leave the jar uncorked for a few days; reserving some of the liquor to replace that which may flow over in the fermentation. Whenever it has done working, bottle it off, but do not use it for six months. If not sufficiently bright and clear, filter it through fine muslin pinned round the bottom of a sieve, or through a white blotting paper fastened in the same manner.

PEACH CORDIAL.—Take the ripest and most juicy free-stone peaches you can procure. Cut them from the stones, and quarter them without paring. Crack the stones, and extract the kernels, which must be blanched and slightly pounded. Put the peaches into a large stone jar in layers. alternately with layers of the kernels, and of powdered loaf-sugar. When the jar is three parts full of the peaches, kernels, and sugar, fill it up with white brandy. Set the jar in a large pan, and leave it uncovered for three or four days. in case of its fermenting and flowing over at the top. Fill up what is thus wasted with more brandy, and then close the jar tightly. Let it stand five or six months; then filter it, and bottle it for use.

Cherry, apricot, and plum cordial may be made in the above manner; adding always the kernels.

ANNISEED CORDIAL.—Melt a pound of loaf-sugar in two quarts of water. Mix it with two quarts of white brandy. and add a table-spoonful of oil of anniseed. Let it stand a week; then filter it through white blotting paper, and bottle it for use.

Clove or Cinnamon Cordial may be made in the same manner, by mixing sugar, water and brandy, and adding oil of cinnamon or oil of cloves. You may colour any of these cordials red by stirring in a little powdered cochineal that has been dissolved in a small quantity of brandy.

ROSE BRANDY.—Nearly fill a china or glass jar with freshly-gathered rose leaves, and pour in sufficient French white brandy to fill it quite up; and then cover it closely. Next day put the whole into a strainer, and having squeezed and pressed the rose leaves and drained off the liquid, throw away the leaves, put fresh ones into the jar, and return the brandy to it. Repeat this every day while roses are in season, (taking care to keep the jar well covered,) and you will find the liquid much better than rose water for flavouring cakes and puddings.

LEMON BRANDY.—When you use lemons for punch or lemonade, do not throw away the peels, but cut them in small pieces, and put them into a glass jar or bottle of brandy. You will find this brandy useful for many purposes.

In the same way keep for use the kernels of peach and plum stones, pounding them slightly before you put them into the brandy.

NOYAU.—Blanch and break up a pound of shelled bitter almonds or peach kernels. Mix with them the grated rinds of three large lemons, half a pint of clarified honey that has been boiled and skimmed, and three pounds of the best double-refined loaf-sugar. Put these ingredients into a jar or demijohn; pour in four quarts of the best white brandy or proof spirit; stop the vessel, and let it stand three months, shaking 't every day for the first month. Then filter it, dilute it with rose water to your taste, (you may allow a quart of rose water to each quart of the liquor,) and bottle it for use.

This and any other cordial may be coloured red by mixing with it (after it is filtered) cochineal, powdered, dissolved in a little white brandy, and strained through fine muslin.

RATAFIA.—Pound in a mortar, and mix together a pound of shelled bitter almonds, an ounce of nutmegs, a pound of fine loaf-sugar, and one grain (apothecaries' weight) of ambergris. Infuse these ingredients for a week in a gallon of white brandy or proof spirit. Then filter it, and bottle it for use.

CAPILLAIRE.—Powder eight pounds of loaf-sugar, and wet it with three pints of water and three eggs well beaten with their shells. Stir the whole mass very hard, and boil it twice over, skimming it well. Then strain it, and stir in two wine glasses of orange flower water. Bottle it, and use it for a summer draught, mixed with a little lemon juice and water; or you may sweeten punch with it.

ORGEAT.—To make orgeat paste, blanch, mix together, and pound in a mortar till perfectly smooth, three quarters of a pound of shelled sweet almonds, and one quarter of a pound of shelled bitter almonds; adding frequently a little orange-flower or rose water, to keep them from oiling; and mixing with them, as you proceed, a pound of fine loaf-sugar that has been previously powdered by itself. When the whole is thoroughly incorporated to a stiff paste, put it into little pots and close them well. It will keep five or six months, and, when you wish to use it for a beverage, allow a piece of orgeat about the size of an egg to each half pint or tumbler of water Having well stirred it, strain the mixture.

To make liquid orgeat for present use; blanch and pound in a mortar, with rose water, a quarter of a pound of sweet and an ounce and a half of bitter almonds. Then sweeten three pints of rich milk with half a pound of loaf-sugar, and stir the almonds gradually into it. Boil it over hot coals, and as soon as it comes to a boil, take it off and stir it fre quently till it gets cold. Then strain it, add a glass of brandy and put it into decanters. When you pour it out for drinking dilute it with water.

———

LEMONADE. — Take fine ripe lemons, and roll them under your hand on the table to increase the quantity of juice. Then cut and squeeze them into a pitcher, and mix the juice with loaf-sugar and cold water. To half a pint of lemon juice you may allow a pint and a half of water, and ten or twelve moderate sized lumps of sugar. Send it round in little glasses with handles.

To make a tumbler of *very good* lemonade, allow the juice of one lemon and four or five lumps of sugar, filling up the glass with water. In summer use ice water.

———

ORANGEADE—Is made of oranges, in the same propor tion as lemonade. It is very fine when frozen.

~~~~~~~~~~~

PUNCH.

ROLL twelve fine lemons under your hand on the table; then pare off the yellow rind very thin, and boil it in a gallon of water till all the flavour is drawn out. Break up into a large bowl, two pounds of loaf-sugar, and squeeze the lemons over it. When the water has boiled sufficiently, strain it from the lemon-peel, and mix it with the lemon juice and sugar. Stir in a quart of rum or of the best whiskey.

Two scruples of flowers of benjamin, steeped in a quart of rum, will make an infusion which much resembles the arrack of the East Indies. It should be kept in a bottle, and a little of it will be found to impart a very fine and fragrant flavour to punch made in the usual manner.

FROZEN PUNCH—Is made as above, omitting one half of the rum or whiskey. Put it into an ice-cream freezer, shaking or stirring it all the time. When it is frozen, send it round immediately, in small glasses with a tea-spoon for each.

ROMAN PUNCH.—Grate the yellow rinds of four lemons and two oranges upon two pounds of loaf-sugar. Squeeze on the juice of the lemons and oranges; cover it, and let it stand till next day. Then strain it through a sieve, add a bottle of champagne, and the whites of eight eggs beaten to a froth. You may freeze it or not.

MILK PUNCH.—What is commonly called milk punch. is a mixture of brandy or rum, sugar, milk and nutmeg, with-without either lemon juice or water. It is taken cold with a lump of ice in each tumbler.

FINE MILK PUNCH.—Pare off the yellow rind of four large lemons, and steep it for twenty-four hours in a quart of brandy or rum. Then mix with it the juice of the lemons, a pound and a half of loaf-sugar, two grated nutmegs, and a quart of water. Add a quart of rich unskimmed milk, made boiling hot, and strain the whole through a jelly-bag. You may either use it as soon as it is cold, or make a larger quantity, (in the above proportions,) and bottle it. It will keep several months.

REGENT'S PUNCH.—Take four large lemons; roll them on the table to make them more juicy, and then pare them as thin as possible. Cut out all the pulp, and throw away the seeds and the white part of the rind. Put the yellow rind and the pulp into a pint of boiling water with one tea-spoonfuls of raw green tea of the best sort. Let all boil together about ten minutes. Then strain it through linen, and stir in a pound of powdered loaf-sugar and a bottle of champagne, or of any liquor suitable for punch. Set it again over the fire, and when just ready to boil, remove it, and pour it into a china bowl or pitcher, to be sent round in glasses.

WINE JELLY.—Clarify a pound of loaf-sugar, by mixing it with half a pint of water and the beaten white of an egg, and then boiling and skimming it. Put an ounce of isinglass (with as much boiling water as will cover it) into a small sauce-pan, and set it in hot coals till the isinglass is thoroughly dissolved. Then when the syrup has been taken from the fire, mix the melted isinglass with it, add a quart of white wine and stir in a table-spoonful or a spoonful and a half of old Jamaica spirits. Stir the mixture very hard, and pour it into a mould. When it has congealed, wrap a cloth dipped in warm water round the outside of the mould; turn out the jelly, and eat it with ice-cream.

SHERRY COBLER.—Lay in the bottom of a tumbler some pieces of the yellow rind of an orange or lemon, pared off very thin; and add a heaping table-spoonful of powdered loaf-sugar. Upon this, place some pounded ice. Pour on sherry wine till the tumbler is one-third, or half full. Hold an empty tumbler inverted or turned downwards, upon the top of that which contains the ingredients; placing the glasses so that their edges exactly meet, and leaving no opening for any portion of the contents to escape. Keep your hands fast on the two tumblers, one above and one below, and turn them up and down, back and forwards, till the articles inside are thoroughly mixed. Then take off the upper tumbler, and let the lower one stand still a few moments before you fill it up with ice-water.

MULLED WINE.—Boil together, in a pint of water, a beaten nutmeg, two sticks of cinnamon broken up, and a table-spoonful of cloves slightly pounded. When reduced to one-half, strain the liquid into a quart of wine, set it on hot coals, take it off as soon as it comes to a boil, and sweeten it. Serve it up hot in a pitcher, surrounded by glass cups, and with it a plate of rusk.

MULLED CIDER.—Allow six eggs to a quart of cider Put a handful of whole cloves into the cider, and boil it. While it is boiling, beat the eggs in a large pitcher; adding to them as much sugar as will make the cider very sweet. By the time the cider boils, the eggs will be sufficiently light. Pour the boiling liquor on the beaten egg, and continue to pour the mixture backwards and forwards from one pitcher to another, till it has a fine froth on it. Then pour it warm into your glasses, and grate some nutmeg over each.

Port wine may be mulled in the same manner.

EGG NOGG.—Beat separately the yolks and whites of six eggs. Stir the yolks into a quart of rich milk, or thin cream, and add half a pound of sugar. Then mix in half a pint of rum or brandy. Flavour it with a grated nutmeg Lastly, stir in gently the beaten whites of three eggs.

It should be mixed in a china bowl.

SANGAREE.—Mix in a pitcher or in tumblers one-third of wine, ale, or porter, with two-thirds of water either warm or cold.   Stir in sufficient loaf-sugar to sweeten it, and grate some nutmeg into it.

By adding to it lemon juice, you may make what is called negus.

———

TURKISH SHERBET.—Put into a large pitcher a pound and a half of the best loaf-sugar, broken small.   Pour on it a quart of clear cold water, and crush and stir the sugar till it is all melted.   Take a dozen large fine ripe oranges, and roll every one under your hand on a table, to increase the juice. Take off the yellow rind in large thin pieces, and cut them neatly into round shapes, the size of a half-dollar.   Squeeze the juice of the oranges through a strainer upon the melted sugar, and stir it well.   Set the pitcher on ice till the sherbet is wanted.   Serve it up in lemonade-glasses, placing in the bottom of each, one of the round pieces of orange-rind, and lay a lump of ice upon it.   Then fill the glasses with the sherbet.   Instead of orange-juice, you may use that of strawberries, raspberries, or currants, pressed through a strainer.

———

BOTTLED SMALL BEER.—Take a quart bottle of the very best brisk porter, and mix it with four quarts of water, a pint of molasses, and a table-spoonful of ginger.   Bottle it, and see that the corks are of the very best kind.   It will be fit for use in three or four days.

———

TO KEEP LEMON JUICE.—Powder a pound of the best loaf-sugar; put it into a bowl, and strain over it a pint of lemon juice; stirring it well with a silver spoon till the sugar has entirely melted.   Boil and skim it.   Then bottle it, sealing the corks, and keep it in a dry place.

ESSENCE OF LEMON-PEEL.—Rub lumps of loaf-sugar on fine ripe lemons till the yellow rind is all grated off; scraping up the sugar in a tea-spoon, and putting it on a plate, as you proceed. When you have enough, press it down into a little glass or china jar, and cover it closely. This will be found very fine to flavour puddings and cakes. The white or inside of lemon-peel is of no use.

CIDER VINEGAR.

Take six quarts of rye meal; stir and mix it well into a barrel of strong hard cider of the best kind; and then add a gallon of whiskey. Cover the cask, (leaving the bung loosely in it,) set it in the part of your yard that is most exposed to the sun and air; and in the course of four weeks (if the weather is warm and dry) you will have good vinegar fit for use. When you draw off a gallon or more, replenish the cask with the same quantity of cider, and add about a pint of whiskey. You may thus have vinegar constantly at hand for common purposes.

The cask should have iron hoops.

A very strong vinegar may be made by mixing cider and strained honey, (allowing a pound of honey to a gallon of cider,) and letting it stand five or six months. This vinegar is so powerful that for common purposes it should be diluted with a little water.

Vinegar may be made in the same manner of sour wine.

WHITE VINEGAR.—Put into a cask a mixture composed of five gallons of water, two gallons of whiskey, and a quart of strong yeast, stirring in two pounds of powdered charcoal. Place it where it will ferment properly, leaving the bung loose till the fermentation is over, but covering the nole slightly to keep out the dust and insects. At the end of four months draw it off, and you will have a fine vinegar, as clear and colourless as water.

SUGAR VINEGAR.—To every gallon of water allow a pound of the best white sugar, and a jill or more of strong yeast. Mix the sugar and water together, and boil and skim it till the scum ceases to rise. Then pour it into a tub; and when it cools to lukewarm heat, put into it the yeast spread on pieces of toast. Let it work two days; then put it into an iron-hooped cask, and set it in a sunny place for five months, leaving the bung loose, but keeping the bung-hole covered. In five months it will be good clear vinegar, and you may bottle it for use.

A cask that has not contained vinegar before, should have a quart of boiling hot vinegar poured into it, shaken about frequently till cold, and allowed to stand some hours.

COMMON CIDER VINEGAR.—Set a barrel of hard sour cider in the sun for a few weeks, or three months, and it will become good vinegar.

PINE-APPLE-ADE.—Pare and slice some very ripe pine-apples; then cut the slices into small pieces. Put them with all their juice into a large pitcher, and sprinkle among them plenty of powdered white sugar. Pour on boiling water, allowing a small half pint to each pine-apple. Cover the pitcher, and let it stand till quite cool, occasionally pressing down the pine apple with a spoon. Then set the pitcher, for a while, in ice. Lastly, strain the infusion into another vessel, and transfer it to tumblers, putting into each glass some more sugar and a bit of ice. This beverage will be found delicious.

PREPARATIONS FOR THE SICK.

CHICKEN JELLY.

TAKE a large chicken, cut it up into very small pieces, bruise the bones, and put the whole into a stone jar with a cover that will make it water tight. Set the jar in a large kettle of boiling water, and keep it boiling for three hours. Then strain off the liquid, and season it slightly with salt, pepper, and mace; or with loaf-sugar and lemon juice, according to the taste of the person for whom it is intended.

Return the fragments of the chicken to the jar, and set it again in a kettle of boiling water. You will find that you can collect nearly as much jelly by the second boiling.

This jelly may be made of an old fowl.

BREAD JELLY.—Measure a quart of boiling water, and set it away to get cold. Take one-third of a six cent loaf of bread, slice it, pare off the crust, and toast the crumb nicely of a light brown. Then put it into the boiled water, set it on hot coals in a covered pan, and boil it gently, till you find by putting some in a spoon to cool, that the liquid has become a jelly. Strain it through a thin cloth, and set it away for use. When it is to be taken, warm a tea-cupful, sweeten it with sugar, and add a little grated lemon-peel.

ARROW ROOT JELLY.—Mix three table-spoonfuls of arrow root powder in a tea-cup of water till quite smooth; cover it, and let it stand a quarter of an hour. Put the yellow peel of a lemon into a skillet with a pint of water, and let it boil till reduced to one half. Then take out the lemon-peel.

and pour in the dissolved arrow root, (while the water is still boiling;) add sufficient white sugar to sweeten it well, and let it boil together for five or six minutes. It may be seasoned (if thought necessary) with two tea-spoonfuls of wine, and some grated nutmeg.

It may be boiled in milk instead of water, or in wine and water, according to the state of the person for whom it is wanted.

———

RICE JELLY.—Having picked and washed a quarter of a pound of rice, mix it with half a pound of loaf-sugar, and just sufficient water to cover it. Boil it till it becomes a glutinous mass; then strain it; season it with whatever may be thought proper; and let it stand to cool.

———

PORT WINE JELLY.—Melt in a little warm water an ounce of isinglass; stir it into a pint of port wine, adding two ounces of sugar candy, an ounce of gum arabic, and half a nutmeg grated. Mix all well, and boil it ten minutes; or till every thing is thoroughly dissolved. Then strain it through muslin, and set it away to get cold.

———

SAGO.—Wash the sago through two or three waters, and then let it soak for two or three hours. To a tea-cupful of sago allow a quart of water and some of the yellow peel of a lemon. Simmer it till all the grains look transparent. Then add as much wine and nutmeg as may be proper, and give it another boil altogether. If seasoning is not advisable, the sago may be boiled in milk instead of water, and eaten plain.

———

TAPIOCA.—Wash the tapioca well, and let it steep for five or six hours, changing the water three times. Simmer it in the last water till quite clear, then season it with sugar and wine, or lemon juice.

GRUEL.—Allow three large table-spoonfuls of oatmeal or Indian meal to a quart of water. Put the meal into a large bowl, and add the water, a little at a time, mixing and bruising the meal with the back of a spoon. As you proceed, pour off the liquid into another bowl, every time, before adding fresh water to the meal, till you have used it all up. Then boil the mixture for twenty minutes, stirring it all the while; add a little salt. Then strain the gruel and sweeten it. A piece of butter may be stirred into it; and, if thought proper, a little wine and nutmeg. It should be taken warm.

OATMEAL GRUEL.—Put four table-spoonfuls of the best grits (oatmeal coarsely ground) into a pint of boiling water. Let it boil gently, and stir it often, till it becomes as thick as you wish it. Then strain it, and add to it while warm, butter, wine, nutmeg, or whatever is thought proper to flavour it.

If you make the gruel of fine oatmeal, sift it, mix it first to a thick batter with a little cold water, and then put it into the sauce-pan of boiling water. Stir it all the time it is boiling, lifting the spoon gently up and down, and letting the gruel fall slowly back again into the pan.

PANADA.—Having pared off the crust, boil some slices of bread in a quart of water for about five minutes. Then take out the bread, and beat it smooth in a deep dish, mixing in a little of the water it has boiled in; and mix it with a bit of fresh butter, and sugar and nutmeg to your taste.

Another way is to grate some bread, or to grate or pound a few crackers. Pour on boiling water, beat it well, and add sugar and nutmeg.

BARLEY WATER.—Wash clean some barley, (either pearl or common,) and to two ounces of barley allow a quart of water. Put it into a sauce-pan, adding, if you choose, an equal quantity of stoned raisins; or some lemon-peel and sugar; or some liquorice root cut up. Let it boil slowly till the liquid is reduced one half. Then strain it off, and sweeten it.

GROUND RICE MILK.—Mix in a bowl two table-spoonfuls of ground rice, with sufficient milk to make a thin batter Then stir it gradually into a pint of milk and boil it with sugar, lemon-peel or nutmeg.

BEEF TEA.—Cut a pound of the lean of fresh juicy beef into small thin slices, and sprinkle them with a very little salt. Put the meat into a wide-mouthed glass or stone jar closely corked, and set it in a kettle or pan of water, which must be made to boil, and kept boiling hard round the jar for an hour or more. Then take out the jar and strain the essence of the beef into a bowl. Chicken tea may be made in the same manner.

MUTTON BROTH.—Cut off all the fat from a loin of mutton, and to each pound of the lean allow a quart of water. Season it with a little salt and some shred parsley, and put in some large pieces of the crust of bread. Boil it slowly for two or three hours, skimming it carefully.

Beef, veal, or chicken broth may be made in the same manner.

Vegetables may be added if approved. Also barley or rice.

MUTTON BROTH MADE QUICKLY.—Cut three chops from the best part of a neck of mutton, and remove the fat and skin. Beat the meat on both sides, and slice it thin. Put into a small sauce-pan with a pint of water, a little salt, and some crust of bread cut into pieces. You may add a little parsley, and a small onion sliced thin. Cover the sauce-pan, and set it over the fire. Boil it fast, skim it, and in half an hour it should be ready for use.

WINE WHEY.—Boil a pint of milk; and when it rises to the top of the sauce-pan, pour in a large glass of sherry or Madeira. It will be the better for adding a glass of currant wine also. Let it again boil up, and then take the sauce-pan off the fire, and set it aside to stand for a few minutes, but do not stir it. Then remove the curd, (if it has completely formed,) and pour the clear whey into a bowl and sweeten it.

When wine is considered too heating, the whey may be made by turning the milk with lemon juice.

RENNET WHEY.—Wash a small bit of rennet about two inches square, in cold water, to get off the salt. Put it into a tea-cup and pour on it sufficient lukewarm water to cover it. Let it stand all night, and in the morning stir the rennet water into a quart pitcher of warm milk. Cover it, and set it near the fire till a firm curd is formed. Pour off the whey from it, and it will be found an excellent and cooling drink. The curd may be eaten (though not by a sick person) with wine, sugar, and nutmeg. The whey should look greenish.

CALF'S FEET BROTH.—Boil two calf's feet in two quarts of water, till the liquid is reduced one half, and the meat has dropped to pieces. Then strain it into a deep dish or pan, and set it by to get cold. When it has congealed, take all the fat carefully off; put a tea-cupful of the jelly into a sauce-pan, and set it on hot coals. When it has nearly boiled, stir in by degrees the beaten yolk of an egg, and then take it off immediately. You may add to it a little sugar, and some grated lemon-peel and nutmeg.

CHICKEN BROTH AND PANADA.—Cut up a chicken, season it with a very little salt, and put it into three quarts of water. Let it simmer slowly till the flesh drops to pieces. You may make chicken panada or gruel of the same fowl, by taking out the white meat as soon as it is tender, mincing it fine, and then pounding it in a mortar, adding as you pound it, sufficient of the chicken water to moisten the paste. You may thin it with water till it becomes liquid enough to drink. Then put it into a sauce-pan and boil it gently a few minutes. Taken in small quantities, it will be found very nutritious. You may add to it a little grated lemon-peel and nutmeg.

VEGETABLE SOUP.—Take a white onion, a turnip, a pared potato, and a head of celery, or a large tea-spoonful of celery seed. Put the vegetables whole into a quart of water, (adding a little salt,) and boil it slowly till reduced to a pint. Make a slice of nice toast; lay it in the bottom of a bowl, and strain the soup over it.

ONION SOUP.—Put half a pound of the best fresh butter into a stew-pan on the fire, and let it boil till it has done making a noise; then have ready twelve large onions peeled and cut small; throw them into the butter, add a little salt, and stew them a quarter of an hour. Then dredge in a little flour, and stir the whole very hard; and in five minutes pour in a quart of boiling water, and some of the upper crust of bread, cut small. Let the soup boil ten minutes longer, stirring it often; and after you take it from the fire, stir in the yolks of two beaten eggs, and serve it up immediately.

In France this soup is considered a fine restorative after any unusual fatigue. Instead of butter, the onions may be boiled in veal or chicken broth.

TOAST AND WATER.—Toast some slices of bread very nicely, without allowing them to burn or blacken. Then put them into a pitcher, and fill it up with boiling water. Let it stand till it is quite cold; then strain it, and put it into a decanter. Another way of preparing toast and water is to put the toasted bread into a mug and pour cold water on it. Cover it closely, and let it infuse for at least an hour. Drink it cold.

APPLE WATER.—Pare and slice a fine juicy apple; pour boiling water over it, cover it, and let it stand till cold.

TAMARIND WATER.—Put tamarinds into a pitcher or tumbler till it is one-third full; then fill it up with cold water, cover it, and let it infuse for a quarter of an hour or more.

Currant jelly or cranberry juice mixed with water makes a pleasant drink for an invalid.

MOLASSES POSSET.—Put into a sauce-pan a pint of the best West India molasses; a tea-spoonful of powdered white ginger; and a quarter of a pound of fresh butter. Se it on hot coals, and simmer it slowly for half an hour; stirring it frequently. Do not let it come to a boil. Then stir in the juice of two lemons, or two table-spoonfuls of vinegar; cover the pan and let it stand by the fire five minutes longer. This is good for a cold. Some of it may be taken warm at once, and the remainder kept at hand for occasional use.

It is the preparation absurdly called by the common people a stewed quaker.

Half a pint of strained honey mixed cold with the juice of a lemon, and a table-spoonful of sweet oil, is another remedy for a cold; a tea-spoonful or two to be taken whenever the cough is troublesome.

FLAX-SEED LEMONADE.—To a large table-spoonful of flax-seed allow a tumbler and a half of cold water. Boil them together till the liquid becomes very sticky. Then strain it hot over a quarter of a pound of pulverized sugar candy, and an ounce of pulverized gum arabic. Stir it till quite dissolved, and squeeze into it the juice of a lemon.

This mixture has frequently been found an efficacious remedy for a cold; taking a wine-glass of it as often as the cough is troublesome.

COCOA.—Put into a sauce-pan two ounces of good cocoa (the chocolate nut before it is ground) and one quart of water. Cover it, and as soon as it has come to a boil, set it on coals oy the side of the fire, to simmer for an hour or more. Take it hot with dry toast. Baker's prepared cocoa is excellent.

COCOA SHELLS.—These can be procured at the principal grocers and confectioners, or at a chocolate manufactory. They are the thin shells that envelope the chocolate kernel, and are sold at a low price; a pound contains a very large quantity. Soak them in water for five or six hours or more, (it will be better to soak them all night,) and then boil them in the same water. They should boil two hours. Strain the liquid when done, and let it be taken warm.

RAW EGG.—Break a fresh egg into a saucer, and mix a little sugar with it; also, if approved, a small quantity of wine. Beat the whole to a strong froth. It is considered a restorative.

SODA WATER.—To forty grains of carbonate of soda, add thirty grains or tartaric acid in small crystals. Fill a soda bottle with spring water, put in the mixture, and cork it instantly with a well-fitting cork.

SEIDLITZ POWDERS.—Fold in a white paper one drachm of Rochelle salts. In a blue paper a mixture of twenty grains of tartaric acid, and twenty-five grains of carbonate of soda. They should all be pulverized very fine. Put the contents of the white paper into a tumbler not quite half full of cold water, and stir it till dissolved. Then put the mixture from the blue paper into another tumbler with the same quantity of water, and stir that also. When the powders are dissolved in both tumblers, pour the first into the other, and it will effervesce immediately. Drink it quickly while foaming

---

BITTERS.—Take two ounces of gentian root, an ounce of Virginia snake root, an ounce of the yellow paring of orange peel, and half a drachm of cochineal. Steep these ingredients for a week or more, in a quart of Madeira or sherry wine, or brandy. When they are thoroughly infused, strain and filter the liquor, and bottle it for use. This is considered a good tonic, taken in a small cordial glass about noon.

ESSENCE OF PEPPERMINT.—Mix an ounce of oil of peppermint with a pint of alcohol. Then colour it by put ring in some leaves of green mint. Let it stand till the colour is a fine green; then filter it through blotting paper. Drop it on sugar when you take it.

Essence of pennyroyal, mint, cinnamon, cloves, &c. may all be prepared in the same manner by mixing a portion of the essential oil with a little alcohol.

You may obtain liquid camphor by breaking up and dissolving a lump in white brandy or spirit of wine.

LAVENDER COMPOUND.—Fill a quart bottle with lavender blossoms freshly gathered, and put in loosely; then pour in as much of the best brandy as it will contain. Let it stand a fortnight, and then strain it. Afterwards, mix with it of powdered cloves, mace, nutmeg and cochineal, a quarter of an ounce of each; and cork it up for use in small bottles. When taken, a little should be dropped on a lump of sugar.

LEAD WATER.—Mix one tea-spoonful of sugar of lead with a quart bottle of rain or river water. Then add three table-spoonfuls of vinegar, and shake it well.

REMEDY FOR A BURN.*—After immediately applying sweet oil, scrape the inside of a raw potato, and lay some of it on the place, securing it with a rag. In a short time put on fresh potato, and repeat this application very frequently. It will give immediate ease, and draw out the fire. Of course, if the burn is bad, it is best to send for a physician.

FOR CHILBLAINS.—Dip the feet every night and morning in cold water, withdrawing them in a minute or two, and

---

* These remedies are all very simple; but the author *knows* them to have been efficacious whenever tried.

drying them by rubbing them very hard with a coarse towel To put them immediately into a pail of brine brought from a pickle tub is another excellent remedy when feet are found to be frosted.

FOR CORNS.—Mix together a little Indian meal and cold water, till it is about the consistence of thick mush. Then bind it on the corn by wrapping a small slip of thin rag round the toe. It will not prevent you from wearing your shoe and stocking. In two or three hours take it off, and you will find the corn much softened. Cut off as much of it as is soft with a penknife or scissors. Then put on a fresh poultice, and repeat it till the corn is entirely levelled, as it will be after a few regular applications of the remedy; which will be found successful whenever the corn returns. There is no permanent cure for them.

WARTS.—To remove the hard callous horny warts which sometimes appear on the hands of children, touch the wart carefully with a new pen dipped slightly in aqua-fortis. It will give no pain; and after repeating it a few times, the wart will be found so loose as to come off by rubbing it with the finger.

RING-WORMS.—Rub mercurial ointment on the ring-worm previous to going to bed, and do not wash it off till morning. It will effect a cure if persevered in; sometimes in less than a week.

MUSQUITO BITES.—Salt wetted into a sort of paste, with a little vinegar, and plastered on the bite, will immediately allay the pain; and if not rubbed, no mark will be seen next day. It is well to keep salt and vinegar always in a chamber that is infested with musquitoes. It is also good for the sting of a wasp or bee; and for the bite of any venomous animal, if applied immediately. It should be left on till it becomes dry, and then renewed.

ANTIDOTE FOR LAUDANUM.—When so large a quantity of laudanum has been swallowed as to produce dangerous effects, the fatal drowsiness has been prevented when all other remedies have failed, by administering a cup of the strongest possible coffee. The patient has revived and recovered, and no ill effects have followed.

GREEN OINTMENT.—Take two or three large handfuls of the fresh-gathered leaves of the Jamestown weed, (called Apple Peru in New England,) and pound it in a mortar till you have extracted the juice. Then put the juice into a tin sauce-pan, mixed with sufficient lard to make a thick salve. Stew them together half an hour, and then put the mixture into gallipots and cover it closely. It is excellent to rub on chilblains, and other inflammatory external swellings, applying it several times a day.

TO STOP BLOOD.—For a prick with a pin, or a slight cut, nothing will more effectually stop the bleeding than old cobwebs compressed into a lump and applied to the wound, or bound on it with a rag. A scrap of cotton wadding is also good for stopping blood. Or wet the place with laudanum. After the blood is stopped, cover the cut with a bit of white or pink court-plaster. The copperas dye in *black* court-plaster will sometimes produce inflammation.

PERFUMERY, ETC.

~~~~~~~~

COLOGNE WATER.

PROCURE at a druggists, one drachm of oil of lavender, the same quantity of oil of lemon, of oil of rosemary, and of oil of cinnamon; with two drachms of oil of bergamot, all mixed in the same phial, which should be a new one. Shake the oils well, and pour them into a pint of spirits of wine. Cork the bottle tightly, shake it hard, and it will be fit for immediate use; though it improves by keeping. You may add to the oils, if you choose, ten drops of the tincture of musk, or ten drops of extract of ambergris

For very fine cologne water, mix together in a new phial oil of lemon, two drachms; oil of bergamot, two drachms; oil of lavender, two drachms; oil of cedrat, one drachm; tincture of benzoin, three drachms; neroli, ten drops; ambergris, ten drops; attar of roses, two drops. Pour the mixture into a pint of spirits of wine; cork and shake the bottle and set it away for use. Use only what is called absolute alcohol.

Another receipt for cologne water is to mix with a pint of alcohol, sixty drops or two large tea-spoonfuls of orange-flower water, and the same quantity of the essential oils of lemon, lavender, and bergamot. The alcohol should be inodorous.

———

LAVENDER WATER.—Mix two ounces of essential oil of lavender, and two drachms of essence of ambergris, with a pint of spirits of wine; cork the bottle, and shake it hard every day for a fortnight. Use absolute alcohol.

HUNGARY WATER.—Mix together one ounce of oil of rosemary and two drachms of essence of ambergris; add them to a pint of spirits of wine. Shake it daily for a month, and then transfer it to small bottles.

ROSE VINEGAR.—Fill a stone or china jar with fresh rose leaves put in loosely. Then pour on them as much of the best white wine vinegar as the jar will hold. Cover it, and set it in the sun, or in some other warm place for three weeks. Then strain it through a flannel bag, and bottle it for use. This vinegar will be found very fine for salads, or for any nice purposes.

THIEVES' VINEGAR.—Take a large handful of lavender blossoms, and the same quantity of sage, mint, rue, wormwood and rosemary. Chop and mix them well. Put them into a jar, with half an ounce of camphor that has been dissolved in a little alcohol, and pour in three quarts of strong clear vinegar. Keep the jar for two or three weeks in the hot sun, and at night plunge it into a box of heated sand. Afterwards strain and bottle the liquid, putting into each bottle a clove of garlic sliced. To have it very clear, after it has been bottled for a week, you should pour it off carefully from the sediment and filter it through blotting paper. Then wash the bottles and return the vinegar to them. It should be kept very tightly corked. It is used for sprinkling about in sick-rooms; and also in close damp oppressive weather. Inhaling the odour from a small bottle will frequently prevent faintness in a crowd.

It is best to make it in June.

This vinegar is so called from an old tradition, that during the prevalence of the plague in London the composition was

Invented by four thieves, who found it a preservative from contagion; and were by that means enabled to remain in the city and exercise their profession to great advantage, after most of the inhabitants had fled.

OIL OF FLOWERS.—A French process for obtaining essential oils from flowers or herbs has been described as follows :—Take carded cotton, or split wadding, and steep it in some pure Florence oil, such as is quite clear and has no smell. Then place a layer of this cotton in the bottom of a deep china dish, or in an earthen pipkin. Cover it with a thick layer of fresh rose leaves, or the leaves of sweet pink. jasmine, wall-flower, tuberose, magnolia blossoms, or and other odoriferous flower or plant from which you wish to obtain the perfume. Spread over the flower-leaves another layer of cotton that has been steeped in oil. Afterwards a second layer of flowers, and repeat them alternately till the vessel is quite full. Cover it closely, and let it stand in the sun for a week. Then throw away the flower-leaves, carefully press out the oil from the cotton, and put it into a small bottle for use. The oil will be found to have imbibed the odour of the flowers.

Keep the scented cotton to perfume your clothes-drawers.

BALM OF GILEAD OIL.—Put loosely into a bottle as many balm of Gilead flowers as will come up to a third part of its height; then nearly fill up the bottle with sweet oil, which should be of the best quality. Let it infuse (shaking it occasionally) for several days, and it will then be fit for use. It is considered a good remedy for bruises of tne skin; also for cuts, burns, and scalds that are not very bad, and should be applied immediately by wetting a soft rag with it; renewing it frequently.

LIP SALVE.—Put into a wide-mouthed bottle four ounces of the best olive oil, with one ounce of the small parts of alkanet root. Stop up the bottle, and set it in the sun, (shaking it often,) till you find the liquid of a beautiful crimson. Then strain off the oil very clear from the alkanet root, put it into an earthen pipkin, and add to it an ounce of white wax, and an ounce and a half of the best mutton suet, which has been previously clarified, or boiled and skimmed. Set the mixture on the embers of coals, and melt it slowly : stirring it well. After it has simmered slowly for a little while, take it off; and while still hot, mix with it a few drops of oil of roses, or of oil of neroli, or tincture of musk.

———

COLD CREAM.—Cut up a shilling cake of white wax; put it into a clean sauce-pan with an ounce of oil of sweet almonds, and two large table-spoonfuls of lard. Boil and stir it well. When you take it off the fire, beat in an ounce of orange-flower, or rose-water. Put it up in gallicups with covers.

———

SOFT POMATUM.—Soak half a pound of fresh lard and a quarter of a pound of beef marrow in water for two or three days; squeezing and pressing it every day, and changing the water. Afterwards drain off the water, and put the lard and marrow into a sieve to dry. Then transfer it to a jar, and set the jar into a pot of boiling water. When the mixture is melted, put it into a basin, and beat it with two spoonfuls of brandy. Then drain off the brandy, perfume the pomatum by mixing with it any scented essence that you please, and tie it up in gallipots.

COSMETIC PASTE.—Take a quarter of a pound of Cas tile soap, and cut it into small pieces. Then put it into a tın or porcelain sauce-pan, with just water enough to moisten it well, and set it on hot coals. Let it simmer till it is entirely dissolved; stirring it till it becomes a smooth paste, and thick ening it with Indian meal, (which even in a raw state is excel lent for the hands.) Then take it from the fire, and when cool scent it with rose-water, or with any fragrant essence you please. Beat and stir it hard with a silver spoon, and when it is thoroughly mixed put it into little pots with covers.

ACID SALT.—This is the composition commonly, but erroneously called salt of lemon, and is excellent for removing ink and other stains from the hands, and for taking ink spots out of white clothes. Pound together in a marble mortar an ounce of salt of sorrel, and an ounce of the best cream of tartar, mixing them thoroughly. Then put it in little wooden boxes or covered gallipots, and rub it on your hands when they are stained, washing them in cold water, and using the acid salt instead of soap; a very small quantity will immediately remove the stain. In applying it to linen or muslin that is spotted with ink or fruit juice, hold the stained part tightly stretched over a cup or bowl of boiling water. Then with your finger rub on the acid salt till the stain disappears. It must always be done before the article is washed.

This mixture costs about twenty-five cents, and the above quantity (if kept dry) will be sufficient for a year or more.

Ink stains may frequently be taken out of white clothes by rubbing on (before they go to the wash) some bits of cold tallow picked from the bottom of a mould candle. Leave the tallow sticking on in a lump, and when the article comes from the wash, it will generally be found that the spot has disappeared. This experiment is so easy and so generally successful that it is always worth trying. When it fails, it is in consequence of some peculiarity in the composition of the ink.

SWEET JARS.—Take a china jar, and put into it three handfuls of fresh damask rose-leaves; three of sweet pinks, three of wall-flowers, and stock gilly-flowers, and equal proportions of any other fragrant flowers that you can procure. Place them in layers; strewing powdered orris-root thickly between each layer.

You may fill another jar with equal quantities of lavender, knotted marjoram, rosemary, lemon-thyme, balm of Gilead, lemon-peel, and smaller quantities of laurel leaves and mint; and some sliced orris-root. You may mix with the herbs, (which must all be chopped,) powdered cloves, cinnamon, and nutmeg; strewing powdered orris-root between the layers.

Flowers, herbs, and spice may all be mixed in the same jar; adding always some orris root. Every thing that is put in should be perfectly free from damp.

The jar should be kept closely covered, except when the cover is occasionally removed for the purpose of diffusing the scent through the room.

SCENTED BAGS.—Take a quarter of a pound of coriander seeds, a quarter of a pound of orris root, a quarter of a pound of aromatic calamus, a quarter of a pound of damask rose leaves, two ounces of lavender blossoms, half an ounce of mace, half an ounce of cinnamon, a quarter of an ounce of cloves, and two drachms of musk-powder. Beat them all separately in a mortar, and then mix them well together Make small silk or satin bags; fill each with a portion of the mixture, and sew them closely all round. Lay them among your clothes in the drawers.

VIOLET PERFUME.—Drop twelve drops of genuine oil of rhodium on a lump of loaf-sugar. Then pound the sugar in a marble mortar with two ounces of orris root powder. This will afford an excellent imitation of the scent of violets. If you add more oil of rhodium, it will produce a rose perfume. Sew up the powder in little silk bags, or keep it in a tight box.

DURABLE INK.—Take, when empty, one of the little bottles that has contained indelible ink, such as is sold in cases, and wash and rinse it clean. Put into it two inches of lunar caustic; fill it up with soft water and cork it tightly. This is the marking ink.

Prepare the larger bottle that has contained the liquid used for the first wash, by making it quite clean. Take a large tea-spoonful of salt of tartar, and a lump of gum arabic the size of a hickory nut. Put them into the wash bottle, and fill it up with clear rain water. Cork both bottles tightly, and set them three days in the sun. Always put them in the sun before using it.

Linen cannot be marked well with durable ink unless the weather is clear and dry. Dip a camel's hair pencil in the large bottle that contains the gum liquid, and wash over with it a small space on a corner of the linen, about large enough to contain the name. Dry it in the sun, and let it alone till next day. Then take a very good pen, and with the ink from the smallest bottle, write the name you intend, on the place that has been prepared by the first liquid. This also must be dried in the sun. See that the bottles are always well corked, and keep them in a covered box.

After the linen is dried, iron it before you write on it.

ANOTHER DURABLE INK.—For the marking liquid—rub together in a small mortar five scruples of lunar caustic with one drachm of gum arabic, one scruple of sap-green and one ounce of rain water. Keep the bottle three days in the sun.

For wetting the linen—mix together a quarter of an ounce of salt of soda, a heaped table-spoonful of powdered gum arabic, and two ounces of hot water.

TO KEEP PEARL-ASH.—Take three ounces of pearl-ash, and put it into a clean black bottle with a pint and a half (not more) of soft water. The proportion is an ounce of pearl-ash to half a pint of water. Cork it very tightly, shake it, and it will be fit for use as soon as all the pearl-ash is dissolved. A table-spoonful of this liquid is equal to a small tea-spoonful of pearl-ash in the lump or powder. Keeping it ready dissolved will be found very convenient.

ALMOND PASTE.—Blanch half a pound of shelled sweet almonds, and a quarter of a pound of bitter ones, and beat them in a mortar to a smooth paste—adding by degrees a jill of rose or orange-flower water. Then beat in, gradually, half a pound of clear strained honey. When the whole is well incorporated, put it into gallipots, pouring on the top of each some orange-flower or rose-water. Keep it closely covered.

This is a celebrated cosmetic for the hands.

MISCELLANEOUS RECEIPTS.

MINCED OYSTERS.—Take fifty fine large oysters, and mince them raw. Chop also four or five small pickled cucumbers, and a bunch of parsley. Grate about two tea-cupfuls of stale bread-crumbs, and beat up the yolks of four eggs. Mix the whole together in a thick batter, seasoning it with cayenne and powdered mace; and with a little salt if the oysters are fresh. Have ready a pound of lard, and melt in the frying-pan enough of it to fry the oysters well. If the lard is in too small a quantity they will be flat and tough. When the lard is boiling hot in the pan, put in about a table-spoonful at a time of the oyster-mixture, and fry it in the form of small fritters; turning them so as to brown on both sides. Serve them up hot, and eat them with small bread rolls.

STEWED BLACK FISH.—Flour a deep dish, and lay in the bottom a piece of butter rolled in flour. Then sprinkle it with a mixture of parsley, sweet marjoram, and green onion; all chopped fine. Take your black fish and rub it inside and outside with a mixture of cayenne, salt, and powdered cloves and mace. Place skewers across the dish, and lay the fish upon them. Then pour in a little wine, and sufficient water to stew the fish. Set the dish in a moderate oven, and let it cook slowly for an hour.

Shad or rock fish may be dressed in the same manner.

FRIED SMELTS.—These little fish are considered extremely fine. Before they are cooked, cut off the heads and tails. Sprinkle the smelts with flour, and have ready in a fry-ing pan over the fire plenty of fresh lard or butter. When it boils, put in the fish and fry them.

BROILED SWEETBREADS.—Split open and skewer the sweetbreads; season them with pepper and salt, and with powdered mace. Broil them on a gridiron till thoroughly done. While they are broiling, prepare some melted butter seasoned with mace and a little white wine, or mushroom catchup; and have ready some toast with the crust cut off. Lay the toast in the bottom of a dish; place the sweetbreads upon it, and pour over them the drawn butter.

PICKLED EGGS.—Boil twelve eggs quite hard, and lay them in cold water; having peeled off the shells. Then put them whole into a stone jar, with a quarter of an ounce of whole mace, and the same quantity of cloves; a sliced nut-meg; a table-spoonful of whole pepper; a small bit of ginger; and a peach leaf. Fill up the jar with boiling vinegar; cover it closely that the eggs may cool slowly. When they are cold, tie up the jar; covering the cork with leather. After it has stood three days pour off the pickle, boil it up again, and return it boiling hot to the eggs and spice. They will be fit for use in a fortnight.

GUMBO SOUP.—Take four pounds of the lean of a fresh round of beef and cut the meat into small pieces, avoiding carefully all the fat. Season the meat with a little pepper and salt, and put it on to boil with three quarts and a pint of water (not more.) Boil it slowly and skim it well. When no more scum rises, out in half a peck of ochras, peeled and sliced.

and half a peck of tomatas cut in quarters. Boil it slowly till the ochras and tomatas are entirely dissolved, and the meat all to rags. Then strain it through a cullender, and send it to table with slices of dry toast. This soup cannot be made in less than seven or eight hours. If you dine at two you must put on the meat to boil at six or seven in the morning. It should be as thick as a jelly.

SHREWSBURY CAKES.—Rub three quarters of a pound of butter into two pounds of sifted flour, and mix in half a pound of powdered sugar, and half a pound of currants, washed and dried. Wet it to a stiff paste with rich milk. Roll it out, and cut it into cakes. Lay them on buttered baking sheets, and put them into a moderate oven.

RICE FLUMMERY.—To two quarts of milk allow half a pound of ground rice. Take out one pint of the milk, and mix the rice gradually with it into a batter; making it quite smooth and free from lumps. Put the three pints of milk into a skillet, (with a bunch of peach leaves or a few peach-kernels,) and let it come to a boil. Then while it is still boiling, stir in by degrees the rice batter, taking care not to have it lumpy; add sugar, mace, and rose brandy to your taste; or you may flavour it with the juice of a large lemon. When it has boiled sufficiently, and is quite thick, strain it, and put it into a mould to congeal. Make a rich boiled custard, (flavoured in the same manner,) and send it to table in a pitcher, to eat with the flummery. Both should be cold. If you mould it in tea-cups, turn it out on a deep dish, and pour the custard round it.

APPLE BUTTER WITHOUT CIDER.—Mix together ten gallons of water, and ten gallons of the best West India molasses. Put it into a large kettle over a good fire; let it come to a hard boil, and skim it as long as any scum continues to rise. Then take out half the liquid, and put it into a tub. Have ready eight bushels of fine sound apples, pared, cored and quartered. Throw them gradually into the liquid that is still boiling on the fire. Let it continue to boil hard, and as it thickens, add by degrees the other half of the molasses and water, (that which has been put into the tub.) Stir it frequently to prevent its scorching, and to make it of equal consistence throughout. Boil it ten or twelve hours, continuing to stir it. At night take it out of the kettle, an set it in tubs to cool; covering it carefully. Wash out th kettle and wipe it very dry.

Next morning boil the apple butter six or eight hours longer; it should boil eighteen hours altogether. Then an hour before you take it finally out, stir in a pound of mixed spice · cloves, mace, cinnamon, and nutmeg, all finely powdered. When entirely done, put up the apple butter in stone or earthen jars. It will keep a year or more

It can, of course, be made in a smaller quantity than that given in the above receipt; and also at any time in the winter; fresn cider not being an ingredient, as in the most usual way of making apple butter.

———

AN APPLE POT PIE.—Make a paste, allowing a pound of butter, or of chopped suet to two pounds and a quarter of flour. Have ready a sufficient quantity of fine juicy acid apples, pared, cored, and sliced. Mix with them brown sugar mough to sweeten them, a few cloves, and some grated lemon-peel. Butter the sides of an iron pot, and line them with paste. Then put in the apples, interspersing them with thin squares of paste, and add a very little water. Cover the whole with a thick lid of paste, cutting a slit in the centre for the water to bubble up, and let it boil two hours. When done, serve it up on a large dish, and eat it with butter and sugar.

PUDDING CATCHUP.—Mix together half a pint of noyau; a pint of sherry or other white wine; the yellow peel of four lemons, pared thin; and half an ounce of mace. Put the whole into a large bottle, and let it stand for two or three weeks. Then strain it, and add half a pint of capillaire or strong sugar syrup; or of Curaçoa. Bottle it, and it will keep two or three years. It may be used for various sweet dishes, but chiefly for pudding-sauce mixed with melted butter.

CURAÇOA.—Grate as much fresh orange-peel as will make two ounces when done; the peel of fresh shaddock will be still better. Mix it with a pint of orange juice. Put it into a quart of the strongest and clearest rectified spirit; shake it, let it infuse-for a fortnight, and strain it. Then make a syrup by dissolving a pound of the best loaf-sugar in a pint of cold water, adding to it the beaten white of an egg, and boiling and skimming it till the scum ceases to rise. Mix the syrup with the strained liquor. Let it stand till next day, and then filter it through white blotting paper fastened to the bottom of a sieve. Curaçoa is a great improvement to punch; also a table-spoonful of it in a tumbler of water makes a very refreshing summer drink.

PATENT YEAST.—Boil half a pound of fresh hops in four quarts of water, till the liquid is reduced to two quarts

Strain it, and mix in sufficient wheat flour to make a thin batter; adding half a pint of strong fresh yeast, (brewer's yeast, if it can be procured.) When it is done fermenting, pour it into a pan, and stir in sufficient Indian meal to make a moderately stiff dough. Cover it, and set it in a warm place to rise. When it has become very light, roll t out into a thick sheet, and cut it into little cakes. Spread them out on a dish, and let them dry gradually in a cool place where there is no sun. Turn them five or six times a day while drying; and when they are quite dry, put them into paper bags, and keep them in a jar or box closely covered, in a place that is not in the least damp.

When you want the yeast for use, dissolve in a little warm water one or more of the cakes, (in proportion to the quantity of bread you intend making,) and when it is quite dissolved, stir it hard, thicken it with a little flour, cover it, and place it near the fire to rise before you use it. Then mix it with the flour in the usual manner of preparing bread.

This is a very convenient way of preserving yeast through the summer, or of conveying it to a distance.

TO DRY HERBS.—By drying herbs with artificial heat as quickly as possible, you preserve their scent and flavour much better than when they are dried slowly by exposing them to the sun and air; a process by which a large portion of their strength evaporates. All sorts of herbs are in the greatest perfection just before they begin to flower. Gather them on a dry day, and place them in an oven, which must not be hot enough to discolour, scorch, or burn them. When they are quite dry, take them out, and replace them with others. Pick the leaves from the stems, (which may be thrown away,) and put them into bottles or jars; cork them ightly, and keep them in a dry place. Those that are used ιn cookery should be kept in a kitchen closet.

PEACH KERNELS.—When peaches are in season, have n a convenient place an old basket or something of the sort, 'n which all the peach stones can be saved ; they are too use- ful to be thrown away. Then have them carefully cracked, so as to extract the kernels whole if possible. Spread them out on a dish for one day. Then put them into a box or jar. and keep them to use as bitter almonds ; for which they are an excellent substitute in flavouring custards, creams and ιakes. Plum stones are worth saving in the same manner.

LEMON-PEEL.—Never throw away the rind of a lemon. Keep a wide-mouthed bottle half full of brandy, and put into it (cut in pieces) all the lemon-rind that you do not imme- diately want. As the white part of the rind is of no use, it will be best to pare off the yellow very thin, and put that alone into the brandy, which will thus imbibe a very fine lemon flavour, and may be used for many nice purposes.

TO KEEP TOMATAS.—Take fine ripe tomatas, and wipe them dry, taking care not to break the skin. Put them into a stone jar with cold vinegar, adding a small thin muslin bag filled with mace, whole cloves, and whole peppers. Ther cork the jar tightly with a cork that has been dipped in melted rosin, and put it away in a dry place. Tomatas pickled in this manner keep perfectly well and retain their colour. For this purpose use the small round button tomatas.

Morella cherries may be pickled thus, in cold vinegar.

ADDITIONAL RECEIPTS

~~~~~~~~~~~~~~~~~~

FRENCH GREEN PEA SOUP.—This soup is made without meat. Put into a soup-pot four quarts of shelled green peas, two large onions sliced, a handful of leaves of sweet marjoram shred from the stalks, or a handful of sweet basil; or a mixed handful of both—also, if you like it, a handful of green mint. Add four quarts of water, and boil the whole slowly till all the peas are entirely to pieces. Then take off the pot, and mash the peas well against its sides to extract from them all their flavour. Afterward strain off the liquid into a clean pot, and add to it a tea-cup full of the juice of spinach, which you must prepare, while the soup is boiling, by pounding some spinach in a mortar. This will give the soup a fine green colour. Then put in a quarter of a pound of the best fresh butter rolled whole in flour; and add a pint and a half more of shelled young peas. If you wish the soup very thick, you may allow a quart of the additional peas. Season it with a very little salt and cayenne; put it again over the fire, and boil it till the last peas are quite soft, but not till they go to pieces.

Have ready in a tureen two or three slices of toasted bread cut into small squares or dice, and pour the soup on it.

This soup, if properly made, will be found excellent, notwithstanding the absence of meat. It is convenient for fast days; and in the country, where vegetables can be obtained from the garden, the expense will be very trifling.

What is left may be warmed for the next day.

————

GIBLET SOUP.—Take three pounds of shin of beef or of neck of mutton. Cut off the meat and break the bones. Then put the meat with the bones into a soup-pot, with a tea-spoon-ful of salt, and three quarts of water. Add a bunch of sweet marjoram, one of sweet basil, and a quarter of an ounce of black pepper-corns, all tied in a thin muslin rag ; a sliced onion, and six or eight turnips and carrots, cut small. Let the whole boil slowly for two or three hours, skimming it well. In the mean time, have ready two sets of goose-giblets, or four of duck. They must be scalded, and well washed in warm water. Cut off the bills, and split the heads ; and cut the necks and giz-zards into mouthfuls. Having taken the meat and bones out of the soup, put in the giblets, with a head of celery chopped. Boil it slowly an hour and a half, or more, taking care to skim it. Make a thickening of an ounce and a half of butter, and a large table-spoonful of flour, mixed together with a little of the soup. Then stir it into the pot, adding a large table-spoonful of mushroom catchup, and some small force-meat balls, or little dumplings. Boil the soup half an hour longer. Then send it to table with the giblets in the tureen.

GUMBO.—Take an equal quantity of young tender ochras and of ripe tomatas, (for instance, a quarter of a peck of each.) Chop the ochras fine, and scald and peel the tomatas. Put them into a stew-pan without any water. Add a lump of but-ter, and a very little salt and pepper ; and, if you choose, an onion minced fine. Let it stew steadily for an hour. Then strain it, and send it to table as soup in a tureen. It should be like a jelly, and is a favourite New Orleans dish. Eat dry toast with it. This gumbo is for fast days.

HAM OMELET.—Take six ounces of cold boiled ham, and mince it very fine, adding a little pepper. Beat separately the whites and yolks of six eggs, and then mix them together add to them gradually the minced ham. Beat the whole very hard, and do not let it stand a moment after it is thoroughly mixed. Have ready some boiling lard in a frying-pan, and put in the omelet immediately. Fry it about ten minutes or a quarter of an hour. When done, put it on a hot dish, trim off the edges, and fold it over in a half moon. Send it to table hot, and covered. It is eaten at breakfast.

If you wish a soft omelet, (not to fold over,) fry it a shorter time, and serve it in a deep dish, to be helped with a spoon.

A similar omelet may be made of the lean of a cold smoked tongue.

BATTER PUDDING.—Take a quart of milk, and stir into it gradually eight large table-spoonfuls of flour, carefully pressing out all the lumps with the back of the spoon. Beat eight eggs very light, and add them by degrees to the milk and flour. Then stir the whole very well together.

Dip your pudding-cloth into boiling water, and then dredge it with flour. Pour in the pudding, and tie it tightly, leaving room for it to swell. Put it into a pot full of boiling water, and boil it hard for two hours. Keep it in the pot till it is time to send it to table. Serve it up with wine-sauce, butter and sugar, or molasses and cold butter.

PEACH MANGOES.—Take free-stone peaches of the largest size, (when they are full grown, but not quite ripe,) and lay them in salt and water for two days, covered with a board to keep them down. Then take them out, wipe them dry, cut them open, and extract the stones. Mix together, to your taste, minced garlic, scraped horse-radish, bruised mustard seed, and cloves; and a little ginger-root soaked in water to soften, and then sliced. Fill the cavity of the peaches with this mixture. Then tie them round with pack-thread, and put them into a stone jar till it is two-thirds full. Strew among them some whole cloves, broken cinnamon, and a little cochineal. Season some cold vinegar, (allowing to each quart a gill of fresh made mustard, and a little ginger, and nutmeg,) and having mixed this pickle well, fill up the jar with it.

BROILED TOMATAS.—Take large ripe tomatas; wipe them, and split them in half. Broil them on a gridiron till brown, turning them when half done. Have ready in a dish some butter seasoned with a little pepper. When the tomatas are well broiled, put them into the dish, and press each a little with the back of a spoon, so that the juice may run into the butter and mix with it. This is to make the gravy. Send them to table hot.

Tomatas are very good sliced, and fried in butter.

PRESERVED TOMATAS.—Take large fine tomatas, (not too ripe,) and scald them to make the skins come off easily. Weigh them, and to each pound allow a pound of the best white sugar, and the grated peel of half a lemon. Put all together into a preserving kettle, and having boiled it slowly for three hours, (skimming it carefully,) add the juice of the lemons, and boil'it an hour longer. Then put the whole into jars, and when cool cover and tie them up closely. This is a cheap and excellent sweetmeat; but the lemon must on no account be omitted. It may be improved by boiling a little ginger with the other ingredients.

TOMATA HONEY.—To each pound of tomatas, allow the grated peel of a lemon and six fresh peach-leaves. Boil them slowly till they are all to pieces; then squeeze and strain them through a bag. To each pint of liquid allow a pound of loaf-sugar, and the juice of one lemon. Boil them together half an hour, or till they become a thick jelly. Then put it into glasses, and lay double tissue paper closely over the top. It will be scarcely distinguishable from real honey.

———

PRESERVED CUCUMBERS.—Your cucumbers should be well shaped, and all of the same size. Spread the bottom and sides of a preserving kettle with a thick layer of vine leaves. Then put in the cucumbers with a little alum broken small. Cover them thickly with vine leaves, and then with a dish. Fill up the kettle with water, and let them hang over a slow fire till next morning, but do not allow the water to boil. Next day, take them out, cool them, and repeat the process with fresh vine leaves, till the cucumbers are a fine green. When cold drain them, cut a small piece out of the flat side, and extract the seeds. Wipe the cucumbers in a dry cloth, and season the inside with a mixture of bruised mace and grated lemon-peel. Tie on with a pack-thread the bit that was cut out.

Weigh them, and to every pound of cucumbers allow a pound of loaf-sugar. Put the sugar into a preserving kettle, a half pint of water to each pound, and the beaten white of an egg to every two pounds. Boil and skim the sugar till quite clear, adding sliced ginger and lemon parings to your taste. When cool, pour it over the cucumbers, and let them lie in it two days, keeping them covered with a plate, and a weight on it to press it down. Then boil up the syrup again, adding one-half as much sugar, &c. as you had at first; and at the last the juice and grated peel of two lemons for every six cucumbers. The lemon must boil in the syrup but ten minutes. Then strain the syrup all over the cucumbers, and put them up in glass jars

If they are not quite clear, boil them in a third syrup.

Small green melons may be preserved in this manner.

APPLE RICE PUDDING.—Wash half a pint of rice, and boil it till soft and dry. Pare, core, and cut up six large juicy apples, and stew them in as little water as possible. When they are quite tender, take them out, and mash them with six table-spoonfuls of brown sugar. When the apples and rice are both cold, mix them together. Have ready five eggs beaten very light, and add them gradually to the other ingredients, with five or six drops of essence of lemon, and a grated nutmeg. Or you may substitute for the essence, the grated peel and the juice of one large lemon. Beat the whole very hard after it is all mixed; tie it tightly in a cloth, (leaving but a very small space for it to swell,) and stopping up the tying place with a lump of flour moistened to paste with water. Put it into a pot of boiling water, and boil it fast for half an hour. Send it to table hot, and eat it with sweetened cream, or with beaten butter and sugar.

BAKED APPLE DUMPLINGS.—Take large, fine, juicy apples, and pare and core them, leaving them as whole as possible. Put them into a kettle with sufficient water to cover them, and let them parboil a quarter of an hour. Then take them out, and drain them on a sieve. Prepare a paste in the proportion of a pound of butter to two pounds of flour. as for plain pies. Roll it out into a sheet, and cut it into equal portions according to your number of apples. Place an apple on each, and fill up the hole from whence the core was extracted with brown sugar moistened with lemon-juice, or with any sort of marmalade. Then cover the apple with the paste, closing it neatly. Place the dumplings side by side in buttered square pans, (not so as to touch,) and bake them of a light brown. Serve them warm or cool, and eat them with cream sauce.

They will be found very good.

––––––

INDIAN LOAF CAKE.—Mix a tea-cup full of powdered white sugar with a quart of rich milk, and cut up in the milk two ounces of butter, adding a salt-spoonful of salt. Put this mixture into a covered pan or skillet, and set it on coals till it is scalding hot. Then take it off, and scald with it as much yellow Indian meal (previously sifted) as will make it of the consistence of thick boiled mush. Beat the whole very hard for a quarter of an hour, and then set it away to cool.

While it is cooling, beat three eggs very light, and stir them gradually into the mixture when it is about as warm as new milk. Add a tea-cup full of good strong yeast, and beat the whole another quarter of an hour—for much of the good-ness of this cake depends on its being long and well beaten. Then have ready a turban mould or earthen pan with a pipe in the centre, (to diffuse the heat through the middle of the cake.) The pan must be very well buttered, as Indian meal is apt to stick. Put in the mixture, cover it, and set it in a warm place to rise. It should be light in about four hours. Then bake it two hours in a moderate oven. When done, turn it out with the broad surface downwards, and send it to table hot and whole. Cut it into slices, and eat it with butter.

This will be found an excellent cake. If wanted for break-fast, mix it, and set it to rise the night before. If properly made, standing all night will not injure it. Like all Indian cakes, (of which this is one of the best,) it should be eaten warm.

It will be much improved by adding to the mixture, a salt-spoon of pearl-ash, or sal-aratus, dissolved in a little water.

PLAIN CIDER CAKE.—Sift into a large pan a pound and a half of flour, and rub into it half a pound of butter. Mix in three-quarters of a pound of powdered white sugar, and melt a small tea-spoonful of sal-aratus or pearl-ash in a pint of the best cider. Pour the cider into the other ingredients while it is foaming, and stir the whole very hard. Have ready a buttered square pan, put in the mixture, and set it immediately in a rather brisk oven. Bake it an hour or more, according to its thickness. This is a tea cake, and should be eaten fresh. Cut it into squares, split and butter them.

TENNESSEE MUFFINS.—Sift three pints of yellow Indian meal, and put one-half into a pan and scald it. Add a good piece of butter. Beat six eggs, whites and yolks separately. The yolks must be beaten till they become very thick and smooth, and the whites till they are a stiff froth that stands alone. When the scalded meal is cold, mix it into a batter with the beaten yolk of egg, the remainder of the meal, a salt-spoonful of salt, and, if necessary, a little water. The batter must be quite thick. At the last, stir in, lightly and slowly, the beaten white of egg. Grease your muffin rings, and set them in an oven of the proper heat; put in the batter immediately, as standing will injure it.

Send them to table hot; pull them open, and eat them with butter.

HOE CAKE.—Beat the whites of three eggs to a stiff froth, and sift into a pan a quart of wheat flour, adding a salt-spoon of salt. Make a hole in the middle, and mix in the white of egg so as to form a thick batter, and then add two table-spoonfuls of the best fresh yeast. Cover it, and let it stand all night. In the morning, take a hoe-iron (such as are made purposely for cakes) and prop it before the fire till it is well heated. Then flour a tea-saucer, and filling it with batter, shake it about, and clap it to the hoe, (which must be previously greased,) and the batter will adhere till it is baked. Repeat this with each cake. Keep them hot, and eat them with butter.

MILK TOAST.—Boil a pint of rich milk, and then take it off, and stir into it a quarter of a pound of fresh butter, mixed with a small table-spoonful of flour. Then let it again come to a boil. Have ready two deep plates with half a dozen slices of toast in each. Pour the milk over them hot, and keep them covered till they go to table. Milk toast is generally eaten at breakfast.

POTATO YEAST.—Pare half a dozen middle-sized potatoes, and boil them in a quart of soft water, mixed with a handful of hops, till quite soft. Then mash the potatoes smooth, not leaving in a single lump. Mix with them a handful of wheat flour. Set a sieve over the pan in which you have the flour and mashed potatoes, and strain into them the hop-water in which they were boiled. Then stir the mixture very hard, and afterwards pass it through a cullender to clear it of lumps. Let it stand till it is nearly cold. Then stir in four table-spoonfuls of strong yeast, and let it stand to ferment. When the foam has sunk down in the middle, (which will not be for several hours,) it is done working. Then put it into a stone jug and cork it. Set it in a cool place.

This yeast will be found extremely good for raising home-made bread.

Yeast when it becomes sour may be made fit to use by stir ring into it a little sal-eratus, or pearl-ash, allowing a small tea-spoonful to a pint of yeast. This will remove the acidity, and improve the bread in lightness. The pearl-ash must be previously melted in a little lukewarm water.

CREAM CHEESE.—The cheese so called, of which numbers are brought to Philadelphia market, is not made entirely of cream, but of milk warm from the cow, (and therefore unskimmed,) mixed with cream of last night. To a small tub of fresh morning's milk, add the cream skimmed from an equal quantity of last evening's milk. Mix the cream and the new milk together, and warm them to about blood-heat or 100 degrees of the thermometer. Have ready a cup of water in which has been soaking, since last night, a piece of rennet, (the salt wiped off,) about the length and breadth of two fingers. Stir the rennet-water into the vessel of mixed milk and cream, and set it in a warm place till the curd has completely formed. Then, with a knife, cut the curd into squares. Next, take a large, thin, straining-cloth, and press it down on the curd so as to make the whey rise up through it. As the whey rises, dip it off with a saucer or skimming dish. When the whey is nearly all out, put the curd into the cloth, and squeeze and press it with your hands till it becomes dry. Next, crumble the curd very fine with your hands, and then salt it to your taste. Then wash the straining-cloth clean, and lay it in the cheese-hoop (a bottomless vessel, about the size of a dinner-plate, perforated with small gimlet-holes) put the crumbled curd into the cloth, and then fold the rest of the cloth closely over it. The cheese-hoop should be set on a clean wooden bench or table. Place on it its round wooden cover, so as to fit exactly ; and lay on the top two bricks or a heavy stone. After it has stood six hours in the hoop or mould, turn it, and let it stand six hours longer.

When you take out the cheese, rub it all over with a little fresh butter. Set it in a dark, dry place, turning it every day, and in four or five days it will be fit for use. When once cut, it should be eaten immediately, if the weather is warm. But while uncut, it may keep a week in a cold place, provided it is turned several times a-day

ALMOND BREAD.—Blanch, and pound in a mortar, half a pound of shelled sweet almonds till they are a smooth paste, adding rose-water as you pound them. They should be done the day before they are wanted. Prepare a pound of loaf-sugar finely powdered, a tea-spoonful of mixed spice, (mace, nutmeg, and cinnamon,) and three-quarters of a pound of sifted flour. Take fourteen eggs, and separate the whites from the yolks. Leave out seven of the whites, and beat the other seven to a stiff froth. Beat the yolks till very thick and smooth, and then beat the sugar gradually into them, adding the spice. Next stir in the white of egg, then the flour, and lastly the almonds. Add the juice of a large lemon.

Put the mixture into a square tin pan, (well buttered,) or into a copper or tin turban-mould, and set it immediately in a brisk oven. Ice it when cool. It is best if eaten fresh.

You may add a few bitter almonds to the sweet ones.

CUSTARD CAKES.—Mix together a pound of sifted flour and a quarter of a pound of powdered loaf-sugar. Divide into four a pound of fresh butter; mix one-fourth of it with the flour, and make it into a dough. Then roll it out, and put in the three remaining divisions of the butter at three more rollings. Set the paste in a cool place till the custard is ready.

For the custard, beat very light the yolk only of eight eggs, and then stir them gradually into a pint of rich cream, adding three ounces of powdered white sugar, a grated nutmeg, and ratafia, peach-water, or essence of lemon, to your taste. Put the mixture into a deep dish; set it in an iron baking pan or a Dutch oven half full of boiling water, and bake it a quarter of an hour. Then put it to cool.

In the mean time roll out the paste into a thin sheet; cut it into little round cakes about the size of a dollar, and bake them on flat tins. When they are done, spread some of the cakes thickly with the custard, and lay others on the top of them, making them fit closely in the manner of lids.

You may bake the paste in patty-pans like shells, and put in the custard after they come out of the oven. If the custard is baked in the paste, it will be clammy and heavy at the bottom.

You may flavour the custard with vanilla.

HONEY GINGER CAKE.—Rub together a pound of sifted flour and three-quarters of a pound of fresh butter. Mix in, a tea-cup of fine brown sugar, two large table-spoonfuls of strong ginger, and (if you like them) two table-spoonfuls of carraway seeds. Having beaten five eggs, add them to the mixture alternately with a pint of strained honey; stirring in towards the last a small tea-spoonful of pearl-ash, that has been melted in a very little vingar.

Having beaten or stirred the mixture long enough to make it perfectly light, transfer it to a square iron or block-tin pan, (which must be well buttered,) put it into a moderate oven, and bake it an hour or more, in proportion to its thickness.

When cool, cut it into squares. It is best if eaten fresh, but it will keep very well a week.

ROCK CAKE.—Blanch three-quarters of a pound of snelled sweet almonds, and bruise them fine in a mortar, but not to a smooth paste as for maccaroons. Add, as you pound them, a little rose-water. Beat to a stiff froth the whites of four eggs, and then beat in gradually a pound of powdered loaf-sugar. Add the juice of a lemon. Then mix in the pounded almonds. Flour your hands, and make the mixture into little cones or pointed cakes. Spread sheets of damp, thin, white paper on buttered sheets of tin, and put the rock cakes on it, rather far apart. Sprinkle each with powdered loaf-sugar. Bake them of a pale brown, in a brisk oven. They will be done in a few minutes.

When cold, take them off the papers.

FROZEN CUSTARD.—Slice a vanilla bean, and boil it slowly in half a pint of milk, till all the strength is extracted and the milk highly flavoured with the vanilla. Then strain it, and set it aside. Mix a quart of cream and a pint of milk, or, if you cannot procure cream, take three pints of rich milk, and put them into a skillet or sauce-pan. Set it on hot coals, and boil it. When it has come to a boil, mix a table-spoonful of flour in three table-spoonfuls of milk, and stir it into the boiling liquid. Afterwards add six eggs, (which have been beaten up with two table-spoonfuls of milk,) pouring them slowly into the mixture. Take care to stir it all the time it is boiling. Five minutes after, stir in gradually half a pound of powdered loaf-sugar, and then the decoction of vanilla. Having stirred it hard a few moments, take it off the fire, and set it to cool. When quite cold, put it into a mould and freeze it, as you would ice-cream, for which it frequently passes.

You may flavour it with the juice of two large lemons, stirred in just before you take it from the fire, or with a quarter of a pound of shelled bitter almonds, blanched, pounded in a mortar with rose-water, and then boiled in half a pint of milk, till the flavour is extracted. Then use the milk only.

———

CHERRY CORDIAL.—Take a bushel of fine ripe cherries, either red or black, or mixed; stone them, put them into a clean wooden vessel, and mash them with a mallet or beetle. Then boil them about ten minutes, and strain the juice. To each quart of juice allow a quart of water, a pound of sugar, and a quart of brandy. Boil in the water (before you mix it with the juice) two ounces of cloves, and four ounces of cinnamon; then strain out the spice. Put the mixture into a stone jug, or a demijohn, and cork it tightly. Bottle it in two or three months.

———

COMMON ICE CREAM.—Split into pieces a vanilla bean, and boil it in a very little milk till the flavour is well extracted; then strain it. Mix two table-spoonfuls of arrow-root powder, or the same quantity of fine powdered starch, with just sufficient cold milk to make it a thin paste; rubbing it till quite smooth. Mix together a pint of cream and a pint of rich milk; and afterwards stir in the preparation of arrow-root, and the milk in which the vanilla has been boiled. Beat it very hard, stir in half a pound of powdered loaf-sugar, beating it very hard again. Then strain it, and put it into a freezer placed in a tub that has a hole in the bottom to let out the water; and surround the freezer on all sides with ice broken finely, and mixed with coarse salt. Beat the cream hard for half an hour. Then let it rest; occasionally taking off the cover, and scraping down with a long spoon the cream that sticks to the sides. When it is well frozen, transfer it to a mould; surround it with fresh salt and ice, and then freeze it over again.

If you wish to flavour it with lemon instead of vanilla, take a large lump of the sugar before you powder it, and rub it on the outside of a large lemon till the yellow is all rubbed off upon the sugar. Then, when the sugar is all powdered, mix with it the juice of two large lemons.

For strawberry ice cream, mix with the powdered sugar the juice of a quart of ripe strawberries squeezed through a linen bag.

PINK CHAMPAGNE JELLY.—Beat up the white of an egg to a stiff froth, and then stir it hard into three wine-glasses of filtered water. Put twelve ounces of the best double-refined loaf-sugar (powdered fine and sifted) into a skillet lined with porcelain. Pour on it the white of egg and water, and stir it till dissolved. Then add twelve grains of cochineal powder. Set it over a moderate fire, and boil it and skim it till the scum ceases to rise. Then strain it through a very fine sieve. Have ready an ounce and a half of isinglass that has been boiled in a little water till quite dissolved. Strain it, and while the boiled sugar is lukewarm mix it with the isinglass, adding a pint of pink champagne and the juice of a large lemon. Run it through a linen bag into a mould. When it has congealed so as to be quite firm, wrap a wet cloth round the outside of the mould, and turn out the jelly into a glass dish; or serve it broken up, in jelly glasses, or glass cups.

Jelly may be made in a similar manner of Madeira, maras-quin, or noyau.

A CHARLOTTE RUSSE.—Boil in half a pint of milk a split vanilla bean, till all the flavour is extracted. Then strain the milk, and when it is cold stir into it the yolks of four beaten eggs, and a quarter of a pound of powdered loaf-sugar.

Simmer this custard five minutes over hot coals, but do not let it come to a boil. Then set it away to cool. Having boiled an ounce of the best Russian isinglass in a pint of watei till it is entirely dissolved and the water reduced to one-half, strain it into the custard, stir it hard, and set it aside to get quite cold.

Whip to a stiff froth a quart of rich cream, taking it off in spoonfuls as you do it, and putting it to drain on an inverted sieve. When the custard is quite cold, (but not yet set or congealing,) stir the whipt cream gradually into it.

Take a circular mould of the shape of a drum, the sides being straight. Cut to fit it two round slices from the top and bottom of an almond sponge-cake; glaze them with white of egg, and lay one on at the bottom of the mould, reserving the other for the top. You can get the mould at a tinner's.

Having thus covered the bottom, line the sides of the mould with more of the sponge-cake, cut into long squares and glazed all over with white of egg. They must be placed so as to stand up all round—each wrapping a little over the other so as to leave not the smallest vacancy between; and they must be cut exactly the height of the mould, and trimmed evenly. Then fill up with the custard and cream when it is just begin ning to congeal; and cover the top with the other round slice of cake.

Set the mould in a tub of pounded ice mixed with coarse salt; and let it remain forty minutes, or near an hour. Then turn out the Charlotte on a china dish. Have ready an icing, made in the usual manner of beaten white of egg and powdered sugar, flavoured with essence of lemon. Spread it smoothly over the top of the Charlotte, which when the icing is dry will be ready to serve. They are introduced at large parties, and it is usual to have two or four of them.

A CHARLOTTE POLONAISE.—Boil over a slow fire a pint and a half of cream. While it is boiling have ready six yolks of eggs, beaten up with two table-spoonfuls of powdered arrow-root, or fine flour. Stir this gradually into the boiling cream, taking care to have it perfectly smooth and free from lumps. Ten minutes will suffice for the egg and cream to boil together. Then divide the mixture by putting it into two separate sauce-pans.

Then mix with it, in one of the pans, six ounces of chocolate scraped fine, two ounces of powdered loaf-sugar, and a quarter of a pound of maccaroons, broken up. When it has come to a hard boil, take it off, stir it well, pour it into a bowl, and set it away to cool.

Have ready, for the other sauce-pan of cream and egg, a dozen bitter almonds, and four ounces of shelled sweet almonds or pistachio nuts, all blanched and pounded in a mortar with rose-water to a smooth paste, and mixed with an ounce of citron also pounded. Add four ounces of powdered sugar; and to colour it green, two large spoonfuls of spinach juice that has been strained through a sieve. Stir this mixture into the other half of the cream, and let it come to a boil. Then put it aside to cool.

Cut a large sponge-cake into slices half an inch thick. Spread one slice thickly with the chocolate cream, and cover another slice with the almond cream. Do this alternately (piling them evenly on a china dish) till all the ingredients are used up. You may arrange it in the original form of the sponge-cake before it was cut, or in a pyramid. Have ready the whites of the six eggs whipped to a stiff froth, with which have been gradually mixed six ounces of powdered sugar, and twelve drops of oil of lemon. With a spoon heap this meringue (as the French call it) all over the pile of cake, &c., and then sift powdered sugar over it. Set it in a very slow oven till the outside becomes a light brown colour.

Serve it up cold, ornamented according to your taste.

If you find the chocolate cream too thin, add more maccaroons. If the almond cream is too thin, mix in more pounded citron. If either of the mixtures is too thick, dilute it with more cream.

This is superior to a Charlotte Russe.

————

APPLE COMPOTE.—Take large ripe pippin apples. Pare, core, and weigh them, and to each pound allow a pound of fine loaf-sugar and two lemons. Parboil the apples, and then set them out to cool. Pare off very nicely with a pen-knife the yellow rind of the lemons, taking care not to break it; and then with scissors trim the edges to an even width all along. Put the lemon-rind to boil in a little sauce-pan by itself, till it becomes tender, and then set it to cool. Allow half a pint of water to each pound of sugar; and when it is melted, set it on the fire in the preserving kettle, put in the apples, and boil them slowly till they are clear and tender all through, but not till they break; skimming the syrup carefully. After you have taken out the apples, add the lemon-juice, put in the lemon-peel, and boil it till quite transparent. When the whole is cold, put the apples with the syrup into glass dishes, and dispose the wreaths of lemon-peel fancifully about them.

————

SOUR MILK.—To recover milk that has turned sour, sti. in powdered carbonate of magnesia, of which allow a heaped tea-spoonful to each quart of milk.

APPENDIX,

~~~~~~~~~~~~

ORANGE CAKE.—Take four ripe oranges, and roll them under your hand on the table. Break up a pound of the best loaf-sugar, and on some of the pieces rub off the yellow rind of the oranges. Then cut the oranges, and squeeze their juice through a strainer. Powder the sugar, and mix the orange-juice with it; reserving a little of the juice to flavour the icing. Wash, and squeeze in a pan of cold water, a pound of the best *fresh* butter, till you have extracted whatever milk and salt may have been in it, as they will impede the lightness of the cake. Cut up the butter in the pan of sugar and orange, and stir it hard till perfectly light, white, and creamy. Sift into a pan fourteen ounces (two ounces less than a pound) of fine flour. Beat ten eggs till they are as thick and smooth as a fine boiled custard. Then stir them, by degrees, into the butter and sugar, alternately with the flour, a little of each at a time. Continue to beat the whole very hard for some time after all the ingredients are in; as this cake requires a great deal of beating. Have ready a large square, shallow pan, well buttered. Put in the mixture, and set it immediately into a brisk oven. It must be thoroughly baked, otherwise it will be heavy, streaked, and unfit to eat. The time of baking must of course be in proportion to its thickness, but it requires a much longer time than pound-cake, queen-cake, or Spanish buns. When it shrinks from the sides of the pan, and looks as if done, try it by sticking in the middle of it, down to the bottom, a twig from a corn-broom, or something similar. If the twig comes out dry and clean, the cake is done; but if the twig remains moist and clammy, let the cake remain longer in the oven. When it is quite done, make an icing of beaten white of egg, and powdered loaf-sugar, mixed with a spoonful or more of orange juice. Dredge the cake with flour, then wipe off the flour and spread on the icing thick and evenly, scoring it in large squares. Before you put it into baskets, cut the cake into squares about the usual size of a Spanish bun. It should be eaten fresh, being best the day it is baked.

This cake will be found very fine. It is, of course, best when oranges are ripe and in perfection, as the orange flavour should be very high. We recommend that at the first trial of this receipt, the batter shall be baked in small tins, such as are used for queen-cake, or Naples biscuit, as there will thus be less risk of its being well baked than if done in a larger pan. When they seem to be done, one of the little cakes can be taken out and broken open, and if more baking is four necessary, the others can thus be continued longer in the oven. After some experience, an orange cake may be baked, like a pound cake, in a large tin pan with a tube in the centre; or in a turban mould, and handsomely iced and ornamented when done. A fine orange cake will, when cut, perfume the table.

Lemon cake may be made and baked in a similar manner. adding also a little lemon juice to the icing.

CITRON CAKE.—Cut a pound of candied citron into slips. Spread it on a large dish. Sprinkle it thickly with sifted flour till it is entirely white with it, tumbling the citron about with your hands till every piece is well covered with flour. Then sift into a pan fourteen ounces (two ounces less than a pound) of flour. Beat together in a deep pan, till perfectly light, a pound of fresh butter cut up in a pound of powdered loaf-sugar. Then add, by degrees, a glass of wine, a glass of brandy, and a table-spoonful of powdered mace and cinnamon mixed, and a powdered nutmeg.   Have ready twelve eggs beaten in a shallow pan till very smooth and thick.   Stir the beaten egg into the beaten butter and sugar, alternately with the flour and citron, a little at a time of each.   Then, at the last, stir the whole very hard.   Butter a large tin pan (one with a tube in the centre will be best), put in the mixture, set it directly in a moderate oven, and bake it at least four hours. Put it on an inverted sieve to cool.

When the cake is cool, ice and ornament it.

Common pound cakes are now very much out of use. They are considered old-fashioned.

BOSTON CREAM CAKES.—From a quart of rich milk or cream take half a pint, and put it into a small saucepan, with a vanilla bean, and a stick of the best Ceylon cinnamon, broken in pieces.   Cover the saucepan closely, and let it boil till the milk is highly flavoured with the vanilla and cinnamon. Then strain it, take out the vanilla bean, wipe it, and put it away, as it will do for the same purpose a second time.   Mix the flavoured milk with the other pint and a half, and let it get quite cold.   Beat very light *the yolks only* of twelve eggs, and stir them into the milk alternately with a quarter of a pound, or more, of powdered white sugar.   Put this custard mixture into a tin pan, set it in a Dutch oven or something similar, pour round the pan some boiling water, enough to reach half-way up its sides, and bake the custard ten minutes.   Instead of vanilla, you may flavour the custard by boiling, in the half pint of milk, a handful of bitter almonds or peach kernels, blanched and broken in half, and stirring into the custard when it has done baking, but is still hot, a wine glass of rose water.

As rose water loses most of its taste by cooking, it is best, when practicable, to add it after the article is taken from the fire.

In the mean time let another mixture be prepared as follows. Sift half a pound of fine flour, cut up half a pound of fresh butter in a pint of rich milk, and set it on a stove or near the fire till the butter is soft but not melted. Then stir it well and take it off. Beat eight whole eggs very light, and stir them gradually into the milk and butter, in turn with the flour. Take care to have this batter very smooth, and quite free from lumps. Having beaten and stirred it thoroughly, put it in equal portions into deep pattypans with plain unscolloped sides, filling them but little more than half, so as to allow space for the cakes to rise in baking. The pattypans must be previously buttered When the mixture is in, sprinkle powdered loaf-sugar over the top of each. Set them immediately into a brisk oven, and bake them about a quarter of an hour, or twenty minutes They must be well browned. When done, take them out, and open in the side of each (while quite hot) a slit or cut, large enough to admit a portion of the custard that has been made for them. Put in with a spoon as much of this custard as will amply fill the cavity or hollow in the middle of each cake. Then close the slit nicely, by pinching and smoothing it with your thumb and finger, and set the cakes to cool. They should be eaten fresh. In summer they will not keep till next day unless they are set on ice. If properly made, they will be found delicious.

CONNECTICUT LOAF CAKE.—For this cake you must prepare, the day before, three pounds of sifted flour, two pounds of powdered white sugar, four nutmegs, and a quarter of an ounce of mace powdered fine; two pounds of stoned raisins, two pounds of currants, picked, washed, and dried (or you may substitute for the currants two additional pounds of raisins), and half a pound of citron cut large. The raisins, currants, and citron must be spread on a large dish, and dredged thickly over with flour, which must be mixed well among them with your hands, so as to coat them all completely. This is to prevent their sinking in a clod to the bottom while the cake is baking, and should always be done with whatever fruit is used in either cakes or puddings. Put the spice into half a pint of white wine, cover it, and let it infuse all night. Next morning, have ready two pounds of the best fresh butter, cut small; six eggs well beaten; a pint of warm new milk; and half a pint of fresh strong yeast, procured, if possible, from a brewer or baker. Rub half the butter into the flour, adding half the sugar; wet it with the milk, and add half of the eggs, and the wine, and the yeast. Stir and mix it thoroughly. Then cover it and set it to rise. It should be perfectly light by evening. Then add the remainder of the butter and the sugar, and the rest of the egg. Mix it well, and set it again to rise till early next morning. Then add gradually the fruit, setting it again to rise for two or three hours. When it is perfectly light for the last time, butter a large deep pan, and put in the mixture. The oven must first be made *very hot*, and then allowed to cool down so as to bake rather slowly. If too hot, it will scorch and crust the cake on the outside, so as to prevent the heat from penetrating any farther, and the inside will then be soddened and heavy. A common-sized loaf-cake may remain in the oven from three to four hours.

CLOVE CAKES.—Rub a pound of fresh butter (cut up) into three pounds of sifted flour; adding, by degrees, a pound of fine brown sugar, half an ounce of cloves ground or powdered, and sufficient West India molasses to wet the whole

into a stiff dough, mixing in at the last a small tea-spoonful of sal-aratus dissolved in tepid water. Roll the dough
out into a sheet of paste, and cut out the cakes with a tin
stamp, or with the edge of a tumbler. Put them in buttered
pans, and bake them a quarter of an hour or more. They will
continue good a long time, if kept dry, and are excellent to
take to sea.

SOFT GINGERBREAD.—Beat to a cream half a pound
of fresh butter cut up in a deep pan, among half a pound of
brown sugar, and at the beginning set near the fire to soften
it a little, but not to melt it. Add two large table-spoonfuls of
ginger, a tea-spoonful of powdered cinnamon, and a tea-spoonful of powdered cloves. Then stir into it, alternately, a pint
of West India molasses, and three pints of sifted flour, and six
well-beaten eggs. Lastly, dissolve a small tea-spoonful of
pearl-ash in a pint of *sour* milk, and stir it, while foaming,
into the mixture. Put it immediately into shallow square tin
pans, well buttered, and place it in an oven not too hot, or it
will burn the outside, and leave the inside raw and heavy.
This cake requires long beating, and much baking.

FINE COOKIES.—Sift into a pan five large tea-cupsful
of flour, and rub into it one tea-cup of fresh butter; add two
cups of powdered white sugar, and a handful or two of carraway
seeds; wet it with an egg well beaten, and a little rose-water
Add, at the last, a small tea-spoonful of sal-aratus dissolved
in a very little lukewarm water. Knead the whole well.
Roll it out into a sheet. Cut it into cakes with a stamp or a
tumbler edge; put them into a buttered pan, and bake them
about fifteen minutes. Instead of carraway seeds, you may
use currants, picked, washed, and dried.

INDIAN CUP CAKES.—Sift a pint and a half of yellow
Indian meal, and mix it with half a pint wheat flour. Beat
two eggs very light, and then stir them gradually into the
meal, in turn with almost a quart of *sour* milk. If you have
no sour milk from the preceding day, you can turn some sweet
milk sour by setting it in the sun. Lastly, dissolve a tea-
spoonful of sal-aratus, or a very small tea-spoonful of pearl-ash
in a little of the sour milk reserved for the purpose. The batter must be as thick as that for a pound-cake. More Indian
meal may be necessary. Stir it at the last into the mixture,
which, while foaming, must be put into buttered cups, or little
tin pans, and set immediately into an oven, brisk but not too
hot. When well baked, turn out the cakes, and send them
warm to the breakfast-table. Eat them with butter.

BRAN BATTER-CAKES.—Mix a quart of bran with a
handful of wheat flour, and a level tea-spoonful of salt. Pour
in sufficient milk-warm water to make a thick batter. Add
two table-spoonfuls of brewer's yeast, or three, if home-made;
and stir it very hard. Cover it, and set it by the fire to rise.
Half an hour before you begin to bake, you may add a salt-
spoonful of soda, melted in a little warm water. Bake it
like buckwheat cakes, on a griddle.

APPLE BREAD PUDDING.—Pare, core, and slice thin,
a dozen or more fine juicy pippins, or bell-flowers, strewing
among them some bits of the yellow rind of a large lemon
that has been pared very thin, and squeezing over them the
juice of the lemon. Or substitute a tea-spoonful of essence
of lemon. Cover the bottom of a large deep dish with a thick
layer of the sliced apples. Strew it thickly with brown sugar

Then scatter on a few very small bits of the best fresh butter. Next strew over it a thin layer of grated bread-crumbs. Afterwards another thick layer of apple, followed by sugar, butter, and bread-crumbs as before. Continue this till you get the dish full, finishing with a thin layer of crumbs. Put the dish into a moderate oven, and bake the pudding well, ascertaining that the apples are thoroughly done and as soft as marmalade. Send it to table either hot or cold, and eat it with cream-sauce, or with butter, sugar, and nutmeg, stirred to a cream. This pudding is in some places called by the homely names of Brown Betty, or Pan Dowdy. It will require far less baking, if the apples are previously stewed soft, and afterwards mixed with the sugar and lemon. Then put it into the dish, in layers, interpersed (as above) with bits of butter, and layers of grated crumbs. It will be much improved by the addition of a grated nutmeg, mixed with the apples.

APPLE CUSTARDS.—Take fine juicy apples, sufficient when stewed to fill two soup plates. Pare, core, and slice them. Add a lump of butter, about the size of a walnut, and the grated peel of a lemon; and stew them with as little water as can possibly keep them from burning. They must be stewed till they are quite soft all through, but not broken. Then mash them well with the back of a spoon, and make them very sweet with fine brown sugar. Squeeze in the juice of a lemon, or add a wine-glass of rose-water. When the apple is quite cold, add a grated nutmeg, a table-spoonful of brandy, and a table-spoonful of cream, mixed with a table-spoonful of finely-grated bread crumbs, and the well-beaten yolk of an egg. Stir the whole very hard. Cover the bottom and sides of two soup plates with thin puff-paste, and put a thick paste round the edges, notching it handsomely. Then fill up with the mixture, and bake it about half an hour. Or you may bake it in cups, without any paste. If for cups, prepare double the above quantity of apple and other ingredients.

Peach custards may be made in a similar manner, of fine ripe free-stone peaches, pared, stoned, quartered, and stewed without any water. Omit the lemon, and add two eggs.

NEW ENGLAND PUMPKIN PIE.—Take a quart of stewed pumpkin. Put it into a sieve, and press and strain it as dry as possible. Then set it away to get cold. Beat eight eggs very light, and stir them gradually into the pumpkin, a little at a time, in turn with a quart of rich cream and a pound of sugar. Mix together a quarter of an ounce of powdered mace, two powdered nutmegs, and a table-spoonful of ground ginger, and stir them into the other ingredients. When all is mixed, stir the whole very hard. Cover the bottom of your pie-dishes with a thin paste, and fill them nearly to the top with the mixture. Cut out narrow stripes of paste with your jagging-iron, and lay them across the tops of your pies. Bake them from an hour to an hour and a quarter. Send them to table cool. They are best the day they are baked. Some persons prefer them without any paste beneath, the dishes being filled entirely with the mixture; and if they have broad edges, a border of thick puff-paste may be laid along the edge, and handsomely notched. We think this the best way; as paste that is baked under any mixture that has milk and eggs in it, is liable, in consequence of the moisture, to become clammy and heavy, and is therefore unwholesome.

WEST INDIA COCOA-NUT PUDDING.—Cut up and skin a large ripe cocoa-nut, and grate it fine. Then put the grated cocoa-nut into a clean cloth, and squeeze and press it till all the moisture is taken out. Spread it on a broad tin pan, and stand it up to dry, either in the sun or before the fire, stirring it up occasionally with your hands. When quite dry weigh a pound of it. Beat very light sixteen eggs (omitting the whites of four) and then beat into them, gradually, a pound of powdered loaf-sugar, and a wine glass of rose-water. Then give the whole a hard stirring. Put the mixture into deep dishes, and lay puff-paste round their edges handsomely notched. Bake them about half an hour. Send them to table cold with white sugar grated over the top.

YANKEE TEA CAKES.—Cut up half a pound of fresh butter in a pint of milk, and warm it a little, so as to soften but not melt the butter. Add, gradually, half a pound of powdered white sugar, in turn with three well-beaten eggs, and a pound of sifted flour, finishing with half a jill of strong fresh yeast. Set the mixture in a warm place to rise. It will most probably be five hours before it is light enough to bake, and it should therefore be made in the forenoon. When it has risen high, and the top is covered with bubbles, butter some cups, and bake it in them about twenty minutes. When done, turn the cakes out on large plates; send them to table hot, and split and butter them. To open these cakes, pull them apart with your fingers.

GELATINE JELLY.—Gelatine is used as a substitute for calves feet in making jelly. It is prepared in light yellow-ish sheets, and can be purchased at the druggists'. The chief advantage in gelatine is, that by keeping it in the house, you can always have it ready for use, and the jelly made with it may be commenced and finished the same day: while, if you use calves' feet, they must be boiled the day before. Also, you may chance to live in a place where calves' feet cannot at all times be procured, and then a box of gelatine, always at hand, may be found very convenient. The cost is about the same, whether the jelly is made of calves' feet or of gelatine. That of calves' feet will generally be the firmest, and will keep two or three days in a cold place or when set on ice; that of gelatine, if not used on the day that it is made, will sometimes melt and become liquid again. Its greatest recommendations are convenience and expedition. The following receipt for gelatine jelly will be found a very good one, if exactly followed.

Soak two ounces of gelatine, for twenty-five minutes, in as much cold water as will cover it. Then take it out, lay it in another vessel, pour on it two quarts of boiling water, and let it thoroughly dissolve. Afterwards set it to cool. Having rolled them under your hand on a table, pare off very thin the yellow rind of four lemons, and cut it into small bits. Break up, into little pieces, two large sticks of the best cinnamon (that of Ceylon is far preferable to any other) and a pound of the best double refined loaf-sugar. Mix together in a large bowl, the sugar, the lemon-rind, and the cinnamon; adding the juice of the lemons, the beaten white of an egg, and a pint of Malaga or any other good white wine. Add to these ingredients the dissolved gelatine, when it is cool but not yet cold. Mix the whole very well, put it into a porcelain kettle, or a very clean bell-metal one, and boil it fifteen minutes. Then pour it warm into a white flannel jelly-bag, and let it drip into a large glass bowl. On no account squeeze or press the bag, or the jelly will be dull and cloudy. After it has congealed in the bowl, set it on ice; but the sooner it goes to table the better. A warm damp day is unfavourable for making any sort of jelly.

You may flavour it with four or five oranges instead of lemons.

If you are averse to using wine in the jelly, substitute a pound of the best raisins, stemmed (but not seeded or stoned) and boiled whole with the other ingredients.

BISCUIT ICE CREAM.—This is the *biscuit glacé* so popular in France. Take some pieces of broken loaf-sugar, and rub off on them the yellow rind of four lemons, or oranges. Then pulverize the sugar, and mix it with half a pound of loaf-sugar already powdered, and moistened with the juice of the lemons. Beat six eggs very light, and stir them gradually into a quart of cream, in turn with the sugar and lemon. Have ready some stale Naples biscuit or square sponge cakes grated very fine, and stir them gradually into the mixture, in sufficient quantity to make a thick batter, which must be beaten till perfectly smooth and free from lumps. Put it into a porcelain stew-pan, and give it one boil up, stirring it nearly all the time. Then put it into a freezer, and freeze it in the usual manner. Afterwards transfer it to a pyramid mould, and freeze it a second time for half an hour or more. When quite frozen, take it out of the mould upon a glass or china dish.

Instead of lemon or orange, you may flavour it with a vanilla bean boiled slowly in half a pint of cream, and then strained out, before you mix it with the other cream.

MACCAROON ICE CREAM.—From a quart of cream take half a pint, and boil in it slowly two ounces of bitter almonds, or peach kernels, previously blanched and broken up. Then, when it is highly flavoured with the almonds, strain the half pint and mix it with the remaining pint and a half of cream, to which add, by degrees, six eggs previously beaten till very light, and half a pound of powdered loaf-sugar. Crumble a sufficient quantity of the best almond maccaroons to make a thick batter when stirred gradually into the mixture of cream, sugar, and eggs, which must be beaten till perfectly smooth. Give it a boil, stirring it well while boiling. Then put it into a freezer, and freeze it as usual. Afterward transfer it to a pyramid mould and freeze it again. It will be found very fine if properly made.

ORANGE WATER ICE. — To four pounds of the best double refined loaf-sugar, allow a quart of water, and four dozen large ripe deep-coloured oranges. Having rolled the oranges on the table under your hand to increase the quantity of juice, wash and wipe them dry. Take pieces of the sugar and rub them on half the oranges till you have taken off on the sugar their yellow rind or zest. Then put that sugar with the remainder into a porcelain kettle, and pour on it a quart of water into which has been beaten the white of one egg. When the sugar is quite melted, set the kettle on the fire, and boil and skim it till the scum ceases to rise, and the orange-zest is entirely dissolved. Then stir in gradually the juice of the oranges, and when all is in, take it directly off the fire, lest the flavour of the juice should be weakened by boiling. Let it cool, stirring it well. Lastly, put it into a freezer surrounded by pounded ice and salt, and stir it hard for the first ten minutes. Take off the lid and repeat the stirring every five minutes till the freezing is accomplished. Turn it out into a glass bowl; having first washed off the ice and salt from the outside of the freezer, lest some of it should chance to get into the inside   Serve it on saucers.

After it has congealed in the freezer, you may transfer it to a pyramid or pine-apple mould, and freeze it a second time, which will require half an hour or more. Of course, while in the mould, it must remain undisturbed. Before you turn it out, hold round the outside of the mould a cloth dipped in cold water.

LEMON-WATER ICE—May be made in the above manner, only that you must allow an additional pound of sugar, and use the zest or yellow rind of *all* the lemons.

STRAWBERRY-WATER ICE.—To each pound of loaf-sugar allow half a pint of water, and three quarts of ripe strawberries. Having broken up the sugar, put it into a preserving-kettle, and pour on it the water in the above proportion. To make the syrup very clear, you may allow to each pint of water half the white of an egg beaten into the water. When the sugar has melted, and been well stirred in the water, put the kettle over the fire, and boil and skim it till the scum ceases to rise. Have ready the strawberry juice, having put the strawberries into a linen bag, and squeezed the liquid into a deep pan. As soon as you take the kettle of syrup from the fire, stir into it the strawberry juice. Then put it into a freezer, surrounded with ice broken small, and mixed with salt; twirl it round by the handles for ten minutes, and then let it freeze, frequently stirring it hard. When done, turn it out into a glass bowl, and serve it on saucers. Or you may give it a second freezing in a pyramid mould.

RASPBERRY-WATER ICE—Is made exactly as above. You may heighten the colour of these ices by adding to the juice a little cochineal, which it is very convenient to keep in the house ready prepared. To do this, mix together an ounce of cochineal (pounded to a fine powder), a quarter of an ounce of powdered alum, and a quarter of an ounce of cream of tartar,

adding a salt-spoonful of pearl-ash, and three ounces of pow
dered loaf-sugar. Boil them all together for ten minutes o)
more. Then put the mixture into a clean new bottle, cork ii
tightly, and stir a little of it into any liquid you wish to colour
of a fine red. With this you may give a red colour to calves'
feet jelly, or blancmange, or to icing for cakes.

GRAPE-WATER ICE—Is made as above, first mash-
ing the grapes with a wooden beetle, before you put them into
the bag for squeezing the juice. Currants for water ice must
also be mashed before squeezing in the bag.

PINE-APPLE WATER ICE.—Having pared and sliced
a sufficient number of very ripe pine-apples, cut the slices into
small bits, put them into a deep dish or a tureen, sprinkle
among them powdered loaf-sugar, cover them and let them set
several hours in a cool place. Then have ready a syrup made
of loaf-sugar, dissolved in a little water (allowing to. every
two pounds of sugar a pint of water beaten with half the white
of an egg), and boiled and skimmed till quite clear. Get as
much pine-apple juice as you can, by squeezing through a
sieve the bits of pine-apple (after they have stood some hours
in the tureen), measure it, and to each pint of the boiled syrup
allow a pint of juice. Mix them together while the syrup is
warm from the fire. Then put it into a freezer, and proceed in
the usual manner.

PEACH-WATER ICE.—Take soft, ripe, juicy, freestone
peaches, pare them, stone them, and cut them in pieces. Put
the pieces into a linen bag and squeeze the juice into a deep
pan. Crack the stones, scald and blanch the kernels, break
them in half, and, naving made a syrup as in the above re-

ieipts, allowing half a pint of water to each pound of loaf-sugar, boil the kernels in the syrup, taking them out when the syrup is done. This infusion of the kernels will add greatly to the flavour. Then measure the peach-juice, allowing a pint of it to each pint of syrup, and mix them together while the syrup is hot. Then freeze it.

A FINE CHARLOTTE RUSSE.—For this purpose you must have a circular or drum-shaped tin mould, or a pair or more of them. The mould should be without a bottom. They can be procured at a tin-store, and are useful for other purposes. The day before you want the Charlotte russe, make a stiff plain jelly by boiling a set of calves' feet (four) in a gallon of water till the meat drops from the bone. It should boil slowly till the liquid is reduced to less than two quarts. Then, having strained it, measure into a pan three pints of the liquid, cover it, and set it away to congeal. Next morning, it should be a solid cake, from which you must carefully scrape off all the fat and sediment. Boil a vanilla bean in half a pint of milk, till the milk is very highly flavoured with the vanilla. Then strain it, and set it away to get cold. Take three pints of rich cream, put it into a shallow pan, set it on ice, and beat it to a stiff froth with rods or a whisk; or churn it to a foam with a little tin churn. Next, add to the cream the vanilla milk, and beat both together. Melt the jelly in a pan over the fire. Beat very light the yolks of six eggs, and then stir gradually into the beaten egg half a pound of powdered loaf-sugar. Next, add, by degrees, the melted jelly to the egg and sugar, stirring very hard. Keep the vessel sitting on ice, and continue stirring till the mixture is firm enough to retain the mark of the spoon. Then stir in the cream as quickly as possible. Have ready the tin mould, lined with the long thin cakes called lady-fingers, or finger biscuits, brushed over with beaten white of egg. They must be laid closely across each other on the bottom of a dish, and be so arranged as to stand up in a circle round the sides of the mould, each wrapping a little over the other. Then carefully put in the mixture, and cover the top with lady-fingers laid closely across. After the whole is nicely arranged, set it on ice till wanted. When you wish to turn out the Charlotte russe, (which must be done with great care,) wrap round the outside of the mould a coarse towel dipped in cold water, and lift it off from the charlotte.

Instead of lady-fingers you may use sponge-cake for the shape or form. Cut two circular slices from a large sponge-cake, one for the bottom, and one for the top of the charlotte, and for the wall or sides arrange tall, square slices of the cake, all of them standing up so as to wrap a little over each other. All the cake must be glazed with beaten white of egg.

A still easier way is to make an almond sponge-cake, and bake it in a drum-shaped mould or pan, or an oval one with straight or upright sides. When cold, cut off the top in one thin slice, and carefully cut out or hollow the middle, so as to make a space to contain the mixture of the charlotte, leaving bottom and sides standing. They must be left thin. Then, when the mixture is ready and quite cold, fill up the cake with it. It must be set on a china or glass dish, and kept on ice till wanted. It will require no turning out; and there is no risk of its breaking. The pieces that come out of the almond-cake when it is hollowed to receive the charlotte mixture, can be used for some other purpose, for instance, to mix with other cakes in a basket, or to dissolve at the bottom of a trifle.

COFFEE CUSTARD.—For this purpose the coffee should be cold drawn. Take a large half pint of fresh ground coffee, which should be of the best quality, and roasted that day. Put it into a grecque or French coffee pot, such as are made with strainers inside, and have a second cover below the lid. Lay the coffee on the upper strainer, pour on it half a pint of *cold* water, and press it down with the inner cover. Put on the outer or top-lid of the coffee-pot, and stop the mouth of the spout with a roll or wad of soft white paper, or with a closely-fitting cork, to prevent any of the aroma escaping.

When the coffee liquid has all filtered down through both the upper and lower strainers, pour it off into a bowl, and return it to the upper strainer to filter down a second time. It will then be beautifully clear, and very strong, notwithstanding that it has been made with cold water.

Have ready a custard-mixture made of eight well-beaten eggs, stirred gradually into a pint of cold rich milk or cream; and three or four table-spoonfuls of powdered loaf-sugar. Stir the cold liquid coffee gradually into it. Put it into cups. Set them in an iron oven or bake-pan with boiling water round them, reaching rather more than half-way up the sides of the cups. Bake them ten minutes or more. Then set them on ice, and send them to table quite cold.

PRESERVED LIMES, OR SMALL LEMONS.—Take limes, or small lemons that are quite ripe, and all about the same size. With a sharp penknife scoop a hole at the stalk end of each, and loosen the pulp all around the inside, taking care not to break or cut through the rind. In doing this, hold the lime over a bowl, and having extracted all the pulp and juice, (saving them in the bowl,) boil the empty limes half an hour or more in alum-water, till the rinds look clear and nearly transparent. Then drain them, and lay them for several hours in cold water, changing the water nearly every hour. At night, having changed the water once more, let the limes remain in it till next day, by which time all taste of the alum should be removed; but if it is not, give them a boil in some weak ginger tea. If you wish them very green, line the sides and bottom of a preserving-kettle with fresh vine-leaves, placed very thickly, put in the limes, and pour on as much clear cold water as will cover them, (spring or pump-water is best,) and fill up with a very thick layer of vine-leaves. Boil them slowly an hour or more. If they are not sufficiently green, repeat the process with fresh vine-leaves and fresh water. They must boil till a twig can pierce them.

After the limes have been greened, give the kettle a com plete washing; or take another and proceed to make the syrup. Having weighed the limes, allow to every pound of them a pound of the best double refined loaf-sugar, and half a pint of very clear water. Break up the sugar and put it into the kettle. Then pour on to it the water, which must previously be mixed with some beaten white of egg, allowing the white of one egg to three pounds of sugar. Let the sugar dissolve in the water before you set it over the fire, stirring it well. Boil and skim the sugar, and when the scum ceases to rise, put in the limes, adding the juice that was saved from them, and which must first be strained from the pulp, seeds, &c. Boil the limes in the syrup till they are very tender and trans- parent. Then take them out carefully, and spread them on flat dishes. Put the syrup into a tureen, and leave it unco- vered for two days.

In the mean time prepare a jelly for filling the limes. Get several dozen of fine ripe lemons. Roll them under your hand on the table, to increase the juice; cut them in half, and squeeze them through a strainer into a pitcher. To each pint of the juice allow a pound and a quarter of the best double refined loaf-sugar. Put the sugar, mixed with the lemon-juice, into a preserving-kettle, and when they are melted set it over the fire, and boil and skim it till it becomes a thick, firm jelly, which it should in twenty minutes. Try if it will congeal by taking out a little in a spoon, and placing it in the open air. If it congeals immediately, it is sufficiently done. If boiled too long it will liquefy, and will not congeal again without the assistance of isinglass. When the jelly is done, put it at once into a large bowl, and leave it uncovered.

The lemon-jelly, the syrup and the limes, being thoroughly done, and all grown cold, finish by filling the limes with the jelly; putting them, with the open part downwards, into wide-mouthed glass jars, and gently pouring on them the syrup. Cover the jars closely, and paste strong paper over the covers. Or seal the corks.

Very small, thin-skinned, ripe oranges, preserved in this manner, and filled with orange-jelly, are delicious.

If, instead of having it liquid, you wish the syrup to crystallize or candy round the fruit, put no water to the sugar, but boil it slowly a long time, with the juice only, clarified by beaten white of egg mixed with the sugar in the proportion of one white to three pounds.

Before squeezing out the juice of the lemons intended to make the jelly, it will be well to pare off very thin the yellow rind, cut it into bits, and put it into a bottle of white wine or brandy, where it will keep soft and fresh, and the infusion will make a fine flavouring for cakes, puddings, &c. The rind of lemons should never be thrown away, as it is useful for so many nice purposes. Apple-sauce and apple-pies should always be flavoured with lemon-peel.

PINE-APPLE MARMALADE.—Take the largest, ripest, and most perfect pine-apples. Pare them, and cut out whatever blemishes you may find. Weigh each pine-apple, balancing the other scale with an equal quantity of the best double refined loaf-sugar, finely powdered. Grate the pine-apples on a large dish, omitting the hard core in the centre of each. Put the grated pine-apples and the sugar into a preserving-kettle, mixing them thoroughly. Set it over a moderate fire, and boil and skim it well, at times stirring it up from the bottom. After the scum has ceased to appear, still stir, till the marmalade is done, which will generally be in half an hour after it has come to a boil; but if not clear, bright, and smooth in that time, continue to boil it longer. When done, put it into a tureen, and cover it closely, while it is growing cold. Afterwards, remove it into tumblers, covering the top of each with double white tissue-paper, cut round so as exactly to fit the inside. Lay this paper closely on the marmalade, and press it down round the edges. Then paste on covers of thick paper.

This preparation of pine-apples is far superior to the usual method of preserving it in slices. It will be found very fine for filling tart-shells, and for jelly-cake.

———

ORANGE DROPS.—Squeeze through a strainer the juice of a dozen or more ripe oranges. Have ready some of the best double refined loaf-sugar, powdered as fine as possible, and sifted. Mix gradually the sugar with the juice, till it is so thick you can scarcely stir it. Put it into a porcelain skillet. Set it on hot coals, or over a moderate fire, and stir it hard with a wooden spoon for five minutes after it begins to boil. Then take it off the fire, and with a silver spoon or the point of a broad knife, drop portions of the mixture upon a flat tin pan or a pewter dish, smoothing the drops, and making them of good shape and regular size, which should be about that of a cent. When cold they will easily come off the tin. They are delicious, if properly made. Never use extract or oil of orange for them, or for any thing else. It will make them taste like turpentine, and render them uneatable. Confectioners form these drops in moulds made for the purpose.

Lemon drops may be prepared in the same manner.

FINE LEMON SYRUP.—The best time for making lemon syrup is early in the spring. Lemons are then plenty, and the syrup mixed with ice-water, makes a pleasant beverage for summer. It is best and cheapest to buy lemons by the box. Before using them *for any purpose*, each lemon should be wiped well, and then rolled hard under your hand upon a table to soften them and increase the juice. Two dozen large ripe lemons will generally yield about a quart of juice if pressed with a wooden lemon-squeezer; but it is best to have a few extra ones at hand, in case they should be required. To a quart of juice allow six pounds of the best loaf-sugar, broken up; on pieces of which rub off the yellow rind or zest of the lemons. The white part of the skin is useless and injurious. Put all the sugar into a large porcelain preserving-kettle. Beat to a stiff froth the whites of two eggs, mix it gradually with a quart of clear soft water, and then add it to the sugar. Stir the sugar while it is melting in the water, and when all is dissolved, place the kettle over the fire, and boil and skim it till perfectly clear, and the scum ceases to rise, and the particles of lemon zest are no longer visible. Meanwhile, squeeze the lemons through a strainer into a large pitcher, till you have a quart of juice. When the sugar has boiled sufficiently, and is quite clear, stir in gradually the lemon-juice, cover the kettle, and let it boil ten minutes longer. When cool put it into clean, clear glass bottles, either quite new ones or some that have already contained lemon syrup. The bottles should first be rinsed with brandy. Cork them tightly and seal the corks. Orange syrup may be made in a similar manner omitting to use the grated yellow rind of the oranges, (it being too pungent for this purpose,) and substituting for it a double quantity of the juice; for instance, allowing two quarts of juice to six pounds of sugar.

CROQUANT CAKE.—Take three quarters of a pound of almonds, (of which two ounces, or more, should be the bitter sort,) and blanch and slice them. Powder three quarters of a pound of fine white sugar. Sift three quarters of a pound of flour, and slice half a pound of citron. Mix together the almond and citron, on a flat dish, and sprinkle among them flour from the dredging-box, till they are white all over. Beat six eggs as light as possible, till they are very thick and smooth. Then mix them gradually with the sugar, almond, and citron, stirring very hard. Lastly, stir in, by degrees, the sifted flour. Butter a tin pan or pans, and put in the mixture about an inch deep. Bake it; and when cool, cut it into narrow slices about an inch wide, and five inches long. To make them keep a long time, lay them on shallow tins, and give them a second baking. Put the cakes into a stone jar, and they will keep a year or more, after this double baking.

SASSAFRAS MEAD.—Mix gradually with two quarts of boiling water, three pounds and a half of the best brown sugar, a pint and a half of good West India molasses, and a quarter of a pound of tartaric acid. Stir it well, and when cool, strain it into a large jug or pan, then mix in a tea-spoonful (not more) of essence of sassafras. Transfer it to clean bottles, (it will fill about half a dozen,) cork it tightly, and keep it in a cool place. It will be fit for use next day. Put into a box or boxes a quarter of a pound of carbonate of soda, to use with it. To prepare a glass of sassafras mead for drinking, put a large table-spoonful of the mead into a half tumbler full of ice-water, stir into it a half tea-spoonful of the soda, and it will immediately foam up to the top.

Sassafras mead will be found a cheap, wholesome, and pleasant beverage for warm weather. The essence of sassafras, tartaric acid, and carbonate of soda, can of course all be obtained at the druggists'.

FINE TOMATA CATCHUP.—Take a large quantity of tomatas, and scald and peel them. Press them through a fine hair-sieve, and boil the pulp in either a porcelain or a bell-metal preserving-kettle, as tin or iron will blacken it. Cover the kettle closely, and keep it at a slow boil during four hours. Then measure the pulp of the tomatas, and to every two quarts allow a tea-spoonful of salt. Boil it an hour after the salt is in, stirring it frequently. Have ready, in equal proportions, a mixture of powdered ginger, nutmeg, mace, and cloves; and to every two quarts of the liquid, allow a large tea-spoonful of these mixed spices, adding a small tea-spoonful of cayenne. Stir in this seasoning, and then boil the catchup half an hour longer. Strain it carefully into a large pitcher, avoiding the grounds or sediment of the spices, and then (while hot) pour it through a flannel into clean bottles. Cork them tightly, and seal the corks. Keep it in a dry, cool place. It will be of a fine scarlet colour.

GREEN TOMATA PICKLES.—Slice a gallon of the largest green tomatas, and salt them over night to your taste. In the morning mix together a table-spoonful of ground black pepper; one of mace; one of cloves; four pods of red pepper, chopped fine; and half a pint of grated horse-radish. Mix them all thoroughly. Have ready a large, wide-mouthed stone jar; put into it first a layer of the seasoning, then a layer of tomatas, then another of seasoning, then another of tomatas, then another of seasoning, another of tomatas; and so on alternately till the jar is filled within two inches of the top, finishing with a layer of seasoning. Then fill up to the top with cold cider vinegar; adding at the last a table-spoonful of sweet oil. Cover the jar closely.

This will be found a very nice pickle, and is easily made, as it requires no cooking. After the tomatas are all gone, the liquid remaining in the jar may be used as catchup.

———

RED TOMATA PICKLES.—Fill three quarters of a jar with small, round, button tomatas when quite ripe. Put them in whole, and then pour over them sufficient cold vinegar (highly flavoured with mace, cloves, and whole black pepper) to raise them to the top. Add a table-spoonful of sweet oil, and cover the jar closely.

———

HASHED VEAL.—Always save the gravy of roast meat. Having skimmed off the fat, and poured the gravy through a strainer into a jar, cover it closely, and set it away in a refrigerator, or some very cold place, till next day. When cold meat is hashed or otherwise recooked, it is best to do it in its own gravy, and without the addition of water.

Take some cold roast veal, and cut it into small mouthfuls Put it into a skillet or stew-pan, without a drop of water. Add to it the veal gravy that was left the preceding day, and a small lump of fresh butter. Cover the skillet, and let the hash stew over the fire for half an hour. Then put to it a large table-spoonful of tomata catchup; or more, according to the quantity of meat. One large table-spoonful of catchup will suffice for as much hash as will fill a soup-plate. After the catchup is in, cover the hash, and let it stew half an hour longer. This is the very best way of dressing cold veal for breakfast. Observe that there must be no water about it. Cold roast beef, mutton, or pork, may be hashed in this manner; but hashed veal is best. You may also hash cold poultry, or rabbits, by cutting them in small bits, and stewing them in gravy, adding mushroom catchup instead of tomata.

FRENCH CHICKEN SALAD.—Take a large, fine, cold fowl, and having removed the skin and fat, cut the flesh from the bones in very small shreds, not more than an inch long. The dressing should not be made till immediately before it goes to table. Have ready half a dozen or more hard-boiled eggs. Cut up the yolks upon a plate, and with the back of a wooden spoon mash them to a paste, adding a small salt-spoonful of salt, rather more of cayenne pepper, and a large tea-spoonful of made mustard. Mix them well together; then add two large table-spoonfuls of salad oil, and one of the best cider vinegar. All these ingredients for the dressing, must be mixed to a fine, smooth, stiff, yellow paste. Lay the shred chicken in a nice even heap, upon the middle of a flat dish. smoothing it, and making it circular or oval with the back of a spoon, and flattening the top. Then cover it thickly and smoothly with the dressing, or paste of seasoned yolk of egg, &c. Have ready a large head of lettuce that has been picked, and washed in cold water; and, cutting up the best parts of it very small, mix the lettuce with a portion of the hard-boiled white of egg minced fine. Lay the chopped lettuce all rouna the heap of shred chicken, &c. Then ornament the surface with very small bits of boiled red beets, and green pickled cucumbers, cut into slips and dots, and arranged in a pretty pattern upon the yellow ground of the coating that covers the chicken. After taking on your plate a portion of each part of the salad, mix all together before eating it.

Do not use for this, or any other purpose, the violently and disagreeable sharp vinegar that is improperly sold in many of the grocery stores, and is made entirely of chemical acids. Some of these employed for making vinegar, are so corrosive as to be absolutely poisonous. This vinegar can always be known by its very clear transparency, and its excessive pungency, overpowering entirely the taste of every thing with which it is mixed; and also by its entire destitution of the least flavour resembling wine or cider, though it is often sold as "the best white vinegar." You can always have good wholesome vinegar by setting in the sun with the cork loosened, a vessel of cider till it becomes vinegar. In buying a keg of vinegar, it is best to get it of a farmer that makes cider.

NORMANDY SOUP.—Take four pounds of knuckle of veal. Put it into a soup pot with twenty common-sized onions, and about four quarts of water. Let it simmer slowly for two hours or more. Then put in about one third of a six-penny loaf grated; adding a small tea-spoonful of salt, and not quite that quantity of cayenne pepper. Let it boil two hours longer. Then take out the meat, and press and strain the soup through a large sieve into a broad pan. Measure it, and to every quart of the soup add a pint of cream, and about two ounces of fresh butter divided into four bits, and rolled in flour. Taste the soup, and if you think it requires additional seasoning, add a very little more salt and cayenne. Always be careful not to season soup highly; as it is very easy for those who like them to add more salt and pepper, after tasting it at table.

Put the soup again over the fire, and let it just come to a boil. Then serve it up. These proportions of the ingredients ought to make a tureen-full. This soup is a very fine one for dinner company. The taste of the onions becomes so mild as to be just agreeably perceptible; particularly in autumn when the onions are young and fresh. In cool weather it may be made the day before; but in this case, when done, it must be set on ice, and the cream and butter not put in till shortly before it goes to table.

Never keep soup (or any other article that has been cooked) in a glazed earthen crock or pitcher. The glazing being of lead would render it unwholesome. Its effects have sometimes been so deleterious as really to destroy life.

TOMATA SOUP.—Take a hind-leg of beef, and cut it up into small pieces. Put the meat with the bones into a soup-pot, and cover it with a gallon of water. Season it with pepper, and a little salt. Boil and skim it well. Have ready half a peck of ripe tomatas cut up small; and when the soup is boiling thoroughly, put them in with all their juice. Add six onions sliced, and some crusts of bread cut small. The soup must then be boiled slowly for six hours or more. When done, strain it through a cullender. Put into the tureen some pieces of bread cut into dice or small squares, and pour the soup upon it.

Tomata soup (like most others) is best when made the day before In this case you may boil it longer and slower. Then having strained it into a stone jar, cover it closely, and set it away in a cold place. Next day, add some grated bread crumbs mixed with a little butter, and give the soup a boil up.

When ochras are in season, this soup will be greatly improved by the addition of half a peck of ochras, peeled and sliced thin.

CALVES' FEET SOUP.—Take eight calves' feet (two sets) and season them with a small tea-spoonful of salt, half a tea-spoonful of cayenne, and half a tea-spoonful of black pepper, all mixed together and rubbed over the feet. Slice a quarter of a peck of ochras, and a dozen onions, and cut up a quarter of a peck of tomatas without skinning them. Put the whole into a soup-pot with four quarts of water, and boil and skim it during two hours. Then take out the calves' feet, and put them on a dish. Next, strain the soup through a cullender, into an earthen pan, and with the back of a short wooden ladle mash out into the pan of soup all the liquid from the vegetables, till they are as dry as possible. Cut off all the meat nicely from the bones into small bits, and return it to the soup, adding a quarter of a pound of fresh butter, divided into four, and rolled in flour. Put the soup again into the pot, and give it a boil up. Toast two or three large thick slices of bread; cut it into small square dice or mouthfuls; lay it in the bottom of the tureen; pour the soup over it, and put on the tureen cover immediately. This soup (which, however, can only be made when tomatas and ochras are in season) will be found excellent. It may be greatly improved by boiling in it the hock of a cold ham: in which case add no salt.

FINE CALVES' HEAD SOUP.—Boil in as much water as will cover it, a calf's head with the skin on, till you can slip out the bones. Then take a fore-leg of beef, and a knuckle of veal; cut them up, and put them (bones and all) into the liquid the calf's head was boiled in; adding as much more water as will cover the meat. Skim it well; and after it has thoroughly come to a boil, add half a dozen sliced carrots; half a dozen sliced onions; a large head of celery cut small; a bunch of sweet herbs; and a salt-spoonful of cayenne pepper. Boil the whole slowly during five hours; then strain it into a large pan.

Take rather more than a pint of the liquid, (after all the fat has been carefully skimmed off,) and put it into a saucepan with two ounces of fresh butter, a bunch of sweet marjoram, a few sprigs of parsley, two onions minced fine, and a large slice of the lean of some cold boiled ham, cut into little bits. Keep it closely covered, and let it simmer over the fire for an hour. Then press it through a sieve into the pan that contains the rest of the soup. Thicken it with a large tea-cupful (half a pint) of grated bread-crumbs; return it to the soup-pot, and boil it half an hour. Unless your dinner hour is late, it is best to make this soup the day before, putting it into a large stone-ware or china vessel, (not an earthen one,) covering it closely and setting it in a cool place.

Have ready some force-meat balls, made of the meat of the calves' head, finely minced, and mixed with grated bread-crumbs, butter, powdered sweet-majoram, a very little salt and pepper, and some beaten yolk of egg to cement these ingredients together. Each ball should be rolled in flour, and fried in fresh butter before it is put into the soup. Shortly before you send it to table, add a large lemon sliced thin without peeling, and a pint of good madeira or sherry, wine of inferior quality being totally unfit for soup, terrapin, or any such purposes. Add also the yolks of some hard-boiled eggs cut in half. Then, after the wine, lemon, and eggs are all in, give the soup one boil up, but not more.

THE BEST CLAM SOUP.—Put fifty clams into a large pot of boiling water, to make the shells open easily. Take a knuckle of veal, cut it into pieces (four calves' feet split in half will be still better) and put it into a soup-pot with the liquor of the clams, and a quart of rich milk, or cream, adding a large bunch of sweet majoram, and a few leaves of sage, cut into pieces, and a head of celery chopped small; also, a dozen whole pepper-corns, but no salt, as the saltness of the clam liquor will be sufficient. Boil it till all the meat of the veal drops from the bones, then strain off the soup and return it to the pot, which must first be washed out. Having in the mean time cut up the clams, and pounded them in a mortar, (which will cause them to flavour the soup much better,) season them with two dozen blades of mace, and two powdered nutmegs; mix with them a quarter of a pound of fresh butter, and put them into the soup with all the liquor that remains about them. After the clams are in, let it boil another quarter of an hour. Have ready some thick slices of nicely-toasted bread, (with the crust removed,) cut them into small square mouthfuls; put them into a tureen; and pour the soup upon them. It will be found excellent. Oyster soup may be made in the same manner.

BAKED CLAMS.—In taking out the clams, save several dozen of the largest and finest shells, which must afterwards be washed clean, and wiped dry. Chop the clams fine, and mix with them some powdered mace and nutmeg. Butter the sides and bottom of a large, deep dish, and cover the bottom with a layer of grated bread-crumbs. Over this scatter some very small bits of the best fresh butter. Then put in a thick layer of the chopped clams. Next, another layer of grated bread-crumbs, and little bits of butter. Then, a layer of chopped clams, and proceed in this manner till the dish is full, finishing at the top with a layer of crumbs. Set the dish in the oven, and bake it about a quarter of an hour. Have ready the clam-shells and fill them with the baked mixture, either leaving them open, or covering each with another clam-shell. Place them on large dishes, and send them to table hot.

Oysters may be cooked in a similar manner; sending them to table in the dish in which they were baked. The meat of boiled crabs may also be minced, seasoned, and dressed this way, and sent to table in the back shells of the crabs.

Clams intended for soup will communicate to it a much finer flavour, if they are previously chopped small, and pounded in a mortar.

———

FINE STEWED OYSTERS.—Strain the liquor from two hundred large oysters, and putting the half of it into a sauce-pan, add a table-spoonful of whole mace, and let it come to a hard boil, skimming it carefully. Have ready six ounces of fresh butter divided into six balls or lumps, and roll each slightly in a little flour. Add them to the boiling oyster liquor, and when the butter is all melted, stir the whole very hard, and then put in the oysters. As soon as they have come to a boil, take them out carefully, and lay them immediately in a pan of very cold water, to plump them and make them firm. Then season the liquor with a grated nutmeg; and taking a pint and a half of very rich cream, add it gradually to the liquor, stirring it all the time. When it has boiled again, return the oysters to it, and simmer them in the creamed liquor about five minutes or just long enough to heat them thoroughly. Send them to the tea-table hot in a covered dish.

If you stew six or eight hundred oysters, in this manner, for a large company, see that the butter, spice, cream, &c., are all increased in the proper proportion.

Oysters cooked in this way make very fine patties. The shells for which must be made of puff-paste, and baked empty in very deep patty-pans, filling them, when done, with oysters.

SPICED OYSTERS.—To four hundred large oysters allow a pint of cider vinegar, four grated nutmegs, sixteen blades of whole mace, six dozen of whole cloves, three dozen whole pepper corns, and a salt-spoonful of cayenne. Put the liquor into a porcelain kettle, and boil and skim it; when it has come to a hard boil, add the vinegar and put in the oysters with the seasoning of spices, &c. Give them one boil up, for if boiled longer they will shrivel and lose their flavour. Then put them into a stone or glass jar, cover them closely, and set them in a cool place. They must be quite cold when eaten.

You may give them a light reddish tint by boiling in the liquor a little prepared cochineal.

TO KEEP FRESH EGGS.—Have a close, dry keg, for the purpose of receiving the eggs as they are brought in fresh from the hen's nests. An old biscuit keg will be best. Keep near it a patty-pan, or something of the sort, to hold a piece of clean white rag with some good lard tied up in it. While they are fresh and warm from the nest, grease each egg all over with the lard, not omitting even the smallest part; and then put it into the keg with the rest. Eggs preserved in this manner (and there is no better way) will continue good for months, provided they were perfectly fresh when greased; and it is useless to attempt preserving any but new-laid eggs. No process whatever, can restore or prevent from spoiling, any egg that is the least stale. Therefore, if you live in a city, or have not hens of your own, it is best to depend on buying eggs as you want them.

A MOLASSES PIE.—Make a good paste, and having rolled it out *thick*, line a pie-dish with a portion of it. Then fill up the dish with molasses, into which you have previously stirred a table-spoonful, or more, of ground ginger. Cover it with an upper crust of the paste; notch the edges neatly; and bake it brown. This pie, plain as it is, will be found very good. It will be improved by laying a sliced orange or lemon in the bottom before you put in the molasses. To the ginger you may add a tea-spoonful of powdered cinnamon.

SOUP À LA LUCY.—Take a large fowl; cut it up, put it with a few small onions into a soup-pot, and fry it brown in plenty of lard. Afterwards pour in as much water as you intend for the soup, and boil it slowly till the whole strength of the chicken is extracted, and the flesh drops in rags from the bones. An hour before dinner, strain off the liquid, return it to the pot (which must first be cleared entirely out) add the liquor of a quart of fresh oysters, and boil it again. In half an hour put in the oysters and mix into the soup two large table-spoonfuls of fresh butter rolled in flour; some whole pepper; blades of mace; and grated nutmeg. Toast some thick slices of bread (without the crust) cut them into dice, and put them into the soup tureen. For the fowl, you may substitute a knuckle of veal cut up, or a pair of rabbits

MINT JULEP.—This can only be made when fresh green mint is in season.

Lay at the bottom of a large tumbler, one or two round slices of pine-apple nicely pared; and cover them with a thick layer of loaf-sugar, powdered or well-broken. Pour on it a glass or more of the best brandy. Add cold water till the tumbler is two-thirds full. Finish with a thick layer of pounded ice till it nearly reaches the top. Then stick down to one side a bunch of fresh green mint, the sprigs full and handsome, and tall enough to rise above the edge of the tumbler. Place, in the other side, one of the small tubes or straws used for drawing in this liquid.

The proportions of the above ingredients may, of course, be varied according to taste.

———

A UNION PUDDING.—The night before you make this pudding, take a piece of rennet, in size rather more than two inches square, and carefully wash off in two cold waters all the salt from the outside. Then wipe it dry. Put the rennet into a tea-cup and pour on sufficient milk-warm water to cover it well. Next morning, as early as you can, stir the rennet-water into a quart of rich milk. Cover the milk, and set it in a warm place till it forms a firm curd, and the whey becomes thin and greenish. Then remove it to a cold place and set it on ice. Blanch, in scalding water, two ounces of shelled bitter almonds, or peach-kernels; and two ounces of shelled sweet almonds. Pound the almonds in a mortar, to a smooth paste, one at a time (sweet and bitter alternately, so as to mix them well); and add, while pounding, sufficient rose-water to make them light and white, and to prevent their oiling. Grate upon a lump of loaf-sugar the yellow rind or zest of two lemons, scraping off the lemon-zest as you proceed, and transferring it to a saucer. Squeeze over it the juice of the lemons, and mix the juice and the zest with half a pound and two ounces of finely-powdered loaf-sugar, adding a small nutmeg, grated. Then put the cold curd into a sieve, and drain it from the whey till it is left very dry, chopping the curd small, that it may drain the better. Beat in a shallow pan the yolks of eight eggs till very light, thick, and smooth Then mix into the egg the curd, in turn with the pounded almonds, and the sugar and lemon. Finish with a glass of brandy, or of Madeira or Sherry, and stir the whole very hard.

Butter a deep dish of strong white ware. Put in the mixture: set it immediately into a brisk oven and bake it well. When done, set it in a cold place till wanted, and before it goes to table, sift powdered sugar over it. It will be still better to cover the surface with a meringue or icing, highly flavored with rose-water or lemon-juice. You may decorate the centre with the word UNION in letters of gilt sugar.

The pudding will be found very fine.

COCOA-NUT CANDY.—Take three cocoa-nuts and grate their meat on a coarse grater. Weigh the grated cocoa-nut, and to each pound, allow one pound of the best double-refined loaf-sugar. Put the sugar into a preserving kettle, and to every two pounds allow a pint of water, and the beaten white of one egg mixed into the water. When the sugar is entirely dissolved in the water, set it over the fire, and boil and skim it. When the scum has ceased to rise, and the sugar is boiling hard, begin to throw in the grated cocoa-nut, gradually, stirring hard all the time. Proceed till the mixture is so thick it can be stirred no longer. Have ready, square or oblong tin pans, slightly buttered with the best fresh butter. Fill them with the mixture, put in evenly and smoothly, and of the same thickness all through the pan. Smooth the surface all over with a broad knife dipped in cold water. Set it to cool, and, when the candy is almost hard, score it down in perpendicularly straight lines with a sharp knife dipped in cold water, the lines being two or three inches apart. These cuts must be made deep down to the bottom of the pan. When it is quite cold and firm, cut the candy entirely apart, so as to form long sticks, and keep it in a cold place.

If any of the grated cocoa-nut is left, you may make it into cocoa-nut maccaroons, or into a cocoa-nut pudding.

PRESERVED GREEN TOMATAS.—Take a peck of button tomatas, full grown, but quite green. Weigh them, and to each pound allow a pound of the best double-refined loaf-sugar, broken up small. Scald and peel them. Have ready ten lemons rolled under your hand on a table, to increase the juice. Grate off, upon lumps of sugar, the yellow surface of the rind, scraping up the grating or zest with a spoon, and transferring it to a bowl. Squeeze over it, through a strainer, the juice of the lemon. Take a quarter of a pound of root ginger, scrape off the outside, grate the ginger and mix it with the lemon.

Put the sugar into a large preserving kettle, and pour water on it; allowing half a pint of water to each pound of sugar. Stir it about with a large, clean wooden spoon, till it melts. Set it over a clear fire, and boil and skim it. After it has boiled, and is very clear, and the scum has ceased to rise, put in the tomatas and boil them till every one has slightly bursted. Next add the lemon and ginger, and boil them about a quarter of an hour longer. Then take them out and spread them on large dishes to cool. Boil the syrup by itself, ten minutes longer. Put the tomatas into jars, about half full and fill up with the syrup. Cover the jars closely, and paste paper round the lids; or tie bladders over them.

Green tomatas, done as above, make an excellent sweetmeat. Ripe or red tomatas may be preserved in the same manner; yellow ones also.

The lemon and ginger must on no account be omitted.

PRESERVED FIGS.—Take figs when perfectly ripe, and wipe them carefully, leaving the stem about half an inch long. Boil them rapidly, for about ten minutes, in water that has a small bag of hickory wood-ashes laid at the bottom of the preserving kettle. Then take them out carefully, so as not to break the skins.- Wash out the kettle, and boil the figs a second time, in clean hot water, for ten minutes. Take them out, spread them separately on large dishes, and let them rest till next morning.

Prepare a syrup, by allowing to every pound of the finest loaf-sugar, half a pint of water, and, when melted together, placing the kettle over the fire. When the syrup has boiled, and is thoroughly skimmed, put in the figs, and boil them about twenty-five minutes or half an hour. Then take them out, and again spread them to cool on large dishes. Afterwards, put them up in glass jars, pouring the syrup over them. Cover the jars closely, and set them in the hot sun all next day. Then seal the corks with the red cement made of melted rosin and bees-wax, thickened with fine brick-dust.

Another way is to cut the stems closely, and to peel off the skin of the figs; and to substitute for the bag of wood-ashes, a little powdered alum. Then proceed as above.

MYRTLE ORANGES PRESERVED.—The small myrtle of the South, makes a very fine green sweetmeat. Lay them three days in weak salt and water.   Then three days in cold water, changed at least three times a day.   Afterwards, put. a layer of green vine-leaves at the bottom of the preserving kettle, and round the sides.   Put in a layer of oranges, sprinkling among them a very little powdered alum, allowing not more than a heaped salt-spoonful of alum to the whole kettle of oranges and vine-leaves.   Then fill up with water; hang them over the fire till they are of a fine green, and boil them till they are so tender that you can pierce them through with a twig from a whisk broom.   When clear and crisp, take them out of the kettle, spread them on flat dishes, and throw away the vine-leaves.   Then wash out the kettle, and, having weighed the oranges, allow to each pound one pound of double-refined sugar, broken small.   Put the sugar into the preserving-kettle, and pour on half a pint of water to each pound of sugar.   When it is quite dissolved, hang it over the fire, and boil and skim it till it is very clear, and no more scum appears on the surface.   Then put in the oranges, and boil them slowly in the syrup till they slightly burst.

Another way is to scoop out all the inside of oranges as soon as they are greened, and make a thick jelly of it, with the addition of some more orange-pulp from other oranges. Press it through a strainer, and, after adding a pound of sugar to each pint of orange juice, boil it to a jelly.   Having boiled the empty oranges in a syrup till they are crisp and tender, spread them out to cool—fill them with the jelly, and put them up in glass jars, pouring the syrup over them.

TO KEEP STRAWBERRIES.—Take the largest and finest ripe strawberries, hull them, and put them immediately into large wide-mouthed bottles, filling them quite up to the top.

Cork them directly, and be sure to wire the corks. Set the bottles into a large preserving-kettle full of cold water. Place them óver the fire, and let the water boil around them for a quarter of an hour after it has come to a boil. Then take out the bottles, drain them, and wipe the outside dry. Proceed at once to seal the corks hermetically, with the red cement made of one-third bees-wax cut up, and two-thirds rosin, melted together in a skillet over the fire, and, when completely liquid, taken off the fire, and thickened to the consistence of sealing-wax by stirring in sufficient finely powdered brick-dust. This cement must be spread on hot over the wired corks. It is excellent for all sweetmeat and pickle jars. Nothing is better. Keep the bottles in boxes of dry sand. When opened, the strawberries will be found fresh and highly flavoured, as when just gathered. They must, however, be used as soon as they are opened, for exposure to the air will spoil them.

Raspberries, ripe currants stripped from the stalk, ripe gooseberries topped and tailed, and any small fruit, may be kept in this manner for many months.

In France, where syrups of every sort of fruit are made by boiling the juice with sugar, and then bottling it, it is very customary to serve up, in glass dishes, fruits preserved as above, with their respective syrups poured round them, from the bottles. They are delicious.

TO KEEP PEACHES.—Take fine ripe juicy free-stone peaches. Pare them, and remove the stones by thrusting them out with a skewer, leaving the peaches as nearly whole as possible. Or you may cut them in half. Put them immediately into flat stone jars, and cement on the covers with the composition of bees-wax and rosin melted togetner, and thickened with powdered brick dust. The jars (*filled up to the top*) must be so closely covered that no air can possibly get to the peaches. Then pack the jars in boxes of sand, or of powdered charcoal, and nail on the box-lid.

Peaches done in this manner, have arrived at California in perfect preservation. But they must be eaten as soon as the jars are opened.

GREEN CORN MUFFINS.—Having boiled the corn, grate it, as if for a pudding. Beat six eggs very light, and stir them gradually into a quart of milk. Then stir in, by degrees, the grated corn, till you have a moderately thick batter. Add a salt-spoon of salt. Butter the inside of your muffin-rings. Place them on a hot griddle, over a clear fire, and nearly fill them with the batter. Bake the muffins well, and send them to table hot. Eat them with butter.

COMPOTE OF SWEET POTATOES.—Select fine large sweet potatoes, all nearly the same size. Boil them well and then peel off the skins. Then lay the potatoes in a large baking-dish; put some pieces of fresh butter among them, and sprinkle them very freely with powdered sugar. Bake them slowly, till the butter and sugar form a crust. They should be eaten after the meat. This is a Carolina dish, and will be found very good.

BAKED HAM.—Soak a nice small Western ham in cold water, from early in the evening till next morning— changing the water at bed-time. (It may require twenty-four hours' soaking.) Trim it nicely, and cut the shank-bone short off. Make a coarse paste of merely flour and water, sufficient in quantity to enclose the whole ham. Roll it out, and cover the ham entirely with it. Place it in a well-heated oven, and bake it five hours, or more, in proportion to its size. When done, remove the paste, peel off the skin, and send the ham to table, with its essence or gravy about it. It will be found very fine.

If the ham is rather salt and hard, parboil it for two hours. Then put it into the paste, and bake it three hours.

MUSHROOM SWEET-BREADS.—Take four fine fresh sweet-breads; trim them nicely, split them open, and remove the gristle or pipe. Then lay the sweet-breads in warm water till all the blood is drawn out. Afterwards, put them into a saucepan, set them over the fire, and parboil them for a quarter of an hour. Then take them out, and lay them immediately in a pan of cold water.

Have ready a quart of fresh mushrooms; peel them, and remove the stalks. Spread out the mushrooms on a large flat dish, with the hollow side uppermost, and sprinkle them slightly with a little salt and pepper. Having divided each sweet-bread into four quarters, put them into a saucepan with the mushrooms, and add a large piece of the best fresh butter rolled in flour. Cover the pan closely, and set it over a clear fire that has no blaze. You must lift the saucepan by the handle, and shake it round hard, otherwise, the contents may burn at the bottom. Keep it closely covered all the time; for if the lid is removed, much of the mushroom-flavour may escape. Let them stew steadily for a quarter of an hour or more. Then take them up, and send them to table in a covered dish, either at breakfast or dinner. They will be found delicious. If the mushrooms are large, quarter them.

PANCAKE HAM.—Cut very thin some slices of cold ham, making them all nearly of the same size and shape Beat six eggs very light, and smooth. Stir them, gradually, into a pint of rich milk, alternately with six table-spoonfuls of sifted flour, adding half a nutmeg, grated. If you find the batter too thick, add a little more milk. For pancakes or fritters, the batter should be rather thin. Take a yeast-pow der; dissolve the contents of the blue paper (the soda) in a little warm water, and, when quite melted, stir it into the batter. In another cup, dissolve the tartaric acid from the white paper, and stir that in immediately after. Have ready, in a frying-pan over the fire, a sufficiency of lard melted and boiling, or of fresh butter. Put in a ladle-full of the batter, and fry it brown. Have ready a hot plate, and put the pan-cakes on it as soon as they come out of the frying-pan, keeping them covered, close to the fire. When they are all baked, pile them evenly on a hot dish, with a slice of cold ham be-tween every two pancakes, beginning with a cake at the bottom of the pile, and finishing with a cake at the top. You may arrange them in two piles, or more. In helping, cut down through the whole pile of pancakes and ham alternately.

In making yeast-powders, allow twice as much carbonate of soda as of tartaric acid. For instance, a level tea-spoonful of soda to a level salt-spoonful of the tartaric acid. Put up the two articles, separately folded in papers of different colours; the former in blue paper, the latter in white.

AN APPLE PANDOWDY.—Make a good plain paste. Pare, core, and slice half a dozen or more fine large juicy apples, and strew among them sufficient brown sugar to make them very sweet; adding some cloves, cinnamon, or lemon-juice. Have ready a pint of sour milk. Butter a deep in baking-pan, and put in the apples with the sugar and spice Then. having dissolved, in a little lukewarm water, a small tea-spoonful of soda, stir it into the milk, the acid of which it will immediately remove. Pour the milk, foaming, upon the apples, and immediately put a lid or cover of paste over the top, in the manner of a pie. This crust should be rolled out rather thick. Notch the edge all round, having made it fit closely. Set it into a hot oven, and bake it an hour. Eat it warm, with sugar.

HONEY PASTE (*for the HANDS.*)—Take half a pound of strained honey, half a pound of white wax, and half a pound of fresh lard. Cut up the wax very small, put it into a porcelain-lined saucepan, and set it over the fire till it is quite melted. Then add alternately the honey and the lard; stirring them all well together. Let them boil moderately, till they become a thick paste, about the consistence of simple cerate, or of lip salve. Then remove the saucepan from the fire, and stir into the mixture some rose-perfume, or carnation, or violet—no other. Transfer the paste, while warm, to gallicups with covers; and paste a slip of white paper round each cover.

For keeping the hands white and soft, and preventing their chapping, there is nothing superior to this paste; rubbing on a little of it, after dipping your hands lightly in water.

GLYCERINE.—This is an excellent and very convenient preparation for the hands. Buy a bottle of it at one of the best druggists, and keep it well corked. After washing your hands with palm or castile soap, empty the basin, and pour in a little fresh water, to which add a few drops of glycerine. Finish your hands with this, rubbing it in hard. It will render them very soft and smooth, and prevent chapping Try it, by all means.

TO KEEP OFF MUSQUITOES.—Before going to bed, put a little eau de cologne into a basin of clean water, and with this wash your face, neck, hands, and arms, letting it dry on. The musquitoes then will not touch you.

It may be necessary to repeat this washing before morning, or about day-light. There is nothing better. You may also do it early in the evening, before the musquitoes begin.

CORN-STARCH BLANCMANGE.—Buy at one of the best grocer's, a half-pound paper of corn-starch flour. Boil a quart of milk, taking out of it a large tea-cup-full, which you may put into a pan. While the milk is boiling, mix with the cold milk four heaping table-spoonfuls of the corn-starch. Beat three eggs very light, and stir them into the mixture. Flavour it with a tea-spoonful of extract of bitter almonds, or of vanilla, or a wine-glass of rose-water. Add a quarter of a pound of powdered loaf-sugar, and stir the whole well together. When the other milk is boiling hard, pour it gradually on the mixture in the pan, which mixture will thicken while the milk is pouring. Transfer it to blancmange moulds, (first wetting them with cold water,) and set them in a cold place till dinner-time. Eat it with cream. Serve up sweetmeats at the same time.

If you use new milk, the mixture will be like a soft custard, and must be sent to table as such. Skim-milk makes it blancmange.

If you wish it as a pudding, use five heaping spoonfuls of the corn-starch powder. Send it to table hot, and eat it with wine sauce. It is a pudding very soon prepared.

Blancmange moulds are best of block tin. Those of china are more liable to stick.

These preparations of corn-starch are much liked.

FARINA—Is the finest, lightest, and most delicate preparation of wheat flour. It is excellent for all sorts of boiled puddings, for flummery, and blancmange. Also, as gruel for the sick.

CINNAMON CAKE.—Take as much of the very best and lightest bread-dough as will weigh a pound. The dough must have risen perfectly, so as to have cracked all over the surface. Put it into a pan, and mix into it a quarter of a pound of fresh butter, melted in half a pint of milk, adding a well-beaten egg, and sufficient flour to enable you to knead the dough over again. Then mix in a heaping tea-spoonful of powdered cinnamon. Next, take a yeast-powder. In one cup, melt the soda or contents of the blue paper, in as much lukewarm water as will cover it; and, when thoroughly melted, mix it into the dough. Immediately after, having dissolved in another cup the tartaric acid, or contents of the white paper, stir that in also, and knead the dough a little while, till the whole is well mixed. Spread the dough thick and evenly in a square pan greased with lard or fresh butter, and with a knife make deep cuts all through it. Having previously prepared in a bowl a mixture of brown sugar, moistened with butter, and highly flavoured with powdered cinnamon, in the proportion of four heaping table-spoonfuls of sugar to two large spoonfuls of butter and one heaped tea-spoonful of cinnamon. Fill the cuts with this mixture, pressing it down well into the dough. Bake the cake half an hour or more, in a rather quick oven. When done, set it to cool; and when cold, cut it in squares, and sift powdered white sugar over it. It is best the day it is baked.

You may, previous to baking, form the dough into separate

round cakes; and in placing them in the pan, do not lay them so near each other as to touch.

By bespeaking it in time, you can get risen bread dough from your baker. For two pounds of dough you must double the proportions of the above ingredients.

THAWING FROZEN MEAT, &c.—If meat, poultry, fish, vegetables, or any other article of food, when found frozen, is thawed by putting it into *warm water* or placing it before the fire, it will most certainly spoil by that process, and be rendered unfit to eat. The only way is to thaw these things by immersing them in *cold* water. This should be done as soon as they are brought in from market, that they may have time to be well thawed before they are cooked. If meat that has been frozen is to be boiled, put it on in cold water. If to be roasted, begin by setting it at a distance from the fire; for if it should not chance to be thoroughly thawed all through to the centre, placing at first too near the fire will cause it to spoil. If it is expedient to thaw the meat or poultry the night before cooking, lay it in cold water early in the evening, and change the water at bed-time. If found crusted with ice in the morning, remove the ice, and put the meat in fresh cold water; letting it lie in it till wanted for cooking

Potatoes are injured by being frozen. Other vegetables are not the worse for it, provided they are always thawed in cold water.

KEEPING MEAT, &c., IN SUMMER.—In summer, meat, poultry, fish, fruit, &c., should always be kept in ice, from the time they are brought from market till it is time to cook them. Families, who have not an ice-house, should have *two* refrigerators; one for meat and poultry, the other for milk, butter, and fruit. If the three last articles are kept in the same refrigerator with meat and poultry, the milk, butter and fruit will imbibe a bad taste.

A barrel of salt fish should never be kept in the same cellar with other articles of food. The fish-smell will injure them greatly, and render them unwholesome; milk and butter particularly.

It is best to buy salt fish a little at a time, as you want it. A fish-barrel in the cellar will sometimes vitiate the atmosphere of the whole lower story of the house, and, indeed, may be smelt immediately on entering the door. In this case, let the barrel and its contents be conveyed to the river and thrown in; otherwise, its odour may produce sickness in the family.

Avoid eating anything that is *in the very least* approaching to decomposition. Even sour bread and strong butter are unwholesome as well as unpalatable. If the bread is sour, or the butter rancid, it is because (as the French, in such cases, unceremoniously say) " putrefaction has commenced." For tunately, the vile practice (once considered fashionable) of eating venison and other game when absolutely tainted, is now obsolete at all good tables. Persons who have had opportunities of feasting on fresh-killed venison, just from the woods, and at a season when the deer have plenty of wild berries to feed on and are fat and juicy, can never relish the hard, lean, black haunches that are brought to the cities in winter.

BROILED SHAD.—Cut off the head and tail, and clean the fish. Wipe it very dry with a cloth, and sprinkle the inside with a little salt and pepper. You may either broil it split open, and laid flat; or you may cut it into three or four pieces without splitting. In the latter case, it will require a longer time to broil. Keep it in ice till you are ready to cook it. Having well greased the bars with lard, or beef suet, or fresh butter, set your gridiron over a bed of clear, bright, hot coals; place the shad upon it (the inside downwards) and broil it thoroughly. When one side is done, turn it on the other with a knife and fork. Have ready a hot dish, with a large piece of softened fresh butter upon it, sprinkled with cayenne. When the shad is broiled, lay it on this dish, and turn it in the butter with a knife and fork. Send it hot to table, under a dish-cover.

APPLE PORK.—Take a fillet of fine fresh pork, and rub it slightly all over with a very little salt and pepper. Score the outside skin in diamonds. Take out the bone, and fill up the place with fine juicy apples, pared, cored, and cut small, and made very sweet with plenty of brown sugar; adding some bits of the yellow rind of a lemon or two, pared off very thin. Then have ready a dozen and a half or more of large apples, pared, cored, and quartered, sweetened well with sugar, and also flavoured with yellow rind of lemon. The juice of the lemons will be an improvement. Put the pork into a large pot, or into an iron bake-oven; fill up with the cut apples the space all round, adding just sufficient water to keep it from burning. Stew or bake it during three hours. When done, serve all up in one large dish.

STEWED SALT PORK.—Take a good piece of salt pork, (not too fat,) and, early in the evening, lay it in water, to soak all night, changing the water about bed-time. In the morning, drain and wash the pork, and cut it in very thin slices, seasoning it with pepper. Put a layer of this pork in the bottom of a large dinner-pot, and then a layer of slices of bread. Next put in a layer of potatoes, pared and cut up; then another layer of pork slices, covered by another layer of sliced bread; and then again potatoes. Proceed till the pot is two-thirds full, finishing with bread. Lastly, pour on just sufficient water to stew it well and keep it from burning. Set it over the fire, and let it cook slowly for three hours. If it becomes too dry, add a little boiling water.

This is a homely dish, but a very good one, particularly on a farm or on ship-board. At sea, you must substitute biscuit for bread.

Cold pork, left from yesterday, may be cooked in this manner.

TO MAKE GOOD TOAST.—Cut the bread in even slices, and moderately thick. When cut too thin, toast is hard and tasteless. It is much nicer when the crust is pared off before toasting. A long-handled toasting-fork (to be obtained at the hardware or tin stores) is far better than the usual toasting apparatus, made to stand before the fire with the slices of bread slipped in between, and therefore liable to be browned in stripes, dark and light alternately; unless the bread, while toasting, is carefully slipped along, so that the whole may receive equal benefit from the fire. With a fork, whose han dle is near a yard in length, the cook can sit at a comfortable distance from the fire, and the bread will be equally browned all over; when one side is done, taking it off from the fork, and turning the other. Send it to table hot, in a heated plate, or in a toast-rack; and butter it to your taste. Toast should neither be burnt nor blackened in any way. You may lay it in even piles, and butter it before it goes to table; cutting each slice in half.

CARVING.

—

THE seat for the carver should be somewhat elevated above the other chairs: it is extremely ungraceful to carve standing, and it is rarely done by any person accustomed to the business. Carving depends more on skill than on strength. We have seen very small women carve admirably sitting down; and very tall men who knew not how to cut a piece of beef-steak without rising on their feet to do it.

The carving knife should be very sharp, and not heavy; and it should be held firmly in the hand: also the dish should be not too far from the carver. It is customary to help the fish with a fish trowel, and not with a knife. The middle part of a fish is generally considered the best. In helping it, avoid breaking the flakes, as that will give it a mangled appearance.

In carving ribs or sirloin of beef, begin by cutting thin slices off the side next to you. Afterwards you may cut from the tender-loin, or cross-part near the lower end. Do not send any one the outside piece, unless you know that they particularly wish it.

In helping beef-steak, put none of the bone on the plate.

In cutting a round of corned beef, begin at the top; but lay aside the first cut or outside piece, and send it to no one, as it is always dry and hard. In a round of *a-la-mode beef*, the outside is frequently preferred.

In a leg of mutton, begin across the middle, cutting the slices quite down to the bone. The same with a leg of pork or a ham. The latter should be cut in *very thin* slices, as its flavour is spoiled when cut thick.

506

To taste well, a tongue should be cut crossways in round slices. Cutting it lengthwise (though the practice at many tables) injures the flavour. The middle part of the tongue is the best. Do not help any one to a piece of the root; that, being by no means a favoured part, is generally left in the dish.

In carving a fore-quarter of lamb, first separate the shoulder part from the breast and ribs, by passing the knife under, and then divide the ribs. If the lamb is large, have another dish brought to put the shoulder in.

For a loin of veal, begin near the smallest end, and separate the ribs; helping a part of the kidney (as far as it will go) with each piece. Carve a loin of pork or mutton in the same manner.

In carving a fillet of veal, begin at the top. Many persons prefer the first cut or outside piece. Help a portion of the stuffing with each slice.

In a breast of veal, there are two parts very different in quality, the ribs and the brisket. You will easily perceive the division; enter your knife at it, and cut through, which will separate the two parts. Ask the persons you are going to help, whether they prefer a rib, or a piece of the brisket.

For a haunch of venison, first make a deep incision, by passing your knife all along the side, cutting quite down to the bone. · This is to let out the gravy. Then turn the broad end of the haunch towards you, and cut it as deep as you can, in thin, smooth slices, allowing some of the fat to each person.

For a saddle of venison, or of mutton, cut from the tail to the other end on each side of the back-bone, making very thin slices, and sending some fat with each. Venison and roast mutton chill very soon, therefore it is usual to eat it with iron heaters under the plates. ·Some heaters are made to contain hot coals, others are kept warm with boiling water, and some are heated by spirits of wine; the last is a very exceptionable mode, as the blue blaze flaming out all around the plate, is to many persons frightful. Currant jelly is an indispensable appendage to venison, and to roast mutton, and to ducks.

A young pig is most generally divided before it comes to table, in which case, it is not customary to send in the head, as to many persons it is a revolting spectacle after it is cut off. When served up whole, first separate the head from the shoulders, then cut off the limbs, and then divide the ribs. Help some of the stuffing with each piece.

To carve a fowl, begin by sticking your fork in the pinion, and drawing it towards the leg; and then passing your knife underneath, take off the wing at the joint. Next, slip your knife between the leg and the body, to cut through the joint; and with the fork, turn the leg back, and the joint will give way. Then take off the other wing and leg. If the fowl has been trussed (as it ought to be) with the liver and gizzard, help the liver with one wing, and the gizzard with the other. The liver wing is considered the best. After the limbs are taken off, enter your knife into the top of the breast, and cut under the merry-thought, so as to loosen it, lifting it with your fork. Afterwards cut slices from both sides of the breast. Next take off the collar-bones, which lie on each side of the merry-thought, and then separate the side-bones from the back. The breast and wings are considered as the most delicate parts of the fowl; the back, as the least desirable, is generally left in the dish. Some persons, in carving a fowl, find it more convenient to take it on a plate, and as they separate it, return each part to the dish; but this is not now the usual way.

A turkey is carved in the same manner as a fowl; except that the legs and wings being larger, are separated at the lower joint. The lower part of the leg, (or drumstick, as it is called,) being hard, tough, and stringy, is never helped to any one, but allowed to remain on the dish. First cut off the wing, leg, and breast from one side; then turn the turkey over, and cut them off from the other.

To carve a goose, separate the leg from the body, by putting the fork into the small end of the limb ; pressing it close to the body, and then passing the knife under, and turning the leg back, as you cut through the joint. To take off the wing, put your fork into the small end of the pinion, and press it closely to the body ; then slip the knife under, and separate the joint. Next cut under the merry-thought, and take it off; and then cut slices from the breast. Then turn the goose, and dismember the other side. Take off the two upper side-bones, that are next to the wings; and then the two lower side-bones. The breast and legs of a goose afford the finest pieces. If a goose is old, there is no fowl so tough ; and if difficult to carve, it will be still more difficult to eat.

Partridges, pheasants, grouse, &c., are carved in the same manner as fowls. Quails, woodcocks, and snipes are merely split down the back; so also are pigeons, giving a half to each person.

In helping any one to gravy, or to melted butter, do not pour it *over* their meat, fowl, or fish, but put it to one side on a vacant part of the plate, that they may use just as much of it as they like. In filling a plate, never heap one thing on another.

In helping vegetables, do not plunge the spoon down to the bottom of the dish, in case they should not have been perfectly well drained. and the water should have settled there.

By observing carefully how it is done, you may acquire a knowledge of the joints, and of the process of carving, which a little daily practice will soon convert into dexterity. If a young lady is ignorant of this very useful art, it will be well for her to take lessons of her father, or her brother, and a married lady can easily learn from her husband. Domestics who wait at table may soon, from looking on daily, become so expert that, when necessary, they can take a dish to the side-table and carve it perfectly well.

At a dinner party, if the hostess is quite young, she is frequently glad to be relieved of the trouble of carving by the gentleman who sits nearest to her; but if she is familiar with the business, she usually prefers doing it herself.

TO DRAW POULTRY, &c.

THOUGH to prepare poultry for cooking is by no means an agreeable business, yet some knowledge of it may be very useful to the mistress of a house, in case she should have occasion to instruct a servant in the manner of doing it; or in the possible event of her being obliged to do it herself; for instance, if her cook has been suddenly taken ill, or has left her unexpectedly.

As all poultry is, of course, drawn in the same manner, it will be sufficient to designate the mode of emptying the inside of a fowl. In winter, if the fowl is frozen, lay it before the fire till it has completely thawed. Then have ready one or more large pieces of waste paper, rolled up loosely into a long wisp; lay the fowl down on a clean part of the hearth, and, taking its legs in your hand, light the paper, and pass it back and forward above the surface of the skin, (turning the fowl on both sides,) so as to singe off all the hairs; doing it so carefully as not to burn or scorch the skin. There should always be a quantity of old newspapers, or other waste paper, kept in a closet or drawer of the kitchen for this and other purposes. Next, lay the fowl upon its back on a clean old waiter or tray, (such as should be kept in every kitchen,) and with a large sharp knife cut off, first the head, and then the legs at the first joint. The next thing is to cut a very long slit in the skin at the right side of the neck, and with your fingers strip down the skin towards the shoulders, till you come to the craw, which you must take out with your hand. Then with your knife make two long deep cuts or incisions on each side of the body, going downward towards the tail. Put your hand into the cut or orifice on the right side, and pull out the heart, liver, gizzard, and then the entrails. Take care not to break the gall-bag, or its liquor will run over the liver, and make it so bitter that it cannot be eaten, and should therefore be thrown away without cooking. Next, to flatten the body, break the breast-bone by striking on it hard with your hand. Then tuck the legs into the lower part of the slits that you have cut on each side of the body. Afterwards with your hand bend or curve inwards the end of the neck-bone, and tuck it away under the long loose piece of skin left there. After this, lay the fowl in a small tub of cold water, and wash it well inside and out: then dry it with a clean towel.

Next, cut open the gizzard, empty it of the sand and gravel, and take out the thick inside skin. Split open the heart, and let out the blood that is in it. Then carefully cut the gall-bag from the liver, so as not to break it. Wash clean the heart, liver, and gizzard, (having trimmed them neatly,) and return the heart to the inside of the breast; putting back also the eggs, if you have found any. Have ready the stuffing, and fill up with it the vacancy from which you have taken the craw, &c., pressing it in hard. Next, taking between your thumb and finger the above-mentioned piece of skin at the top of the neck.

draw it down tightly towards the back of the fowl, (folding it nicely over the bent end of the neck-bone,) and fasten it down between the shoulders with a skewer, which must be stuck in so as to go lengthways down the back. This will prevent any of the stuffing from getting out, and will keep all compact and nice.

Then run a skewer through both the wings and the upper part of the body, tucking in the liver so as to appear from under the right pinion, and the gizzard (scoring it first) on the left. Both pinions must be bent upwards. Lastly, secure all by tying two strings of small twine tightly round the fowl; one just above the skewer that confines the legs; the other just below that which passes through the wings.

Of course, the strings and skewers are removed before the poultry is sent to table.

Turkeys, geese, and ducks are always trussed in this manner, the legs being cut off at the first joint. So are fowls for boiling. But when fowls are to be roasted, some cooks leave on the whole of the legs and feet, (scraping and washing them clean,) and drawing the feet up quite to the breast, where they are tied together by a string.

Pigeons, pheasants, partridges, &c., are all trussed as above, with the legs short.

To draw a little roasting pig, cut the body open by one long slit, and before you take out what is inside, loosen it all with a sharp knife; then extract it with your hands. Empty the head also. Afterwards wash the animal clean, (inside and out,) and fill the vacancy with stuffing. Having bent the knees under, skewer the legs to the body, and secure the stuffing by tying twine tightly several times round the body; first fastening the slit by pinning it with a wooden skewer. Having boiled the liver and heart, chop them to enrich the gravy.

FIGURES EXPLANATORY OF THE PIECES INTO WHICH THE FIVE
LARGE ANIMALS ARE DIVIDED BY THE BUTCHERS.

Beef

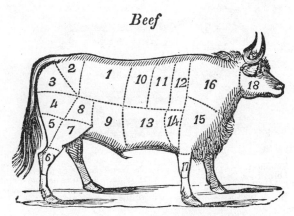

1. Sirloin.
2. Rump.
3. Edge Bone.
4. Buttock.
5. Mouse Buttock.
6. Leg.
7. Thick Flank.
8. Veiny Piece.
9. Thin Flank.
10. Fore Rib: 7 Ribs.
11. Middle Rib: 4 Ribs
12. Chuck Rib: 2 Ribs.
13. Brisket.
14. Shoulder, or Leg of Mutton Piece.
15. Clod.
16. Neck, or Sticking Piece.
17. Shin.
18. Cheek.

Veal.

1. Loin, Best End.
2. Fillet.
3. Loin, Chump End.
4. Hind Knuckle.
5. Neck, Best End.
6. Breast, Best End.
7. Blade Bone.
8. Fore Knuckle.
9. Breast, Brisket End.
10. Neck, Scrag End.

Mutton.

1. Leg.
2. Shoulder.
3. Loin, Best End.
4. Loin, Chump End.
5. Neck, Best End.

6. Breast.
7. Neck, Scrag End.
   Note. A Chine is two Loins; and a Saddle is two Loins and two Necks of the Best End.

Pork.

1. Leg.
2. Hind Loin.
3. Fore Loin.

4. Spare Rib.
5. Hand.
6. Spring.

Venison.

1. Shoulder.   4. Breast.
2. Neck.   5. Scrag.
3. Haunch.

INDEX.

517

NEW RECEIPTS.

A CATALOG OF SELECTED DOVER
BOOKS IN ALL FIELDS OF INTEREST

CONCERNING THE SPIRITUAL IN ART, Wassily Kandinsky. Pioneering work by father of abstract art. Thoughts on color theory, nature of art. Analysis of earlier masters. 12 illustrations. 80pp. of text. 5⅜ x 8½.   23411-8 Pa. $4.95

ANIMALS: 1,419 Copyright-Free Illustrations of Mammals, Birds, Fish, Insects, etc., Jim Harter (ed.). Clear wood engravings present, in extremely lifelike poses, over 1,000 species of animals. One of the most extensive pictorial sourcebooks of its kind. Captions. Index. 284pp. 9 x 12.   23766-4 Pa. $14.95

CELTIC ART: The Methods of Construction, George Bain. Simple geometric techniques for making Celtic interlacements, spirals, Kells-type initials, animals, humans, etc. Over 500 illustrations. 160pp. 9 x 12. (USO)   22923-8 Pa. $9.95

AN ATLAS OF ANATOMY FOR ARTISTS, Fritz Schider. Most thorough reference work on art anatomy in the world. Hundreds of illustrations, including selections from works by Vesalius, Leonardo, Goya, Ingres, Michelangelo, others. 593 illustrations. 192pp. 7⅛ x 10¼.   20241-0 Pa. $9.95

CELTIC HAND STROKE-BY-STROKE (Irish Half-Uncial from "The Book of Kells"): An Arthur Baker Calligraphy Manual, Arthur Baker. Complete guide to creating each letter of the alphabet in distinctive Celtic manner. Covers hand position, strokes, pens, inks, paper, more. Illustrated. 48pp. 8¼ x 11.   24336-2 Pa. $3.95

EASY ORIGAMI, John Montroll. Charming collection of 32 projects (hat, cup, pelican, piano, swan, many more) specially designed for the novice origami hobbyist. Clearly illustrated easy-to-follow instructions insure that even beginning papercrafters will achieve successful results. 48pp. 8¼ x 11.   27298-2 Pa. $3.50

THE COMPLETE BOOK OF BIRDHOUSE CONSTRUCTION FOR WOODWORKERS, Scott D. Campbell. Detailed instructions, illustrations, tables. Also data on bird habitat and instinct patterns. Bibliography. 3 tables. 63 illustrations in 15 figures. 48pp. 5¼ x 8½.   24407-5 Pa. $2.50

BLOOMINGDALE'S ILLUSTRATED 1886 CATALOG: Fashions, Dry Goods and Housewares, Bloomingdale Brothers. Famed merchants' extremely rare catalog depicting about 1,700 products: clothing, housewares, firearms, dry goods, jewelry, more. Invaluable for dating, identifying vintage items. Also, copyright-free graphics for artists, designers. Co-published with Henry Ford Museum & Greenfield Village. 160pp. 8¼ x 11.   25780-0 Pa. $10.95

HISTORIC COSTUME IN PICTURES, Braun & Schneider. Over 1,450 costumed figures in clearly detailed engravings—from dawn of civilization to end of 19th century. Captions. Many folk costumes. 256pp. 8⅜ x 11¾.   23150-X Pa. $12.95

PERSPECTIVE FOR ARTISTS, Rex Vicat Cole. Depth, perspective of sky and sea, shadows, much more, not usually covered. 391 diagrams, 81 reproductions of drawings and paintings. 279pp. 5⅜ x 8½. 22487-2 Pa. $7.95

DRAWING THE LIVING FIGURE, Joseph Sheppard. Innovative approach to artistic anatomy focuses on specifics of surface anatomy, rather than muscles and bones. Over 170 drawings of live models in front, back and side views, and in widely varying poses. Accompanying diagrams. 177 illustrations. Introduction. Index. 144pp. 8⅜ x11¼. 26723-7 Pa. $8.95

GOTHIC AND OLD ENGLISH ALPHABETS: 100 Complete Fonts, Dan X. Solo. Add power, elegance to posters, signs, other graphics with 100 stunning copyright-free alphabets: Blackstone, Dolbey, Germania, 97 more–including many lower-case, numerals, punctuation marks. 104pp. 8⅛ x 11. 24695-7 Pa. $8.95

HOW TO DO BEADWORK, Mary White. Fundamental book on craft from simple projects to five-bead chains and woven works. 106 illustrations. 142pp. 5⅜ x 8. 20697-1 Pa. $4.95

THE BOOK OF WOOD CARVING, Charles Marshall Sayers. Finest book for beginners discusses fundamentals and offers 34 designs. "Absolutely first rate . . . well thought out and well executed."–E. J. Tangerman. 118pp. 7¾ x 10⅝. 23654-4 Pa. $6.95

ILLUSTRATED CATALOG OF CIVIL WAR MILITARY GOODS: Union Army Weapons, Insignia, Uniform Accessories, and Other Equipment, Schuyler, Hartley, and Graham. Rare, profusely illustrated 1846 catalog includes Union Army uniform and dress regulations, arms and ammunition, coats, insignia, flags, swords, rifles, etc. 226 illustrations. 160pp. 9 x 12. 24939-5 Pa. $10.95

WOMEN'S FASHIONS OF THE EARLY 1900s: An Unabridged Republication of "New York Fashions, 1909," National Cloak & Suit Co. Rare catalog of mail-order fashions documents women's and children's clothing styles shortly after the turn of the century. Captions offer full descriptions, prices. Invaluable resource for fashion, costume historians. Approximately 725 illustrations. 128pp. 8⅜ x 11¼. 27276-1 Pa. $11.95

THE 1912 AND 1915 GUSTAV STICKLEY FURNITURE CATALOGS, Gustav Stickley. With over 200 detailed illustrations and descriptions, these two catalogs are essential reading and reference materials and identification guides for Stickley furniture. Captions cite materials, dimensions and prices. 112pp. 6½ x 9¼. 26676-1 Pa. $9.95

EARLY AMERICAN LOCOMOTIVES, John H. White, Jr. Finest locomotive engravings from early 19th century: historical (1804–74), main-line (after 1870), special, foreign, etc. 147 plates. 142pp. 11⅜ x 8¼. 22772-3 Pa. $10.95

THE TALL SHIPS OF TODAY IN PHOTOGRAPHS, Frank O. Braynard. Lavishly illustrated tribute to nearly 100 majestic contemporary sailing vessels: Amerigo Vespucci, Clearwater, Constitution, Eagle, Mayflower, Sea Cloud, Victory, many more. Authoritative captions provide statistics, background on each ship. 190 black-and-white photographs and illustrations. Introduction. 128pp. 8⅞ x 11¾. 27163-3 Pa. $14.95

PHOTOGRAPHIC SKETCHBOOK OF THE CIVIL WAR, Alexander Gardner. 100 photos taken on field during the Civil War. Famous shots of Manassas Harper's Ferry, Lincoln, Richmond, slave pens, etc. 244pp. 10⅝ x 8¼. 22731-6 Pa. $9.95

FIVE ACRES AND INDEPENDENCE, Maurice G. Kains. Great back-to-the-land classic explains basics of self-sufficient farming. The one book to get. 95 illustrations. 397pp. 5⅜ x 8½. 20974-1 Pa. $7.95

SONGS OF EASTERN BIRDS, Dr. Donald J. Borror. Songs and calls of 60 species most common to eastern U.S.: warblers, woodpeckers, flycatchers, thrushes, larks, many more in high-quality recording. Cassette and manual 99912-2 $9.95

A MODERN HERBAL, Margaret Grieve. Much the fullest, most exact, most useful compilation of herbal material. Gigantic alphabetical encyclopedia, from aconite to zedoary, gives botanical information, medical properties, folklore, economic uses, much else. Indispensable to serious reader. 161 illustrations. 888pp. 6½ x 9¼. 2-vol. set. (USO) Vol. I: 22798-7 Pa. $9.95
Vol. II: 22799-5 Pa. $9.95

HIDDEN TREASURE MAZE BOOK, Dave Phillips. Solve 34 challenging mazes accompanied by heroic tales of adventure. Evil dragons, people-eating plants, blood-thirsty giants, many more dangerous adversaries lurk at every twist and turn. 34 mazes, stories, solutions. 48pp. 8¼ x 11. 24566-7 Pa. $2.95

LETTERS OF W. A. MOZART, Wolfgang A. Mozart. Remarkable letters show bawdy wit, humor, imagination, musical insights, contemporary musical world; includes some letters from Leopold Mozart. 276pp. 5⅜ x 8½. 22859-2 Pa. $7.95

BASIC PRINCIPLES OF CLASSICAL BALLET, Agrippina Vaganova. Great Russian theoretician, teacher explains methods for teaching classical ballet. 118 illustrations. 175pp. 5⅜ x 8½. 22036-2 Pa. $5.95

THE JUMPING FROG, Mark Twain. Revenge edition. The original story of The Celebrated Jumping Frog of Calaveras County, a hapless French translation, and Twain's hilarious "retranslation" from the French. 12 illustrations. 66pp. 5⅜ x 8½. 22686-7 Pa. $3.95

BEST REMEMBERED POEMS, Martin Gardner (ed.). The 126 poems in this superb collection of 19th- and 20th-century British and American verse range from Shelley's "To a Skylark" to the impassioned "Renascence" of Edna St. Vincent Millay and to Edward Lear's whimsical "The Owl and the Pussycat." 224pp. 5⅜ x 8½. 27165-X Pa. $5.95

COMPLETE SONNETS, William Shakespeare. Over 150 exquisite poems deal with love, friendship, the tyranny of time, beauty's evanescence, death and other themes in language of remarkable power, precision and beauty. Glossary of archaic terms. 80pp. 5³⁄₁₆ x 8¼. 26686-9 Pa. $1.00

BODIES IN A BOOKSHOP, R. T. Campbell. Challenging mystery of blackmail and murder with ingenious plot and superbly drawn characters. In the best tradition of British suspense fiction. 192pp. 5⅜ x 8½. 24720-1 Pa. $6.95

THE INFLUENCE OF SEA POWER UPON HISTORY, 1660–1783, A. T. Mahan. Influential classic of naval history and tactics still used as text in war colleges. First paperback edition. 4 maps. 24 battle plans. 640pp. 5⅜ x 8½. 25509-3 Pa. $14.95

THE STORY OF THE TITANIC AS TOLD BY ITS SURVIVORS, Jack Winocour (ed.). What it was really like. Panic, despair, shocking inefficiency, and a little heroism. More thrilling than any fictional account. 26 illustrations. 320pp. 5⅜ x 8½. 20610-6 Pa. $8.95

FAIRY AND FOLK TALES OF THE IRISH PEASANTRY, William Butler Yeats (ed.). Treasury of 64 tales from the twilight world of Celtic myth and legend: "The Soul Cages," "The Kildare Pooka," "King O'Toole and his Goose," many more. Introduction and Notes by W. B. Yeats. 352pp. 5⅜ x 8½. 26941-8 Pa. $8.95

BUDDHIST MAHAYANA TEXTS, E. B. Cowell and Others (eds.). Superb, accurate translations of basic documents in Mahayana Buddhism, highly important in history of religions. The Buddha-karita of Asvaghosha, Larger Sukhavativyuha, more. 448pp. 5⅜ x 8½. 25552-2 Pa. $12.95

ONE TWO THREE . . . INFINITY: Facts and Speculations of Science, George Gamow. Great physicist's fascinating, readable overview of contemporary science: number theory, relativity, fourth dimension, entropy, genes, atomic structure, much more. 128 illustrations. Index. 352pp. 5⅜ x 8½. 25664-2 Pa. $8.95

ENGINEERING IN HISTORY, Richard Shelton Kirby, et al. Broad, nontechnical survey of history's major technological advances: birth of Greek science, industrial revolution, electricity and applied science, 20th-century automation, much more. 181 illustrations. ". . . excellent . . ."–*Isis.* Bibliography. vii + 530pp. 5⅜ x 8¼. 26412-2 Pa. $14.95

DALÍ ON MODERN ART: The Cuckolds of Antiquated Modern Art, Salvador Dalí. Influential painter skewers modern art and its practitioners. Outrageous evaluations of Picasso, Cézanne, Turner, more. 15 renderings of paintings discussed. 44 calligraphic decorations by Dalí. 96pp. 5⅜ x 8½. (USO) 29220-7 Pa. $4.95

ANTIQUE PLAYING CARDS: A Pictorial History, Henry René D'Allemagne. Over 900 elaborate, decorative images from rare playing cards (14th–20th centuries): Bacchus, death, dancing dogs, hunting scenes, royal coats of arms, players cheating, much more. 96pp. 9¼ x 12¼. 29265-7 Pa. $12.95

MAKING FURNITURE MASTERPIECES: 30 Projects with Measured Drawings, Franklin H. Gottshall. Step-by-step instructions, illustrations for constructing handsome, useful pieces, among them a Sheraton desk, Chippendale chair, Spanish desk, Queen Anne table and a William and Mary dressing mirror. 224pp. 8⅛ x 11¼. 29338-6 Pa. $13.95

THE FOSSIL BOOK: A Record of Prehistoric Life, Patricia V. Rich et al. Profusely illustrated definitive guide covers everything from single-celled organisms and dinosaurs to birds and mammals and the interplay between climate and man. Over 1,500 illustrations. 760pp. 7½ x 10⅛. 29371-8 Pa. $29.95

Prices subject to change without notice.

Available at your book dealer or write for free catalog to Dept. GI, Dover Publications, Inc., 31 East 2nd St., Mineola, N.Y. 11501. Dover publishes more than 500 books each year on science, elementary and advanced mathematics, biology, music, art, literary history, social sciences and other areas.

NO 01 '00